Kingship and Conversion in Sixteenth-Century Sri Lanka

When the Portuguese arrived on the shores of Sri Lanka in 1506, they opened an era in which religious identity became central to struggles for power on the island. During the reign of King Bhuvanekabāhu VII (1521–51), they became the first European empire to dominate Lankan politics. This book sets out to explain the behaviour of the Portuguese and the Sinhalese as their relationship evolved over the century. Topics covered include the nature of Portuguese imperialism and indigenous state power in the earlier decades, the impact of Catholic missions on this Buddhist society and how this was shaped by local principles of caste, land tenure and religious thought, and the issue of identity. It reveals how indigenist, dynastic and religious loyalties shaped the increasingly violent conflicts of the later decades. The principal concern is the sacred legitimization of kingship: why was Christian monarchy never truly established in Sri Lanka?

ALAN STRATHERN is a Research Fellow in History at Clare Hall, Cambridge.

University of Cambridge Oriental Publications 66

Kingship and Conversion in Sixteenth-Century Sri Lanka

Kingship and Conversion in Sixteenth-Century Sri Lanka

Portuguese Imperialism in a Buddhist Land

ALAN STRATHERN

CAMBRIDGE
UNIVERSITY PRESS

CAMBRIDGE UNIVERSITY PRESS
Cambridge, New York, Melbourne, Madrid, Cape Town, Singapore, São Paulo

Cambridge University Press
The Edinburgh Building, Cambridge CB2 8RU, UK

Published in the United States of America by Cambridge University Press, New York

www.cambridge.org
Information on this title: www.cambridge.org/9780521860093

First published 2007

Printed in the United Kingdom at the University Press, Cambridge

A catalogue record for this publication is available from the British Library

ISBN 978-0-521-86009-3 hardback

Reciprocally, to M. S.

CONTENTS

	List of maps	*page* viii
	List of plates	ix
	Acknowledgements	xi
	List of abbreviations	xiv
	Introduction	1
Part I	**The temporal**	**19**
1	The kingdom of Kōṭṭe	21
2	Portuguese imperialism	35
3	Imperialism in action	49
4	Bhuvanekabāhu's sovereignty	61
Part II	**The spiritual**	**83**
5	The mission	85
6	Missionary mentality	113
7	The Buddhism of the Sinhalese	125
Part III	**The temporal and the spiritual**	**139**
8	The religious obligations of kingship	141
9	The consequences of royal conversion in Kōṭṭe and Sītāvaka	164
10	Christianity and Buddhism resurgent	194
	Conclusion: some final thoughts on indigenism, identity and kingship	235
	Appendix: Regnal dates of rulers in Sri Lanka	252
	Bibliography	254
	Index	271

MAPS

PLATES

The following plates are all photographs of ivory caskets produced in Kōṭṭe in the sixteenth century. For the sake of consistency and easy orientation, I have referred to them by their dates as suggested by Jaffer and Schwabe 1999. However, as I discuss in the footnotes, these datings are contested and provisional.

1. Left end of casket, *c*. 1543. Residenz, Munich, Schatzkammer, inv. no. 1241
   Thanks to Bayerische Verwaltung der staatlichen Schlösser, Gärten und Seen for reproduction permission, and to Annemarie Jordan Gschwend for the use of the photograph *page* 28
2. Front of casket, *c*. 1543
   Thanks to Bayerische Verwaltung der staatlichen Schlösser, Gärten und Seen for reproduction permission, and to Annemarie Jordan Gschwend for the use of the photograph 67
3. Rear of casket, *c*. 1543
   Thanks to Bayerische Verwaltung der staatlichen Schlösser, Gärten und Seen for reproduction permission, and to Annemarie Jordan Gschwend for the use of the photograph 68
4. Right end of casket, *c*. 1543
   Thanks to Bayerische Verwaltung der staatlichen Schlösser, Gärten und Seen for reproduction permission, and to Annemarie Jordan Gschwend for the use of the photograph 69
5. Front of casket, *c*. 1547. Residenz, Munich, Schatzkammer, inv. no. 1242.
   Thanks to Bayerische Verwaltung der staatlichen Schlösser, Gärten und Seen for reproduction permission, and to Annemarie Jordan Gschwend for the use of the photograph 74
6. Right end of casket, *c*. 1547
   Thanks to Bayerische Verwaltung der staatlichen Schlösser, Gärten und Seen for reproduction permission, and to Annemarie Jordan Gschwend for the use of the photograph 76

7. Left end of casket, *c.* 1547
Thanks to Bayerische Verwaltung der staatlichen Schlösser, Gärten und Seen for reproduction permission, and to Annemarie Jordan Gschwend for the use of the photograph 77
8. Top view of 'Robinson' casket, *c.* 1557. Victoria and Albert Museum, London, inv. no. IS. 41–1980
© V&A Images/Victoria and Albert Museum 137
9. Rear of 'Robinson' casket, *c.* 1557
© V&A Images/Victoria and Albert Museum 199
10. Right end of 'Robinson' casket, *c.* 1557
© V&A Images/Victoria and Albert Museum 200
11. Top of casket, *c.* 1578–80. Museum für Indische Kunst, Berlin inv. no. MIK I-9928.
© Bildarchiv Preussischer Kulturbesitz, Berlin, Museum für Indische Kunst. Photo by Ute Franz-Scarciglia, Museum für Indische Kunst, Staatliche Museen zu Berlin 201
12. Left end of casket, *c.* 1578–80
© Bildarchiv Preussischer Kulturbesitz, Berlin, Museum für Indische Kunst. Photo by Ute Franz-Scarciglia, Museum für Indische Kunst, Staatliche Museen zu Berlin 202
13. Front of casket, *c.* 1578–80
© Bildarchiv Preussischer Kulturbesitz, Berlin, Museum für Indische Kunst. Photo by Ute Franz-Scarciglia, Museum für Indische Kunst, Staatliche Museen zu Berlin 203
14. Rear of casket, *c.* 1578–80
© Bildarchiv Preussischer Kulturbesitz, Berlin, Museum für Indische Kunst. Photo by Ute Franz-Scarciglia, Museum für Indische Kunst, Staatliche Museen zu Berlin 204
15. Right end of casket, *c.* 1578–80
© Bildarchiv Preussischer Kulturbesitz, Berlin, Museum für Indische Kunst. Photo by Ute Franz-Scarciglia, Museum für Indische Kunst, Staatliche Museen zu Berlin 205

ACKNOWLEDGEMENTS

C. R. de Silva, the presiding scholar of the 'Portuguese period' of Sri Lankan history, has been a mentor from afar ever since my interest in the field was first aroused, and I have benefited a great deal from his expertise and continuing support. A glance at the footnotes should reveal my debt to his work and to that of the other expert in the field, Jorge Manuel Flores, who has also been very helpful. Peter Carey has offered invaluable support from my undergraduate years onwards. As a co-supervisor of the D.Phil. thesis that formed the basis for this book, he provided a model both of rigorous scholarship and of direct engagement with the contemporary reality of the region one studies. I am very grateful too to my other supervisor, Tom Earle, who went beyond the call of duty in working to improve my Portuguese and check translations.

Zoltán Biedermann began work in Lisbon on Portuguese Sri Lanka at the same time as I did, and he has been a tremendous aid in navigating both Portugal and the burgeoning Portuguese scholarship. We have developed a close working relationship, and I am particularly grateful to him for allowing me to profit from his archival labours in the later sixteenth-century material at a time when I was not able to travel. Michael Roberts has become a regular sounding-board, and the galvanizing influence of his work on my later chapters will be evident to those who know it. John Rogers has been unfailingly generous with his time and advice, particularly on theoretical matters such as caste. Jonathan Walters has acted as an insightful reader for related work. Susan Bayly has sharpened my thinking on a number of issues and, crucially, encouraged me to expand the book beyond its 1521–51 remit. Joan-Pau Rubiés has offered timely advice for many years. John Clifford Holt from the earliest days, and Kitsiri Malalgoda more recently, have always been ready to help with religious and textual queries. Other scholars who have gracefully received harassment on particular topics include: Richard Gombrich, David Washbrook, Sanjay Subrahmanyam, Anne M. Blackburn, Antoni M. Ucerler, Stephen Berkwitz, and Nuno Vassalo e Silva.

This book also depends on the work of people who have opened up the world of Sinhala texts for me. Rohini and K. D. Paranavitana, K. N. O. Dharmadasa, Nihal Kiriella, K. M. P. Kulasekera and Sandadas Coperahewa have all helped me a great deal with translations of important texts. My research in Sri Lanka was made possible by a grant from the Arts and Humanities Research Board (who also funded my D.Phil. research) and the hospitality and generosity of relations by marriage, the Gunasekera family: Anura, Malini, Isuru, Mihirini, Lahiru, Achi and Siya. They have continued to help my work in so many ways over the years. Lorna Dewaraja facilitated my research at a time when it was apparently not easy for Western students to obtain research visas for Sri Lanka. I am grateful too to many scholars there for the welcome and assistance they extended to a young researcher from abroad: M. D. Rohandeera, H. B. M. Ilangasinha, Martin Quéré, A. V. Suraveera, R. Amarasinghe, K. D. G. Wimalratne, H. A. P. Abeyawardena, D. G. B. De Silva, and Douglas Ranasinghe. This includes Vito Perniola, a living link to the long tradition of Jesuit scholarship. His translations of the contemporary letters have allowed me to refer English readers to the principal body of source material for the early decades.

My research in Portugal was made possible by the institutional generosity of the Fundação Calouste Gulbenkian and made pleasant by the personal kindness of Zoltán Biedermann and Andreia Martins de Carvalho. I am very grateful to Annemarie Jordan Gschwend for her discussions of the caskets, and in particular for the loan of her photographs of them used in this book. I thank the Museum für Indische Kunst, Berlin, the Schatzkammer of the Residenz, Munich, and the Victoria and Albert Museum, London, for allowing me to reproduce images of their caskets. In Oxford, Nick Davidson and David Parrot gave encouragement when it was most needed, and the staff at the Indian Institute Library and Bodleian suffered me with patience. The Cecil Lubbock Memorial Scholarship awarded by Trinity College was important in sustaining me for a fourth year. Latterly, an Old Dominion Research Fellowship at Clare Hall, Cambridge, has provided an exceptional opportunity to pursue further research, a tolerant environment in which to do it, and even a valuable reader for some arduous spin-off work in Geoffrey Hawthorn. I also want to thank my editor, Michael Sharp, for his patient fielding of queries, and everyone else at CUP for all their help.

I have to reserve my highest thanks for Nilmini Dissanayake, who has helped my research in more ways than I can do justice to here. Her daughter, Samanthi, is the reason why I begun in the first place, and why I have emerged from it with sanity apparently still intact.

A note on style

The conventions followed here are determined by ease of comprehension. I therefore refer to the island as 'Sri Lanka', even though that only became its official name in 1972. Strictly speaking, 'sixteenth-century Sri Lanka' is anachronistic. It is not entirely inappropriate however, given that the use of the honorific ('Siri Laka') was alive and well among Sinhalese in the sixteenth century. While I use 'Sri Lanka' and 'Lanka' interchangeably, I often use 'Lankan' for the adjectival form. The Portuguese referred to the island as 'Ceilão', but to use the English equivalent 'Ceylon' might insensibly evoke the British period of rule. I use the common term 'Sinhalese' for the people, and 'Sinhala' for the language. I have pluralized Sinhala nouns as if they were English. Sinhala diacritics follow the system used in www.omniglot.com, with a couple of adjustments as advised by Charles Hallisey. I have tended not to use diacritics for Indian names and have refrained from allowing Portuguese noblemen their 'Dom' and mendicants their 'Fr'.

ABBREVIATIONS

AGS-SP	Archivo General Simancas, Secretarías Provinciales, Portugal.
AHU	Arquivo Histórico Ultramarino, Lisbon.
APO	*Archivo Portuguez-Oriental*, ed. J. H. da Cunha-Rivara (8 vols.). Nova Goa, 1857–77, vol. III.
Alakeśvarayuddhaya	A. Suravira (ed.), *Alakeśvarayuddhaya*. Colombo, 1965.
Azevedo	[Agostinho de Azevedo], 'Estado da India e aonde tem o seu principio', printed as an anonymous document in *Documentação Ultramarina Portuguesa* 1, 1960, I: 197–263.
BA	Biblioteca da Ajuda, Lisbon.
Barros; Couto	D. Ferguson (ed. and trans.), *The History of Ceylon from the Earliest Times to 1600 AD*. New Delhi, 1993. (First published by the *Journal of the Ceylon Branch of the Royal Asiatic Society* 1908, this is an annotated English translation of the 'Decadas' by João de Barros and Diogo do Couto.)
Biker	J. F. Júdice Biker, *Collecção de Tratados e Concertos de Pazes que o Estado da Índia Portugueza Fez com os Reis e Senhores com Quem Teve Relações nas Partes da Ásia e África Oriental desde o Principio da Conqusita até ao Fim do Século XVIII* (14 vols.). Lisbon, 1881–7.
BL	British Library, London.
Bocarro	T. B. H. Abeyasinghe (ed. and trans.), 'António Bocarro's Ceylon', introduction by C. R. De Silva, *Journal of the Royal Asiatic Society of Sri Lanka* n.s. 39, 1995 (published 1996).
Bocarro, *Decada*,	António Bocarro, *Década 13 da História da India*, ed. Rodrigo José de Lima Felner. Lisbon, 1876.
Bouchon, Doc,	'Documents', in Geneviève Bouchon, '*Regent of the Sea': Cannanore's Response to Portuguese Expansion, 1507–1528*. Delhi, 1988.

Caração	Geneviève Bouchon (ed.), 'A Letter: Cristóvão Lourenço Caração, to D. Manuel, Cochin 13 Jan 1522', *Mare Luso-Indicum* 1, 1971.
Castanheda	Fernão Lopes de Castanheda, *História do Descobrimento e Conquista da Índia pelos Portugueses* (9 vols.). Coimbra, 1924–33.
Conquista	Fernão de Queiros, *Conquista Temporal e Espiritual de Ceylão*, ed. P. E. Pieris. Colombo, 1916.
Correia	'The Portuguese in Ceylon in the First Half of the Sixteenth Century. Gaspar Correa's Account', trans. D. Ferguson, *Ceylon Literary Register* 4, 1935–6.
Correia, *Lendas*	Gaspar Correia, *Lendas da Índia*, ed. Rodrigo José de Lima Felner (4 vols.). Lisbon, 1858–64.
Couto	See Barros above for D. Ferguson translation (1993).
CS	Luís de Albuquerque e José Pereira da Costa, 'Cartas de Serviços da Índia (1500–1550)', *Mare Liberum* 1, 1990.
Cūḷavaṃsa	Geiger, W. (ed. and trans.) *Culavamsa, Being the More Recent Part of the Mahavamsa*, trans. from the German into English by C. M. Rickmers, part II. Colombo, 1953.
DI	J. Wicki (ed.), *Documenta Indica* (18 vols.). Rome, 1948–88.
DPM	*Documentos sobre os Portugueses em Moçambigue e na África Central, 1497–1840* (9 vols.). Lisbon, 1962–.
EZ	*Epigraphia Zeylanica, Being Lithic and other Inscriptions of Ceylon*, Ceylon Archaeological Survey (4 vols.)., vols. I–III, ed. Don Martino de Zilva Wickremasinghe, vol. IV, ed. H. W. Codrington and S. Paranavitana. London, 1904–43.
Flores, Doc	'Documentos', in Jorge Manuel Flores, *Os Portugueses e o Mar de Ceilão: Trato, Diplomacia e Guerra (1498–1543)*. Lisbon, 1988.
IAN/TT	Instituto dos Arquivos Nacionais/Torre do Tombo.
Knox	Robert Knox, *An Historical Relation of the Island of Ceylon*, ed. J. H. O. Paulusz (2nd edn. including interleaved notes) (2 vols.), vol. II. Dehiwala, 1989.
Linschoten	J. H. van Linschoten, *The Voyage of John Huyghen van Linschoten to the East Indies from the Old English Translation of 1598*, ed. A. C. Burnell and P. A. Thiele, vol. I. London, 1885.
Miranda	Jorge Manuel Flores (ed.), *Os Olhos do Rei: Desenhos e Descrições Portuguesas da Ilha de Ceilão (1624, 1638).* Lisbon, 2001. (Contains Constantino de Sá de Miranda's text of 1638.)

Nevill	K. D. Somadasa, *Catalogue of the Hugh Nevill Collection of Sinhalese Manuscripts in the British Library* (7 vols.). London, 1987–95.
Queyroz	Fernão de Queyroz, *The Temporal and Spiritual Conquest of Ceylon*, trans. with introduction by S. G. Perera, 3 vols. First published 1930; reprint, New Delhi, 1992.
Rājaratnākaraya	*Rājaratnākaraya*, ed. S. de Silva. Colombo, 1930.
Rājāvaliya	*Rājāvaliya*, trans. A. Suraweera. Sri Lanka, 2000.
Ribeiro	João Ribeiro, *The Historic Tragedy of the Island of Ceilão*, ed. and trans. P. E. Pieris. Colombo, 1948.
SH	*Sītāvaka Haṭana*, ed. Rohini Paranavitana. Colombo, 1999.
Spilbergen	Spilbergen, Joris van, *Journal of Spilbergen, The First Dutch Envoy to Ceylon, 1602*, ed. and trans. K. D. Paranavitana. Colombo, 1997.
SR	A. da Silva Rego (ed.), *Documentação para a História das Missões do Padroado Português do Oriente* (12 vols.). Lisbon, 1947–58.
SV	Georg Schurhamer and E. A. Voretzsch (eds.), *Ceylon zur Zeit des Konigs Bhuvaneka Bahu und Franz Xavers, 1539–1552* (2 vols.). Leipzig, 1928.
Trindade	Paulo da Trindade, *Conquista Espiritual do Oriente*, ed. Fernando Félix Lopes (3 parts). Lisbon, 1962–7.
VP	Vito Perniola (ed.), *The Catholic Church in Sri Lanka, The Portuguese Period*, vol. I, *1505–1565*. Dehiwala, 1989. vol. II, *1566–1619*. Dehiwala, 1991. Vol. III, *1620–1658*. Dehiwala, 1991. Where no volume number is given, vol. I is referred to.

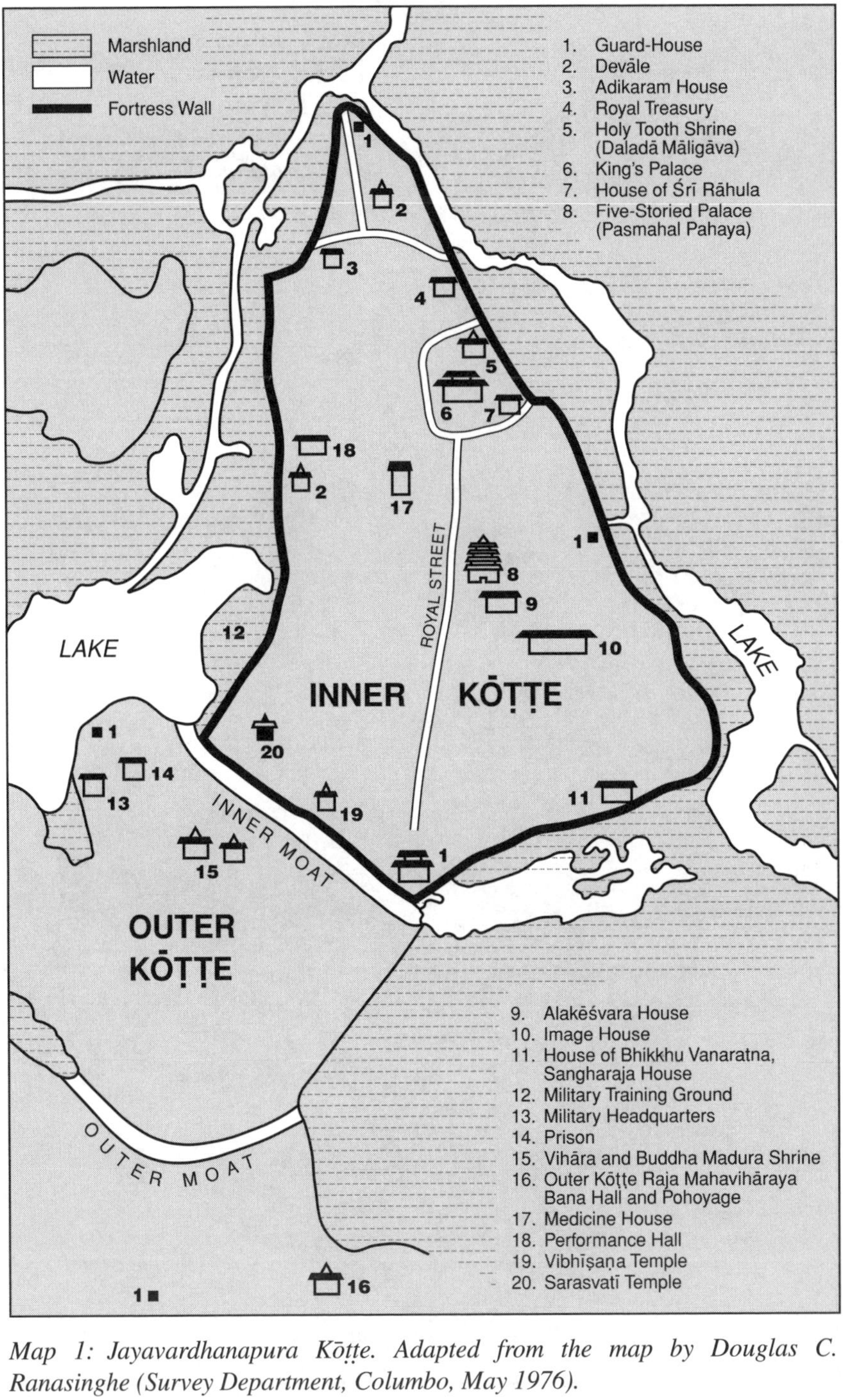

Map 1: Jayavardhanapura Kōṭṭe. Adapted from the map by Douglas C. Ranasinghe (Survey Department, Columbo, May 1976).

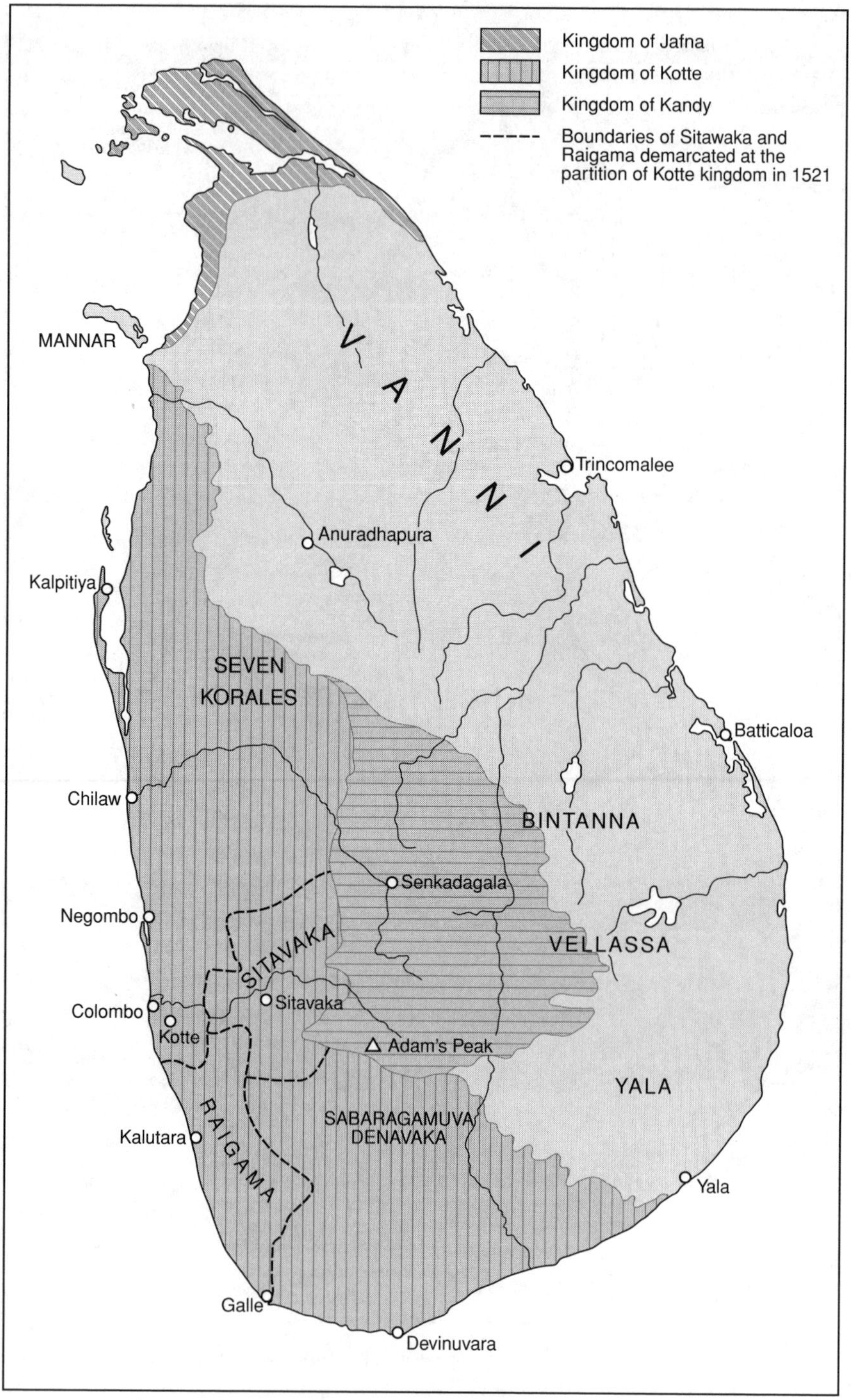

Map 2: Sri Lanka in the mid-sixteenth century.

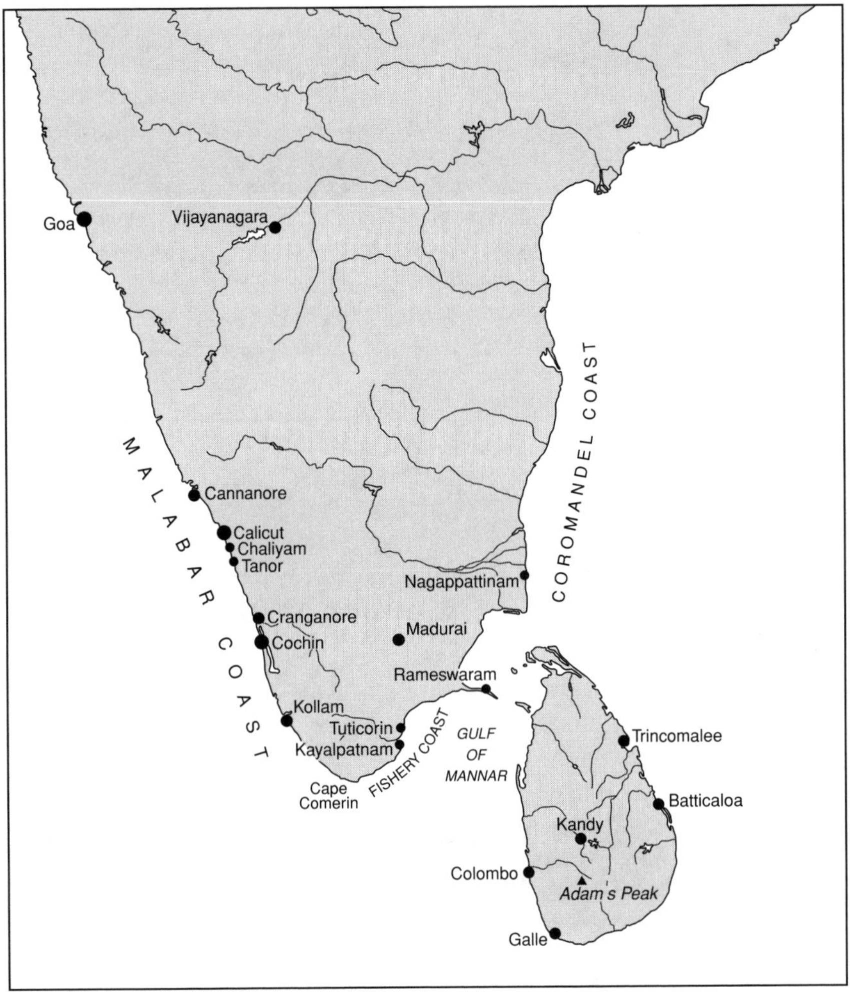

Map 3: South India and Sri Lanka.

INTRODUCTION

A short way into his adventures, Don Quixote sees two large dust-clouds approaching each other and in his mind they become two armies gathering for battle. He imagines that they belong to a heathen emperor of 'the great Ínsula Taprobane' – a legendary island often identified with Sri Lanka – on the one side and a Christian king on the other.[1] The emperor had asked for the hand of his opponent's daughter, but she was refused to him unless he renounced his false prophet and turned to Christ. Don Quixote decides to join the campaign to defend this point of principle. The knight's perceptions are the least reliable in literature, and his creator a very remote observer.[2] But his ravings were at least fortuitous. Cervantes was writing just as the sixteenth century expired, a century which had indeed seen Iberians going into battle in Sri Lanka in the name of baptized kings against 'heathen' rulers who styled themselves emperors. A few years before, a Sinhalese Christian princess had even been forced to wed the apostate king Vimaladharmasūriya I (1591–1604). The banners of religious identity had come to be flown above political struggles.

Two features of the sixteenth-century Portuguese maritime expansion in Asia are worth emphasizing for those familiar with other kinds of empire. First, territorial conquest was often eschewed. The preferred means of protecting their mercantile strongholds was typically to make vassals or allies of the surrounding rulers. Second, the pursuit of commercial and political power was intimately associated with religious ideals and missionary concerns. This book examines what happened when this wave of expansion reached the Sinhalese kingdoms of Sri Lanka.[3]

[1] Cervantes 2005: 126–30.

[2] Sri Lanka was commonly identified with that ancient island in Portugal (see the letter of King Manuel to the Pope, 25 September 1507, announcing the discovery of Ceylon as Taprobane, VP: 5; and, writing in the 1590s, Couto: 80), but there was a long-running debate in Europe over its identification. Don Quixote lived through classical and chivalric texts, and he is drawing on their exotic image of 'Taprobane' rather than on contemporary realities to fuel his imagination. The hapless knight imagines the heathen emperor to be a Muslim and accords all the protagonists absurd and bombastic names. However, Cervantes had served as a spy in Portugal during the early 1580s, so it is plausible that he knew something of Lankan affairs.

[3] Since this book is primarily concerned with the Sinhalese kingdoms, we shall not reflect on the controversial issue of the origins of the Jaffna kingdom in the north of the island.

The first two parts are rooted in the mid century. Many broader themes are broached there – such as the nature of state power in Sri Lanka – but they are used to provide the context for a fine-grained analysis of the reign of King Bhuvanekabāhu VII of Kōṭṭe (1521–51). This is where those readers should turn who want a case-study of how early Portuguese imperialism worked and how an Asian ruler responded to it, or of what kind of impact the arrival of a small Christian mission could have in a Buddhist land. The third and largest part is quite different, taking in the latter half of the sixteenth century and a decade or two beyond in order to reflect on themes of identity. The central argument concerns the religious identity of kings, but we shall also explore how dynastic loyalties and ethnic and cultural antagonisms were played out over the whole of the century.

Some characters and controversies

Bhuvanekabāhu VII's reign is where the long history of European imperial involvement in Sri Lanka's history has its origins. At least one previous king had sworn some sort of vassalage to the Portuguese, but it was only under Bhuvanekabāhu that the Portuguese came to acquire real power on the island and it was at his personal invitation that the first Christian mission arrived on its shores. One might expect then that he would have been eulogized by a writer such as Fernão de Queirós, the Portuguese Jesuit whose massive chronicle, 'The Temporal and Spiritual Conquest of Ceylon' narrated the whole 'Portuguese period' of Lankan history (1506–1658).[4] But for Queirós, Bhuvanekabāhu presented a dilemma: this king had also resisted all attempts to procure his baptism. He turned out to be the very symbol of resolute paganism. In Queirós' text, Bhuvanekabāhu's characterization is therefore ambiguous; he is blessed with the qualities of gentleness and kindness and even honour, but he is no great man, he is weak and timorous, afraid to convert for fear of alienating his subjects.

That is the image that has come down to us today, largely because of the way in which Queirós' text was embodied in the highly influential work of P. E. Pieris in the early twentieth century.[5] Pieris, a pronounced Sinhalese patriot, had his own reasons for affirming Queirós' judgement of Bhuvanekabāhu as a man endowed with 'the more feminine virtues' but not the masculine qualities of leadership: for him, as for many others, Bhuvanekabāhu was at fault for facilitating the establishment of colonial power in Ceylon.[6] In this Pieris was also following the lead of the Sinhalese chronicle, the *Rājāvaliya*, which had already castigated him as a traitor

[4] I have used a modernized version of 'Queirós' in the main text, but the English translation will be cited according to its rendering, 'Queyroz'.

[5] Pieris 1983–92 (first published 1913–14), upon which many popular works continue to rely. It is ironic therefore that some nationalist interpretations have their origins in the idiosyncratic preoccupations of this Portuguese Jesuit, see Malalasekera 1994: 258–61; Weerasooriya 1970; Sankaranarayan 1994: 59; Panabokke 1993: 192–207; Rambukwelle 1996, who explicitly acknowledges his dependence on Pieris and Queirós.

[6] Pieris and Fitzler 1927b: 23; Roberts, Raheem and Colin-Thomé 1989: 5; J. A. Will Perera 1956.

in the late seventeenth century.[7] This image of a feeble, vacillating creature, principally propelled by terror of his ambitious younger brother Māyādunnē (1521–81), of the vigorous Portuguese and of his own subjects has become a cliché of subsequent historical writing.[8]

Of course, if that is the posterity meted out to the last independent king of Kōṭṭe, one would one not expect much of the reputation of his thoroughly dependent successor, his young grandson Dharmapāla (1551–97), who did convert to Christianity early on in his reign and spent decades confined to his capital in an impotent and claustrophobic relationship with the Portuguese. While Dharmapāla is the extension of all that was forlorn or pathetic in his predecessor, so too Rājasiṃha I (1581–93), the terrible lion of the rival kingdom of Sītāvaka, tends to be seen as the epitome of all that was patriotic and warlike in his father Māyādunnē.[9]

In the writing of sixteenth-century history, such character-sketches have been attractive explanatory devices, but they are difficult to establish in contemporary evidence. Take Bhuvanekabāhu: his 'goodness' or friendliness is a theme that one can trace back to the earliest Portuguese chroniclers.[10] It may reflect his actual reputation at the time; it certainly reflects his status as a generally reliable Portuguese ally. But when we turn to the contemporary letters we find that the received characterization dissolves into a slender and ambiguous assemblage of perspectives. To observers at the Kōṭṭe court he is crafty or prone to tears.[11] To a Portuguese governor, wearily intent on maintaining the status quo, he may be 'a man of good disposition', but to an aggrieved Portuguese settler he is a tyrant and sodomite, to a friar pushing Kandyan claims he is an opium and arrack-addict, and to another friar angered by his recalcitrance he is a duplicitous servant of the devil.[12]

The standard characterizations slip easily into the modern imagination.[13] To the man in the street in Sri Lanka, the colonial Portuguese still tend to bear an awful reputation as religious vandals. And for writers with nationalist sympathies that reputation remains a powerful symbol of the evils of foreign interference, as a raft of editorials and comments regarding the recent quincentennial of the Portuguese arrival in Sri Lanka revealed (this was widely held to be 2005, although most professional historians agree that it was more likely that the Portuguese first arrived in 1506 rather than 1505). When one collective wanted to impress on their readership the image of the then Prime Minister Ranil Wickremasinghe as a

[7] *Rājāvaliya*: 73–7. [8] See Bourdon 1936; G. G. Perera 1951: 33: Quéré 1988a: 74.

[9] Māyādunnē can sometimes be blamed as a 'causer of disunity' (interview with Douglas Ranasinghe Colombo, Feb. 2000), but more often he is something of a hero.

[10] Correia: 211, 267; Barros: 74; Couto: 140; Castanheda, VI. 296. The letter of Miguel Ferreira reported by Queyroz: 231–3, may be a fictitious creation.

[11] VP: 10, 130. [12] VP: 192, 118, 205, 239.

[13] A local tradition of Church history, carried forward by S. G. Perera, W. L. A. Don Peter, Vito Perniola, and Martin Quéré, has taken issue with the anti-Christian perspectives while developing the critique of Portuguese imperialism that is present in the earliest Portuguese letters and chronicles. In the twentieth century this was transformed into the notion that Catholicism was actually damaged by its association with the Portuguese.

'Betrayer of the Sinhala Nation' for his attempts to come to a political settlement with the LTTE (Liberation Tigers of Tamil Eelam), they concluded by comparing him to Dharmapāla – with no further explanation deemed necessary.[14] But it is not a modern idiosyncrasy to draw religious differences into political violence. From the 1560s the Portuguese set out to destroy sacred sites in an attempt to symbolically undermine the authority of Sinhalese states and concretely undermine morale. For Sinhalese today, who have seen Tamil Tigers attack the Srī Mahābōdi and the Temple of the Tooth with very similar aims, the Portuguese policies must feel horribly familiar. But aggression was met with aggression, then as now. As early as the 1550s, the Sinhalese prince Vīdiyē Baṇḍāra led a rebellion intent on destroying Christian targets.

Another tendency is to see the arrival of the Portuguese as the first in a long line of malign and disordering Western influences whose weight can be felt as a burden in this globalized age, and again we can find this prefigured in some texts from the late sixteenth and seventeenth century and their descriptions of the chaos wrought by the Portuguese presence. If the historian arriving from abroad can discern traces of the present in the past, he or she must also be amazed and humbled by how strongly the past lives in the Sri Lankan present, by the capacity of sixteenth-century events to arouse debate in national newspapers or internet sites. But the corollary of this is that the past is often understood in the same terms as the present. (Even this tendency seems ancient in its fashion.) It can appear squashed within the limits of the twentieth- or twenty-first century mind. In this book we shall try to let the sixteenth century breathe for itself, and fill out into perhaps unexpected forms. To that end, extensive quotations from primary sources have been retained.

While Portuguese imperialism still resounds in the popular imagination – much more vibrantly than the more recent experience of Dutch rule, for example – it has barely registered in the minds of recent theorists of Sri Lankan history and society. One important strand of theory, which has been described usefully as 'post-Orientalist', emphasizes how European writings have constructed or fixed the contemporary contours of caste, religion and ethnicity in Asia.[15] These arguments often rely on evidence from eighteenth- to twentieth-century British India. What can our more fragmentary sources tell us about the nature of these phenomena *before* the British or the modern era, when a quite different kind of European first began to make their appraisals?

One aim of this book is to introduce sixteenth-century material into the debates that have acquired such significance over the last twenty years of post-colonial predicament and bitter civil war. There is simply not the space here to do justice to the variety of different positions taken up in these debates, but it can help to isolate intellectual principles from political positions. For our purposes, then, we can imagine a spectrum defined by two opposing approaches to the past.

[14] Singhaputhra-Coalition 2004.
[15] See the overviews by Rogers 1994, 2004a, and Roberts 2001.

The 'traditionalist' view is concerned to emphasize the continuity and idiosyncrasy of Sri Lankan history. It draws on an exceptionally long-lived, if not exactly continuous, indigenous tradition of historical writing. As early as the sixth century AD the Buddhist monks of the Mahāvihāra fraternity were composing the Pāli chronicle known as the *Mahāvaṃsa*, a text that apparently drew on earlier works (such as the *Dīpavaṃsa*) and would receive later additions (sometimes known as the *Cūḷavaṃsa*). These texts are presented as elaborating a distinctive religious and political worldview, sometimes referred to as the '*vaṃsa* ideology', although features of it are discernible in Sinhala works such as the *Rājāvaliya*. According to the *Mahāvaṃsa*, the Buddha had visited the island of Lanka and made it radiant with the *dhamma* (Buddhist teachings), and just before he drew his last breath had requested Śakra, the lord of gods, to give it especial protection as a land destined for the flourishing of his religion.[16] Just as the Buddha had taken possession of Lanka, so it was the destiny of the Sinhalese kings to conquer and rule over the whole island. These rulers would reign over a unified state that was dedicated to the preservation of Buddhist ideals. In the words of one writer, this mythology exhibited a 'constant strain to identify the religion with the state and the Buddhist state in turn with a Buddhist society'.[17] Traditionalism takes this worldview to be representative of a Sinhalese culture that prevailed throughout the island for two millennia.

The 'historicist' approach is concerned to emphasize discontinuities, to make supposed structures of the very *longue durée* contingent on smaller moments of history. It demands a more critical view of the monastic literature, rendering such works reflections of the particular conditions of their production rather than embodiments of 'Sinhala culture' *per se*, as prescriptive rather than descriptive. There was then no coherent '*vaṃsa* ideology'. The conflation of state, people and religion can be teased apart. One can explore the great transformations in the nature of the state and the changing extent of state dominions across the centuries, undermine the notion that a coherent sense of ethnic identity was a significant factor in Sri Lankan history before the nineteenth century, and question the hegemony of Theravāda Buddhism as the ground of Lankan culture in favour of a more fluid and accommodating mixture of religious forms.[18]

These terms are intended primarily as tools for doing scholarship rather than for describing it.[19] They should not be taken as euphemisms for particular political

[16] *Mahāvaṃsa*, ed. Geiger: 1993: 8–9, 55. This is now often glossed as rendering Sri Lanka *dhammadīpa* (island of the *dhamma*). Collins 1998: 598–9, and Walters 2000: 147, argue that this gloss is recent and carries inappropriate connotations of exclusivity. Nevertheless, the basic symbolism remains that of an island consecrated, reconstituted and enduringly transformed by the Buddha's presence.

[17] Tambiah 1976: 521, qualified and complicated in Tambiah 1992.

[18] See the index for topics where these terms are introduced.

[19] See Strathern 2004 for more. It makes little sense then to describe a given work as either 'traditionalist' or 'historicist'. Such empty terms often attract unintended interpretations. A quite different understanding of historicism is normally employed in Sri Lankan studies (e.g. Hallisey 1995: 36–7). I use the *Concise Oxford Dictionary* definition: the 'theory that social and cultural phenomena are determined by history'. Also see the conceptual dichotomies proposed by Rogers 1994 (primordialist/modernist) or Spencer 1995 (primordialist/constructionalist).

viewpoints, and nor does this book set out to demonstrate the superiority of one over the other.

Some contexts and concepts

The period of Portuguese influence may have remained on the periphery of theoretical developments, but there exist excellent historical accounts of it, such as can be found principally in the work of C. R. de Silva, T. B. H. Abeyasinghe and Jorge Manuel Flores.[20] Rather than provide a comprehensive narrative, then, this book sets out to provide a series of explanatory contexts for the events of this time, to make them more comprehensible and meaningful. In Part One, the political context is at issue: what was the nature of this early wave of European expansion; what kind of imperial pressure did the Portuguese exert? What legal vehicles did it work through, and how much did central policy matter? And with what did it interact: what sort of state was the Kingdom of Kōṭṭe? What real room for manoeuvre was left for vassals such as Bhuvanekabāhu?

Part Two explores the religious developments of the mid century. A comparatively modest conversion movement along the southwest coast seems to have caused disproportionate socio-political disruption. These patterns can best be understood through a consideration of the indigenous institutions of caste and land tenure. Chapter Five also analyses what Bhuvanekabāhu's policies were in dealing with this new threat. Incidentally, it should be pointed out that the term 'conversion' as used in this book is not intended to convey any assumptions about the interior lives of individuals. It is analytically more helpful to see converts as simply those who accepted their identification as such.[21] However porous the boundaries of religious belief and practice, we shall see that crossing the boundaries of religious *identity* was highly significant. But Chapter Six asks how the missionaries thought about such matters: what did they think they were doing in Sri Lanka? How did they accommodate their consciences to the business of 'theological diplomacy'? Chapter Seven, which relies on secondary sources much more than other chapters, is intended to provide the context of local religiosity, enquiring into the state of Buddhism in the island at that time, and how the Sinhalese may have interpreted the Christian message.

Part Three is the largest and most important, and it is where the twin themes of kingship and conversion come together. As we proceed into the later decades of the century, many of the other contexts fall away. In particular, there is no room to follow in any detail the evolution of the Portuguese state from the mid century into the great Iberian mammoth of the Period of the Two Crowns (1580–1640), or of the transformation of the Portuguese presence in Sri Lanka from lieges to conquerors. Readers interested in these processes, and many others, can consult the

[20] See, principally, C. R. de Silva 1995, Flores 1998, and also now Biedermann 2005a and their further works in the bibliography. Bourdon 1936; Schurhammer 1973–82; and Da Silva Cosme 1990 also have detailed narratives.

[21] See Hefner 1993.

illuminating new research by Zoltán Biedermann.[22] Instead the central concern of Part Three is the implications of conversion for the legitimacy of rulers. What role did Buddhist or Indic conceptions of the relationship between kings and subjects play in determining the decision as to whether to convert or not? And it is for the later decades that the historian can begin to offer insights on such resonant themes as rebellion, patriotism, and religious antagonism.

This book locates the primary grounds for Lankan political activity in the capacity of its state-forms to generate conflict. However grandiose the imagery of kingship, the king himself was vulnerable to a ceaseless jostling for status on the part of his family members and noble factions manoeuvring for succession at the centre, or forming breakaway courts in the regions, and it is these conflicts that sucked the Portuguese into their affairs. This is one reason why it is often misleading to think of sixteenth-century Lanka in terms of the modern understandings of the nation and nationalism. Particularly in the later decades, nobles and officials were apparently ready to switch their allegiances between different dynasties. However, it would be a mistake to reduce Lankan politics to the intrigue of elite factions or the playing out of a heroic warrior ethos. In the later chapters, I have tried to discern how much broader – even popular – sentiments helped to determine the nature and success of factions and pretenders. One of these, which gained some influence in the latter half of the century, could be described as 'indigenism'. At its simplest, this means a favouring of indigenous or traditional peoples, political forms, customs and religious practices over their foreign equivalents. At its weakest, it functions simply as an undefined flip side of anti-Portuguese, anti-Christian sentiment. An associated term used here is patriotism, which assumes a natural association between a territory and a society. This sentiment need not depend on any political mediation – it may ignore state boundaries entirely – but it does have political implications, rendering foreign claims to dominion illegitimate.

What both terms leave open is the extent to which these sentiments are merely aspects of a strong sense of Sinhalaness. This is because if the Portuguese are the 'them', the evidence is often not rich enough to clarify whether the 'us' were imagined to be the Sinhalese or simply the traditional communities of Sri Lanka. However, some sources do suggest that Sinhalaness was significant, and this is entirely plausible.[23] Whether we refer to this as an 'ethnic' consciousness turns on one's definitions. A narrow definition of ethnicity renders it an axiomatic identity rooted in beliefs of shared blood or ancestry.[24] In Sri Lanka, the strongest primordial or lineage-based identities may have been based on caste.[25] Yet, cultural features can be constructed as markers of a felt community without fixed beliefs in ancestry. Nor need a group conform to state boundaries to feel that its interests are opposed to those of another group. One of the most powerful forces here is

[22] Biedermann 2005a. This also has a great deal on the early decades, but I decided not to use that material here, so that it can speak for itself: a dialogue rather than a synthesis.

[23] See Conclusion. [24] On this issue, Obeyesekere 1995a and b; Pollock 1998.

[25] Rogers, 1994:17, 1995.

the experience of war.[26] Evoked as they are by particular contexts, the salience of such identities waxes and wanes: they are, in this sense, 'soft', sometimes more germane to elites than to the masses, and co-existing with all manner of other loyalties and categorizations.[27] But they could acquire very hard edges. And it would be wrong to imagine that the forms of communication and mobilization in pre-modern societies were inherently too weak to sustain any such ties of solidarity.[28] Michael Roberts has argued this case powerfully, and his work displays the most fully developed appreciation of the way in which group boundaries can be subtle, messy, contradictory and shifting, and yet of deep significance at the same time. If one had to characterize the conjuncture of the later sixteenth century in a word, one might eventually settle for militiarization. If this served to strengthen the hand of indigenist or ethnic sentiments, it also threatened to pull apart the long-term norms of rulership – threatened to, but eventually did not.

Some comparisons

Sixteenth-century Sri Lanka is presented here as a case-study for a comparative argument as to why rulers do or do not convert to new religions. Conversion is always potentially a dilemma for monarchs: by attempting to redefine what a legitimate king should be, they risk bringing the whole edifice of kingship crashing to the ground. Move too far beyond the norms of their subjects – which they are, after all, supposed to embody and represent, affording a society a vision of who it is and what it holds dear – then they may cease to be a king. But I have argued that in those societies which were heirs to the religious transcendentalist traditions of the Axial Age, these considerations were particularly highly charged and thus their rulers more impervious to pressures to convert.[29]

At first sight, 'transcendentalism' refers to a bewildering variety of philosophies and religions that have their roots in the societal convulsions of first-millennium BC Greece, Israel, China and India.[30] These convulsions were not the birth-pangs of

[26] E.g. the mobilization of a pre-existing 'Greek' identity based on a common culture during the Persian wars (fifth century BC), at a time when the Greeks were divided into tiny and fiercely competitive city-states.

[27] See Lieberman 2003: 41, following Prasenjit Duara. Compare with Gunawardana's 'archaic' ethnicity (1995: 4), which, however, confines ethnic consciousness to the literate elite. The general approach to ethnicity in Sabaratnam 2001 is sensible (e.g. 9–10) but its comments on the decline in ethnic salience in the Portuguese period (e.g. 40) must be revised in the light of the material here.

[28] Roberts 2004, and Strathern 2005 on the problems with modernization theory.

[29] See Strathern (2007b) for a much more comprehensive theoretical defence of the proposition: 'When faced with the dilemma of whether to undergo a wholesale conversion to a religion introduced from an external source, a ruler of a society shaped by established transcendentalist religion is more likely to resist conversion than a ruler of a society in which transcendentalist religion has had a superficial or negligible impact.' Strathern 2007a, summarizes elements of this book to act as a short case-study.

[30] See Eisenstadt 1986; Eisenstadt and Schluchter 1998; Eisenstadt, Kahane and Shulman 1984; Schwarz 1975. Collins 1998: 20–9, finds 'transcendentalism' a useful tool, but not the language of this- and other-worldly realms, which is deemed Christocentric. But the 'other world' may be a transcendentalist state of being.

civilization *per se* but the challenges to pre-existing Eurasian civilizations caused by rapid social change and conflict. Powerful modes of second-order thinking and a new consciousness of epistemological plight developed as a result. This was alleviated by recourse to a vision of a transcendental order of reality that existed in a state of tension with the mundane. Where that vision was expressed within a religious framework, this generated a new set of 'otherworldly' norms that must be abided by in order to attain the newly distant divine state of being – to achieve salvation from a mundane existence which was now seen as irredeemably unsatisfactory. Such teachings were codified and set down in writing, and those writings were interpreted and represented by an institutionalized priesthood or clerisy. Christianity, Islam and Buddhism were 'secondary breakthroughs', reviving the initial spirit of challenge and questioning the established mediation of the transcendental order expressed by Judaic and Upanishadic teachings.

In the societies that established themselves upon these great traditions, the sacred and secular realms were now separated according to a firm conceptual dichotomy. It was a hierarchical dichotomy, too: the sacred was superior because it represented the ultimate fortunes and purposes of men as opposed to merely their current concerns. This allowed its priestly representatives to call secular power to account. They could mould the consciousness of whole populations and establish standards of behaviour that applied no less to kings than to subjects. One sees this very clearly in the continuing moral and epistemological authority of the *saṃgha* in contemporary Sri Lanka. Where the institutions of transcendentalist religion became deeply rooted and widespread in a society, they could shape popular sentiments necessitating the religious fidelity of the king. Missionaries hoping to replicate in parts of Asia the top-down conversion movements of first-millennium Europe or the recent successes in Africa would often be doomed to fail.

This truncated version of the argument requires many qualifications and clarifications which cannot be addressed here. Clearly, religions based on transcendentalist traditions also accommodate large areas of non-transcendentalist practice, as the popularity of deity-worship among Sri Lankans testifies.[31] Naturally, monotheistic and Indic traditions conceptualized the breach between the transcendent and the mundane in contrasting ways.[32] One result was a much less exclusivist understanding of religious identity in Indic societies, and we shall see in Chapters Seven and Eight how the royal courts in particular played host to a creative interweaving of Indian traditions (that would later be – and is hereafter – referred to as Hinduism) with Buddhism. Indeed, some observers may even want to describe the 'identity' that rulers were loath to forgo as Hindu-Buddhist.

[31] The new science of religion (e.g. Atran 2002) would emphasize this of course.

[32] Eisenstadt 1986: 16, refers to the distinction 'between the monotheistic religions in which there is a concept of God standing outside the universe and potentially guiding it and those systems, like Hinduism and Buddhism, in which the transcendental, cosmic system was conceived in impersonal almost metaphysical terms, and in a state of continuous existential tension with the mundane system'. The implications of this are mainly important for Chapter Seven.

Syncretism flourished; so too did cosmopolitanism. Rulers in early modern Asia often claimed sovereignty over diverse religious groups, and the Lankan kings were no exception. But, however many different moral communities the royal cult must respond to, the principle of transcendentalist intransigence remains in place. The king's collective ritual and particularly ethical responsibilities will stand in the way of the kind of wholesale conversion demanded by monotheism. Ultimately, then, the intransigence of Sinhalese kings does not depend on the particular balance in their public life between *vaṃsa*-esque Buddhist norms and divinizing Hindu forms. Nevertheless, one could describe the Buddhist subjects of the king as constituting his 'primary moral community', which would always present certain limits to the eclecticism and innovation of the royal cult.

None of this is to suggest that religious propriety was the sole determinant of legitimacy. It was one of a number of principles to which Sinhalese kings appealed, thus: (1) ritual and ethical conduct; (2) their proclaimed ancestry and that of their queens, which should be of *kṣatriya* origin and include a host of illustrious forebears; (3) their right of inheritance according to principles of succession; (4) their military prowess, success and popularity;[33] (5) their possession of a capital city, the Tooth Relic and other sacra and regalia. In this book, we shall see each one rise in and out of prominence as the decades wear on.

The above constitutes one of three comparative aims of this book. The second is to begin to compare and contrast the Portuguese and the Sinhalese. This is not pursued in a systematic manner, but any analysis of their interactions has to reflect a little on the different ways the Portuguese and the Sinhalese drew conceptual boundaries in the areas of politics (around the state, sovereignty, jurisdiction) and religion (around religious identity and belief).[34] It is not always a question of contrast.[35] Christianity and Buddhism were both transcendentalist traditions that produced religious virtuosi (whose function is to act as exemplary embodiments of otherworldliness) and organized them into established monastic traditions. When the Portuguese friars met the Sinhalese *bhikkhus*, they would have found themselves face-to-face with men who performed eerily similar social roles to their own.

This third aim takes in both comparative and connective history, by placing the kingdom of Kōṭṭe in the context of the principalities of the Malabar Coast of southwest India (see Map 3), with a particular focus on Cochin. A number of key issues – geopolitical pressures, the legal implications of vassalage to the Portuguese, the way that principles of caste and land-tenure shaped conversion patterns – are best explored in the light of this comparative perspective. Flores' work has already

[33] This might include the accumulation and dispensation of wealth, although here we shift into the grey area between legitimacy and power. Consider Queyroz: 517: 'but any Chingalâ, when he sees himself with a few Larins, at once presumes that he has the means to become a King and to carve a little [kingdom] for himself.'

[34] See Silber 1995 for a systematic comparative sociology of medieval Lanka and Catholic Europe.

[35] Broad similarities can enable rough-and-ready communication or working misunderstandings. See e.g. Lockhart 1994: 218–19.

demonstrated the value of situating Sri Lanka in a broader geography, in this case in the 'Sea of Ceylon' region, which connects the island with the southern tip of the Indian littoral and the Maldives.[36] But what grounds are there for turning to the Malabar principalities for context?

The connections between the two regions were strong enough, particularly through commerce, dynastic congress and military aid. As for comparisons, they shared such features as: the dispersion of sovereignty through the royal family; routine contestation of succession; complex systems of land tenure in which the king's authority predominated; certain aspects of sacred kingship. These in turn led to similar modes of interaction with the Portuguese. Indeed, the nature of the Portuguese presence in these areas also had much in common: the settlers and officials remained within the official world of the *Estado da Índia* (State of India) while the rajas yet retained a nominal or subordinated form of independence. In both places the Portuguese had arrived during the early phase of Manueline imperialism, and they felt a particular debt to those rulers who gave them welcome and shelter and were in turn rewarded with a personal relationship with the King of Portugal.

Some anthropology of kingship

One comparative road which this book does not take would lead into the plains of sacred kingship theory, which have been cultivated by anthropologists beginning with James Frazer and A. M. Hocart.[37] It would take another book to analyse all the material here in that light. Instead, I have grouped some reflections here, which should deepen our understanding of the essentially historical analysis that follows.

The nature of the king's identity vis-à-vis his subjects is intrinsically paradoxical: kings are imagined as outside society and at its centre at the same time. This is so in at least two ways. First, a compelling way of creating a being who is deeply connected to *everyone* in society, is to see him transcend all the normal means by which one is connected to *some* people.[38] This is why so often in the symbolism of king-creation deployed in installation rituals and the myths of dynastic origin (for example, the Sinhalese tale of Vijaya's advent in Lanka), kings are represented as committing transgressive acts that break kinship rules such as incest, parricide and so on, as well as wider social norms.[39] Second, rulers of states must create social order by exercising the disordering power of violence; in this very particular sense, then, kings represent or contain both the antithesis to order and its absolute source. Marshall Sahlins has emphasized the way in which this is conceived of in socio-geographic terms, so that power is seen as originating in the realms beyond the society, which are associated with the non-human, the animal, the uncanny.

[36] Besides Flores' work, see C. R. de Silva (2001–2).
[37] Hocart 1927, 1933; Frazer 1922. [38] Quigley 2005b.
[39] There is a comprehensive symbolic rupture with the domestic order: Heusch 2005: 33.

The task of kingship is to harness that power, draw it inside, and domesticate it.[40] Sahlins offers this as an explanation for the wide prevalence of stranger-king myths (among which, again, we must count Vijaya), in which a miscreant prince from abroad arrives and defeats the indigenous people to create a new political community and a higher standard of civilization. Both the king and his people are civilized through this union, but kings are never entirely domesticated for they must always be ready to grapple with the outside forces that threaten to destroy the community: to vanquish them by meeting them on their own terms. When Vijaya's father Siṃhaba commits parricide by slaying the lion, he is at once demonstrating the same sort of brute force embodied by the lion he has slain and also taming, neutralizing that force.[41]

To repeat, these points concern certain aspects of the symbolism of king-creation. In practice, the royal family is more typically estranged from their subjects by an emphasis on royal blood, which can only be maintained by intermarriage with foreign equivalents. If some of the above sketch still looks a little peculiar and extreme, it is probably because it draws upon theory largely derived from kingship in non-transcendentalist societies. With the arrival of Axial Age discourses, a quite new means of thinking about and legitimizing power became available.[42] But these discourses are often lain over the older ones, which remain in a subdued form – particularly in the Indic cultures which managed to accommodate more of the pre-existing substrata of kingship ideology than did monotheism.[43] While transcendentalism allows new ways of processing the paradoxes of kingship – including the ethical and philosophical as well as the mythic and symbolic – it does not resolve them. Doctrinal Buddhism's reprehension of violence is unusually unremitting and it is a major function of much of the Lankan literary tradition to somehow find a place for the exercise of mundane power within the renunciative framework of Buddhist virtues.[44]

For Bruce Kapferer, the exercise of mundane power in the form of the state has also been situated within the framework of Buddhist ideas about the workings of the human personality. Kapferer's insistence on the homology and interdependence of state and personhood may sometimes have been pushed too far, but it is echoed, again, in the Vijaya myth.[45] When Buddha cleanses Sri Lanka of demons to prepare it for Vijaya's civilizing rule, there is a clear connection between the erection of socio-political order by the king and the maintenance of psychological order by

[40] Sahlins 2006, and 1985: 90: 'the same creative violence that institutes society would be dangerously unfit to constitute it.'

[41] Thus what Kapferer explores as a feature of Indic cosmology – 'the demonic and destructive conditions of existence are also the source of the regeneration of the hierarchical order of society' (1988: 11) – can be seen as a version of a much more basic principle. What might be particularly Indic is the ceaseless instability of the two states, the same beings slipping between chaos and order as they move up and down the cosmological hierarchy.

[42] Thus it is an insufficiency of much anthropological theory of sacred kingship that the revolutionary consequences of the Axial Age remain unappreciated.

[43] Hence the persistence of the Vijaya myth.

[44] Tambiah 1976, Smith 1978a.

[45] Kapferer's presentation of a perennial ontology is certainly pushed too far, but compare with Smith 1978*c*: 55–6.

exorcism and the light of *dhamma*. It is particularly Buddhist that the threats to both are often characterized in terms of passion or greed. This is not a universal, for one could equally represent enemy agents as being cold and unemotional. But, in the *Sītāvaka Haṭana*, the Portuguese are characterized by dirty, insatiable appetites. They are thus like the *prētas*, the fallen spirits of ungoverned desire, but they are also akin to the harrying thoughts and impulses that each of us must master in order to achieve the one-pointedness of meditative calm. From this perspective, the battle between order and chaos, without and within, is ceaseless.

This is germane to the persisting paradox of the persisting ideal unity of Lanka and its actual fragmentation. In Sinhalese myths, unity cannot be assumed – just as in their political practices the loyalties of one's vassals must be renegotiated rather than inherited. The basic existential unity of the state (which European kings of the early modern period could increasingly start to take for granted) must be continually re-created. In the foundational story of Duṭugämunu, we hear of a king who starts out a violent force in the margins but moves to the centre of the state and restores Buddhist order.[46] In the sixteenth century, Bhuvanekabāhu and his brothers would be displaced from Kōṭṭe, mount opposition from the regions, re-enter the capital city and sack it, killing their father, Vijayabāhu VII.[47] I do not want to push a particular connection between the mythic-textual and the actual here – one could, if one wished, merely see the former as an epiphenomenon of long-lasting institutional and political structures. But in such a history-conscious world, these stories might help us to understand why it was rather typical for rulers to feel it justifiable to throw the land into chaos in the name of a new order.

That has particular resonance for the rebellions against Portuguese or Christian rulers, for Duṭugämunu's war was one against a foreign occupation of the centre.[48] It needs stressing that it was not the foreign origin of the Portuguese that was so troubling here but their foreign comportment: they remained an obstreperously undomesticated, uninidigenized power.[49] As such, instead of constituting a centre of order and civility diffusing outwards to the margins, their opponents could feel they had allowed chaos to settle at the heart of the state. But chaos can emerge from within too, and some representations of Rājasiṃha I evoke a man who has failed to harness his own drives: his sheer power compels the kind of awe that is appropriate for kings, but its untamed exertion arouses disgust too.[50] Kings can fail at kingship: there is no contradiction then between kings being regarded as sacred and yet vulnerable to murder, not so much in the Lankan case because of the persistence of some Frazerian logic of the sacrificial-king, but simply because the process of turning the pathetic creature that is man into the perfect being that is

[46] Kapferer 1988: 58–62. [47] *Rājāvaliya*: 71–2.

[48] Tambiah 1992: 150, and see Kapferer 1988: 81.

[49] Obeyesekere and Tambiah have written much on such domestication processes, and see C. R. de Silva and Bartholomeusz 1998: 17 on the unintegrated as polluting.

[50] Rājasiṃha could also be associated with foreignness in some ways, obviously through his Saivism. Obeyesekere 1995a: 240, refers to the tradition that he was the son of a dancing woman a.k.a. Tamil.

king is highly fraught.[51] Indeed, the more divine that vision is, the easier it will be for opponents to point to the gaping disharmony between the 'king's two bodies'.[52] In non-transcendentalist societies that vision is primarily a matter of ritual felicity; in transcendentalist ones it acquires an ethical and soteriological dimension.

If some anthropological models have dwelt on kingship as an imprisoning office of subjection to society, Sahlins' account of eighteenth-century Polynesia seeks out its opposite. He makes history there the slave of kings – to subvert Tolstoy.[53] We shall see that in sixteenth-century Sri Lanka rulers sometimes appeared to exhibit this 'heroic mode of historicity', transforming society by acting on its behalf: the turns towards Christianity and Saivism could be considered in this light. But structure was normally too strong for such agency. Perhaps Polynesian kings could take their peoples with them through the baptismal waters, but Lankan kings usually had to shed their subjects as well as their sins. Equally, the concept of 'hierarchical solidarity', whereby 'the collectivity is defined by its adherence to a given chief or king rather than by distinctive cultural attributes', might gesture to the dominance of dynastic loyalties in our period and the violence generated by the struggles to command them.[54] Nevertheless, it too quickly finds its limits in a situation where a great literary tradition was quite able to insist on the cultural and religious particularities of the Sinhalese, and where those particularities could acquire a political relevance.[55] In short, if a spectrum exists with heroic politics on one end and national politics on the other, we must find a place for sixteenth-century Sri Lanka somewhere in between the two.[56]

A note on sources

One reason for focusing most attention on Bhuvanekabāhu's reign is that the history of Sri Lanka is illuminated for the first time by an abundance of contemporary letters, nearly all in Portuguese. Most of them were collected in Schurhammer and Voretzsch in 1928, a publication which has formed the bedrock of all subsequent research in the period.[57] The great majority of these letters have recently been re-edited and translated as part of Vito Perniola's documentation of the history of the Catholic Church in Sri Lanka.[58] The early-to-mid sixteenth century is also

51 On Frazerian logic: Quigley 2005b: 13.

52 Schnepel 1995, following Kantorowicz 1957.

53 Contrast Sahlins' emphasis (1985: 41) on the disproportionate historical agency of kings in the heroic mode with Tolstoy, *War and Peace* (1997: 666): 'The higher a man stands on the social ladder, the more people he is connected with and the more power he has over others, the more evident is the predestination and inevitability of his every action. "The King's heart is in the hands of the Lord." A king is history's slave.'

54 Sahlins 1985: 45.

55 The 'division of labour in cultural and historical consciousness' in heroic societies (Sahlins 1985: 49), by which the masses are left with no sense of history while the courts maintain dynastic genealogies, is not transferable to Sri Lanka where religious and historical texts and oral stories circulated among its wider population.

56 Lankan politics looks most 'heroic' in the turmoil of the 1580–90s. Sahlins himself refers to some fundamental differences between Polynesia and South Asia in 1995: 4–5.

57 SV.

58 Because this is widely available in Sri Lanka, I have used it for my citations (as VP), except for quotations which are usually my own translation from SV (a VP reference follows in brackets if it

somewhat better than later periods in exciting the attention of the Portuguese chroniclers. The official chronicle, or *décadas*, of the empire compiled by João de Barros (1496–1570) and Diogo do Couto (1543–1616) devote considerable space to the description and history of Sri Lanka.[59] It is rarely noticed that much of the latter material contained in Couto's 'Fifth Decade' has been lifted, largely verbatim and unacknowledged, from the work of an Augustinian friar, Agostino de Azevedo's remarkable 'Estado da India e aonde tem o seu principio' (1603, relevant material written in 1580s).[60]

While occasionally unreliable, Gaspar Correia's *Lendas da Índia* is vital for the 1520s and 30s. As a man of India himself he offers a distinctively local perspective that retains plausible details and insights lacking in the other chroniclers.[61] Turning to the chronicles of the religious orders, the Franciscan texts constitute a corrective to the Jesuit predominance in letter-writing. A crucial section of the voluminous material on Sri Lanka in Paulo da Trindade's *Conquista Espiritual do Oriente* draws on Francesco Gonzaga's earlier chronicle of the Franciscan order. This in turn was based on notes compiled by Gaspar de Lisboa, who was the Custodian in India (1584–91).[62] But it was a Jesuit who provided Sri Lanka with its own chronicle in Fernão de Queirós' exhaustive work first published in 1687. This is an immensely important source for the period of Portuguese involvement in Sri Lanka's history, based on a variety of textual and oral sources now lost to us. It is also complex and confounding, so apart from the discussion of the *Conquista* in Chapter Nine, readers will have to refer to another paper for the sustained source-criticism it deserves.[63] We can simply mention that, in a peculiar mirroring of the

differs to my own). I have only referenced details of the letter where particularly noteworthy. Most letters of the SV collection not published in VP can be found in (unreliable) translation in Pieris and Fitzler 1927a, and in Da Silva Cosme 1986. Other relevant letters beyond SV include Caração; CS; *DPM*; Pessoa 1960; Biker; Flores, Doc; Bouchon, Doc. See below, pp. 162–3, for the question of the mediation of Bhuvanekabāhu's letters.

59 Barros; Couto. Fernão Lopes de Castanheda's chronicle is also used here. Faria e Sousa 1665–75, and Andrada 1976, are rarely relevant. The chronicles of Pierre Du Jarric, João de Lucena and Joseph-François Lafitau (see Bibliography) generally only repeat and embellish events associated with Francis Xavier. Given that the narrative of events is reasonably well established, I have not sought to reference each point with all its traces in the various chronicles, except where they differ significantly.

60 Azevedo may have previously been a soldier who had served in Kōṭṭe in 1558 (Queyroz: 341), as Schurhammer 1973–821, II: 615 suggests. Hence his particular interest in Sri Lanka, and his fairly detailed knowledge of the early sixteenth century (240). See also Loureiro 2007.

61 See Kriegel and Subrahmanyam 2000: 52–3, on Correia's strengths. Correia served in India as a secretary of Albuquerque and then as a *feitoria* scribe in 1512–27 and 1530–63. He was probably among the viceroy's retinue that put into Colombo in 1518 and throughout Bhuvanekabāhu's reign Correia was making sketches for his *Lendas* ('legends').

62 Trindade, III. 28, n. 5. Much of the relevant material in Gonzaga is in VP, which will be referenced unless I need to draw attention to the Latin original, Gonzaga 1603. Gaspar de Lisboa's memorial has not survived, see his entry in Lopes 1949: 99. Lopes 1962 reproduces letters by Lisboa to Gonzaga; one mentions his scrupulous methods in compiling the memorial (75). Schurhammer 1973–82, II: 422, is unaware of Lisboa's mediation. Monforte 1751, is a 1696 chronicle of the Province of Piety. Beyond such Franciscan chronicles as Lisboa 2001 (a facsimile of the 1614–15 edition), Monforte must have drawn on the specific histories of the *piedosos* now in the archives of Ajuda, BA 51-II-20 (a Latin work from 1606), and IAN/TT, Manuscritos da Livraria no. 1104 (a Portuguese work from 1649).

63 See Strathern 2005 (which includes material from Strathern 1998, 2000); Abeyasinghe 1980–1.

Azevedo–Couto relationship, Queirós also reproduced without acknowledgement large stretches of one source for much of his ethnological material, Constantino de Sá de Miranda's report on Sri Lanka from the 1630s.[64] The current taste for distinguishing 'multiple voices' in texts thus has a very concrete application for the vast, agglomerative chronicles we are faced with.

As we move into the latter half of the century (Chapters Nine, Ten and Conclusion), sources are used only for their relevance to particular themes.[65] Both letters and chronicle accounts dwindle in these decades and we become more dependent on Couto, Queirós and Trindade, but the arrival of Dutch commentators such as Linschoten and particularly Joris Van Spilbergen affords a valuable perspective quite independent of Portuguese concerns. But, given that various aspects of identity are our focus here, can European eyes be trusted to read the political emotions of the Lankans? The question is a fair one, but only if we recognize that our Portuguese and Dutch commentators were writing before the development of modern Western discourses of the East, and while the conceptual apparatus of race and nation was still in the early stages of its construction. Between 1580 and 1640, for example, the Portuguese were part of a sprawling seaborne expansion that had become merged with the Spanish empire under the Habsburg dynasty, and which governed many different European peoples under diverse political arrangements. Thus for many decades, the king in Madrid was also attempting to deal with consequences of maintaining dynastic rights over the Netherlands – which had only been formally independent for a short time when it in turn produced commentators on Sri Lanka such as Spilbergen.[66]

In a depressing reflection of the changing dynamics of power, the new life brought by the Portuguese sources comes somewhat at the expense of the old: Sri Lanka's impressive literary traditions dry up somewhat. Few texts or archaeological remains have survived: see Map 1 for what has been discerned from the ruins of Kōṭṭe city.[67] In chapters Seven and Eight, this means that we need to supplement our depiction of the religious context with evidence from the preceding and following centuries. However, the later chapters in particular are much enriched by two crucial Sinhala texts, the *Alakeśvarayuddhaya* and *Sītāvaka Haṭana*. Once again, they are so important that their source-criticism has to be addressed in

[64] MS 13, Biblioteca Universitária, Universidad de Zaragoza, published in Miranda. An early digestion of the Miranda material can be found in a draft in the BA in Lisbon: MS *Descripção Historica, geographica, e topographica da Ilha de Ceilão* (call-mark 51-VII-27, no. 27, fol. 266–81), along with one of the two surviving manuscripts of the Conquista entitled *Livro Premeiro da Historia de Ceylao Pello P.e Fernao de queiros* (Codex 51-VII-40).

[65] My use of material for these decades is not exhaustive, then, but is fairly comprehensive for the themes pursued. Those interested in the narrative history of this period and other themes should consult Biedermann 2005a. Indeed, Biedermann's hard work is the source for the archival citations in my later chapters, for which I remain very grateful. His researches turned up very few new letters for the pre-1552 period (2005a: 25).

[66] The States-General declared sovereignty in 1590. The differences between seventeenth-century Portuguese and eighteenth-century Dutch notions of group or national identity also require attention.

[67] On the archaeology, see Ranasinghe 1969; E. W. Perera 1910; Schurhammer, 1973–82, II: 415–20.

other publications. The *Alakeśvarayuddhaya* is a chronicle of the Kōṭṭe kings that seems to have been continued by Sītāvakan writers from *c.* 1557 onwards. It is the source for much of the information up to the early 1560s contained in the better-known late seventeenth-century *Rājāvaliya*.[68] The epic poem *Sītāvaka Haṭana* appears strikingly similar in tone to the later *haṭanas* (war-poems) from the mid-to-late seventeenth century, and its partisan qualities contrast with the neutral *Alakeśvarayuddhaya* – to the extent that one might wonder at the authenticity of its advertised date of 1585. But the best explanation for this is that the later war poems used the *Sītāvaka Haṭana* as a genre-template, resurrecting its staunch defence of indigenous traditions and dynasties.[69] It can be taken then as a priceless, unmediated expression of the Sītāvakan perspective, as a section of Chapter Nine reveals. I have drawn on the services of several translators for the quotations provided here, but they must be seen as subject to revision by experts in early modern Sinhala.

The *Rājaratnākaraya* (or 'Mine of the Gem of Kings'), a eulogy of the King of Kandy, is the only substantial Sinhala source from Bhuvanekabāhu VII's reign, but contains little relevant information.[70] The catalogue notes to the Hugh Nevill collection of *ola* manuscripts supplied useful material, but there is a mass of folk texts here that would surely repay the labours of a dedicated Sinhalese specialist in the future.[71] We are also fortunate to have a series of caskets bearing detailed ivory relief-work, produced at the Kōṭṭe court throughout the century. The form of these caskets is derived from the Portuguese travelling box, but they display ivory-work of an indigenous style that came to acquire European motifs from the 1540s and

[68] And again for the events of 1593. See Strathern 2006a, which suggests that the portion up to 1557 was first written by a Kōṭṭe Christian, and the next portion up to 1562 by a Sītāvakan courtier. The Nevill collection contains numerous related *ola* texts, including Or. 6606(106, 107).

[69] The *SH* would then reflect a reification of Sītāvakan resistance by Rājasiṃha II. There are further reasons to doubt the date, but Strathern (forthcoming b) gives various reasons why it is probably authentic, the most concrete being a reference (verse 1003) to the cult of Upulvan at Devinuvara, which was destroyed after the sacking of Devinuvara in 1587. If that date is wrong, then the *SH* can be taken as evidence of an early modern rather than Sītāvakan mentality.

[70] The author was the Mahā Thēra of Valgampāya. Ilangasinha 1992: 114, gives a late fifteenth-century composition date. However, the text gives a list of Kōṭṭe kings which includes Bhuvanekabāhu VII (*Rājaratnākaraya*: 47; Upham 1833: 114), and it focuses on the patronage of the King of Kandy, whom it describes coming to the throne in 2085 of the Buddhist era (AD 1541). Hence Godakumbura 1955: 127, suggests it was written in the 1540s. Somaratna 1975: 29–30, points out that its chronology is unreliable. Moreover, the narrative context suggests the relevant king is rather the founder of Kandy, Senāsammata Vikramabāhu (1469–1511). However, the vagueness of both this text and the *Cūlavaṃsa*, II: 220–3, which depends on the *Rājaratnākaraya* here, allows his successor, Jayavīra (1511–52, who also had the name Vikramabāhu) to be a candidate too. Thanks to K. N. O. Dharmadasa for translating relevant sections of the text for me. Further, Pieris 1910–12: 169–80; Codrington, in *EZ*, III: 62–3; and Somaratna 1975: 188, date four *sannas* (royal decrees) to Bhuvanekabāhu's reign. Bell 1904: 91–4, prefers Bhuvanekabāhu V (1371–1408). To these one can add the copper-plate *Palkum̆bura Sannasa* (*EZ*, III: 240–6) from the reign of a Bhuvanekabāhu, which Codrington identifies as that of Bhuvanekabāhu VII on the bassis of its sixteenth-century script. This should not be confused with the *Palkum̆bura Vihāra Sannasa* of 1804 (Lawrie 1896–8, II: 687–8) which merely refers back to Bhuvanekabāhu VII's time.

[71] Relevant texts: Or. 6605(3); 6606(3, 34, 50, 65, 77, 86, 106–7, 128, 130–2, 145, 150–2, 156, 177); 6609(147); 6611(59).

stand as some of the finest of this type.[72] There is a question as to how far their iconography can be read as specific projections of Kōṭṭe propaganda, and how far it was determined in a less coherent way by the aesthetic tastes of the European private market for Eastern luxury objects.[73] Lastly, there are the texts which I shall refer to as the 'unverified sources'. The *Mandārampura-Puvata*, the *Sitāvaka Rājasiṃha Rājja Kālaya*, the *Asgiriye Talpatha*, and some documents associated with the Māniyamgama temple in Avissāvēlla, may turn out to be valuable and challenging additions to the corpus. If they are authentic, they would enhance our understanding of the internal affairs in Sītāvaka and Kandy and require us to adjust the accepted chronology of these years. But note the conditional: there are major question marks hanging over them.[74] As a result I have not sought to draw on them for support. If verified, it does not appear that they would pose any problems for the major arguments advanced here; they would rather tend to strengthen them.

72 See Plates; Jaffer and Schwabe 1999; Jaffer 2004: 86, 108, 255–6; Schwabe 2000; Gschwend 1996; P. H. De Silva 1975; Coutinho 1972; Schurhammer, 1973–82, II: 232.

73 See Vassallo e Silva 2007 for the latter view. The 1543 casket is so clearly associated with the embassy to Lisbon that its political import is undeniable. Later caskets may have been commissioned for European buyers, but I have tended to interpret them here as nonetheless generally expressive of the political culture of Kōṭṭe.

74 The relevant portion of the *Mandārampura-Puvata* portion claims to date to 1647. But Malalgoda 1999 (followed, provisionally, by C. R. de Silva 2000: 289; Roberts 2004: 116) has advanced compelling arguments for its inauthenticity. C. R. de Silva 1995: 12, has likewise questioned the *Asgiriye Talpatha*. See Amarasinghe 1998 for the other texts.

I

The temporal

1
The kingdom of Kōṭṭe

Capitulations to the Portuguese across Malabar and Sri Lanka

The first context through which to understand Bhuvanekabāhu's alliance with the Portuguese is the regional balance of power between the Portuguese and the Māppiḷas – indigenous Malayālam-speaking Muslims (*mouros da terra*) based in the ports along the Malabar Coast and in Colombo. War between these two seafaring groups repeatedly flared into life throughout the 1520s and 1530s.

In the cosmopolitan port cities encountered by the Portuguese in Asia, the functions of war and commerce were often dominated by foreign specialists. It might be tempting then to see the Portuguese as merely one more element slotting into this Asian division of labour. But they pursued an exclusive dominion over both the mercantile and the military with an altogether original degree of ambition and success.[1] The irresistible naval power of the Portuguese is a fact of great importance for understanding the history of Malabar and Sri Lanka in the sixteenth century. Any coastal fortress could be protected indefinitely with a Portuguese fleet in support, almost regardless of the hostility or otherwise of indigenous rulers. At the height of his power, when almost the whole island was in his hands, Rājasiṃha I (1581–93) never succeeded in taking Colombo, indeed no Sinhalese king ever did. Even the combined power of the Ottoman Turks and the Gujaratis could not take the Indian fortress of Diu from the Portuguese in the 1530s and 1540s.[2]

But the seaborne power of the Portuguese had its challengers. Of particular interest to us is the resistance mounted by the Māppiḷas. It was the Māppiḷas who stood to lose most from the arrival of the Portuguese, for they had been the chief agents of the pepper and cinnamon trade which the Portuguese were trying to monopolize. Indeed, Portuguese policy in general aimed at destroying the extensive Muslim trade networks across Asia. So, naturally, it was the Muslims who opted to fight. The Hindu and Buddhist rulers who played host to these trading communities had to decide which side they should back. Within Malabar, the Hindu Samorin of Calicut had the most invested in the status quo, overseeing a very profitable

[1] This military superiority has been attributed to the fact that Portuguese ships alone were sturdy enough to mount cannon, but recent commentators prefer to emphasize organizational or technical advantages: Willis 2000; Arnold 2000.

[2] Bethencourt and Chaudhuri 1998: 179; Winius and Diffie 1977: 293.

port and claiming overlordship over most of the other rajas. When a group of Māppiḷa merchants led by Pate Marakkar sought his support (having failed to receive protection from Portuguese harassment in Cochin) he was happy to shelter them. Yet he was also open to diplomatic negotiations with the Portuguese, no doubt wary of the threat the Muslim seafarers presented to his own position.[3]

Before the offensive of Pate Marakkar, it had been the Māppiḷa community of Cannanore led by one 'Mamale', who had taken on the Portuguese, largely over the shipping of the Maldives and Laccadives but also over the Coromandel and Sri Lanka trade. During the siege of Colombo in 1521, it seems that Mamale was directing the Kōṭṭe war effort to some extent, providing them with artillery and establishing plans to frustrate Portuguese trade.[4] Before Mamale's ascendancy, the Hindu Kōḷaṭhiri of Eli, or the King of Cannanore as the Portuguese knew him, had vacillated between the two naval powers. In 1501, Pedro Álvares Cabral had sailed into an instant welcome from the king who was clearly looking to counterbalance the influence of the Muslim merchants.[5] A factory and a fortress were established soon afterwards.[6] In 1507, the raja, seeing that a Muslim attack on the Portuguese fortress had failed, wrote a letter of allegiance to the king of Portugal, confirming himself as 'an enemy to your enemies and a friend to your friends'.[7]

What the Kōḷaṭhiri Raja really wanted was a guarantee of independence from his feudatory overlord, the Calicut Samorin. The same is true for the two other great dynasties of Malabar, both of whom accepted Portuguese alliance and the construction of forts, the royal family of Vēṇād (known to the Portuguese by its principal city of Kollam or *Coulão*), and the rulers of Perumpadappanud (known as the rajas of Cochin), and for other lesser princes such as the rulers of Chaliyam and Cranganore. Kollam was a particularly unstable ally under the control of an extended royal family who ruled a great part of the southern tip of the Indian littoral and whose complex divisions of rulership could be exploited variously by both the Portuguese and the Māppiḷas. A trading post or 'factory' (*feitoria*) was built very early on, but was soon subject to attacks, being rebuilt with a fortress after the signing of the peace treaty of 1516.[8] Cranganore had also quickly sought to place itself under Portuguese protection, caught as it was in contentious ground between Calicut and Cochin. A fort was eventually built there in 1536.[9]

Lastly we come to the rajas of Cochin, the most successful dynasty to adopt this strategy. At the start of the sixteenth century the raja was a rather dejected vassal of Calicut subject to periodic invasions from the Samorin who tended to manipulate the very complicated process of royal succession.[10] Through firm alliance with the Portuguese, Cochin shrugged off and eventually surpassed its overbearing

[3] See Flores 1998: 174–7, on signs of antagonism between the Māppiḷas and the Samorin.
[4] Caração: 164–8. [5] Bouchon 1988: 54. [6] J. M. Correia 1998: 51. [7] SR, I: 62.
[8] Biker, III: 33–7. The fortress was besieged in the early 1520s, contemporaneously with the attacks on the fortress of Colombo. During the rest of the decade Kollam was used as a safe port for the Māppiḷa counter-offensive, see Bouchon 1987: 175.
[9] Oliveira e Costa 1994: 129, 135. See also Bouchon 1987: 176, on the fort built in Chaliyam (or *chalé*) in 1531.
[10] Barbosa 1918–21, II: 94–5.

neighbour. The Portuguese threat intensified internal divisions as well as polarizing foreign relations: the collaborationist rajas in Cochin came from the Mutha branch of the ruling family who had been excluded from the succession while the Samorin favoured the rival Elaya branch.[11]

In this context, the responses of the Sinhalese rulers seem unremarkable, determined as they are by the same two factors: their relationship with the Muslim merchant community on the one hand and their struggles with dynastic rivals on the other.[12] From very early on the dimly perceived opportunities of the Portuguese presence were perturbing Sinhalese politics. In 1513 Afonso de Albuquerque reported that two brothers were in conflict over succession to the Kōṭṭe crown. One of them had appealed to him for military assistance in exchange for permission to build a fortress.[13] It was probably Vijayabāhu VI (1513–21) anticipating conflict with his brother Sakalakalāvallaba.[14] Even the brother of Vijayabāhu VI who had led attacks against the Portuguese in 1518 was prepared to cut a deal with them if he was promised the throne.[15] In the face of these internal challenges it is not difficult to see why Vijayabāhu agreed when the governor Lopo Soares de Albergaria came to request permission to build a fort in Colombo in 1518.[16] However, once the walls had reached a certain height, the Portuguese stepped up their demands for rights over the cinnamon trade and an affronted Vijayabāhu allowed an attack on the fortress to proceed. When the attack was repelled Vijayabāhu was compelled to accept vassalage.[17]

But the prime mover behind the attacks on the fortress in 1518 and 1521 was probably the small Muslim trading community goaded by the agents of Mamale of Cannanore, their numbers swelled by those who had faced persecution on the mainland.[18] Following the second attack, there was a palace coup in which Bhuvanekabāhu VII came to the throne. What has received little comment is that the ousted faction fled to the fortress and begged for Portuguese help, promising

[11] Tavim 1997: 21. [12] See also Bouchon 1999: 233.

[13] Albuquerque, Cannanore, 30 November 1513, in *Alguns Documentos* . . . 1892: 295–8; Barros: 40. Rohandeera 1996, has challenged the chronology of this period, arguing that Vīra Parākramabāhu ruled 1490–1509, followed by Vijayabāhu 1509–21, and that Dharma Parākramabāhu IX was only a minor prince who tried to represent himself as emperor to the Portuguese. However, there is conclusive Portuguese evidence that Rohandeera's 'real king', Vijayabāhu, was a vassal from 1518 to 1521 (e.g. Bouchon, Doc: 190–205, 'The Inquiry set up in Ceylon by Lopo de Brito Regarding the Tribute and the Cinnamon', Colombo, Jan. 1522; Caração: 167). Nonetheless, our sources for these decades are vague and rather contradictory, partly because kingship itself was so fractured at this time. In particular, we need to explain why the *Rājaratnākaraya*: 47 does not mention Dharma Parākramabāhu in its list of kings. Was the omission of the first Sinhalese king to associate with the Portuguese a deliberate snub? But it does not ignore more firmly established vassals: Vijayabāhu VI, Bhuvanekabāhu VIII. The *Alakeśvarayuddhaya*: 29 does mention Dharma Parākramabāhu.

[14] Somaratna 1991: 23.

[15] Only in Correia: 196–7, who was in Sri Lanka in 1518; Somaratna 1975: 221.

[16] Barros: 40, also reports that he saw how much the King of Cochin had profited from the Portuguese presence, confirmed by the Raja of Cochin (Biker, III: 11).

[17] This was the classic method for turning allied kings into vassals, as described in the *Livro das Cidades* . . . in Luz 1953: 66.

[18] Bouchon, Doc. 2: 186–8; Bouchon 1988: 156, 163, on context.

the captain of the fortress that they would turn over all the treasure of the island if he helped them avenge the murder of Vijayabāhu.[19] Bhuvanekabāhu, already middle-aged by 1521, would have lived through all of this.[20] It was clear that the cinnamon trade and the strategically crucial Sea of Ceylon were becoming battlegrounds, and one had to decide whom to back. Thus far the Portuguese had won each round. When they put pressure on him to expel the Muslim traders in 1526 Bhuvanekabāhu did so. He was calculating – he was forced to calculate – in exactly the same way as other coastal rulers in this part of South Asia.

However, in Sri Lanka the Muslims had somewhere else to go, the court of Māyādunnē who had by now set himself up in opposition to his elder brother. For the next thirteen years he was an ally of the Calicut Māppiḷas. It ought to be recognized that the involvement of the Muslims also brought complications and compromises of autonomy, but Māyādunnē, in parallel with Bhuvanekabāhu, turned to outsiders in his hour of need.[21] More revealing is the fact that when the Māppiḷas were no longer viable allies Māyādunnē was not above trying to form an agreement with the Portuguese himself.[22] What he wanted from the Portuguese was military support in the shape of 200 fully armed soldiers and an extension of his territorial control and a seaport.[23] These were universally appealing objectives. The King of Kandy asked for all of these too (plus a factor in permanent residence). The Prince of the Seven Kōralēs and the chiefs of Trincomalee and Batticaloa were of the same mind.[24]

The point here is very simple. By the 1540s every prince in Sri Lanka wanted what Bhuvanekabāhu had, the commercial and military advantages offered by alliance with the Portuguese. They may have imagined a more robust independence within those terms, but what we should not do is assume that Bhuvanekabāhu's confession of vassalage, his acceptance of the Portuguese factory, and his hospitality towards Portuguese officials and clerics represented an unusual capitulation or a necessary reflection of personal weakness. Rather these were prizes that exuded glamour and a power equally irresistible to his rivals on the island and many of his peers across the straits.

But is it meaningful to place the kingdom of Kōṭṭe in the context of the rajas of Malabar or the lesser princes in Sri Lanka? The Malabar rajas were generally minor rulers perching on the coast, subordinate to the great territorial powers of the interior such as Vijayanagar, and drawing their wealth from the profitable currents of trade that swept across their shores. On the other hand, the great monarchs of

[19] João Garcês, Cochin, 2 Jan. 1529, in CS: 329.

[20] Queyroz: 293, tells us he was 83 when he died in 1551.

[21] In the mid fourteenth century a Muslim chief controlled Colombo, see Kulasuriya 1976: 150. In Dharma Parākramabāhu's time a Muslim ruler from Kayalpatinam seized Chilaw in order to exploit the pearl fishery and had to be beaten off by the king's brother (*Rājāvaliya*: 67–8; Somaratna 1975: 167–8). In 1539, Māyādunnē only lured Pate Marakkar to Sri Lanka by promising him the rights to the revenues of Negombo.

[22] See below, pp. 73, 80. [23] VP: 230–1.

[24] And the Kōṭṭe princes, chiefs of Vellassa and 'Cauralle': VP: 62, 112, 154, 166, 211–13, 220–1, 229, 287.

South Asia, who aspired to the status of *cakravarti* ('ruler of the four quarters' or 'world conqueror') paid less attention to trade or indeed the activities of the Portuguese.[25] Is this not the suitable context for the King of Kōṭṭe, who claimed the imperial title of *cakravarti*?[26] His dominion stretched, in theory, over the whole of the hinterland, and he drew his wealth primarily from the soil rather than the vicissitudes of oceanic trade. Surely Bhuvanekabāhu could have afforded to act with greater disdain?

The sovereignty of Kōṭṭe, in theory and practice

However, a historicist critique would prompt us to ask what the *cakravarti* title really meant in this period – indeed what was the nature of royal authority in general? Here we shall answer that question from an abstracted, outsider's viewpoint. Those who want an insider's perspective, to see what these principles looked like when expressed as living political emotion, should turn to the analysis of the *Sītāvaka Haṭana* in Chapter Nine.

It has been argued that Sinhalese imperial rhetoric was first given proper articulation as part of a project to assert an overlordship that would cross the seas and subsume South India, although the term *cakravarti* was not used until the tail end of this dynamic in the late twelfth century.[27] Then centuries lapsed. The paradigmatic *cakravarti* figure for our epoch was Parākramabāhu VI (1411–67). He subdued the entire island, an extremely rare feat by this time, but went no further. His feats must have lingered in the minds of his successors. The significance of the language of universal empire may have lingered on in the odd monarchical boast, but it was now wedded to a quite unusual conception of bounded hegemony, in which the domination of the island of Lanka was the precondition – or fulfilment – of the *cakravarti* ideal.[28] From the literature of the post-Polonnaruva period (i.e. after the early thirteenth century) it becomes clear that the *cakravarti* image was no mere generational whim; indeed it had become entrenched as a master symbol drawn upon to express the ideal of comprehensive mastery in religious or literary terms too.[29]

This point is worth emphasizing in the face of a weighty historicist critique of pre-modern South and South East Asian statehood that tends to concentrate on the blurry or porous quality of such polities: their sovereignties shade into

[25] Pearson 1976. But Subrahmanyam 1993: 12–29; 2005a: 62, resists the emphasis on the distinction between small trading states and massive agrarian ones, providing examples of the latter which were concerned with commerce and the Portuguese.

[26] His *sannas* refer to him as *trīsiṃhalādhiśvara* and *cakravarti*, see *EZ*, III: 247; Bell 1804: 91; Pieris 1910–12. The *cakravarti* title was likely drawn from neighbouring Indian conceptions rather than a revival of its ancient Buddhist meaning, see Holt 2004: 42.

[27] Walters 2000: 132–45.

[28] See Goonewardena 1977. Collins 1998: 20, 85, refers to this unusual sense of territorial boundedness as 'a kind of proto-nationalism'.

[29] Hallisey 2003: 708–18.

one another, their reach continually expands and contracts.[30] We shall emphasize the value of that insight for our period soon enough, but two caveats must be registered immediately. The first is that there remains a great deal of work to be done to establish just how the 'blurry' geography of sovereignty existed alongside a very precise personal and administrative local geography – by which I mean the care with which individual property rights and village or departmental limits were delineated in the popular and royal consciousness.[31] Indeed, there is a genre of 'boundary books' (*kaḍaim pot*) from the fourteenth century onwards concerned with precisely that.[32]

Secondly, Sri Lanka appears to be a case in which a very obvious geographical feature – the surrounding sea – was constructed as a significant and durable political boundary. A similar principle seems to have been fundamental to political legitimacy in the Maldives, conceptually united under the symbolic centre of Male.[33] In Kōṭṭe the *cakravarti* title was routinely associated with equivalent titles such as *trīsiṃhalādhiśvara* (lord of the three Sinhalas, i.e. the whole island), and it seems as if there was a higher form of consecration ritual (*svarṇābhiṣēka*) that could only be claimed by those with rightful dominion over all the territories of Lanka.[34] In this way Sinhalese kings expressed their dominion over all the peoples of Lanka, encompassing the Sinhalese, the Tamils of Jaffna and elsewhere, the väddās, the Muslim Māppiḷas and other South Indian merchant communities.[35]

Yet by the time Bhuvanekabāhu came to this exalted throne, one could be forgiven for imagining that all this was entirely academic. Jaffna in the north and Kandy in the central highlands had broken away under new monarchies. Then there was a great, if often very sparsely populated swathe of territory covering most of the north and the east that resided under the control of the *vanniyār* chiefs. In this region there appear to have been at least two substantial principalities, which the Portuguese referred to as Yala (*Jala*) and Batticaloa (*Batecalou*).[36] Therefore the dominions of Vijayabāhu VI, which modern historians call 'the Kingdom of Kōṭṭe', had been confined to the south and west of the island, stretching from Malvatu Oya in the north to beyond the Valavē Gaṅga in the South (see Map 2).[37] Worse

30 Nissan and Stirrat 1990: 25; Craig Reynolds 1995: 425–30; Schnepel 2005.

31 See below, pp. 51–2 on the robust administrative system and pp. 101–2 on property rights.

32 Abeyawardhana 1999: a collection of popular/vernacular texts of boundary divisions that demands theoretical attention. See also D. G. B. De Silva 1996.

33 See C. R. de Silva 2001–2.

34 Goonewardena 1977 argues for the continuing relevance of the *svarṇābhiṣēka* ideal drawing on the Gaḍalādeniya slab inscription from 1463–9 AD (*EZ*, IV: 26) and Dutch accounts. The evidence for the intervening period is more circumstantial. Goonewardena argued that Rājasiṃha II of Kandy (1635–87), despite achieving *de facto* rule over the great bulk of the country, never ceased in his designs on Kōṭṭe and Colombo partly so that he could claim this higher sovereignty.

35 See Roberts 2004: ch. 4, on multi-ethnic dominion in the Kandyan period, and p. 159 on possible Sinhala terms for 'all-island overlordship'.

36 VP: 211. Barros: 37, reporting nine different kingdoms on the island, also refers to the 'kingdoms' of Vellasa ('Vilacem') and Trincomalee ('Triquinámale').

37 A more detailed discussion of the boundaries of Kōṭṭe, in C. R. de Silva 1975: 79–82; also Ribeiro: 3–5.

still, until fairly recently many works of history described the palace coup of 1521 as resulting in a further division of these homelands into three separate kingdoms.

However, it is now clear that Bhuvanekabāhu assumed the imperial title and the royal centre at Kōṭṭe, while his two brothers were installed as the rajas of Sītāvaka and Rayigama under him.[38] These arrangements are illuminated by one of our rare items of artistic evidence from the Kōṭṭe court, an ivory travelling box with detailed pictorial relief-work made by a Sinhalese artist either in anticipation or commemoration of the embassy that Bhuvanekabāhu sent to Lisbon in 1542.[39] The most splendid depiction is that of Bhuvanekabāhu at the moment of his coronation, surrounded by insignias of all-island imperial authority such as the *rāja siṃha* and the white parasol of state hanging above the elevated throne (Plate 1). The choice of this scene is significant for it allows Māyādunnē and Rayigam Baṇḍāra to be present: they are depicted in attendance, mundane mortal size, waiting in the wings. Their inferiority, the stratification of power, is emphatic. Indeed, the claim later made by the Portuguese Crown that all of Sri Lanka came under its rightful dominion was based on Dharmapāla's bequest of this title to King Felipe II.[40] A letter from Bhuvanekabāhu to the Portuguese court in 1543 unambiguously refers to Kandy and Jaffna as properly part of his dominion.[41] From the perspective of the Kōṭṭe court, all of Lanka fell under its sovereignty.

But this ideal of Lankan unity was contested by other rulers and it is here that historicist questions about the *nature* of political unity are very much to the point.[42] Nissan and Stirrat have argued that pre-modern polities were defined by the centre rather than the periphery: beyond the core lands, various regions and diverse ethnic groups enjoyed a considerable autonomy, connected to the state essentially through the recognition of sacred overlordship.[43] This draws on a raft of influential theoretical scholarship, and has broad similarities with works guided by a contrasting dichotomy of East versus West, such as Geertz's much-cited work on the Balinese 'theatre state'.[44] Tambiah's 'galactic polity', which he sees as having prevailed in the Theravādin regions of pre-colonial South and South East Asia, offers a more specific vision.[45] Occasionally, these could take a strong form and achieve a temporary centralization of power.[46] But the weak state was more typical, in which the *cakravarti*'s centre was surrounded by minor courts that replicated the centre's attributes on a lesser scale.[47] The overlord placed great

[38] See *Rājāvaliya*: 72–3; Barbosa 1918–21, II: 117; Queyroz: 101, 204, 263; Bouchon 1971: 68–70, n. 30.

[39] Jaffer and Schwabe 1999.

[40] Saldanha 1991.

[41] 28 November 1543, VP: 48. Dharmapāla was referred to as 'Great King' in 1552, SV, II: 585.

[42] In Kandyan perspective Bhuvanekabāhu was only 'formerly emperor', see VP: 200.

[43] Nissan and Stirrat 1990. In South Asian studies this insight is associated with the rubric of the segmentary or decentred state, see Price 1996: 14–19.

[44] Geertz: 1980.

[45] Tambiah 1976: 102–32; Tambiah 1985: ch. 7. Although Tambiah uses the Kandyan kingdom as his case-study, the model is suggested as relevant to all pre-colonial Sri Lankan kingdoms.

[46] A more genuine centralization could remain an ideal, therefore, and was perhaps achieved in the contracted 1640s Kandy.

[47] Tambiah 1992: 173–5.

Plate 1: Left end of c. *1543 casket, Residenz, Munich, Schatzkammer. This casket was either made for the occasion of the 1542 embassy to Lisbon or in commemoration of it. Here we see Bhuvanekabāhu VII on his throne. Are the figures flanking him Māyādunnē and Rayigam Baṇḍāra?*

significance on the presentation of fealty from these vassals while neglecting the implementation of an administrative machinery to directly exploit or control their lands. And if he failed to assert his strength, the peripheral territories were liable to be sucked into the embrace of competing 'pulsating centres'.

We can pause here for a comparison with Portuguese kingship, which need not be conducted only in grand distinctions between East and West. In one sense, Sri Lankan and Portuguese states shared key features as dynastic monarchies relying on personal acts of homage from their vassals. Was it only the process of territorialization that Portugal underwent in the early modern period that opened up such a conceptual gulf between them? Zoltán Biedermann has drawn our attention to the way in which Portugal under João III (1521–57) was settling into and reifying its borders at the same time as it was dispatching its first adventurers and officials to Sri Lanka.[48] We shall see that seventeenth-century Portuguese commentators found the political idiosyncrasies of the Sinhalese more remarkable than their compatriots of the previous century.

However, the Portuguese kings had been less at the mercy of grandees or usurpers for some time. Succession and factional disputes tended to be resolved at the centre, without constantly initiating a resurgence of regional powers. The assumption of royal insignia by regional nobility would be treasonous and, by this time, almost unthinkable. The borders of Portugal were firmly established in the political imagination. In the Sinhalese worldview, the boundaries of Lanka (*lakdiva*) itself were rich with meaning, but rarely corresponded to those of actual political authority. In sixteenth-century Sri Lanka, kings stood within a continuum of kingship, and the whole system of political relationships was imbued with a more profound sense of contractualism. The ties of vassalage required constant attention and re-negotiation.

It is clear that Kōṭṭe overlordship was primarily expressed through an insistence on the presentation of fealty. Hence, when the founder of Kandy, Senāsammata Vikramabāhu (1469–1511), proclaimed himself *trīsiṃhalādhiśvara* and *cakravarti*, the kings of Kōṭṭe launched repeated attacks on him with the overriding aim of simply forcing him to withdraw those proclamations, which he eventually did.[49] When Jayavīra (1511–52) began to assert his independence in the early 1540s Bhuvanekabāhu's invasion of his lands was then an entirely traditional response.[50] And what did he intend to do with the highland territories? To create, in effect, a new sub-kingdom by placing them under the rule of a disgruntled prince (probably Jugo), who had just been disinherited and threatened to disrupt the succession.[51]

At the same time, the King of Kandy was busy establishing his own form of overlordship, competing with the King of Kōṭṭe for recognition from the largely autonomous *vanniyār* principalities. What scant evidence there is indicates that Kandy was more successful in establishing itself as the principal authority in the east.[52] There is one neglected piece of evidence, the *Kaňdurē Baṇḍāravaliya*,

[48] Biedermann 2005a: 312–27, whose illuminating comparison of Portuguese and Sinhalese concepts of territoriality has also informed the next paragraph.

[49] Abeyasinghe 1995: 141–3. [50] VP: 68. [51] Correia: 323.

[52] In the Gaḍalādeniya inscription (*EZ*, IV: 15), Vikramabāhu (1469–1511) claimed sovereignty over the modern Eastern, Central and Uva provinces, and the Tamankaduva district. Somaratna 1975: 192.

which suggests that Bhuvanekabāhu was raising his status in the eastern lands through the judicious use of marriage alliance with recently arrived noble families from Malabar.[53] If reliable it would indicate that Bhuvanekabāhu's political reach extended further than is generally assumed.[54] Turning to 'Greater Kōṭṭe', it is clear that Māyādunnē and Rayigam Baṇḍāra were left to rule over and appropriate the resources of their territories with a great deal of autonomy. At this point, however, the galactic polity model loses some of its usefulness, for Māyādunnē always seemed to have recognized the higher value of the dynastic imperial title. As a result what is most compelling about this period is not the rivalry of 'pulsating centres', but a struggle for access to the legitimating traditions of one centre.

In all monarchical systems the moment of succession is liable to become a crisis, the crux point upon which factional forces are brought to bear. But Sinhalese kingship appears to have been particularly fissiparous because it lacked an authoritative principle of succession: it could always be disputed whether the title should pass from brother to brother or from father to son.[55] The result was that civil wars and palace coups were rather the norm. The practice of the kings of Kōṭṭe of relying heavily on other members of the royal family or granting them sub-kingdoms outright owed much to a desire to avert succession crises. Cristovão Lourenço Caração, a Portuguese scribe who was present in the last years of the reign of Vijayabāhu VI, gives us an interesting outsider's perspective on the kind of shared sovereignty that could result. We are told that Vijayabāhu was in fact the youngest of three brothers, the elder two having retired from the succession. Yet Vijayabāhu himself rarely left the city of Kōṭṭe, never failed to consult his brothers before any important undertaking, and gave one of them the command of the army.[56] The principle of endowing members of the royal family with fiefdoms extended to much lesser rulers, as Duarte Barbosa's report of 1517 makes clear.[57] The ruler of the Seven Kōralēs, a large stretch of territory in the north of 'Greater Kōṭṭe', was the most important of these and he often seems to have acted with considerable independence in the 1540s and 1550s.[58]

[53] Nevill: Or. 6606(77.III), says that Kaňdurē Baṇḍāra and his six brothers arrived in the reign of 'Bhuvanekabāhu' – apparently the seventh, since after his death Kaňdurē Baṇḍāra went over to the King of Sītāvaka. Some of the brothers seized lands around Bintänna and Vellassa which were highly valued as army recruiting grounds. Bhuvanekabāhu won Kaňdurē Baṇḍāra over by taking his sister as a concubine. See D. de Silva 1996: 162–80.

[54] But it derives from oral tradition not written down until well over 100 years later, which may serve later land-claims.

[55] Somaratna 1991: 17–32, concludes that the succession of only one of the nine kings of Kōṭṭe was undisputed.

[56] Caração: 167. Compare with power-sharing under Dharma Parākramabāhu IX (1483–1513), *Rājāvaliya*: 67–8.

[57] Barbosa 1918–21, II: 117, says that the main ports of the island were under the rule of nephews of the emperor. See Barros: 24–5, on the lord of Galle, whom Bhuvanekabāhu would refer to as 'of noble family and somewhat related to me', VP: 252.

[58] A Portuguese describes him as not acknowledging 'any subjection to the king of Ceilam or his brother, but only to one that brings them *fanams* [a gold coin of South Asia]', VP: 71, also 62. Taniyavallabāhu of Mādampe, also seems to have maintained his position into the 1540s, see Somaratna 1975: 188; C. R. de Silva 1971.

As regards how power really operated through this complicated political landscape, we remain largely ignorant. At least in terms of resources, the arrangements of 1521 had left Bhuvanekabāhu in command of the largest and richest territory in Sri Lanka.[59] This remained so even when Māyādunnē annexed Rayigama with Bhuvanekabāhu's ratification in 1538. When Māyādunnē was on the warpath, however, many of these resources undoubtedly flowed back to Sītāvaka.[60] A brief glance at the location of the lands Māyādunnē ruled shows how easy it would have been for him to cut off Bhuvanekabāhu's control of the south (Map 2). As for inscriptional evidence, there are a small number of *sannas* or royal decrees (the *Ganēgoḍa*, *Goḍagama*, and *Palkuṁbura Vihāra Sannas*) issued by a 'Bhuvanekabāhu' – probably but not certainly our king – which bestow rights to lands located in this southern region.[61] This would suggest that there were parties there who still conceived legitimization from Kōṭṭe to be worthwhile in the late 1540s. Our conclusion is that Bhuvanekabāhu could still draw on considerable revenue from the land, more than any of his rivals, but his image as a great territorial ruler was more aspired to than real.

The development of military dependency

Two features of the military history of Lanka before the advent of European colonialism stand out: its kings rarely tried to develop a significant naval presence and they tended to rely on Indian mercenaries for armed might.[62] Sri Lanka was a richly endowed island caught in the major trade routes between the eastern and western halves of the Indian Ocean.[63] The absence of a navy therefore made her vulnerable to external interference, a fact of particular pertinence to Kōṭṭe, which was easily accessible from the coast, being a mere two leagues up the Kälaṇi river. This was a crucial difference between the kingdom of Kōṭṭe and the great principalities of the subcontinent.

It seems that the location of the royal centre close to Colombo was determined by the desire to take advantage of the burgeoning cinnamon trade.[64] Could we then see Kōṭṭe as akin to the port-based, commercially orientated polities of Malabar and island South East Asia? Maritime commerce was significant for Kōṭṭe in a way that it had not been for the irrigation-based kingdoms of the past, and its kings certainly sought to protect and extend their economic rights. Yet easily the

59 Bhuvanekabāhu had 2,800 villages (and all the seaports) compared to Māyādunnē's 1,880: C. R. de Silva 1975; 1995: 63.

60 Including sometimes from ports on the western coast, VP: 14–15.

61 Pieris 1910–12: 169–80, argues that the *Ganēgoḍa Sannasa* and *Goḍagama Sannasa* were issued in the 26th and 29th years respectively (1547, 1550) of Bhuvanekabāhu VII's reign. The former refers to a village of 'Valatura' in the Sabaragamuva district, but also interestingly seems to acknowledge Māyādunnē's authority. The *Palkuṁbura* decree refers to a grant of land in Divigoḍa (Gālu Kōraḷē): *EZ*, III: 240–6.

62 See Muttukumaru 1987; Codrington 1959: 98–9.

63 Correia: 157, is clear on the strategic value of the Palk straits.

64 Kiribamune 1987; C. R. de Silva 1990.

most significant source of revenue was still the land, and there was only the most rudimentary bureaucracy devoted to trade.[65] The chronicler Castanheda seems to have understood this, judging by the speech which he puts into the mouth of the Moorish representative trying to persuade Vijayabāhu not to allow the construction of Portuguese fortress in 1518: '. . . nor will you lose anything [by refusing the fortress], since the land itself provides you with your wealth and not the sea, as is the case with the King of Calicut.'[66] In Kōṭṭe, then, we find a particular irony at work: as vulnerable to Portuguese seaborne power as any of the Malabar ports, yet less able to derive the same economic profits from association with the Portuguese.

The Kōṭṭe kings did have a system for levying native troops, as is reflected in the high court status of the *sēnāpati* (commander) and other military officials.[67] However, there was no standing army as such and in practice the kings often tended to rely largely on South Indian mercenaries, who were rewarded with land rights. From the *Mukkara Haṭana* we learn that Karāva mercenaries were brought over in 1508 to oppose an attack by Mukkuvās, and the *Kandurē Baṇḍāravaliya* suggests that Bhuvanekabāhu continued to welcome South Indian emigrants into Kōṭṭe.[68] In the early sixteenth century, Sinhalese society would have appeared as rather less militarized than the Malabar Coast where the rajas could tap a ready supply of specialized warrior groups, principally the Nayars.[69]

This must be partly responsible for the general view among Portuguese commentators in the first half of the sixteenth century that the Sinhalese were unwarlike and ineffective soldiers. The earliest writer, Duarte Barbosa, stated that the Sinhalese 'pay no attention to matters of weapons, nor do they possess them'.[70] Such generalizations about Asiatic peoples invite our suspicion, of course, and it has been argued that the Portuguese assumed a certain cowardliness among the Sinhalese.[71] However, the Portuguese did not assume that all Asian peoples were so unwarlike and it is plausible that Duarte Barbosa, Ludovico di Varthema and Marco Polo before them were informed by impressions of Sri Lanka prevalent on

[65] Flores 1998: 90–5. Bhuvanekabāhu was very concerned about his revenue from the ports. He desired to place the highly contested Mannar pearl fishery under his control, and the Portuguese settlers in his realms complained of the effects of a 'fiscally penetrative state', but Kōṭṭe remained focused on the land: see VP: 14–20, 238–40. C. R. de Silva 2000 refers to the lowly status of merchants, and 1995: 60 to trade as less than 25 per cent of overall revenue.

[66] Castanheda, IV: 451, confirmed by a letter of Valentim Fernandes, 1510, in Brásio 1960: 19.

[67] C. R. de Silva 1995: 28, on the military levy system. See Map 1, nos. 12 and 13, for the military headquarters and training ground.

[68] On the *Mukkara Haṭana*, translated in Raghavan 1961: 15–24, possibly of late seventeenth-century provenance. See also Roberts 1995: 19, 24–5. It is possible that its emphasis on the martial origins of the Karāva reflects a later process of kṣatriyaization. See too *Kaňdurē Baṇḍāravaliya* (Nevill: Or. 6606(77.III) and *Kīravälle Rajamula* (Or. 6606(50) – thanks to C. R. de Silva for referring me to the latter.

[69] And the St Thomas Christians: Bayly 1989: 248–55.

[70] Barbosa 1918–21, II: 110. Castanheda, IV: 452 reports that Vijayabāhu submitted to vassalage partly because, 'a sua gente não ser boa de guerra', similarly, Castanheda, VI: 296; Correia: 160.

[71] C. R. de Silva 1994: 316, 320.

the mainland.[72] They may also have drawn on first-hand observation by Portuguese stationed there. The testimony of Caração is very illuminating here: 'The people are very weak, because the most that this king [Vijayabāhu] and his brother can muster to fight when they go to war is 1,500 or 2,000, and the best of these are from Coulam [Kollam] who go to these kings as mercenaries.'[73] This presents a pragmatic explanation for military weakness: the small size of the levies and dependence on foreigners. Diogo do Couto must have been correct in suggesting that it was continual conflict with the Portuguese that precipitated the more militarized and pugnacious Sinhalese communities of the later sixteenth century.[74]

When Bhuvanekabāhu came to the throne he was hardly taking charge of a powerful war machine. Yet, in the first few years, he did not need one. Nor did he need military protection. Therefore, the presence of the Portuguese fortress did not serve his interests, and his policy was to work towards its removal. He had seen his father Vijayabāhu try and fail to destroy the fort by brute force. Instead, he rendered it economically futile by making it clear that while it stood the Portuguese would not get their hands on the cinnamon they desired. He reneged on the tribute (in cinnamon and elephants), or gave up only poor-quality cinnamon and allowed the Muslims to smuggle it out of Kōṭṭe.[75] His strategy appeared to succeed: the fort was dismantled in 1524 as part of a wider policy of dispensing with non-essential military bases. Nuno Álvares' interesting letter indicates that Bhuvanekabāhu's thinking was more ambitious still: now the fortress had been eliminated, he was arguing for the removal of the factory.[76] Álvares suggests that it was the King of Portugal who was in debt to the King of Kōṭṭe for providing protection to twenty-five or thirty Portuguese who were otherwise in danger of being captured by the Muslims. There is no suggestion here that Bhuvanekabāhu was dependent, militarily or otherwise, on the Portuguese.

In fact it was the removal of the fortress that left him vulnerable, as Māyādunnē and the Māppiḷas launched their assaults on Kōṭṭe, over the next few years. Only the arrival of the Portuguese fleet in 1528 under Martim Afonso de Melo Juzarte saved the day. Hence we find that a few months later Bhuvanekabāhu sent his ambassador to Cochin to ask for a tower to be built on the site of the former fortress for defence against Māyādunnē! The Captain of Cochin wrote to Lisbon to support this plan because it would also strengthen the position of the factor and his men, who, when the Portuguese fleet was absent, still had to run to the Kōṭṭe palace for protection

[72] Varthema 1997: 73; Marco Polo 1986: 259 (*The Travels*). Corriea refers to his use of indigenous oral sources in general, particularly those of Cannanor, see Kriegel and Subrahmanyam 2000: 54. See Rubiés 2000, for an extended argument that European travellers such as Marco Polo participated in Asian ethnographic discourses.

[73] Caração: 167. In the attack on the fortress in that year, Barros: 53, reports that the Sinhalese managed to muster 150 horsemen and 25 war elephants.

[74] Couto: 72, and Queyroz: 96–100.

[75] Thus many Portuguese urged that the best way to get good cinnamon was to destroy the fortress: see António da Fonseca, Oct. 1523, in *DPM*, VI: 205; Queyroz: 206; and Flores 1995: 69, n. 10.

[76] CS: 314–17. See Chapter Four for more detail.

when the Māppiḷa ships appeared on the horizon.[77] A crucial shift had occurred. From resenting a Portuguese imperial presence, Bhuvanekabāhu was now actively requesting it. He thereby joined the company of the Raja of Cochin, who had long been convinced of the value of Portuguese fortifications.[78]

In the 1530s, the pattern of a desperately besieged Kōṭṭe saved by Portuguese ships only repeated itself with greater intensity. We should be wary of assuming that he was quite as defenceless and beholden to the Portuguese as the chroniclers' depiction of him suggests. They appear to have routinely underestimated the role of Kōṭṭe forces, who had an outstanding military leader in Vīdiyē Baṇḍāra, in the wars with Sītāvaka and Kandy, especially in the land-based campaigns of the 1540s.[79] But with the naval conflict of the 1520s and 1530s, both Bhuvanekabāhu and Māyādunnē were forced to rely on external forces.[80] The former gradually lost the power to raise troops of his own; the numbers of his levies dwindled still further and his dependence on the Portuguese grew more complete.[81] The *Rājāvaliya* gives the simple facts of the matter:

> King Bhuvanekabāhu, not having any means of attack, assuming that there was no king among the kings of the whole of *Dambadiva* [India] equal to the king of *Pratikala* [Portugal] (in power), despatched letters along with many presents.[82]

In courting overseas might Bhuvanekabāhu was acting traditionally, but his new allies did not appear to know their lines: they would follow a different script to that used by the mercenaries of old.

[77] Flores, Doc: 349.

[78] Flores, Doc: 341–2, which asks (1526) for more fortifications and stresses his total dependence on Portuguese force. The Raja rarely attempted any military undertaking without first securing Portuguese aid.

[79] Vīdiyē Baṇḍāra and the men of Kōṭṭe emerge as much stronger forces in the often neglected parts of Queirós' narrative, see, for example Queyroz: 273, where we have him ('Tribule') apparently raising a large army (although the figure of 40,000 is clearly in error, as the introduction to SV: 47, indicates).

[80] If we can trust Queyroz: 265, in the 1540s Māyādunnē was still arranging for 'Badagas' (or *vadugai*, Telugu-speaking South Indian mercenaries) and some foreign Muslims to fight for Sītāvaka.

[81] C. R. de Silva 1991a: 231. Compare with the decline in Cannanore's military capability after they became dependent on the Māppiḷas.

[82] *Rājāvaliya*: 73, derived from *Alakeśvarayuddhaya*: 33.

2
Portuguese imperialism

What was the nature of the beast that Bhuvanekabāhu invited into Kōṭṭe? There is a tendency to see it as simply the earliest manifestation of a generic European imperialism, and there is truth in this: the Portuguese came – like those who would come after – to exploit the resources of the island by whatever means they could. But in order to capture what was distinctive about the sixteenth-century encounter we need to have a much better understanding of the idiosyncrasies of Portuguese expansion.

Contrary to the modern connotations of its name, the *Estado da Índia* (State or perhaps Estate of India) referred to the whole of the Portuguese empire in the East, stretching from Zanzibar on the east coast of Africa to the Moluccas in the Indonesian archipelago.[1] Its key nodes were established with great swiftness during the governorship of Afonso de Albuquerque (1509–15), who was guided by the objective of controlling the traffic of spices throughout Asia. The authority of the *Estado* sprang from the sea and only a few strategic positions on land were needed to govern the great trade routes. Consequently it combined the most extreme geographical spread with a tiny degree of territorial control, a fact that is reflected in the small numbers of Portuguese stationed beyond the Cape of Good Hope: in 1540 one contemporary estimated that there were no more than six to seven thousand.[2] As Luís Filipe F. R. Thomaz has remarked, it was then, in essence, a network, a system of communication between far-flung strongholds.[3] Upon this central fact rest three key features of the *Estado da Índia*: first, it necessarily became involved in complex legal and political relationships with the territories surrounding its nodal points; second, dispersed over such great distances, it suffered from a lack of technological or bureaucratic machinery with which to exercise effective vigilance over the Portuguese diaspora; third, the interests of the *Estado* often failed to prevail over those of the individual Portuguese. The following pages will sketch out some of the consequences of these principles for the Portuguese presence in Sri Lanka,

[1] Thomaz 1985: 515. Although the phrase *Estado da Índia* was not current until the later sixteenth century, it is a useful analytical term for the earlier period. The Portuguese expansion in the Atlantic and the New World is best considered as a quite separate political phenomenon, akin to colonization.
[2] Subrahmanyam 1993: 74.
[3] Some have argued that 'empire' is a misleading characterization of the Portuguese expansion: see Disney 2001.

and, by way of comparison, along the Malabar Coast. They will also be seen to underlie much of Chapters Three and Four.

Vassalage, friendship and extra-territoriality in Kōṭṭe and Cochin

The first context here is the impact of legal vehicles on the relationship between the Portuguese and the kings of Kōṭṭe, and it is best brought into focus through comparison with the situation in Cochin. The jurisdictional arrangements between the Portuguese and the territorial rulers were *ad hoc* and exceedingly various. Direct rights of conquest were sometimes imposed, but given that the Portuguese generally recognized the theoretical legitimacy of non-Christian sovereignty, in most cases treaties were established which aimed at a suspension of hostilities and the permission to erect a trading post (*feitoria*) with commercial rights and privileges.[4] These treaties encompassed many different kinds of relationship, from an acceptance of parity to clear subordination.[5]

If the King of Kōṭṭe cannot be straightforwardly distinguished from the Malabar princes on account of the magnitude of his dominion, it might be argued that he had entered into a much more demeaning and subordinate form of relationship with the Portuguese than that enjoyed by his Hindu peers. After all, they were *friends* of the Crown of Portugal, while he was a *vassal*. Recent scholarship has sought to isolate the various legal principles expressed in the Portuguese treaties with eastern rulers and the degrees of inequality they entailed. Vassalage was defined by the implication that the vassal's authority was *derived* from that of his liege, and was a status that was unilaterally imposed – normally after military defeat was experienced or threatened.[6] Its most characteristic feature was the obligation to make a regular payment of *páreas* or tribute.

In attempting to determine the nature of the contract of vassalage acceded to by the Kōṭṭe kings we find our path strewn with traps, largely deposited there by Fernão de Queirós. To begin with, the diplomatic implications of the gift offered by Dharma Parākramabāhu IX (1489–1513) to the Portuguese embassy in 1506 remain unclear.[7] The Portuguese may have subsequently interpreted it as an offering of tribute, but for the Sinhalese such gifts could denote a range of relationships.[8] Certainly, Dharma Parākramabāhu did not feel any obligation to make regular

4 Although the legitimacy of non-Christian sovereignty was a matter of debate: Thomaz 1985: 530.
5 See Saldanha 1997, 1991.
6 Saldanha 1997: 385–7.
7 Somaratna 1975: 214–16; C. R. de Silva 1995: 17.
8 The reference in Queyroz: 181, to vassalage is probably misleading. Correia: 148–50, appears the most plausible account of the Portuguese perspective, in which the latter propose something like a fraternal *amizade*, with an element of maritime military protection guaranteed in return for fidelity expressed by payment of tribute. Along with gift-exchange, the *Alakeśvarayuddhaya*: 29 seems to record an acknowledgement of Portuguese superiority (the language here is ambiguous, but the text uses the same phrases in the context of recounting Vijayabāhu's 'honouring' of the Portuguese; see also *Rājāvaliya*: 69), although, as C. R. de Silva 1994: 312–14 suggests, the narrative generally accords Dharma Parākramabāhu IX a more authoritative and active role than the Portuguese accounts do. See also the discussion in Biedermann 2005b and 2005a: 106–11, including his new translation of a key German source (Letter of Valentim Fernandes, 1510, in Brásio 1960: 19).

payments. What is certain is that in 1518 Vijayabāhu VI (1513–21) was forced to become a vassal after his defeated attempt on the fortress. Barros describes the contract thus:

> . . . at last he (Vijayabāhu) agreed to become a vassal of the King Manuel, with a yearly tribute of 300 *bahares* of cinnamon . . . and besides twelve rings of rubies and sapphires from those that were dug from the gem-pits of Ceylon, and six elephants for the service of the factory at Cochin, all to be paid to the captain of the fortress . . . And that the King Manuel should be obliged to protect and defend him, the king, from his enemies as his vassal, along with further conditions which are set forth in the agreement of that treaty, of which Lopo Soares had one copy and the king retained the other, written on leaves of beaten gold (according to their usage) and ours on parchment.[9]

In 1554, Simão Botelho remarked that no such document of vassalage could be found and that is still the case today.[10] Queirós claimed to have access to a copy drawn from the archives of Colombo, but his quotation only adduces a long and bombastic list of titles claimed by the King of Kōṭṭe which is probably fabricated.[11] Nevertheless, the state of vassalage was held to transfer automatically on succession, and in his letters Bhuvanekabāhu explicitly referred to himself as vassal of King João III.[12]

Vassalage tended to be distinguished from less hierarchical forms of alliance encompassed by the rubrics of *amizade* (friendship) and *irmandade* (brotherhood).[13] This language of parity and personal loyalty was particularly useful in the first years of empire when the Portuguese were in great need of safe ports on the Malabar Coast.[14] Cochin, for example, was not, properly speaking, a vassal, but was rather a 'protected' state of the Portuguese Crown. Although this naturally implied a disparity between a superior protector and a beholden protected one, it did not technically compromise the full sovereignty of the inferior state, which remained *sui generis*. In liberating Cochin from subservience to Calicut, the Portuguese decided to confer full sovereignty on the rajas, renouncing the overlordship they had attained to make the rajas free and perfect kings.[15]

The problem is that such juridical distinctions were liable to be undermined by the fluidity of the Portuguese discourse of international relations, which was not codified into a systematic corpus of legal theory. For example, the obligation to pay

[9] Barros 1988: 30v/Barros: 44. Other descriptions of the treaty, giving different amounts of tribute, are found in the letter of Diogo Lopes de Sequeira from 1518 (*DPM*, V: 599), and Castanheda, IV: 542.

[10] Felner 1868.

[11] As Somaratna 1975: 223–4 argues, contrary to the confidence of Saldanha 1997: 606, and Pieris 1983–92, I: 54. Queyroz: 234, rendition of the *ola* of vassalage supposedly submitted in the embassy to Lisbon in 1542, which has a very similar structure, is equally dubious.

[12] VP: 98. [13] Saldanha 1997: 374.

[14] See SR, I: 4. Correia: 148, has it that in 1506 Diogo de Almeida explained to Dharma Parākramabāhu IX that the Portuguese, 'towards their good friends, they have a friendship like that of very brothers'. Correia extends this fraternal tone to describing relations with the vassals Vijayabāhu VI (189, 201) and Bhuvanekabāhu VII himself (265, 267).

[15] Thomaz 1985: 531; Saldanha 1997: 588, 635. See the precise words of Castanheda, II: 256.

tribute seems to be the chief distinguishing manifestation of vassalage. Yet it was in fact far from definitive in this regard, for we find that it was also widely requested of allies as recognition of Portuguese control over navigation, an acknowledgement of 'protection'.[16] Hence the status of allies such as the Raja of Cochin could easily become forgotten or confused. This is why although Cochin under Rāma Varma (?1505–45) was nominally a protected state, commentators from the early seventeenth century to the present day have often simply described it as a vassal.[17] And if one enquires closely into the substance of the relationships with the Portuguese maintained by the kings of Cochin and Kōṭṭe they can seem remarkably similar.

Both kings were consistently eager to point out that they and the resources of their kingdoms were at the service of the king of Portugal. This was entirely to be expected from a vassal who was obliged to render services.[18] Moreover, the notion of *serviço* would perhaps have translated into the Sinhalese term *mehe (meheya)* which we find being used in the internal context of obligations to monarchs in sixteenth-century inscriptions and texts.[19] Turning to Cochin, while protected states were not required to provide services on demand, the ties of protection created a similar – if less formalized – sense of obligation, as we find expressed in the raja's oath on his coronation: 'throughout his life his services would be a testament to this love.'[20] A letter by the raja from 1513 shows how seriously this was taken. He proclaimed that King Manuel should consider Cochin in the same way he considered Lisbon: as his possession.[21]

The contract of vassalage also established binding obligations on the liege. As indicated by Barros' account of Vijayabāhu's contract, the fidelity of the lord lay in defending the estate of his vassal and upholding his claims to rule. Exactly the same guarantees were established by the contract of protection. It is important to note that military dependence was, therefore, an integral element of the rhetoric as well as the reality of the relationship that the kings of Kōṭṭe and Cochin entered into with the Portuguese. The corollary of this was that the powers of the *Estado* were potentially tied to the interests of the inferior state, which now had a right to call on military assistance. In honouring the oath of protection, the *Estado* could be dragged into all sorts of projects beyond its immediate interests. Both kings tried to enlarge their dominions by recourse to such claims.[22]

The language of *amizade* and *irmandade* was equally prevalent in their letters. These were immensely flexible and general terms that could be employed to describe any form of alliance and mutual obligation.[23] They, did, however, retain connotations of parity and they also expressed the specifically personal qualities that defined King Manuel's conception of international relations, as if he was creating a family of monarchs ranging across the seas. This was not an alien way of thinking to a world where, as one Portuguese commentator put it, the various

16 Saldanha 1997: 640–50.
17 See Mathew and Ahmed 1990: ii.
18 Saldanha 1997: 615.
19 Gunasekera 1978: 125–6, refers to the Alutnuvara slab inscription (*EZ*, IV: 261–70). The Gaḍalādeniya slab-pillar inscription (*EZ*, IV: 16–27) refers to military *kāriya* or service.
20 Barros 1988: 115v.
21 Biker, III: 10. Also SR, II: 141; Flores, Doc: 342.
22 Saldanha 1997: 619–26, on Cochin.
23 Saldanha 1997: 372, 635.

rulers in Sri Lanka 'are all relatives and friends'.[24] This personalization of politics via the imagery of blood-ties was one key homology between South Asian and Portuguese conceptions of political relationships in the early sixteenth century.[25] Nor were these sentiments purely rhetorical. They were cultivated through a regular exchange of correspondence.[26]

The relationship between the kings of Kōṭṭe and the kings of Portugal did not quite have the antiquity of that enjoyed by the rajas of Cochin, nor could it boast of such amicable origins. Yet throughout the first two decades of Bhuvanekabāhu's reign an equivalent sense of shared interest and loyalty did develop and he took avidly to letter writing.[27] Emissaries and gifts were also keenly desired markers of friendship.[28] After the embassy of 1542 the sense of a personal link between the royal families was intensified. Thereafter Bhuvanekabāhu could direct correspondence to Prince Luís and Queen Catarina.[29] If this relationship did not translate into friendly behaviour by Portuguese officers, yet he would 'bear everything . . . for the old and strong friendship which I have cherished, still cherish and will always cherish with my king my lord'.[30]

The distinction between vassals and 'friends' or 'protected' rulers was also blurred by the fact that both were liable to be formally invested as kings (normally through coronation) by a representative of the Portuguese sovereign. Rāma Varma, the Raja of Cochin, owed his succession to the Portuguese. When it seemed that a Calicut-leaning heir was to ascend to the throne, Albuquerque pressured the retiring king to disinherit him and appoint Rāma Varma instead.[31] This was ratified by a Portuguese ceremony, in which the raja received a gold crown from 'the hand of King Manuel . . . lord of the coronation of him and all would come to reign in Cochin'.[32] While this did not make him a vassal in any formal sense, the symbolism of investiture was heavily redolent of the central concept of vassalage: that one's power was derived from a superior authority. It also entailed similar obligations on the part of the lord by reinforcing the sense that the Crown was responsible for maintaining the dignity of the indigenous dynasty and the proper operation of succession.[33] When Bhuvanekabāhu decided to have a statue of Dharmapāla crowned in Lisbon during the 1542 embassy, he and his advisers may well have taken inspiration from the glorious coronation of the Raja of Cochin several decades before.

If the juridical category of Cochin as an autonomous state under the protection of the Portuguese was not always symbolically manifest, António Vasconcelos de

[24] Tomé Pires 1978: 359 (*A Suma Oriental*); C. R. de Silva 1995: 24.

[25] Portuguese political language, see Saldanha 1997: 359–61, 376.

[26] Biker, III: 10–14.

[27] When this was obstructed by the factor in 1548, Bhuvanekabāhu said that as a vassal unable to draft letters to his lord he was as good as dead, see VP: 241–2. Like the king of Cochin, Bhuvanekabāhu had stood firm against Māppiḷa requests to hand over Portuguese in his care, in 1525, see Castanheda, VI: 296.

[28] As perceived by the Governor Estevão da Gama (1540–2), VP: 12.

[29] VP: 47–8, 249, 259–60; SV: 543.

[30] VP: 261, and see also 135.

[31] Thereby subverting the normal principles of succession: SR, I: 228–9.

[32] Barros 1988: 115v.

[33] Saldanha 1997: 621.

Saldanha has argued that it was reflected in the history of Portuguese interaction with the raja.[34] The Portuguese continued to recognize their oath to safeguard all his rights and honour, and allowed Cochin to function with its sovereignty largely intact.[35] The Raja of Cochin was therefore treated with a degree of forbearance that was not granted to Bhuvanekabāhu. However, the strength of his position vis-à-vis the *Estado* derived from many factors, particularly the influence of the independently minded group of Cochin *casados* with whom his commercial interests dovetailed so effectively. The profits of both depended on the trade that poured through the bustling cosmopolitan city in much greater volumes than that of Colombo.[36] As we shall see, if the raja often enjoyed the favour of the *Estado*, this did not necessarily translate into respect for his dignity and authority. The tendency for Portuguese influence to extend itself beyond the fortress walls and deep into the fibres of indigenous government was not held at bay.[37]

The main legal mechanism that facilitated this was the principle of extraterritoriality. At first sight the jurisdictional boundaries of the *Estado da Índia* appear to be territorial, along the lines of the explicit agreement that separated the Portuguese settlement of Santa Cruz de Cochim from the old city of the raja, for instance.[38] However, it was often a basic assumption of the treaties established by the Portuguese that their officers or settlers – wherever they were – would always be subject to Portuguese law rather than local jurisdiction.[39] Hence the factor took on the function of 'chief magistrate'. Equally, the Portuguese officials had no right to arrest or dispense justice to the subjects of the native king. This is especially clear in the treaties made with the rulers of Kollam (*Coulão*): 'if it happens that some Portuguese or native Christians commit some crime, then they will be brought to the captain of the fortress for punishment; and also if it happens that some people of the land, whether Moors or Pagan or any other kind, are also committing such things. Then the captain of the fortress will hand him over to the *adigar* [local official] for him to pronounce justice.'[40]

The fact that Bhuvanekabāhu was a vassal made no difference to this arrangement because the contracts of vassalage established in the East did not place fiefdoms under the internal law of the sovereign liege, but allowed local justice to remain intact.[41] Hence we find Bhuvanekabāhu complaining that 'the chief guard likes to lay his hands on some people, a thing which goes against my will and

[34] Saldanha 1997: 633–7.

[35] Ostensibly because they felt a particular debt towards the dynasty that had sacrificed so much in the first days of empire, see e.g. *Livro das Cidades* . . . in Luz 1953: 66–8.

[36] Flores, Doc: 341; Correia, *Lendas*, IV: 388–9.

[37] See Thomaz 1985: 531, on the process by which the hinterland turns into an 'insidious protectorate' ('protectorado larvado'). The thrust of the argument here runs counter to the contrast of Cochin and Kōṭṭe presented by Winius and Diffie 1977: 295.

[38] SR, I: 148–9; *Livro das Cidades* . . . in Luz 1953: 66, 71.

[39] Thomaz 1985: 530.

[40] This is from the treaty of 1543 (Biker, III: 95), reaffirming earlier statements to this effect from 1516 (p. 35) and 1520 (p. 39).

[41] This distinguishes 'imperial vassalage' from vassalage within medieval Europe, see Saldanha 1997: 393.

he cannot do this simply because he is my guard and factor.'[42] We even know of occasions where Bhuvanekabāhu issued proclamations that were meant to be binding on everyone, both Portuguese and Sinhalese alike.[43] But he had no rights of enforcement. If a Portuguese contravened a Sinhalese law, on what grounds would the factor take up the case? This inviolability was explicitly referred to by the Kōṭṭe ambassador in 1551; 'the Portuguese enjoy as much liberty in his [Bhuvanekabāhu's] realm as if they were on their own farms and houses.'[44]

In one sense little of this was innovative. Merchant communities (particularly Muslims) had long enjoyed similar concessions from Asian rulers.[45] Now, however, this principle operated in favour of an expansionist imperial presence. The legal basis for the establishment of the *feitoria* or fortress tended to matter less than the dynamics of power that subsequently developed between the two parties. The Portuguese settlements, as isolated little enclaves surrounded by territorial principalities, can seem to us immensely vulnerable. But if the Portuguese sometimes lived in fear of being overwhelmed, it was usually because they were nervously watching the seas. When the naval power at their backs felt irresistible, this sensation of military supremacy could spill over into a wider arrogation of authority within the supposedly sovereign hinterland.

Distance and vigilance

The sprawling dispersion of the *Estado da Índia* presented extreme logistical problems. In terms of sailing time Goa was four times further away from Lisbon than the Americas were. It could take years to send a letter and receive a reply. The danger was that in the outer reaches of the *Estado*'s influence the Portuguese communities would become a law unto themselves.

The king's chief representative in the East was the governor or, if a higher status was called for, the viceroy.[46] While many royal letters sent to Sri Lanka in our period conceded that judgement on critical matters could not be sensibly made in Portugal, governors themselves were allotted a tenure of only three years in which to acquire experience – a fact widely bemoaned in the East.[47] And it often seemed that they were more interested in lining their own pockets than managing the state efficiently.[48] Inevitably, the governor himself was heavily dependent on accounts

[42] SV: 400 (VP: 183).

[43] E.g., a decree outlawing trade with Māyādunnē in 1547, see VP: 240. There is one puzzling piece of evidence regarding jurisdiction, in Duarte Teixeira letters of 1545 (SV: 163–8). He states that while he was factor Māyādunnē had stolen some unspecified goods and that Teixeira therefore had a '*sentença*' made against him but could not act on it owing to lack of support. '*Sentença*' implies a decision made by an acknowledged authority. Unless this came from the Governor (which we do not hear of from any other source), it must have come from a Kōṭṭe authority. If this is correct then Teixeira was using Sinhalese law for redress, and the same law also claimed authority over Māyādunnē.

[44] VP: 279. [45] Boxer 1969: 48. [46] Winius and Diffie, 1977: 324–31.

[47] See VP: 142 (King João III to João de Castro, 1546); Flores, Doc: 341; VP: 282; Winius 2000.

[48] See the popular satire of the *capitães-mores* who succeeded Afonso de Albuquerque and Francisco de Almeida as 'jokers' (*rideiros*) in João Garcês, CS: 328.

of the small Portuguese community in Sri Lanka and, above all, on the perceptions of the factor of Colombo, the diplomatic and commercial agent of the king.

Once the fortress had been dismantled and its military commanders decommissioned in 1524 the factor was in command of the Portuguese on the island. His tenure was normally for three years but this could vary considerably. Since the governor could only nominate candidates for the higher offices, any appointment was merely *de facto* – and therefore often unpaid – until it was confirmed by the king: a major incentive to turn to unofficial means of reimbursement.[49] It was a highly desirable office and there was often a backlog of royal appointees for the position in Sri Lanka who had been promised it years in advance.[50] The factor normally held the position of chief magistrate (*alcaide-mor*) as well, in which capacity he was supported by a judge (*ouvidor).* At the factory in Colombo there were perhaps a dozen minor administrative posts under the factor's supervision and there was also a probate judge (*provedor dos defuntos*) who ensured the proper execution of wills.[51]

This little administrative set-up was not perhaps literally a long way from Goa, yet the monsoons made navigation across the Sea of Ceylon very risky or actually impossible for large parts of the year. The safest time was September to November when the cinnamon ship sailed. It is this comparative detachment that led Jorge Flores to characterize the Sea of Ceylon area as 'a kind of social frontier' mid-way between the entirely private arm of Portuguese expansion, the 'shadow empire' further east, and the centres of established *Estado* control on the west coast of India. Sri Lanka was unlikely to see the forms of insurrection or independence that could break out farther east, but it was too far away for efficient state control.[52] A certain latitude in the representation of events also followed: there were comparatively few pressures on either Portuguese or Lankans to be truthful in their letters to Goa and Lisbon.

As a result a genuine cacophony of voices issued from the island. João de Castro (1545–8), returning from the great siege of Diu in 1546, found letters relating to the complicated events in Kandy 'that differ so much that I cannot find out the real truth'.[53] How could the governor discriminate between these missives when they disagreed, or test their integrity when they conspired in agreement? Perhaps the most effective – if rarely used – mechanism was to dispatch an ambassador who could then report directly back to the governor. This proved decisive in 1545 when João de Castro sent Duarte Barbudo to the Kōṭṭe court and subsequently paid far more attention to his report than to complaints of the resident missionaries and

49 Winius and Diffie 1977: 327.

50 IAN/TT, *Chancelaria de D. João III*, livro 25, fol. 54v; livro 31, fol. 34, on nominations of Miguel de Carvalho and Manuel Rodrigues Coutinho.

51 Nuno Álvares in CS: 315.

52 Hence the island could be listed among those places 'that are much removed from India' in 1549: SR, IV: 558. Yet, while lacking a fort and a fleet, it was still seen as part of the legitimate official world by 'statists' such as Cosme Anes: SR: III. 540.

53 VP: 194.

settlers.[54] Another option was to dispatch the *ouvidor geral*, who was in charge of the administration of justice throughout the *Estado*, to investigate specific crimes. Yet this never occurred in Bhuvanekabāhu's reign. Beyond this, the *Estado* seems to have lacked any formal auditory institutions that could have maintained a check on the factors.

In the absence of such, the captain of the cinnamon ship, who dropped anchor at Colombo every autumn to collect the tribute, was often directed to help enforce central policy.[55] At other times he was drawn into the role of arbitrator. Even if he only stayed for a month or two, he represented the only Portuguese counterweight to the factor's influence and a rare alternative line of communication to the rest of the empire. In the 1520s, Bhuvanekabāhu had expressed a desire to deal only with this captain rather than contend with the year-round supervision of the factor.[56] It seems likely that the *fidalgo* (nobleman) Duarte Teixeira de Macedo, who drew up the long list of charges against the factor and the Portuguese community in 1541, had arrived on the island in this capacity, and the following year he accompanied Bhuvanekabāhu's ambassador to Lisbon.[57] Indeed, he may have introduced the idea of the embassy at the Kōṭṭe court.[58] From 1542 the captain was Francisco de Ayora, who also developed a good understanding with Bhuvanekabāhu.[59] Within four years he was dispatched to Goa as an ambassador of Kōṭṭe no less, expressing Bhuvanekabāhu's dissatisfactions with the permanent officials on the island.[60]

The weightiest mechanism of state vigilance was a visit by the governor in person. The only one to do so, once by accident in 1550 and secondly by design in 1551, was Afonso de Noronha. Interestingly, his most emphatic annoyance at the marginal liberty of Colombo was aroused not by the officials but by the small community of *moradores*, or Portuguese settlers.[61] Many of them would have been *casados*, men who settled down and married local women and were generally exempt from military duty, although they could be called upon in an

54 VP: 65–77, 191, 232–3.

55 He could set up official enquiries, as João Fernandes de Vasconcelos did in 1548, VP: 250.

56 CS: 315.

57 The memorial concludes by asking for Duarte Teixeira de Macedo to be installed as factor of Sri Lanka, VP: 14–20. Incidentally, he should not be confused (as Flores 1994: 135; Pieris and Fitzler 1927b: 17, do), with Duarte Teixeira. VP: 61, 69, refers to Teixiera de Macedo being in Portugal when we know that Duarte Teixeira was in Sri Lanka. He was still apparently in the East in 1546, see Schurhammer 1973–82, III: 319, n. 18.

58 The resulting decrees were directed towards all Portuguese officials, but it appears that the captain of the cinnamon ship was envisaged as the principal vehicle of royal will, to judge by the marginalia in IAN/TT, *Cartas dos Vice-Reis da Índia*, no. 100. This document was brought to my attention by Andreia Martins de Carvalho, and I have come across no references to it elsewhere. The copy of this letter used by SV is *Fragmentos*, Maço 1. SV also refers to a second copy, 'B', which contains marginal notes by the State Secretary Pedro de Alcaçova Carneiro beginning halfway through. I suggest that the extract found in *Cartas dos Vice-Reis* is the *first half* of 'B'.

59 It was he who brought the ambassadors back to Sri Lanka in 1543, see Correia: 321–3 and the *Crónica* of Andrada 1976: 865.

60 VP: 181–6. Moved perhaps by a gift of ten bahars of cinnamon: Schurhrammer 1973–82, II: 324; and see SV: 395–6.

61 In the 1520s these consisted of only around 30 to 50 souls: CS: 314–15.

emergency and sometimes played an important strategic role.[62] Often they would only help if the project was demonstrably in their interest, but sometimes they could contribute to more indirectly profitable ventures.[63] In the main, though, they were businessmen, trading in elephants, precious stones, horses, and so on. Shipbuilding also seems to have been a major activity and this was expanding through the 1540s.[64] However, the term *casado*, with its implications of a settled and legitimate role within the Portuguese imperial project, is not to be used unreservedly; some would have remained unmarried and some were engaged in illegitimate trans-Asian trade, drawing them closer to the lifestyles of the merchant types in the informal expansion east of Sri Lanka, the *chatins* and *lançados*.

Viceroy Noronha reported that in Sri Lanka there was no semblance of justice or order, with men scattered all about the island and routinely evading customs duty.[65] A few years before, the *casados* had claimed they were loyal subjects but ones 'removed from the service of the King our Lord, since we are not so close as those of Cochin'.[66] Noronha, confirming his reputation as a centralizer, ordered all unmarried men, clearly the biggest trouble-makers, to be sent to India, while the remaining Portuguese would be forced to reside together in Colombo under official scrutiny. He ordered that their trade be properly taxed, forbade the use of royal ships for private purposes and advised the construction of a strong fort. It is unlikely that the *moradores*' lifestyle changed much in response.

So local politics were of the essence. For long stretches of time the factor was the sole point of contact between the *Estado da Índia* and the King of Kōṭṭe. A great deal rested on the character of whoever was in office at the time. He could become a trusted friend of Bhuvanekabāhu or a source of immense unhappiness and frustration.[67] As we shall see in the following chapter, it was Bhuvanekabāhu in particular who suffered from the relative insignificance of high diplomacy. In the late 1520s, one Portuguese voiced the Kōṭṭe king's sentiments, saying that his compatriots felts so strong in their factory that they acted with no sense of accountability, and 'the friendship of Your Highness [with Bhuvanekabāhu] has no force on the factor nor anyone there.'[68]

Self-interest vs central interest

The *Estado* often failed to maintain a powerful hold over the interests and aims of private individuals. What we would consider today as corruption naturally prevailed. The notoriously poor and decidedly erratic payment of salaries engendered a feeling that unofficial profit-making was only to be expected.[69] The theme of

[62] Flores 1998: 174.
[63] Miguel Fernandez and António Gonçalves, *casados* of Colombo, both gave support to the expeditions to Kandy, see VP: 160, 175–8.
[64] Flores 1998: 63. [65] VP: 263–73. [66] SV: 496 (VP: 240). [67] Flores 1998: 178.
[68] CS: 315, echoed by the raja of Cochin in 1513, see Biker, III: 13.
[69] SR, IV: 562–3; Winius 1985.

greed is emphatic in later chroniclers and contemporary letters alike, in which it could become intermingled with a fear that the Portuguese were 'going wild' and losing their civility among the natives.[70]

As early as 1522 the Apostolic Commissary to the East, the titular Bishop of Dume, described a cultural shift that seemed to accompany the rounding of the Cape of Good Hope. He reports the advice of many leading men that there was no point in preaching restitution, for example, because such a notion simply conflicted with the ruling principles of life in the East:

> The Portuguese change their quality and nationality in this land and they become like the natives in their way of life, desiring nothing but sensuality . . . They leave Portugal with this intent which is followed by persons of every state and condition, so that I tell your Highness that India is going out of control, for none comes to serve your Highness in these parts but only with their own interests in mind.[71]

In Sri Lanka the head of the Franciscan mission, João de Vila do Conde, would evince a similar despair at the systemic avarice of the Portuguese expansion.[72] In the eyes of clerics, Christian morality was struggling to find a purchase in this new world.[73]

For large numbers of Portuguese, then, it was neither profitable nor were they compelled to place the interests of the *Estado* above their own immediate self-interest.[74] At one extreme this meant that many Portuguese left the bounds of the *Estado* altogether to start trading in the private Portuguese settlements which began to spring up east of Sri Lanka or even to join the service of native – sometimes enemy – rulers.[75] At the same time, the royal recognition and status conferred by holding office in the *Estado* still exerted an attraction, and it is often difficult to make distinctions between 'rebels' and 'loyal' individuals constantly tacking forth between the private and public.[76] We shall see below in Chapter Three how the factors and other officials were often the biggest culprits of nefarious commerce.

For military expeditions, the *Estado da Índia* was generally represented by appointed captains who were no more reliable as official agents. The *laissez-faire* approach of the state was partly to blame by making the leaders of these expeditions pay their own expenses, resulting in an overriding concern for personal remuneration. The negotiations with the King of Kandy in 1546 collapsed under the weight of this concern, inducing the accompanying friar to remark that 'here everything is greed for money.'[77] The leader of the next expedition, António Moniz

70 SR, II: 370–2; VP: 242–4, 257–63; Correia, *Lendas*, III: 652, IV: 338–9.
71 *DPM*, VI: 71–3, 79. 72 VP: 118.
73 However, this was part of an agenda to remake the East as a 'new world' of true Christianity in these days of religious reform: see Xavier 2004: 783–805.
74 See Winius and Diffie 1977: 334.
75 In 1527, *c.* 400 Portuguese defected to the court of Vijayanagar, disgusted with the pay and provisions produced by the *Estado*: CS: 314.
76 Flores 1993: 27–8; 1994: 128–30. 77 VP: 188.

Barreto, a hero from the siege of Diu no less, took out his embarrassment for its failure by humiliating Bhuvanekabāhu in public.[78]

The thrust of recent scholarship has therefore been to emphasize the heterogeneity of Portuguese expansion: the cleavages between Lisbon and Goa, between the governor and the local factors or captains, between officials and the merchant community, between those inside and those outside the pale of state influence, between loyalists and renegades, religious and secular, *fidalgos* (nobles) and commoners and so on.[79] However, within Sri Lanka this approach has not filtered down to a widespread view of 'the Portuguese period' as expressed particularly in non-specialist works, which allow a notion of empire (and perhaps resistance) drawn from the relative efficiencies of nineteenth-century British dominion to inform our perception of the early sixteenth-century Portuguese. In particular, many narratives assume that the comparatively ramshackle *Estado da Índia* had a coherent long-term policy of conquest and the means to execute it.

For example, one is sometimes given the impression that the Portuguese were responsible for the discord between Kōṭṭe, Sītāvaka and Kandy which left Sri Lanka so vulnerable to external interference. One recent work tells us that the Portuguese 'effected internecine warfare in the country and demanded that the king place more faith in them and act according to their demands'.[80] Many Portuguese were indeed opportunists of the highest order and saw as well as anybody the advantages of divide and rule. The attempt to support the pretensions of the King of Kandy in the mid-1540s is probably the best example.[81] Afonso de Noronha, who led an unusually rapacious expedition to the island, remarked that 'as it seemed more in the interest of Your Highness that the island should not be unified under one single ruler, but rather that it should be divided among several, former governors did not interfere in this matter and left the rulers to go on with their quarrel.'[82] This does not mean, however, that they were the fundamental cause of such dissension, or that they pursued any long-term policy towards creating it. Nor does it mean that there was agreement about when and how to take advantage of it. For there had been systemic contradictions at the heart of the imperial project from its inception.

Systemic contradictions

There was an underlying tension between, first, the desire to keep a tight control over all navigation and trade in the Indian Ocean in order to raise direct profits

[78] One Portuguese commented to the viceroy: 'If your lordship was to hear what the King suffered at the hands of António Moniz [Barreto], how he was humiliated and put to shame, you would find enough to be horrified.' VP: 241; Queyroz: 272.

[79] As a general survey, see Oliveira e Costa and Rodrigues 1992. Flores 1998: 166, and C. R. de Silva 1991a: 220, have applied this to Sri Lanka.

[80] Panabokke 1993: 201; Malalasekera 1994; Weerasooria 1970: 222, 233. The origin probably lies in the work of P. E. Pieris. For example, Pieris and Fitzler 1927b: 15: 'The Portuguese deliberately adopted that policy [of inculcating jealousy and self-seeking]; by fomenting domestic quarrels they wrecked the country.'

[81] See the comment of the factor (VP: 68). but there were many other reasons too for this policy.

[82] VP: 292.

for the Crown via royal monopolies of crucial spices; and second, the realization that a significant proportion of the basic income sustaining the empire was drawn from customs dues which depended on a freedom of trade. This was but one manifestation of a debate about the very nature and purpose of Portuguese expansion that had wracked the court of King Manuel, split as it was, to borrow Thomaz's terms, between *imperialist* and *liberal* factions. The former, inspired by the politico-religious ideal of crusade, envisaged a programme of expansion with a powerful redistributive state at its heart; the latter saw the East as an immense opportunity for individual liberty, whether in the form of private commerce or the piratical derring-do of freewheeling *fidalgos*. The appointment of administrators to the *Estado* has been plausibly linked to the power struggles of these two broad factions. The victory of the 'liberalists' was most notoriously evident in the appointment of Lopo Soares de Albergaria (1515–18), and his 'Gran Soltura' – the great liberation or release of private energies.[83] One can watch this debate persist and mutate in the reign of King João too.[84]

It is not easy to relate the shifts of factional hegemony to the tenor of relations in Sri Lanka, although Flores has shown that it was the more mercantilist governors who tended to give strategic priority to the island, attracted by its lucrative trade with the Coromandel.[85] Yet we certainly can catch glimpses of how the Portuguese community in Sri Lanka itself was divided by these strikingly different understandings of what they were doing in Asia. What was required here: imperial vigilance and military intervention or the more peaceful diplomacy in which trade flourishes?[86] In the 1520s, some argued for a military solution to the conundrum of Sri Lanka. After the long siege of 1521, a scribe at the factory argued that the governor should come in person, 'with all the power of India', seize the kingdom, appropriate its revenues, and replace the king with one of the princes from South India.[87] Again in 1529, João Garcês wrote a letter to King João III, expressing considerable anger at the dismantling of the fortress in 1524, and urging military conquest: 'and now this same Island is in such a state that, if the captains wanted to, they could certainly take it, because the brothers [The three inheritors of Kōṭṭe] fight amongst themselves and all the people of this land are frightened of them and wish to see them die.'[88]

But João Garcês was a lowly interpreter, expressing the statist predilections of many commoners; his views carried little weight and official policy such as it

[83] Correia: 158–9, offers an illuminating contrast of the centralizing Afonso de Albuquerque and his successor Lopo Soares de Albergaria.

[84] Thomaz 1998: 73.

[85] Flores 1998: 137–9. This explains the apparent irony that it was the liberalist Lopo Soares who finally carried through King Manuel's instruction to construct the fort in Colombo, while the centralizing Vasco da Gama ordered its destruction.

[86] The conflict between the practice of granting trading licences and the need to collect tribute offers a further manifestation: in 1525 a Moorish merchant carrying such a licence had sailed to Colombo and bought up the cinnamon, leaving very little to provide the tribute: see Flores, Doc: 344–5.

[87] Caração: 167.

[88] CS: 329. Fernão de Queirós, an apologist for the territorial ambitions of the later empire, is partly responsible for the idea that the Portuguese had always been thus motivated: see Queyroz: 227.

was drifted in an entirely different direction. Weightier officials had counselled the fortress' destruction. Some went even further. Nuno Álvares, who served in the island at about the same time, argued that even the factor should be removed from the island as an unnecessary expense that only served to irritate the King of Sri Lanka. Only one 'black' need serve there all the year round, the sole permanent vestige of imperial imposition.[89] Moreover, in the late 1540s when the internecine troubles were at their height, a prominent *casado* and former factor of Sri Lanka wrote in a report for the incoming Governor Garcia de Sá that

> if there is war in Ceylon I say that in no way can one collect any cinnamon, even if there is a fortress there, because it is harvested by the native people and in many parts of the island in the interior, because when there is discord in the land between him and his brother one cannot collect as much except with much work on the part of the factor and the Portuguese there, and so much more when there is war.[90]

One could not wish for a more telling comment on the way in which the economic priorities of empire could conflict with pretensions to political control through military interference.

In the following chapter we shall see how the tensions and frailties of central authority could benefit or undermine the vassals and allies of the Portuguese. The general failure of discipline was a prominent theme of the chroniclers. In Sri Lanka, the Portuguese empire came and went and Queirós, for one, argued that the rot had never been stopped: 'We could have been masters of India, if we had been masters of ourselves.[91]

[89] CS: 315.

[90] That is to say, civil discord was a great hindrance to cinnamon harvesting and actual war an even greater obstacle. It is likely that António Pessoa was also worried about the profitability of his shipbuilding business: see Pessoa 1960: 37–9. My thanks to C. R. de Silva for referring me to this document. The viceroy, João de Castro, advanced a similar cautious concern for the cinnamon trade in 1546, VP: 193.

[91] Queyroz: 280.

3
Imperialism in action

Symbiosis

While the bulk of this chapter will be given over to exploring the ways in which the Portuguese began to intrude into Kōṭṭe and frustrate its ruler, we ought to begin by acknowledging that the nature of Portuguese expansion in this epoch could also bring benefits to indigenous rulers. This was largely because many Portuguese found the patronage offered by such rulers to be more generous and reliable than that offered by the *Estado*. While Albuquerquian centralism hung over Colombo in the shape of the fortress, Bhuvanekabāhu's dealings with the Portuguese were rather sour. But once the fortress was dismantled in 1524 and its errant Captain Fernão Gomes de Lemos arrested, relations greatly improved.[1] For the next fifteen years of Bhuvanekabāhu's reign there was a genuine symbiosis, a crucial fact for understanding his subsequent policy.

The new factor Nuno Freire de Andrade's repeated bravery in defence of Kōṭṭe in the 1520s demonstrated the best of what vassalage had to offer, and in return he profited handsomely from Bhuvanekabāhu's largesse.[2] Nuno Álvares also established a close relationship with the king. We have already heard him arguing in 1527 for a radical reduction of the permanent imperial presence in Sri Lanka.[3] At the same time, he argued that Sri Lanka be given a much more central role in the empire, as a base where the fleet could winter and undergo repairs. Pointing to the support Bhuvanekabāhu had given to some men who had suffered a shipwreck ('he supplied them with food and gave them some money, in the manner of your highness, except he paid them rather better'), he openly contrasted the beneficence of the King of Kōṭṭe with that of the King of Portugal. Álvares is clearly articulating the view from the court of Kōṭṭe, yet he was also an imperial official, as probate judge in Colombo for five or six years in the early 1520s.[4]

More typically slippery in their loyalties were the careers of Duarte Teixeira and António Pessoa. Pessoa had taken the Colombo factorship by 1533, during

[1] Correia: 204. [2] This relationship is detailed in Strathern 2002: 62–3.
[3] CS: 315; and above, p. 48.
[4] And, if he is the 'Nun'Allverez' referred to in March 1524 (Flores, Doc: 328), also *almoxarife* of the fortress.

which he signed the important cinnamon contract of that year, then moved quickly to Bassein and returned to the post in Sri Lanka for 1541–3.[5] This time he became the culprit in Bhuvanekabāhu's complaints to the Lisbon court. Later on in the decade he appears as one of the key players in the shipbuilding industry which was causing so much aggravation to the Kōṭṭe king. However, in his report to Garcia de Sá of 1548 we find him clearly supporting a peaceful and tolerant policy towards Bhuvanekabāhu, and arguing for submission to his wishes regarding the regulation of timber-cutting and cinnamon collection. By 1552, he was a reliable supporter of Kōṭṭe stability.[6] Duarte Teixeira (factor, 1539–41) had undoubtedly also precipitated Bhuvanekabāhu's ire in the 1541 memorial, but he swiftly 'changed colours' once he lost office, perhaps simply because he failed to win another position.[7] In 1545, Teixeira was at the Kōṭṭe court testifying in Bhuvanekabāhu's favour, and by 1547 he became (along with a 'Master Luís') one of his chief advisers, helping him in his preparations for war.[8]

Bhuvanekabāhu also sought to express his independence by bestowing patronage on men who were sidelined or rejected by the *Estado* such as the maverick Gonçalo Vaz Coutinho.[9] As Kōṭṭe and Goa drew apart in the later 1540s, Bhuvanekabāhu was in greater need of Portuguese middlemen to press his case. The clearest example here is Jorge de Castro, a *fidalgo* of very high standing, who sought refuge at Kōṭṭe.[10] His marginality with regard to the *Estado* was not, therefore, a function of his pedigree but the result of a feud with the governor Garcia de Sá. This was turned on its head when Castro's nephew, Jorge Cabral, became governor (1549–51). Castro was able to persuade him to support a campaign against Māyādunnē led by himself and financed by Bhuvanekabāhu. In other words, Castro had brought about a sudden reversal of Goan policy, bringing Bhuvanekabāhu briefly back into favour.

Without a doubt the two Portuguese closest to the King of Kōṭṭe in this turbulent decade were his interpreter, António Pereira, and his secretary António da Fonseca.[11] They, along with others such as Teixeira, found themselves quite out of tune with the prevailing mood of opinion among the *casados*, who claimed that the latter was 'more loyal to him [Bhuvanekabāhu] than to the king and lord of the

[5] The identity between the Pessoa of 1533 (Flores, Doc: 350) and Bassein (*DPM*, VI: 436), and the Pessoa of 1541–3 (VP: 182) is not proven. Pessoa received a grant to make ships in Ceylon in March 1547: see *Livro das Mercês* . . . , in Baião 1925: 315 (and 301).

[6] Testifying in Dharmapāla's favour: VP: 297.

[7] His conflict with Pessoa caused them both to be brought before the governor, who installed Simão Botelho as factor (Correia: 320). Teixeira claimed that Pessoa bought his office from the *vedor da fazenda*, SV: 63–9. Martim Afonso de Sousa then sent António Pessoa to resume his factorship, but shortly afterwards Manuel Rodrigues Coutinho replaced him. In the 1520s, Duarte Teixeira had been treasurer of Cochin (Correia, *Lendas*, III: 114, 335).

[8] VP: 240.

[9] On Coutinho's story see Correia: 320; Subrahmanyam 1993: 253–4, and Dejanirah Silva Couto 2000: 178–201.

[10] See VP: 254; Couto: 133–6.

[11] The aged Pereira, another member of the 1541 embassy, had a family in Colombo.

land of their birth'.[12] By the mid 1540s the Portuguese community was polarized between this small group clustered around the King of Kōṭṭe and an expanding body of men who regularly ignored his authority or actively sought his downfall.[13]

In truth, from the end of the 1530s the friendship of Bhuvanekabāhu had begun to seem less appealing than other routes to prosperity. As King João's reign wore on, increasing numbers of Portuguese sailed to South Asia to make their fortune outside of the official opportunities of the *Estado*.[14] By 1547, one principal official could write to the king that the chief disservice he received in the East was this scattering of his countrymen beyond state purview, their harassment of the locals destroying the reputation of the Portuguese.[15] The royal control of cinnamon was eroded as the spice trade was liberalized in the 1540s and the governor Martim Afonso de Sousa (1542–5) displayed a marked preference for aristocratic adventure over state and commercial protocol.[16] But, already by 1539, Miguel Ferreira was warning, 'I assure Your Highness that if you do not provide Ceylon with some little justice to the best of my judgement it will last but a very short time.'[17] One can distinguish three developments in Portuguese behaviour: an increasingly domineering presence at court, a disregard for local law, and the extension of diplomacy to other centres in the island. Through Bhuvanekabāhu's eyes they would appear as arrogance, criminality and treachery.

The micro-politics of court

The kingdom of Kōṭṭe had a highly developed administrative system with an array of ministers in charge of everything from the royal treasury (the *mudalnāyaka*) to the keeping of the royal elephants (the *gajanāyaka*). The council of ministers discharged an advisory role. There were both territorial and departmental administrative hierarchies which were sophisticated enough to endure throughout the Portuguese and Dutch periods.[18] As Caração remarked, in the Kōṭṭe palace Vijayabāhu had

> the estate of kingship and palace officials exactly as Your Highness does, even though they are not as perfect, in that he has *vedores* and clerks of the treasury and a *vedor* of the palace, and chief and minor *estribeiros* and a secretary and all the other officers belonging to a royal palace.[19]

[12] VP: 240. At the same time, Teixeira was hoping to profit from secretive communications with the King of Kandy (VP: 69–73), and in late 1546/early 1547 he was angling to be made the chief guard and tutor to the son of the King of Kandy (VP: 216), although possibly only once the rapprochement between Kōṭṭe and Kandy was established in early 1547.

[13] VP: 238–40. [14] See SR, II: 250–3.

[15] Therefore native rulers deserved all possible support and assistance from the Portuguese captains: SR: III. 539–40; and in 1549: SR, IV: 470.

[16] Flores 1998: 167. [17] SV: 91.

[18] C. R. de Silva 1995: 24–31; Siriweera 1993/5; Ariyapala 1968: chapter 3; Flores 1998: 87–9.

[19] Caração: 167–8.

This comparison with European courts should remind us of a simple point: that Bhuvanekabāhu was not the totality of Kōṭṭe government, which was rather dominated by a group of close family members. The king's nephew, Tammiṭa Sembaha Perumāl, held the post of chief chamberlain for life.[20] His elder brother was none other than Vīdiyē Baṇḍāra, who was also son-in-law to Bhuvanekabāhu, having married his daughter Samudrādēvi in the mid 1530s and produced the heir to the throne, Dharmapāla.[21] During Bhuvanekabāhu's reign Vīdiyē Baṇḍāra was the *sēnāpati* or commander-in-chief of the Sinhalese military. Lastly there was the *purōhita* or chaplain, Śrī Rāmarakṣa Paṇḍita, whose stock rose considerably after his triumphant embassy to Lisbon in 1542.[22]

These officers, and more particularly the ranks of nameless lesser courtiers, must have found the atmosphere of courtly life profoundly altered by the Portuguese who came to frequent the Kōṭṭe palace. This was not simply because they represented an alien intrusion, for there had long been foreigners enjoying high status at the Kōṭṭe court. There were two specific institutions that seem to have paved the way for Portuguese influence. The first is the role of *mahaveleńda-na*, or chief-of-merchants, who represented the interests of the predominantly Muslim merchants at the court of Vijayabāhu.[23] Once the Muslims were expelled the Portuguese factor would have slotted easily into this role. Secondly, there was the royal guard, which was traditionally made up of foreign mercenaries: kings looked abroad in order to attract men who, having no connections of caste or kinship with the entrenched Sinhalese aristocracy, would have loyalty only to their royal person. They had tended to rely on South Indian soldiers, particularly the Karāvas, who were given extensive land along the Kōṭṭe coast in return for their services.[24]

Bhuvanekabāhu requested a Portuguese guard for much the same reasons. His stated rationale was that a guard would give him some purchase over the lawless Portuguese. But the guard would also strengthen his hand against the noble factions that had troubled him in the 1520s and 1530s.[25] It was widely appreciated that the Portuguese had replaced the South Indians as the most attractive warriors in the region. Bhuvanekabāhu did not get what he bargained for. A body of Portuguese were assembled but they were not placed under his immediate control. Rather, Manuel Rodrigues Coutinho, who had been assured the post of factor and chief magistrate in 1541, travelled to Sri Lanka with the further office of the 'chief guard' (*guarda-mor*).[26] Just as the factor was far more intrusive than

[20] VP: 34, (and see n. 2 which gives the variety of names by which he was known).

[21] *Rājāvaliya*: 73–5; Ribeiro: 10. Queyroz: 333, gives a slightly different genealogy, which Pieris 1983–92: 78, tries to resolve.

[22] In 1545, we find him boasting that all the affairs of the kingdom are in his hands: see VP: 61.

[23] C. R. de Silva 1995: 26.

[24] Knox 114: Rājasiṃha II of Kandy (1635–87) had a guard of black men 'in whom he imposeth more confidence than in his own people'.

[25] VP: 19, 20. See also below, p. 78.

[26] IAN/TT, *Chancelaria de D. João III*, livro 25, folio 54v. Later factors – Belchior Botelho, Miguel Carvalho and Gaspar de Azevedo – are not explicitly referred to as having this title. At times someone else may have assumed the role: see VP: 185.

any chief-of-merchants, so the *guarda-mor* was an altogether novel pressure on Bhuvanekabāhu. Here Portuguese imperialism worked by appropriating and transforming existing institutions.

The intimacy and informality of relations with the king afforded by these positions was important; the Portuguese could thereby circumvent his public persona, the court ritual and magnificent adornments that served to elevate him above the merely mortal.[27] The royal audience was a ceremony of major significance. In the time of Parākramabāhu VI (1411–67), the king was seated at the far end of the room while ministers sat on both sides singing on his entrance and exit.[28] It is hardly surprising then that their first encounter with the King of Kōṭṭe made a strong impression on the Portuguese, who sent a detailed description of the occasion to King Manuel. He in turn relayed it with pride in a letter to the Pope in 1507. Queirós takes his description of the audience hall from this letter, dwelling on the sumptuous fabrics and treasures and the elaborate nature of the obsequies.[29] Later reports from Kōṭṭe, Sītāvaka and Kandy confirm the formality, ritual intricacy and high pomp of these occasions.[30]

But the Portuguese factor and chief guard were not confined to such ritually circumscribed encounters. Their sense of military superiority was therefore allowed to express itself in a superiority of comportment, a general disrespect for indigenous honour. This was a common problem, and one angrily bemoaned by Queirós.[31] In Sri Lanka, it makes its first significant appearance with the first major demonstration of Portuguese military power into the interior of the island. Miguel Ferreira's expedition of 1539 drove deep into Sītāvaka for the first time, and Ferreira finished by holding aloft the heads of his enemies, the Māppiḷa captains. This decisive victory represented something of a watershed in relations between the Portuguese and Bhuvanekabāhu. For long stretches the king had been holed up in Kōṭṭe with the factor, Pero Vaz Travassos.[32] In this intimate situation Travassos had not behaved decorously. Ferreira wrote that

> . . . in my presence the factor spoke and acted in a very unbecoming way. He showed great disrespect to the king and used foul language against him. The king felt very humiliated and I saw tears trickling down his beard at the insults of Pero Vaz.[33]

Only the chance arbitration of Ferreira and the visiting Franciscan Commissary facilitated his removal. In the 1540s the factor's tenure became more erratic and short-lived, perhaps as a result of the growing venality attached to the office, and

[27] See Plate 1. The fifteenth-century *sandēśa* poems are good on the glamour of royal processions and buildings: see Ariyapala 1968: 61. Dewaraja 1988: 266–7, comments on the limitations of court theatrics.

[28] Siriweera 1993/5: 9. [29] Queyroz: 180.

[30] Flores 1998: 86. The description in 'Referir de Francesco del Bocchier' of 1518 in Aubin 1974, is very close to Bhuvanekabāhu's reign – my thanks to C. R. de Silva for making his translation available. See Ralph Fitch's comments on Sītāvaka from 1589 in Foster 1921: 43; and Miranda: 186. Dutch reports: Goonewardena 1977. However, sometimes foreign ambassadors were placed in a different category for whom the normal procedures did not apply: Dewaraja 1988: 271–3.

[31] Queyroz: 288–9. [32] Correia: 268–9. [33] VP: 10.

mutual understanding rarely developed. Bhuvanekabāhu's letters become a litany of complaints. The nadir was probably reached with Gaspar de Azevedo, who took office in 1548 and whose conduct scandalized even the Portuguese community in Cochin. The influential *vedor da fazenda* was moved to write that 'till now they had not placed there a man as factor and chief magistrate who was a greater drunkard and more arrogant and a greater thief than him.'[34]

Bhuvanekabāhu found ways of fighting back, using diplomatic leverage or withholding the cinnamon tribute to influence the selection of officers.[35] And as we have seen, there were a few Portuguese still interested in symbiosis. The court, therefore, became the scene of struggle, in which Bhuvanekabāhu's secretary and interpreter became the objects of a tug-of-war between the king and the factor. The interpreter, António Pereira, was difficult to remove as he had a decree from the King of Portugal guaranteeing him the office for life.[36] The factor's response was simply to refuse to pay him.[37] The secretary, more vulnerable, was subject to regular attempts to have him shipped out of the island.[38] An analogous process can be seen in the later Cochin courts where the secretary, given his unusual closeness to the king and potential role as voice of resistance, functioned as a diplomatic pivot.[39] In late 1546 we get a vivid sense of the way in which the chief guard and factor were intruding into court business: Bhuvanekabāhu complained that they insisted on being present when he was composing his letters and forced him to write certain things against his wishes![40] Yet in the same year Bhuvanekabāhu, all too aware of the menace which his new guard represented, had purged it of all Portuguese in a strong reassertion of his authority.[41] It would seem then that the court was characterized by subtly shifting ebbs and flows of power limited only by the loose framework of higher diplomacy.

Indeed, when we compare him with some other vassals and allies of the Portuguese, Bhuvanekabāhu can appear relatively precious about his royal presence. Sebastião Pires, the Vicar of Cochin, gives us a snapshot of the kind of domestic unhappiness into which the Raja of Cochin's relationship with the Portuguese could descend in 1527.[42] The raja had found himself very 'disfavoured by and unhappy with the captain and controller of the treasury, Afonso Mexia, because of the many harsh words that he has said to him, such as that he is only king while the Portuguese want him to be'. He was so upset that he had been refusing to come to the fortress for many days and had even threatened to abdicate. This indicates that the usual state of affairs was a very close association and that it was normal for the raja to leave his palace and consult with the Portuguese on their home ground. Whatever court protocol Bhuvanekabāhu was willing to forgo, we very rarely hear of him leaving his palace behind altogether.[43]

[34] VP: 242. [35] Flores, Doc: 344–5; VP: 11 (regarding Manuel de Queirós). [36] VP: 33.
[37] VP: 185. [38] VP: 251. [39] Tavim 1997: 60. [40] VP: 184, 186.
[41] VP: 118. Notice that the royal guard was still largely foreign at this time. Bhuvanekabāhu was also quite able to deny indigenous Christians access to the palace regardless of Portuguese protestations: see below, p. 106.
[42] SR, II: 142.
[43] For one exception, see VP: 251; but see the haughty snub of Noronha in Queyroz: 288–91.

Disregarding local law

Many Asian rulers who submitted to the principle of extra-territoriality naturally found that the Portuguese felt little compunction to abide by local norms or laws, but more worrying still was their inability to protect even their own delimited sphere of jurisdiction. We have heard Bhuvanekabāhu articulate this very clearly.[44] This process was not confined to comparatively isolated lands such as Ceylon, for we find it among the allied principalities of Malabar too.[45] The authority of native kings was perhaps most regularly undermined by the refusal to pay customs dues, a revealing point when one considers the tight connection between sovereignty and revenue rights in both Asia and Europe at this time.[46] The Kōḷaṭhiri Raja of Cannanore complained in 1518 that the Portuguese were directly imposing their laws on his subjects.[47] By 1545, the situation was much worse. The Kōḷaṭhiri wrote a letter describing the bullying tactics displayed by the captain of the Malabar fleet, Belchior de Sousa Chichorro.[48] The captain's conduct was so offensive that the Muslim merchants felt compelled to abandon Canannore altogether and, on taking office, João de Castro immediately dispatched the *ouvidor geral* to direct an investigation there.[49]

The trading community in Colombo was more likely to be antagonistic to the king than in Cochin if only because Colombo was much less lucrative as a centre of commerce. In Cochin the *casados* formed a powerful interest group, helping the *Estado* when it was relevant to their trading prospects and resisting mightily when they perceived that imperial policy had other concerns, notably under the centralizing yokes of Albuquerque and João de Castro.[50] The economy of the city was directed firmly towards private interests, and pepper smuggling was the norm.[51] The interests of the *casados* and those of the raja often intertwined; both wanted a liberal attitude to trade, preference over the trading rival of Goa and a policy of aggression towards Calicut. By contrast, only occasionally can one discern an explicit expression of united interests among the merchants and the state in Kōṭṭe.[52] The Colombo settlers, having less opportunity to make huge fortunes by legitimate means, may have been more intent on generating profit through nefarious activities.

Again it is Bhuvanekabāhu's memorial of 1541 which throws light on their misdemeanours: refusing to pay customs dues, forcing locals to buy unwanted goods or selling them at an unfairly low price, entering and stealing from Sinhalese houses and all manner of book-keeping scandals. Moreover, an illicit slave trade had come into existence, with children and adults being kidnapped and shipped away.[53] The memorial also shows how difficult it is to separate the behaviour

44 See above, p. 41.
45 Already in 1509, the Raja of Cochin complained that the Viceroy was hanging people without reference to his authority: SR, I: 74–5.
46 An outraged Raja of Cochin complained in 1526–7, see Flores, Doc: 34; SR, II: 141.
47 Bouchon 1988: 155–6.
48 Bouchon, Doc: 212–17; Goertz 1989: 8–10.
49 Goertz 1986: 63–78.
50 See Biker, IV: 52, 1513, on the powerful pro-Cochin Portuguese lobby.
51 See Tavim 1995: 95.
52 Both wanted private ships to be forced to stop at Colombo: see VP: 184, and Pessoa 1960: 38.
53 VP: 14–20.

of the settlers from the officials who were supposed to be regulating them. The latter were actively co-operating with the more rapacious businessmen and indeed running rackets of their own.[54] One way of circumnavigating Bhuvanekabāhu's authority was to conduct business in the other coastal towns along the western seaboard. Already in 1529 a canny Lusitanian had pointed to the profit to be made in these ports and offered his services as a roaming commercial agent, buying up the cinnamon and tar unavailable to the Colombo-bound factors.[55] But ten years later the factor had sent his own men to the ports. They bullied their way into dominating commerce, refused to pay any customs dues, fixed prices, and used their authority to corrupt justice. Faced with such pressure, Bhuvanekabāhu's subjects began to desert the coastal towns.[56]

If the memorial evokes the dangers of extra-territoriality, it was also intended as a solution to it, indeed the only possible solution: to elicit the passing of Portuguese decrees that would mimic those of local jurisdiction. It succeeded marvellously, bearing fruit in the ten decrees issued by King João III in March 1543.[57] In this way, the presumably brief contract of vassalage was supplemented by a comprehensive set of arrangements that resembled the negotiated settlements contained in the treaties of *amizade* established by the Malabar kings. The same issues – cutting down palm trees, quarrelling with natives – recur in both. Undoubtedly, the Lisbon court did not realize quite how far-reaching some of these decrees were. One granted that when the Portuguese purchased some land 'they shall pay the rents and discharge the obligations and customs to which were subject those who sold the lands'.[58] The reference to 'obligations and customs' seems innocuous enough, but it thereby tied Portuguese settlers into the complex traditional system of land tenure that prevailed in Kōṭṭe which required land-holders to provide specified services. Given that the most common form of service was military, any Portuguese who acquired land outside of Colombo was theoretically liable to become a militiaman of Bhuvanekabāhu. The foundation of Sinhalese sovereignty in the dominion and organization of land and labour could not but conflict with the extra-territorial thrust of Portuguese imperialism.

The sentiment in Lisbon was clearly that the Portuguese community in Sri Lanka must be brought under central control.[59] The decrees had simply made Portuguese misbehaviour a question of internal discipline within the *Estado da Índia*. After 1543, the factor or the *ouvidor* would have had the power to prosecute cases under these provisions. But, in the most important demonstration of

[54] VP: 16, 19: the captain of the fishery coast was charged with usurping the dues owed to Bhuvanekabāhu from the pearl beds off Kalpitiya and Chilaw.

[55] CS: 329. [56] VP: 136, 183, 250. [57] VP: 24–34. [58] SV: 114 (VP: 28).

[59] The sympathy of Lisbon for Bhuvanekabāhu's situation is evident not just in the ten decrees, but in the initial response of the State Secretary Pedro de Alcaçova Carneiro, who suggested various ways to check the factor's power, for example that any Portuguese would have to obtain the permission of both the Portuguese governor and the King of Kōṭṭe if they wanted to reside on the island. If any Portuguese already resident failed to obtain permission they would be deported by the captain of the cinnamon ship: IAN/TT, *Cartas dos Vice-Reis da Índia*, no. 100.

the weakness of high diplomacy, the decrees were routinely disregarded.[60] New *ouvidores* came, proclaimed the 'great corruption and licentiousness' of the land, and largely failed to make an impact or even succumbed to the same practices themselves.[61] Bhuvanekabāhu turned sarcastic: 'you should be amazed that I have not yet gone insane and that I am not already wandering in the forest.'[62] Towards the end of his reign Bhuvanekabāhu became more desperate, writing to Prince Luís of the pecuniary obsession of the Portuguese:

> For they by all the cunning devices and ways they can summon, and in spite of the order of their king and of their governor, do what they will without fear of reprisal. [The captains] permit this among all the Portuguese who reside in my lands, without chastising them but rather favouring them.[63]

The chronicler Gaspar Correia would echo Bhuvanekabāhu's denunciations in the strongest of terms.[64]

This image of a descent into quasi-anarchy over the 1540s is confirmed by the reports of two Jesuits, Manuel Morais and António Dias, who arrived at Colombo in the wake of Bhuvanekabāhu's death in 1551. They saw a community on the periphery of Christian morality: 'These [Portuguese], being in the island and far from the governor, were in the habit of disobeying the law of God and man, committing many evils.'[65] If this reflects a typical clerical anxiety about the unreformed pastoral life, some Sinhalese had begun to make their own judgements as to the dissolution of the Colombo Portuguese, withdrawing from the city and leaving it for the newcomers.[66]

The extension of diplomacy

It is also in the memorial of 1541 that we see the first glimmerings of another arena of discontent, in the terse request for an order for the Portuguese to cease contact with Māyādunnē. In the coming years it would be Kandy rather than Sītāvaka that attracted controversy, but the principle is here at the beginning of the fifth decade: the Portuguese were starting to look beyond Kōṭṭe, to extend relations to other

60 This may be partly because King João III often seemed on the verge of abrogating the decrees on account of Bhuvanekabāhu's failure to convert: see VP: 261.

61 VP: 75, and 181–5, for further complaints by Bhuvanekabāhu of illicit shipbuilding, evasion of customs dues and enslavement of his subjects. The chief guard (A. Ferreira) who arrived with the *ouvidor* (Álvares), soon succumbed to cinnamon stealing: see Figueiredo in SV: 395–6. Apparently, Ferreira and his brother Estevão were even planning to mint coins in Kōṭṭe.

62 VP: 136.

63 SV: 540 (VP: 261).

64 Correia: 265, who also says that Bhuvanekabāhu was so oppressed 'that he would long ago have left the kingdom, if he had any place to go to', which seems an echo of Bhuvanekabāhu's letter of 1546, quoted above.

65 VP: 318, and compare with 293.

66 VP: 337. In 1555 another Jesuit (VP: 342) commented that 'as the Portuguese who come to these parts come for no other purpose than somehow to enrich themselves, then go back home, they have no real interest in this country.'

kings. Such promiscuity – consorting with his rebellious vassals – is the third way in which the Portuguese began to displease Bhuvanekabāhu.

Officers and settlers may have been grinding down the Kōṭṭe–Portugal alliance with their pursuit of profit but neither they nor the authorities in Goa were the real conductors of Portuguese diplomacy on the island. As C. R. de Silva has remarked, it was the individual entrepreneur out to make his fortune regardless of state policy who drove so much of the action in Sri Lanka.[67] Indeed, given the short tenure of officials, it was often only such independent operators who could build up substantial local expertise. But official policy was hardly irrelevant, because ultimately these adventurers could do little without the military or symbolic support of the state.

Rather it was that the *Estado* was always responding in an *ad hoc* manner to processes set in motion by individuals. In this way 1540s Sri Lanka has much in common with Sanjay Subrahmanyam's characterization of parts of the Portuguese empire in the later sixteenth century as a time when 'peripheral initiatives came to dominate a system in place of a central motor' – peripheral initiatives set in motion by enterprising Portuguese inserting themselves into favourable positions at indigenous courts.[68] This was intensified in the geographical frontier regions which were also social frontiers where lower-born men could find the liberty to better themselves. Such 'sub-imperialism' came early to Sri Lanka, no doubt largely because its fractured local conditions were so conducive. Moreover, it makes sense to see the Sea of Ceylon region as a 'halfway house' once more: these adventurers were not operating in complete independence as happened on the wilder shores of the Portuguese expansion, yet they also exercised a greater freedom to dictate and interpret the course of events than men of equivalent status in areas more properly under imperial vigilance.

The classic example of the kind of man who grew to prominence in such an environment is Miguel Ferreira. His long career operating both under and beyond the aegis of the *Estado* has inspired a detailed study by Jorge Flores, so we shall move on swiftly to the two most influential adventurers of the 1540s, Nuno Álvares Pereira and André de Sousa.[69] Sousa had amassed considerable experience in Asia before we find him trying his luck in Colombo in the 1530s, and a few years later he maintained he was there by the order of the governor Martim Afonso de Sousa, though in what capacity we do not know.[70] André de Sousa was the main engine

[67] C. R. de Silva 1991a: 229; Flores 1994: 135.

[68] Subrahmanyam 1990. Winius 2000 makes such peripheral dynamism an essential characteristic of the *Estado da Índia*. Flores 1994: 139, has already remarked on the way in which Sri Lanka fits Subrahmanyam's paradigm. Indeed that article offers an analysis of much of the material presented here and affords many further insights.

[69] Flores 1993. While Ferreira was very influential in the Sea of Ceylon region, these two misfits exerted a greater power in the internal events of Sri Lanka.

[70] VP: 109; Flores, Doc: 351, n. 73. We know that an André de Sousa was an inhabitant of Colombo in 1533 (Flores, Doc: 351), although the brief biography in Coutinho 1972: 97, asserts that our Sousa was fighting in Diu in 1531 and was a fleet commander 1534–7. By 1539 he was attending Bhuvanekabāhu's court, VP: 10. For other details, see Schurhammer 1973–82, II: 532, n. 345, and VP: 111, n. 2.

behind the affair of the Kōṭṭe princes in 1544 which did so much damage to relations with Kōṭṭe (discussed in detail below in Chapter Five). He claimed to have converted them and whisked them to safety in Goa, and the correspondence that he then wrote on their behalf included the extraordinary request that he be made the captain and governor of all their lands for the rest of his life.[71]

Shortly afterwards André de Sousa managed to win an official position as the head of the expedition sent out to connect with the King of Kandy. However, the man responsible for inducing the governor to send the expedition was Nuno Álvares Pereira, who had boldly set forth on the hazardous journey to Kandy in 1541/2. Nuno Álvares was a man of ambiguous background. It has been suggested that he was a bastard son of the Conde de Feria who arrived with Martim Afonso de Sousa in 1541.[72] He certainly had motive enough to force a leap in status by becoming the key man at the centre of a rising power in Sri Lanka. We must turn to the testimony of the friar Padrão to drive a sceptical wedge between the complicities and duplicities of Sousa and Pereira. It transpires that Pereira had engineered the correspondence, leading the king to believe that 'the governor would crown him and make him emperor of the island, that all would kiss his foot and become his vassal and tributaries'. To Goa, he promoted the equally misleading image of the perfect Christian neophyte.[73] After 1546, he somewhat fades from sight, but not before establishing this beguiling mirage of a Christian vassal in the highlands of Sri Lanka, an image that would eventually assume a somewhat shaky reality in the 1560s.

It was also in the interests of André de Sousa to keep that vision alive. He arrived in Kandy in 1546 after the king had been baptized. Well aware of the reflected glory that a royal baptism entailed, he still tried to claim the credit for it, insisting that it was the result of particularly persuasive letter he had written to the king from Galle.[74] In Kandy, Padrão claimed that Sousa began to assume an authority to which he was not entitled, styling himself a captain, quite contrary to the official letter carried by the friar.[75] Once again Sousa was improvising. Here the distorting effect of the distance from the centre worked in reverse: now it was the intentions of the *Estado* whose representation became malleable.

In the comparatively open diplomatic field of the later 1540s, the more disreputable opportunists could play Kōṭṭe and Sītāvaka off one another. Hence we have João Fernandes de Vasconcelos, who threatened that he would go over to Māyādunnē unless Bhuvanekabāhu wrote off a great sum in loans.[76] We know of at least one Portuguese who did firmly attach himself to the court of Sītāvaka. Previously Diogo de Noronha had sought his fortune in Bhuvanekabāhu's court but had apparently caused some sort of outrage, for he was forced to flee to Māyādunnē,

[71] VP: 89, 90, 101–11. As VP: 116, n. 6, points out, the governor was appropriately wary of Sousa and directed someone else, Vasco da Cunha, to oversee the princes' installation in Sri Lanka.
[72] SV: 148, n. 1. See VP: 76, for a report of his 'honourable' status. But the friar Padrão (188) described him as 'a poor practical soldier'. Perhaps he was a disinherited or illegitimate *fidalgo*.
[73] VP: 187–8. [74] A claim undermined by VP: 152; also Bourdon 1936: 47, n. 2.
[75] VP: 168–70. [76] VP: 261.

'who was enlisting Portuguese', according to the Kōṭṭe ambassador, thereby placing himself beyond the sympathies of the *Estado* at that time.[77] However, it so happened that his uncle, Afonso de Noronha, was installed as the new viceroy who turned up in Sri Lanka in 1551. Diogo had his chance: he pressed Māyādunnē's case to his uncle and was probably instrumental in turning him against Bhuvanekabāhu. In fact, his story illustrates the same principle as Jorge de Castro's (see above, Chapter 3): how alienated Portuguese *fidalgos* could seek patronage at an indigenous court and then, with a change of administration, find themselves suddenly close to the centre of the *Estado*. But for this family connection, Diogo might well have ended up entirely divorced from the state's interests.

True rebels (*aleventados*) tended to leave only shadowy records of themselves. We do have one glimpse of an out-and-out renegade in our period, although it is offered to us by the chronologically unreliable Queirós.[78] His name was Paulo Chainho and he was apparently an influential adviser of Māyādunnē, spurring him in his wars and even, according to some reports, abjuring the faith to take up the religion of his adopted kingdom. We are told that in 1549 he arrived in Goa as Māyādunnē's ambassador, was recognized for the renegade that he was, and hanged without further ado.

In this early phase of Portuguese–Sinhalese relations, the numbers of Portuguese operating in the island were tiny. Yet they had a disproportionately large impact. For every one of them to a greater or lesser extent had the weight of the Portuguese empire behind him, and moved about with a kind of diplomatic inviolability. At the same time, these men rarely experienced that weight as a burden or a bureaucratic force to which they were accountable. That is the nature of the Portuguese imperialism to which the island was becoming subject in these decades before outright conquest: small-scale, disorganized, far from comprehensive, yet disruptive nonetheless. It is in the interstices that Bhuvanekabāhu's authority resided and that is the theme of the following chapter.

[77] VP: 277.

[78] Queyroz: 281, and 335, for another renegade, Afonso Rasquinho, a native of the Algarve: see Conclusion, p. 000 below.

4
Bhuvanekabāhu's sovereignty

A historiographical problem: puppet-king or tyrant?

With the litany of abuses and frustrations described in the last chapter still fresh in our minds, it is easy enough to see why many writers have seen fit to follow the Portuguese chroniclers in representing Bhuvanekabāhu as a man weak by disposition and increasingly pathetic by circumstance, crushed as he was between the more dynamic forces of Māyādunnē and the Portuguese. His own melancholic letters can seem to reinforce that image. Can we concur that his sovereignty was fatally undermined?

This is what has often been concluded from the decrees of 1543.[1] It is argued that they were not simply an attempt to gain some legal purchase over the Portuguese; they also conceded an inability to rule as sovereign over the people of Kōṭṭe. Why else would Bhuvanekabāhu need to have recourse to distant Lisbon in order to ratify the succession of his grandson Dharmapāla?[2] However, the truth is that the theoretical arbitration of succession had been already conceded to the crown of Portugal when Vijayabāhu became a vassal in 1518. The same could be said for all allies who had been invested by the Portuguese. Indeed, Portugal was, in a sense, *obliged* to oversee and safeguard their modes of succession.[3]

Nor did these contractual bonds remain in the realm of theory. They allowed the Portuguese to exploit the conflicts of succession that seemed so characteristic of the states encountered in the East. Afonso de Albuquerque in particular saw the potential: a malleable candidate could be upheld and at the same time held in check by the threat of ratifying a rival. In 1512 Albuquerque did not merely manipulate ambiguities in Cochin, he literally abolished the customary rule of succession which stated that when the retired king (the 'Muppil') died the current monarch must take his place in retirement. In this way he kept his preferred choice, Rāma Varma, on the throne. When Rāma Varma tried to abdicate the Portuguese put him in prison, saying that he could only abdicate with their permission. Two

[1] Da Silva Cosme 1990: 2–3.
[2] Coutinho 1972: 70, states that these decrees show that King João was recognized by all as the true sovereign of Sri Lanka. In a specific sense he was Bhuvanekabāhu's liege, but we shall argue that the latter's sovereignty remained intact.
[3] Saldanha 1997: 620–2.

years later we find Albuquerque threatening that if the raja did not toe the line there was always his disinherited uncle waiting in the wings, eager to do business with the Portuguese.[4]

Bhuvanekabāhu would have been only too aware of the way in which the Portuguese tended to insert themselves into the cracks that opened up at moments of succession. He did not expect his will to hold sway over either the Portuguese or the ambitions of Māyādunnē after his death.[5] It is for the same reason that he wanted a decree confirming the hereditary office of his chamberlain, promoting his status as an effective go-between with the Portuguese and ensuring that Dharmapāla would not be sidelined during his minority. These requests may reflect the fact of vassalage, but they do not suggest a particularly craven dependence on it.

Again, though, the dismal picture presented in his letters throughout the 1540s appears to draw us towards that conclusion. Above all, they contrive to emphasize his vulnerability in the face of the overweening Portuguese or the ever-present threat emanating from Sītāvaka. In 1543, he wrote to Prince Luís, 'I live always in fear and I do not know to whom to turn.'[6] One specific aspect of this vulnerability is the way in which the Portuguese were arrogating his very sovereignty: 'In this he [the factor] deprives me of my power and authority [*poder e senhorio*],' wrote Bhuvanekabāhu.[7] A couple of years later he claimed that 'it is I who have least power in this land and the reason for this is my loyalty to your highness.'[8] This seems like first-hand evidence for the king's declining authority, and it cannot be easily dismissed. But close attention to Bhuvanekabāhu's language suggests that the state of his 'sovereignty' is used as a general index of his unhappiness. After an enquiry vindicated his charges against the factor, Bhuvanekabāhu wrote, 'now I can say with reason that I am the real king.'[9] In reality his sovereignty was not won or lost so easily, but, when writing direct to his fellow monarch, King João, it was an effective rhetorical device.[10]

A key function of these letters was to retain Portuguese goodwill at a time when it could not be taken for granted. It seems that Bhuvanekabāhu was adopting a position of supplication that emphasized his weakness in contrast to the strength of his liege, a verbal formulation of physical prostration. We see the motif of 'suffering for the love of Your Highness' in an early letter by the Raja of Cochin, and Bhuvanekabāhu and his advisers were also employing it.[11] We should recall that the relationship of vassalage/protection was founded on military dependence

[4] SR, I: 228–31.

[5] Compare with the thoughts of the governor Estevão da Gama (1540–2) in VP: 12.

[6] VP: 48.

[7] VP: 184. As C. R. de Silva 1995: 73, relates, Bhuvanekabāhu is here referring to the decree that stipulated that ships could only be built in Sri Lanka with the permission of the governor and the King of Kōṭṭe. Initially intended to stop Portuguese from bypassing his authority, by 1546, it was being interpreted to mean that Bhuvanekabāhu could not order any ship to be built without the Portuguese governor's permission.

[8] VP: 250. See also comments from Cochin: 241–2.

[9] VP: 250.

[10] Bhuvanekabāhu's emphasis on his own vulnerability is always more marked in his letters to Lisbon than in his letters to Goa.

[11] SR, I: 75.

and inferiority. By highlighting the threats ranged against their sovereignty these kings were in fact making a plea to their lord to honour his oath of protection.

We should further note the dissonance that is sometimes revealed between these images of helplessness and his other ambitions. In the same letter of 1543 in which Bhuvanekabāhu announced his friendless confusion he also asked for Portuguese assistance to return the long-seceded kingdoms of Kandy and Jaffna to his rule – and these ambitious plans were duly approved.[12] This sense of dissonance becomes unavoidable when we turn to consider some statements from the missionaries and *moradores* in Colombo. In late 1547, just as Bhuvanekabāhu's protestations were reaching their height, they wrote to the governor that 'this king, who calls himself a friend of the Portuguese, is the greatest enemy that we have here. So long as we do not defend ourselves against him, he worries us with impunity.'[13] How does Bhuvanekabāhu get away with this? 'The king always strives to satisfy the captains of the cinnamon ship which comes here and some other powerful people, so that he may be able to do to us all the evil deeds and injuries that he wants, without your Lordship and the other governors being informed of the truth.' It is they who were suffering in their distance from the centre of the *Estado*, a small isolated community tyrannized by a heathen king. Those who tell the governor different are 'dependent' on the king, men such as Duarte Teixeira. João de Vila do Conde spoke for many when he pronounced Bhuvanekabāhu to be no less than a servant of the devil drawing unsuspecting Portuguese into a satanic allegiance.[14]

If we can believe these claims, throughout the 1540s Bhuvanekabāhu continued to exploit the frailties of the *Estado* with dastardly skill, leeching the loyalties of weak Portuguese, his protestations of vulnerability no more than propaganda. This presents us with a historiographical dilemma, one that could potentially overturn the emphasis of the last chapter on Portuguese exploitation. This dilemma is a result of the polarization of Colombo-Kōṭṭe, intensified by the arrival of the friars, into pro- and anti-Bhuvanekabāhu groups, so that we now find it difficult to see beneath their contradictory agendas. If we have portrayed the visit by the captain of the cinnamon ship as a rare chance for the *Estado* to audit what was happening in Sri Lanka, should we now view it as simply a means by which the king could disseminate a false version of events to Goa?

With such doubts in mind, should we then re-interpret Bhuvanekabāhu's requests for someone to be stationed in Kōṭṭe who could supervise (or advertise) the conduct of the Portuguese? For a closer reading reveals that he envisaged these men as operating under his direct command. The guard of fifty men requested in 1541, 'will not be obliged to do what your factor commands them, but only what I command them in what regards the service of your highness'.[15] In 1546, Bhuvanekabāhu requested an official who could reside in the island to make sure that the decrees were being observed; he would be approved by Bhuvanekabāhu and 'serve God

[12] VP: 48, 142, 144. [13] SV: 494–5 (VP: 238–40). [14] VP: 118.

[15] VP: 20. According to one copy of the 1541 memorial Bhuvanekabāhu was still requesting that there be no factor at all on the island: SV: 106. This is apparently confirmed by Correia: 323, who must, however, be wrong in stating that King João granted him a decree to this effect.

and the King my Lord and my authority' – implicitly not the factor or viceroy.[16] Were these requests an attempt to force local politics to abide by high diplomacy, to establish the kind of auditory institution that the *Estado* lacked, or were they simply intended as instruments of his will?

The distinction between bribery and patronage was, of course, a highly subjective one.[17] It is equally clear that what looked like bribery from the settlers' viewpoint could seem like extortion from Bhuvanekabāhu's, who wrote that it was only when he showered the Portuguese officials with gifts and rewards that they conducted themselves properly.[18] As for the charges of the settlers, on examination their most specific resentment concerned local tax, expressing a great sense of grievance that they should not be exempt from indigenous commercial regulations 'as is done in other parts and ports'.[19]

However, the strongest argument that Bhuvanekabāhu was the main victim in this war of representations derives from the evidence that the Portuguese were trying to silence the king by threatening his scribe and interpreter.[20] It transpires that in 1548 there were even attempts to control the 'nephew of the king' sent on an embassy to Goa: he was forbidden to speak without an agent of the factor present.[21] In that year Bhuvanekabāhu requested that a judge be sent to Ceylon who was 'above suspicion' to enquire into his complaints.[22] Bhuvanekabāhu undoubtedly wanted officials under his pay and command for his own reasons of *realpolitik*, but if he was being systematically disingenuous it is difficult to see why he would consistently invite more Portuguese to penetrate his affairs. It seems that the Portuguese had more to lose from independent scrutiny than Bhuvanekabāhu did. Yet the weighing up of mendacity and fidelity will only take us so far: the contradictory nature of our sources derives also from a genuine conflict of worldviews.

Bhuvanekabāhu's understanding of vassalage and overlordship

Whatever the disjunctures between Sinhalese and Portuguese political worldviews, there was at least one aspect in which they seemed to shade into one another.[23] To recall the indigenous ideas about vassalage within Sri Lanka that we broached in Chapter One, Bhuvanekabāhu was himself a liege, his title proclaiming him 'world ruler', king of kings. We have seen that his position was conceived in terms of 'tributary overlordship', maintained by ritual acts of obeisance and tribute-payments.[24] It is important to recognize that in their external affairs the Portuguese monarchs could draw on a roughly equivalent conception of overlordship, if it

[16] SV: 400 (VP: 183).

[17] Accusations of bribery were a common way of defaming one's opponents, see, for example, SV: 440–1. In 1546 there were rumours that Bhuvanekabāhu had bribed the factor António Ferreira not to give assistance to the Kandy expedition, but a reliable source, the *casado* Miguel Fernandes, contradicts this, see VP: 155, 160–1, 176.

[18] VP: 260–2, supported by the Kōṭṭe ambassador: 27.

[19] VP: 239.

[20] See above, p. 000.

[21] VP: 241–2.

[22] VP: 251; SV: 523.

[23] Pearson 1992: 147, suggests that Europe and India shared a basic tributary mode of production.

[24] The phrase is from Roberts 2004: 60–3.

was but one option among many forms of domination. The Lisbon embassy of 1542 was such a glorious success partly because both sides understood it to be hugely important in terms of their own coding of the liege–vassal relationship. Bhuvanekabāhu would have understood that tribute and *ad hoc* services were required. The equation between authority, the right to levy funds and the obligation to protect one's vassals did not need spelling out.

What may have run counter to Sinhalese expectations was the way in which Portuguese vassalage had become the vehicle for a more intrusive form of imperialism. In Sri Lanka, as in Malabar, indigenous overlordship did not necessarily entail much practical control or economic exploitation.[25] Kōṭṭe had no mechanism of expansion analogous to the Portuguese version because the peripheral territories were already conceptually incorporated under the *cakravarti* ideal.[26] Bhuvanekabāhu's hegemony resists categorization as 'imperialism' because the vassal territories were not differentiated enough from the centre symbolically, and were not impinged upon enough politically.[27]

When we turn from this system of *internal* vassalage to previous relations of *external* vassalage, we only encounter rather distant and unobtrusive forms of overlordship extending little beyond the payment of tribute. In truth, the latter exceeded even its Portuguese equivalent in diplomatic ambiguity. It could denote simply friendship or an entirely ritualized marker of trust used to facilitate trade.[28] It could equally represent a formal recognition of maritime hegemony, a short-term need to 'buy off' a threatening force, or indeed to draw it in to shore up internal authority. The meaning of the vassalage sworn by fifteenth-century Sinhalese kings to the emperors of China during the days when the admiral Cheng Ho sailed his great junks through the Indian Ocean (1405–34), probably shifted between all of these.[29] The 1542 embassy to Portugal thus had clear antecedents in the regular missions sent to present tribute at the court of the Ming emperor.

The possibility that the Gampola and Kōṭṭe kings had also accepted a form of subordination to the Hindu empire of Vijayanagar is less often noted.[30] Moreover, by the time the Portuguese arrived, the Kōṭṭe kings were also paying tribute to Kollam, apparently as a means of securing a ready supply of mercenaries.[31] None of these relationships, nor the distant association that Dharma Parākramabāhu IX (1489–1513) had with the Portuguese, entailed any great practical compromises of sovereignty. Indeed, rites of submission to external authorities could

[25] See above, Chapter One, and on Malabar, see Bayly 1989: 248.

[26] That is, they were conceptually incorporated according to the perspective of the Kōṭṭe court. For the King of Kandy, Bhuvanekabāhu, was only 'formerly emperor' (VP: 200).

[27] See Doyle 1986 for the distinction between hegemony (control over foreign policy) and imperialism (control over internal policy).

[28] Across South East Asia tribute was a gesture with few implications for internal sovereignty: Reid 1988–93, II: 234.

[29] See Werake 1987.

[30] Walters 1991–2. However, Vijayanagar's influence in the island was brought to an end in the mid fifteenth century: Pillay 1963: 110–12, and Pathmanathan 1982: 43.

[31] As Tomé Pires 1978 mentions; Biedermann 2005a: 101–2.

be understood as means of servicing and strengthening internal authority.[32] This is why Bhuvanekabāhu never stopped representing himself as a *cakravarti*; his decrees maintained the full quotient of imperial titles without reference to any higher authority.[33] This self-image appears to be confirmed by the artistic evidence of the ivory-carved casket associated with the 1542 embassy.[34] The front of the casket displays two fascinating scenes depicting the events in Lisbon. In the left panel we see Dharmapāla paying homage to King João III, and in the right panel we see the coronation of Dharmapāla (Plate 2). In each case, standing behind Dharmapāla is a Sinhalese figure, representing either the Sinhalese ambassador or Bhuvanekabāhu himself. These figures are exactly the same size and equally resplendent as the King of Portugal.[35] The iconography of this casket as a whole is arguably dominated by Bhuvanekabāhu.[36]

Most importantly, the carvings bring out the continuity of the Sinhalese dynastic authority that will be conferred on Dharmapāla. What is striking, indeed unique, about this representation, is that it depicts a distinctively Buddhist conical crown being lowered onto his head; all other Asian princes whom we know were crowned in this way knelt to receive a gold crown fashioned in Portugal.[37] Contrary to the accounts of the Portuguese chroniclers who tell us that the golden effigy of Dharmapāla was crowned 'in the fashion of Portugal' ('ao modo do Reino'), the prince is here dressed in the costume of a *dēva* and bears a lotus flower in one hand to indicate his descent from the solar dynasty.[38] Dharmapāla would be no Raja of Cochin, bending his head to receive a foreign crown. The iconography appears to assert that one could be emperor and vassal at the same time, that association with the Portuguese did not undermine the dignity of the Kōṭṭe dynasty but somehow upheld it.

All this helps to explain an otherwise odd feature of Bhuvanekabāhu's letters, which seem to assume that the factor and his men have an obligation to serve and obey him. He complained, for example, about the factor Gaspar de Azevedo,

32 Walters 2000: 145, suggests this was a new kind of monarchical identity formulated under the shadow of Vijayanagar.

33 *EZ*, III: 247; Bell 1904: 91; Pieris 1910–12.

34 Previously the casket was identified as the 'rich coffer' that our literary sources tell us was sent to Lisbon. Jaffer and Schwabe 1999: 7, and Saldanha 1997: 595, argue that it was made in commemoration of the embassy. But if, P. H. De Silva 1975: 71, is correct to identify the figures in Plate 3 as Padmā and her sons, we can at least say that the casket was constructed before the murder of one of those sons, Prince Jugo, in late 1544. After that date, it is unlikely Padmā, the mother of one murdered usurper and another living rival in Goa, and someone with pro-Christian sympathies herself, would be celebrated in such style. See VP: 76, on the deteriorating relationship between Bhuvanekabāhu and this secondary queen.

35 *Rājāvaliya*: 73; Couto: 118–19; Queyroz: 234–5. Trindade, III: 38–9, adds that a larger effigy of Bhuvanekabāhu was also sent.

36 Jaffer and Schwabe 1999: 7.

37 Saldanha 1997: 588. Couto: 440, says that Dharmapāla was crowned with a gold crown sent from Kōṭṭe.

38 Diogo Do Couto (*Década Quinta*) 1936: 440; *Conquista*: 185 – but, puzzlingly, as Saldanha 1997: 594, points out, coronation was not a feature of the formal investiture of the Portuguese kings. P. H. De Silva 1975: 81.

Plate 2: Front of c. *1543 casket.*
The left-hand panel represents the act of homage by which Dharmapāla affirms his vassalage. The right-hand panel represents a coronation of Dharmapāla. Notice the conical crown.

Plate 3: Front of c. *1543 casket.*
The lower panels represent dancing scenes. The central woman is perhaps a queen of Bhuvanekabāhu's. In the left-hand panel of the lid, Jaffer and Schwabe 1999 see a representation of Śiva mounted on the sacred bull.

Plate 4: Right end of c. *1543 casket.*
This may well be Bhuvanekabāhu riding an elephant.

that 'he was unwilling to do anything that I would order him'.[39] This was partly because the post of chief guard meant that the factor or another Portuguese official did have a clear obligation to 'serve' the King of Kōṭṭe in a very intimate sense.[40] In a more general sense, Bhuvanekabāhu may have been drawing on experiences

[39] VP: 261 (see also 250). We have seen how the occupation of land might draw Portuguese back into the theoretical sovereignty of the King of Kōṭṭe. Yet this seems to be different: a general presumption of obedience as opposed to an expectation of *rājakāriya*.

[40] Hence Bhuvankebāhu refers to him as 'my guard and factor', SV: 400.

of the earlier state of alliance under Vijayabāhu VI and the observed relations with the Malabar kings who had signed treaties of *amizade*.[41] Some of these agreements did oblige Portuguese officers to render active service.[42]

We also need to consider how Bhuvanekabāhu would have experienced the reality of vassalage throughout the 1520s and 1530s. Even when the Portuguese presence was established in the aggressive guise of the fortress, Bhuvanekabāhu did not take the obligations of his fealty seriously, and simply reneged on his tribute. Many Portuguese at the time thought that only a military solution, gaining control of the Sea of Ceylon in order to blockade the transportation of rice from the Coromandel to Kōṭṭe, would make Bhuvanekabāhu produce the required amount and quality of cinnamon.[43] When the decision came to dismantle the fortress, this would have had a great impact on Bhuvanekabāhu's interpretation of his status. For most of Bhuvanekabāhu's reign there was no visible symbol of his subjection. In contrast to other 'friends' of His Highness, the King of Kōṭṭe suffered only a *feitoria* and its small staff.[44]

This did not mean that he immediately became a dutiful payer of tribute. In 1525 a Muslim merchant had managed to obtain a sea pass (*cartaz*), sail to Kōṭṭe and buy up the good cinnamon, leaving little left for the payment of tribute (*páreas*).[45] It was probably a result of this that King João III issued a strident decree reinforcing his monopolistic claims to the cinnamon trade and ordering his governor to extract the full amount of tribute from Bhuvanekabāhu.[46] This fits entirely with the tenor of that remarkable letter of Nuno Álvares from 1527, which indicates that Bhuvanekabāhu had been pressing for the removal of official presence altogether and for only seven or eight Portuguese to remain – and these under Bhuvanekabāhu's command.[47] Indeed, the prevailing model of Portuguese–Sinhalese relations was as much indigenous as imposed with Bhuvanekabāhu's attempt to draw the newcomers into his own multi-ethnic patronage.

Then, as we have seen, the King of Kōṭṭe was thrown into a real dependence on the forces of the Portuguese. In turn, a greatly indebted Bhuvanekabāhu became a more dependable supplier of cinnamon, expelling the Muslim traders and ceding ever more privileges to his allies. The 1533 cinnamon contract capped this developing economic union: the tribute was to be raised and a low fixed price of excess cinnamon was established, but Bhuvanekabāhu was assured that the Portuguese would purchase all the cinnamon he offered.[48] It now appeared appropriate to sacrifice commercial independence in order to retain his grip on power. The relationship of 'protection' suited both parties: the military superiority of

[41] Correia: 194, tells us that the Portuguese captain told Vijayabāhu that 'the captain and men who might be in the fortress would serve him on land in all that he should command like his native servants, as did the captains of the other fortresses which existed on the coast of India.'

[42] The treaty with the ruler of Kollam, 1520: Biker, III: 39. Correia's narrative is clear on the assumption that the Raja of Cochin should be 'served' by Portuguese officers, see e.g. Correia, *Lendas*, IV: 389.

[43] Flores 1995: 60.

[44] See Thomaz 1985: 530, for Portuguese recognition that the symbolic import of a fortress could be difficult to reconcile with relations of friendship and alliance.

[45] Flores, Doc: 345. [46] Flores, Doc: 338. [47] CS: 315. [48] C. R. de Silva 1991b.

the Portuguese obliged them to exert considerable effort in the defence of their protégé, who in turn was obliged to render commercial advantages and compensation. This macro-diplomacy seems to have been matched by the micro-politics of the Kōṭṭe court. As we demonstrated in Chapter One, in these early years the Portuguese presence was small, generally well-behaved and dominated by those seeking the patronage or at least friendliness of the King of Kōṭṭe.[49]

There was thus a strong vortex of indigenous forces sucking in outsiders: as soldiers servicing a comparatively un-militiarized society; as agents in the ceaseless struggles of galactic polities and their routine succession disputes; as means of protecting kingship against a predatory aristocracy (recall the royal bodyguard); as commercial specialists to enhance royal revenues in the absence of a dynamic indigenous entrepreneurial class. But precedent allowed Bhuvanekabāhu to assume that such outsiders would be somehow duty-bound to protect his kingship and magnify his power. In the 1540s these values would come to seem tragically anachronistic.

Diplomatic manoeuvres

The state of alliance naturally entails compromises in the exercise of foreign policy. Treaties of *amizade* regularly included a clause to the effect that the two parties must now share friends and enemies.[50] Nevertheless, the ability to act within the international sphere, to pursue an 'external' policy, is often taken to be a crucial indicator of political independence.[51] Can we say then that the rajas of Cochin were pursuing a foreign policy proper, whereas Bhuvanekabāhu was merely concerned with internal affairs, fighting rearguard actions against secessionists? In fact, the complex political boundaries of South Asian states render the distinction between an expansionist 'foreign policy' and a defensive 'internal policy' somewhat problematic.[52] To be sure, the Raja of Cochin was motivated by a desire to become the 'chief king of India' and to revenge himself against Calicut.[53] But he also represented himself as defending or reinstating ancient tutelary and territorial rights of his own. Moreover, both the raja and Bhuvanekabāhu saw their association with the Portuguese not just as an opportunity to protect their sovereignty but to expand it.[54] Alliance and vassalage constituted tools of foreign policy as well as limitations of it; indeed some have presented them as central features of pre-colonial South Asian statecraft. Bhuvanekabāhu's approach to such matters is encapsulated by this definition of the principle of *upajāpa* described in the *Arthaśāstra*, 'comprising conciliation, gift-giving, sowing dissension among and 'winning over' of an enemy's local supporters, and involving the use of force only secondarily'.[55]

A full examination of Bhuvanekabāhu's 'diplomatic manoeuvres' would involve re-telling the narrative of the 1540s, a complex weave of events that is accessible

[49] This is echoed by Flores 1994: 140. [50] E.g. the treaty of 1516 with Kollam, Biker, III: 35.
[51] Saldanha 1997: 378. [52] Nissan and Stirrat 1990: 25. [53] Biker, III: 10–14.
[54] VP: 47–8, 142; Saldanha 1997: 624. [55] Price 1996: 18, quoting André Wink.

in other works.[56] Instead, we need only draw out some pertinent conclusions. First, Bhuvanekabāhu sometimes deployed anti-Portuguese propaganda in order to obstruct other princes forming alliances with the Portuguese. In 1544 the developing relations with Kandy threatened all the major players: while Māyādunnē and Caṇkili of Jaffna (1519–61) threatened death to anyone facilitating this communication, Bhuvanekabāhu wrote directly to Kandy dwelling on how much he had suffered from the alliance and what untrustworthy thieves the Portuguese were.[57] Again in 1546 he helped scupper André de Sousa's expedition by writing a similar letter on the evils of conversion.[58]

Second, Bhuvanekabāhu tried hard to retain his official status as an ally and vassal of Portugal, which meant that he had to keep certain Portuguese parties happy through exploiting the deficiencies in the chains of communication and mutual interest that were maintained between them.[59] His awareness of the advantage that could be gained from bypassing the hierarchies of the *Estado da Índia* and cultivating a relationship with Lisbon was perhaps unusual.[60] It was also, of course, important to preserve his standing with the governor or viceroy, with João de Castro being a favoured target for his letters. Within Sri Lanka itself, the missionaries, most likely to be alienated by his religious policy and possessing their own channels of communication reaching up to the highest circles, could find themselves subject to the occasional charm offensive. While Bhuvanekabāhu was penning his warning letters to Kandy in 1546, we hear from Vila do Conde that the king had managed to conceal his anger from the court and was suddenly enraptured by what the friar had to say, being uncommonly yielding.[61]

Thirdly, when the Portuguese alliance seemed doomed, Bhuvanekabāhu quickly sought alternatives. In late 1545, with the princes in Goa expected to arrive with armed might at any minute, Bhuvanekabāhu's personal relations with the Portuguese took a sharp turn for the worse.[62] Duarte Teixeira was struck by the sudden coldness that had come over him and his noblemen: there were daily disagreements with the factor, the Portuguese had been banished from the royal guard, converts were being refused entry to the palace, the settlers were afraid of a physical attack.[63] This is when Bhuvanekabāhu wrote his least supplicatory letter, to the Governor João de Castro. It contained an implicit threat regarding the princes in Goa: 'if they were to come, it would be impossible to serve the King of Portugal as I desire. As long as they do not come here, you can do as you like.'[64] Bhuvanekabāhu was least inclined to play the part of the subservient vassal when he thought that the Portuguese were not playing the role of faithful liege. This

[56] A more detailed sense of these events can be garnered from pp. 104–10.

[57] VP: 84–5. [58] VP: 206, and 164. [59] See also C. R. de Silva 1998: 112.

[60] As Flores 1998: 189, notes, very few major Asian kings managed to orchestrate the dispatch of an actual embassy to Lisbon.

[61] One observer remarked, 'he tells the Portuguese [at Kōṭṭe] that he is resigned to it all, and hence they report this in their letters,' SV: 368 (VP: 164).

[62] VP: 75.

[63] VP: 70, 86–7, 117–19. According to João de Vila do Conde, Bhuvanekabāhu had written an equally 'bold' letter to the King of Portugal himself.

[64] VP: 97.

rare hauteur owed much to the new diplomatic understanding that had grown to fill the vacuum, the alliance with Māyādunnē. As we shall see below in Chapter Five, this was a serious league directed at a war with Kandy that was still ongoing in early 1546. Later the friar António Padrão would reflect that the two brothers 'were gradually forcing us out of the land'.[65]

The fourth point is that Bhuvanekabāhu's religious and diplomatic policy in the late 1540s, principally his efforts (some real, some merely alleged) to frustrate the various Portuguese missions to Kandy, meant that he often lost the sympathies of Portuguese opinion-formers and decision-makers.[66] He responded to this predicament energetically. After being blamed for the failure of the Barreto mission in 1547, Bhuvanekabāhu first attempted to patch up the diplomatic façade, by offering to pay the war expenses and sending his nephew as ambassador to Goa. Secondly, he made preparations to wage war on Māyādunnē.[67] This was probably a defensive measure rather than an expansionist one, but it stands as an example of Bhuvanekabāhu taking the military initiative without securing Portuguese assistance.[68] To no avail. In 1548, Māyādunnē was acknowledged as an official vassal, receiving the banner of King João III. This meant that, in theory, the sovereignty of Māyādunnē was equally worthy of Portuguese protection as Bhuvanekabāhu's. The Crown of Portugal was now placed in the position of arbiter, obliged to maintain peace and justice between its vassals.[69] Perhaps only the death of João de Castro halted vigorous intervention against Bhuvanekabāhu, while his successors showed themselves liable to favour either one of the two brothers.

The tone of this later phase of Kōṭ̤ṭe diplomacy may be reflected in a second ornamental casket. If Jaffer and Schwabe are correct, the central image on the front (Plate 5) depicts a Kōṭ̤ṭe ambassador engaged in diplomatic intercourse with João de Castro.[70] A sense of equivalence between the two powers is invoked. While the

65 VP: 200, 234, and see 175.

66 The events of these later years are confused, hence Queyroz: 272–9, goes to the unusual length of reproducing two accounts, one from Francisco Negrão and the other from Bento da Silva (both lost works).

67 VP: 240.

68 Although he did ask the captain of the cinnamon ship to stay in anticipation of Māyādunnē's attack. VP: 251.

69 King João III gave explicit instructions to this effect to Afonso de Noronha, VP: 291. The Sītāvakan kings were very quick to pick up on the obligations they were owed as vassals: see the requests made by the young prince Rājasiṃha in VP: 268.

70 Jaffer and Schwabe 1999: 7–8, argue that it has scenes loosely related to a series of tapestries made between 1555 and 1560 which portray events from Castro's victorious relief of the siege of Diu in 1546. We only know of one diplomatic mission from Castro's tenure, that carried out by a nephew of Bhuvanekabāhu after the battle of Diu in late 1547/early 1548 when relations with the Portuguese were at their lowest ebb (VP: 241–2). Could this 'nephew' even be Vīdiyē Baṇḍāra, the commander of the Kōṭ̤ṭe military forces? Jaffer and Schwabe suggest that the Sinhalese figure is not the ambassador Srī Rāmarakṣa Paṇḍita as is normally claimed, but the ambassador 'Sri Proytila Rala' who met De Castro in early 1547. But these are the same man (see VP: 15, n. 3) and there is no record of such a meeting in our sources. Bhuvanekabāhu is also shown, on a panel on the back, receiving homage from his ambassador depicted on the front. However, Gschwend 1996: 105–7 argues that the casket was commissioned by the Lisbon court directly after the 1542 embassy in order to celebrate it, and that the two principal figures are Bhuvanekabāhu and João III.

Plate 5: Front of c. *1547 casket, Residenz, Munich, Schatzkammer.*
Jaffer and Schwabe 1999 suggest a date of 1547, and that the central figures at the table represent a Sinhalese ambassador and the Portuguese viceroy, João de Castro. Annemarie Jordan Gschwend considers this casket was made around the same time as the c. *1542 casket and is another representation of the embassy to Lisbon.*

carvers have drawn freely on European motifs and models, the two end panels are entirely within the traditions of Sinhalese kingship, portraying the same scenes as their equivalents on the *c*. 1543 casket, but with a distinctly martial emphasis. Now the elephant that Bhuvanekabāhu rides is plated with armour and he sits in his throne room eschewing the gestures of Buddhist piety for a sword grasped in his right hand (Plates 6 and 7). If this does date to Castro's tenure, Bhuvanekabāhu was preparing for war with Sītāvaka at this time: the friendship between Kōṭṭe and the Portuguese is emphasized, but a more aggressive note is sounded too.

Bhuvanekabāhu's policy was never motivated by the desire to rid himself of the Portuguese. It was only when he felt that the alliance was already endangered by the successive threats to the status quo issuing from the princes in Goa, the King of Kandy and then Māyādunnē, that he decided to take risks with it. Nevertheless, he played the diplomatic game that became so compelling during this decade with a freer hand than one might expect. In doing so he sometimes lost the backing of the *Estado da Índia* altogether. While Bhuvanekabāhu's letters became more pathetic towards the end of his reign, his diplomatic policy expressed a more vigorous independence. In 1550, Jorge de Castro's disastrous defeat in Kandy, in which, according to Couto, 400 Portuguese died, had engendered a new self-confidence among all Sinhalese parties.[71] When Noronha arrived in that year he found a Kōṭṭe rather different, both more antagonistic and more volatile than that of the previous decade.[72] The most impressive measure of Bhuvanekabāhu's increasing awkwardness to the Portuguese may well lie in his death. It seems most likely that the shot which killed him at Kälaṇiya in 1551 was fired by a Portuguese assassin. He had been shot while approaching a window onto a veranda where Portuguese soldiers were eating. Queirós tells us of a report that a slave, António de Barcelos, had been left behind by the viceroy and had perpetrated the murder on his master's orders.[73] Among the burghers of Goa, Noronha's guilt was taken as fact.[74]

Popular opposition

What impact did the encroachments of the Portuguese have on Bhuvanekabāhu's relationship with his own subjects? If the monarch's duty to maintain social and political order was seen as a responsibility of cosmic proportions, might not his legitimacy be damaged by a failure to curtail these disruptive and anarchic newcomers? This book has stressed the tolerance of or appetite for external cultural influences and external military support, particularly from South India, in the later Kōṭṭe period. Contrary to the implications of some recent scholarly opinion, this may in fact have little bearing on ethnic differentiation: it need not tell us much about the 'existence' or otherwise of Sinhalaness. However, it does suggest that such identities were not yet readily inflated into an instinctive generic xenophobia. And we have seen that the Portuguese were very far from being instantly

[71] Couto: 136–46, Noronha estimates only 200: see VP: 265–6, 277. [72] VP: 290.
[73] Queyroz: 293–4; Couto: 146–7. [74] SV: 618; C. R. de Silva 1995: 82–3.

Plate 6: Right end of c. *1547 casket.*
Bhuvanekabāhu on his throne again, but holding a sword: compare with Plate 1.

Plate 7: Left end of c. *1547 casket.*
Again the rider is probably Bhuvanekabāhu, but note that in contrast with Plate 4, the elephant is armoured.

repudiated or mistrusted. The fascinating record of 'first encounter' – the 1506 meeting – which made its way into the *Alakeśvarayuddhaya* and thence the *Rājāvaliya* reveals some awe and possibly disquiet.[75] But the subsequent tone of this portion of the *Alakeśvarayuddhaya*, perhaps written in *c.* 1557 by a Kōṭṭe Christian, betrays no anti-Portuguese sentiment, treating the newcomers as a military power with whom it is simply pragmatic to come to terms.[76]

This should influence how we interpret evidence of internal opposition. Particularly interesting is the chronicle of Gaspar Correia, who was already rewriting the first draft of his *Lendas da Índia* when Bhuvanekabāhu died (it was completed in 1563).[77] During the attack of Ali Hassan in 1525, we are told that Bhuvanekabāhu hid amongst the Portuguese 'as he feared that the Moor might incite treachery against him among his people, and he was ever on guard against his own followers, and trusted only in the Portuguese'.[78] This is reinforced by a letter from Cochin in 1528, which describes the situation in Sri Lanka: 'This king is very devoted to Your Majesty, and places more confidence in us than in his own people, and only this year, in terror of his brother he placed himself, his treasure and his jewels under the protection of the factor.'[79]

But who were these people or followers of whom Bhuvanekabāhu was so afraid? At this point, it makes the most sense, following a historicist emphasis on class or a 'galactic political' evocation of perennial rebellion and contested succession, to imagine the movements of disgruntled noble factions.[80] The problem of a powerful and sometimes recalcitrant nobility was a perennial one for Sinhalese kings.[81] Bhuvanekabāhu himself came to power as the result of a coup, and it seems clear that the murderous scenes in the palace in 1521 had their origins in court factionalism rather than popular revolt.[82] Nor is it then surprising that Bhuvanekabāhu had to contend with a rebellion in the Hāpiṭigam Kōraḷē led by the party in Vijayabāhu's court who had backed the failed succession plans. The leaders included a nephew of the murdered king, Vīrasūriya, and the king's equerry and possibly someone referred to as the Prince of Chilaw (*chilão*).[83] It is also clear that the Muslim merchants had some strong connections among the Sinhalese nobility given that they were able to instigate actions against the Portuguese regardless of the king's wishes.[84] The decision to expel the Muslims was controversial, and a hawkish

[75] *Alakeśvarayuddhaya*: 29/*Rājāvaliya*: 69. Michael Roberts in Roberts, Raheem and Colin-Thomé 1989: 2–5, argues that the terms of admiration contain a sub-text of mockery.

[76] See Strathern 2006a. [77] Schurhammer 1973–82, II: 608–10.

[78] Correia: 160 (Correia's chronology is off at this point). We are told he hides again for the same reasons in 1539, see Correia: 268.

[79] Flores, Doc: 349. [80] Gunawardana 1990: 67; Somaratna 1975: 142–8.

[81] Somaratna 1991. The King of Kandy faced opposition and revolt from his leading captains in the mid 1540s, see VP: 202.

[82] See Somaratna 1975: 182.

[83] *Rājāvaliya*: 72–3. Vīrasūriya or Pilässe Vīdiyē Baṇḍāra may be the same as the *ēkanāyaka* (chief minister) who orchestrated the failed succession plans along with a noble named Kaňdurē Baṇḍāra (Queyroz: 204). The Prince of Chilaw is mentioned as one of the nobles who threw themselves at the mercy of the Portuguese captain of the fortress in 1521 and presumably survived (CS: 329).

[84] Correia: 159–61, 189–99.

group of *mudaliyārs* threatened to go over to Sītāvaka. In other words, it was the expulsion of one unassimilated group as much as the welcoming of another one that precipitated discontent.

Succession was another prodigious generator of factional conflict. Besides Māyādunnē, there were various offspring of Bhuvanekabāhu who saw their hopes dashed by the decision to make Dharmapāla the heir-apparent in the late 1530s. The figurative carvings on the *c*. 1543 casket give us a sense of these struggles for status in the Kōṭṭe court. The whole rear panel of the casket is given over to a depiction of Padmā, the *yakaḍadoli* or junior queen of Bhuvanekabāhu (Plate 3).[85] She is attended by her two sons, Prince Jugo and the other later baptized as Luís. By contrast, the two figures of Samudrādēvi (Dharmapāla's mother) and the chief queen of Bhuvanekabāhu are relegated to a small section to the upper left of the front panel. In reality, the relative importance of these two parties was the reverse: the very mission celebrated by the casket would undermine the dynastic pretensions of the two princes. Perhaps court politics demanded a figurative restoration of status.[86] Merely figurative restorations, however, would not suffice and Bhuvanekabāhu cast around for a more substantial sop to their frustrated ambitions. In 1543 he wrote to the governor asking for assistance to retake Kandy and Jaffna.[87] Correia alone tells us why: he intended to give these lands to one of his sons (probably Jugo), who was dissatisfied with his current rule over a much lesser kingdom and threatened to quarrel with Dharmapāla's succession.[88] When this came to nothing Jugo planned to woo Portuguese support and was assassinated. Other disinherited offspring fled to Goa, followed by many supporters.

But can aristocratic factionalism account for the successes of Māyādunnē, who represented the largest threat to Bhuvanekabāhu's sovereignty? Queirós tells us that many nobles defected because of a family squabble precipitated by Vīdiyē Baṇḍāra, that this was even Māyādunnē's initial pretext for war.[89] By 1541, we know that he had managed to seize the greater part of Kōṭṭe, appropriating the revenues from the lands and ports for himself.[90] In 1545, we hear one Portuguese commentator making the striking claim that, 'Madune is more feared here than the rightful King of Ceilão, who, I assure your Lordship, has no more kingship than the name.'[91] Some five years later the Kōṭṭe ambassador reported that Māyādunnē had been

[85] P. H. De Silva 1975: 71, identifies her by her battle-axe (which I cannot discern), an indication of her *yakaḍadoli* status, and the three flowers in the picture that may denote her name.

[86] Jaffer and Schwabe 1999: 7, seem to imply that Padmā dominates these representations because she was Bhuvanekabāhu's favourite Queen. Padmā is also featured in an earlier casket identified by Jaffer and Schwabe: 4–5, as being pre-1542.

[87] VP: 47–8.

[88] Although the narrative of Correia: 322–3, is confused. Andrada (*Crónica*) 1976: 890, who seems to be relying on Correia for his account, confuses things still further by merging the events of 1543 and 1544.

[89] Queyroz: 223; a similar story is told about the late 1540s (254, 262). Here Queirós has probably received information about the same event from two different sources but failed to identify them as such.

[90] VP: 14, 15. [91] VP: 74.

secretly winning over Bhuvanekabāhu's captains to his designs and lording it over lands he had last dominated in the 1530s.[92]

A common interpretation has been that many Sinhalese were becoming disenchanted with Bhuvanekabāhu's alliance with the Portuguese and were thus drawn towards the banner of Māyādunnē. The Portuguese activities described in the last chapter would have caused disruption to anybody involved in trade in Colombo and the other western ports and to many innocents living in the immediate environs. In the 1541 memorial Bhuvanekabāhu makes the intriguing claim that this could result in insurrections in Jaffna and Sītāvaka and Kandy.[93] However, the only direct evidence that Māyādunnē profited from this dissatisfaction comes from Queirós, who tells us that he proclaimed himself emperor in 1539 and portrayed himself as a 'liberator' who 'was anxious to extinguish in Ceylon the name of Christ and the power of the Portuguese'.[94] But Queirós was perhaps subject here to what must have seemed a very minor anachronism in the 1680s – conflating the 1540s with the later 1550s.[95]

The most important point here is simply that Māyādunnē himself regularly wanted to cut a deal with the Portuguese in the 1540s. In 1543, he detained Nuno Álvares Pereira and caused him to write to the governor, 'regarding the friendship he was anxious to establish with the King of Portugal and the tribute he would pay. It seemed to him that the King of Portugal was already his friend.'[96] In 1547, Māyādunnē tried again, intriguing with António Moniz Barreto and writing to the governor that he had desired Portuguese vassalage for many years.[97] By March 1548 he had succeeded.[98] Therefore the battle lines are too blurred to discern any real 'ideological' motives at this stage. For example, the extraordinary claim about Māyādunnē's power made in 1545 refers to a period when Bhuvanekabāhu was actually in league with Māyādunnē and *repudiating* the Portuguese. It may be that Māyādunnē was sometimes able to harness some embryonic anti-Portuguese sentiment in the 1540s, but we cannot know if the various territories of Kōṭṭe submitted to his advance willingly, or were bribed, or were simply compelled to do so.

If Queirós' picture of widespread public grief at Bhuvanekabāhu's death is more than a literary conceit then he clearly retained a great deal of personal loyalty from many who would desert Kōṭṭe during the reign of his grandson.[99] It is in Dharmapāla that we see a king who really failed to command public support, and in the following decades that we see 'indigenist' sentiment arrive as a political force.

It is now acknowledged that the acquiescence of the rajas of Cochin in their subordination to the Portuguese did not make them mere quislings. Rather they were pursuing a successful strategy, transforming the fortunes of their state from a minor principality under the thumb of Calicut into one of the dominant economic centres of Kerala over the course of the sixteenth century and ensuring impressively

[92] VP: 273.
[93] VP: 19, and see 250. Kandy is only mentioned in one copy of the memorial: SV: 104.
[94] Queyroz: 262, and see 223, 280, 334–6. [95] See below, pp. 174–5. [96] VP: 82.
[97] VP: 230. [98] VP: 291. [99] Queyroz: 296; C. R. de Silva 1995: 83 concurs.

long reigns for the incumbents of the crown.[100] What is interesting is how the rajas manoeuvred within the terms of their relationship of 'protection' to promote their interests.[101] The trajectory taken by the kingdom of Kōṭṭe was not so blessed. Yet we know now that Bhuvanekabāhu was able to turn the Portuguese presence to his advantage, particularly in the early years, and he was not as emasculated as some Portuguese chroniclers and later historians have assumed. Bhuvanekabāhu's own letters are partly responsible for this unflattering posterity, but we have seen that they are far from transparent or naïve. They are yet more reliable guides to the deteriorating relations in Kōṭṭe than the protestations of the Portuguese.

100 Subrahmanyam 1987. 101 Tavim 1997: 59–62.

II

The spiritual

5
The mission

The troublesome Pious ones

One can consider the political upheaval that characterized the 1540s as the result of a single development: the advent of Christian mission, which scrambled the usual signals of diplomacy through its new and insistent focus on religious identity.[1] Indigenous rulers could now use the theological predilections of the newcomers to further their own political ambitions: Bhuvanekabāhu's rivals suddenly had the opportunity to lever apart his association with the Portuguese.

Events in Sri Lanka are consonant with a broader pattern, for across the Asian regions of Portuguese influence spiritual priorities were beginning to find a new purchase during the 1540s.[2] The religious affiliation of allies and vassals acquired a new significance, a little ideological shift quickly exploited by a number of Asian princes. Tabarija, the King of Maluku, had undergone baptism in 1537. In 1545 hope rose higher. Along with several Sri Lankan rulers whom we shall encounter in the following pages, the kings of the Indian principalities of Tanor and Chaul had also requested baptism in return for Portuguese backing. A strong gust of optimism swept through the clerical community: through these baptisms the ancient idolatry of India was about to give way to the Cross.[3] The 1540s dynamic acquired a particular intensity in Sri Lanka because of the Portuguese misunderstanding that Bhuvanekabāhu had instructed his ambassadors in Lisbon to convey his own desire to convert. Perhaps due only to a slip of the interpreter's tongue, the significance of his own religious affiliation was multiplied. Christian rhetoric should not merely be conceived as a sanctimonious gloss to diplomatic manoeuvres. There were no overwhelming temporal motivations for the *Estado* to become involved in the schemes of André de Sousa and the princes of Kōṭṭe, or of Nuno Álvares Pereira and the King of Kandy.

There was rather a newly invigorated sense of mission. Although this is normally associated with the arrival of the Jesuits and the Counter-Reformation, for

[1] Flores 1998: 195.

[2] The fine detail of the mid-sixteenth-century Sri Lankan mission, its reflections of wider missionary developments, and a study of the *piedosos*, has had to be hived off into another publication: see Strathern unpublished.

[3] SR, III: 241, and also see 257; in 1547, SV: 455–8.

a few years much of the impetus in South Asia came from a branch of reformed Franciscans known as *piedosos*.[4] They had their origin in the resurgence of mendicant spirituality in late fifteenth- and early sixteenth-century Iberia. There, a number of institutions had sprung up to allow Franciscans to go beyond the strictures of the mainstream Observants in their emphasis on poverty, asceticism and meditation. These discalced (barefoot) friars displayed a commitment to mission from the start. The Spanish branch of the *piedosos*, established as the Province of San Gabriel de Estremadura, had worked hard to preach the gospel to the *moriscos* of Granada, and in 1524 they were chosen to form the first mission to Mexico under Martín de Valencia. It may have been this glamorous role in the conquest of New Spain that aroused the interest of the Lisbon court in the sister branch in Portugal. From the early 1530s onwards a number of crucial ecclesiastical posts and missionary tasks in the East were allocated to the *piedosos*.

It was, of course, also this movement that furnished Sri Lanka with its first Christian mission. Before its arrival in 1543, priests and friars tending to the Portuguese flock had overseen a small 'organic' conversion movement, as some locals accepted baptism as a form of social lubrication with the Portuguese settlers. But the *piedosos* were intent on penetrating deep into heathen society. We have to be careful about vague estimates of conversion rates, as they were often made as part of a highly pointed rhetorical agenda.[5] Perhaps Gonzaga's figure of some 3,000 is not too far off the mark as an estimate of those who accepted baptism at some point, with a general pattern of initial success hampered by a worsening political climate.[6] We can certainly say that the Franciscans managed to extend the mission outside of the Colombo–Kōṭṭe locale: by 1552 they had established churches in five seaports along the south-west coast, each one with a friar to baptize and teach converts.[7] In other words, we have moved from a picture of a few dozen opportunistic converts huddled next to the Portuguese settlement to a genuine missionary drive into the trading and fishing communities of the coast.

Bhuvanekabāhu had personally invited these men into his kingdom on the occasion of the great embassy to Lisbon of 1542. But he had done so on the basis of his experience of the modest activities of the one or two Observant Franciscans in Kōṭṭe. These mendicant friars, their behaviour, appearance, and function in life, would have been strongly familiar to the Sinhalese. By virtue of their Axial Age heritage, they shared with the *bhikkhus* the common language of asceticism. As much later King Senarat of Kandy would remark in a letter to Philip III, '. . . for though we are Heathens, we well understand that virtue consists in the disregard of the things of this earth and of the riches of the world.'[8] On one level the *piedosos* would merely have reinforced that sense of familiarity. The use of fasting was a marker of otherworldliness common to both sets of virtuosi, as was the strictly

[4] On the origins of the Province of Piety see also Monforte 1751, Book 1.

[5] The claims in VP: 105, 110, 122, 246, cannot be taken at face value.

[6] Gonzaga 1603: 1208.

[7] Colombo, Galle, Negombo, Beruwela, Weligama, see VP: 311.

[8] Queyroz: 711; also in Trindade, III: 80–1. This may possibly reflect the perspective of the Portuguese friar who drafted the letter.

vegetarian diet, a strong symbol of spiritual cleanliness in South Asia and potentially a source of immediate respect.[9] Even their bare feet would have served to emphasize their closeness to the *bhikkhu* role. But it soon became apparent that these ultra-Franciscans were radically unusual as well as strikingly familiar. One aspect of their behaviour would have jarred almost immediately. Bhuvanekabāhu offered the new mission his munificence in the shape of a considerable sum of money to support them in Colombo. In an equally grand gesture, they rejected it.[10] They continued to reject it for five or six months until the king stopped asking. For the friars this was a perfect opportunity to display their commitment to the literal observance of the Rule of Saint Francis, to advertise their position in the debate over ascetic purity that had defined the fractious history of their order.

But Sinhalese traditions of monastic asceticism did not place quite the same emphasis on the corrupting nature of financial patronage.[11] For Bhuvanekabāhu the traditional means of ensuring religious harmony had been rudely dismissed. Sinhalese kings had bestowed their patronage on a variety of Buddhist and Hindu institutions. The new faith was not then immediately perceived as repugnant or threatening. Bhuvanekabāhu had merely extended his patronage to Christianity, furnishing lavish gifts on the church in Colombo.[12] In a multi-religious environment, the affiliation of religion and state can be maintained when what matters is outward form and ritual observance. The discalced friars now changed the frame of reference: patronage was not enough – indeed it was despised – what was needed was an exclusivist transformation of interiority. The transcendentalist fixation of the *piedosos* had a profound effect on the hardening of court politics between 1543 and 1545. 'He who is against my faith is against me,' wrote António Padrão, a telling phrase and one that leaves any diplomatic imperatives for dead.[13] According to the Governor João de Castro, they were largely responsible for Bhuvanekabāhu's ill-will, harassing him with 'such harsh ways as to cause astonishment'.[14] In 1545 direct control of the Sri Lanka mission passed over to the Observant Custodian António do Casal.[15] This may have been a deliberate decision to restore some stability to the Kōṭṭe scene, for there is a marked dissonance between the anti-Bhuvanekabāhu sentiments of the *piedosos* in Sri Lanka and the more temperate judgements of their Observant superior, who told his workers in Ceylon not to be 'unduly worried' by the failure of the king to convert.[16]

The particular spiritual traditions of the discalced friars formed a serious obstacle to rapprochement with Bhuvanekabāhu. Their propulsion of Portuguese diplomacy away to the courts of his rivals constituted a further massive affront. But there were other reasons why, after many years of comfortable co-habitation with Christianity, the king's religious policy began to take on a much darker aspect – a shift that had serious implications for his position as an ally of the Portuguese. As with so much else concerning Bhuvanekabāhu's reign, the first clues are to be found in the long

[9] The *capuchos* fasted on Wednesdays, Fridays and Saturdays, and spent $2\frac{1}{2}$ hours each day meditating: Schurhammer 1973–82, II: 155.
[10] See VP: 38–41, 96, 181–2. [11] Silber 1995: 113. [12] VP: 182, 193 [13] VP: 234.
[14] VP: 192–3. [15] Trindade, I: 101–6, n. 1; Schurhammer 1973–82, III: 599. [16] VP: 256.

list of requests carried by the king's ambassadors as they set out on their perilous journey to Europe early in 1542. While the ambassadors were under instructions to request the dispatch of a Franciscan mission, the document they carried indicates that the conversion process was already beginning to disrupt social and political arrangements. Once again, the underlying structures behind these perturbations were common to Kōṭṭe and the coastal states of Malabar. First we shall see how the latter responded to this challenge, and then we shall consider how the particularly Lankan caste and property systems inflected the process.

Loyalties, caste and conversion in Malabar

In 1566, the Rector of the Jesuit College of Cochin began his letter to his superior in Rome with the following observations:

> First of all, the main obstacle which prevents the rapid growth of Christianity in these parts is the pagan kings and rulers whose subjects become Christians. For those kings say that their subjects embrace the Christian religion not so much because they are really convinced that their old religion is false and the Catholic religion is true, but because they see that the Portuguese are powerful and are masters of the sea and free them from the tyrannies of their oppressions both present and future. At the same time, the kings see that as soon as their subjects become Christians, they feel more obliged to serve the captains in whose territory they are than their own kings whose subjects they are. And if their kings and rulers demand any tyrannical service [*tirania*] which they used to demand, the Christians immediately complain to the Fathers and to the captains, who side with them: and to this the kings take strong objection. Similarly in some regions the Christians do not pay the royal dues to the pagan kings, causing them much loss. Again those same kings and their officers of justice suffer another loss: when those people were pagans and committed an offence, their kings and judges imposed a fine which they now lose when their people become Christians, since after baptism they become subject either to the secular jurisdiction of the captains or to the ecclesiastical jurisdiction of the Fathers.[17]

These obstacles would remain, the rector argued, until the Portuguese followed the Muslim strategy of conquest in regions such as Gujarat and Sri Lanka. Alliance or even vassalage to the Portuguese clearly did not make indigenous rulers favourable to Christianity. But in the first Portuguese settlements new kinds of social and legal arrangements did spring up in an effort to contain some of the chaos unleashed by its arrival.

Cochin in particular can be seen as paradigmatic. As the first town to develop a sizeable convert community, the arrangements hammered out there necessarily exerted an influence over negotiations elsewhere in Asia. In *c.* 1509, the Raja of Cochin reported a crucial development: all Christians who committed a crime would be dealt with by the Portuguese captain, while he would administer justice

[17] M. Nunes Barreto to J. Miron, Cochin, 29 Jan. 1566, in *DI*, VI: 677; VP, II: 2–3.

to the 'moors and pagans'.[18] This reflected an ancient European legal principle of 'personality of law', by which the relevant jurisdiction was determined not by the political power to which an individual was subject but by his social or cultural status.[19] How damaging this could be was quickly brought home to the Raja of Cochin when his *arel* (harbourmaster) converted in 1510. Many of the seafaring groups who worked under him, his relatives and associates, followed him into the faith – up to 1,000 people.[20] Beyond conferring on him the full privileges of a *fidalgo*, the Portuguese captains also granted him full legal authority over all those who converted. The raja was distraught. Just as converts were being legally separated from pagan society, so there was an accompanying process of spatial separation. It is often pointed out that Christians flocked to the Portuguese settlement as destitutes repudiated by their own society.[21] However, for Afonso de Albuquerque in 1512 the main problem was rather the reverse: the number of unconverted kith and kin living *with* the baptized Indians.[22] Albuquerque saw them as a threat to the stability of the Portuguese settlement, which was regularly set on fire. At his request, the raja demarcated a portion of land that would be entirely reserved for the Portuguese and the local converts: *Cochim de Baixo* [Lower Cochin] was established as a Christian-only town.

The principle of extra-territoriality was now extended beyond the Portuguese themselves to those who converted to their faith. From then on the choice to baptize could not but entail the choice to switch from local to Portuguese jurisdiction. What needs emphasizing, however, is that this did not necessarily mean that converts had ceased to be subjects of their traditional rulers. Indeed, when Miguel Vaz pressed the case of persecuted Christians to the Raja of Cochin in 1542, his argument was precisely that people did not cease to be subjects of the raja when they converted, rather they were all the more deserving of his protection.[23] Or we could take the case of the Saint Thomas Christians who were placed under Portuguese jurisdiction by the treaty signed with the rulers of Kollam in 1516 and were even considered to be vassals of the Portuguese Crown, yet who remained obliged to pay local taxes.[24] To modern eyes, the political status of the converts, much like that of the Portuguese themselves, appears deeply ambiguous: as Christians they were subject to Portuguese law, but as residents or holders of land, they could be subject to the service and fiscal obligations owed to the native lord.

[18] SR, I. 74–5.

[19] Santos 1999: 308; Oliveira e Costa and Rodrigues 1992: 105–6. In 1518 (SR, I: 341), the Vicar of Cochin referred to the status of converts under ecclesiastical and then *Estado* jurisdiction.

[20] SR, I: documents 22, 40, 42, 75, 103, and particularly 43 (p. 116).

[21] Silva Rego 1949: 112.

[22] SR, I: 148–9. That is, the problem seems to have been not that native society had cast the converts out but that the converts had drawn in too much of native society behind them. Mundadan 1984: 365, interprets this as referring to the problem of converted prostitutes receiving unconverted clientele.

[23] SR, II. 329, and see the explicit remark of João III that converts remain the vassals of the Raja of Cochin: SR, III: 318.

[24] Biker: 35, reaffirmed in the peace treaty of 1541, and see 95. See also Anriques' letter of 1561 regarding putative arrangements in Jaffna in VP: 380.

Not that this distinction always held good in the eyes of contemporaries: as Barreto's letter makes plain, convert communities in some parts apparently assumed that they had no obligations at all to their territorial lord. Already in 1507, the Raja of Cannanore was complaining to the King of Portugal that when low-caste workers converted they no longer yielded revenue to their Nayar overlords.[25] Despite legal arrangements to the contrary, many Portuguese themselves were not averse to the idea that communities deserved a political leader of the same faith as themselves.[26] In particular, the conception of the Portuguese king as the 'protector' of Christians in the East meant that at the very least converts could always appeal to him against perceived injustices. Barreto's letter is particularly illuminating as to just how broadly those injustices could be conceived. The extract betrays an uneasy tension between an acknowledgement that converts were transgressing the rules of the land and the sense that this was yet akin to a process of liberation whereby the converts would be 'freed from oppressions past and future'.

The Paravas are an interesting, if atypical, case in this regard, given that they were only loosely bound by the local hegemonies of Sri Vira Ravivarma, the King of Travancore, and the Nāyaks of Madurai, vassals of Vijayanagar.[27] The 'tyrannies' to which they were subject came in the form of Nāyak and Māppiḷa attempts to wrest the control of the pearl fishery from them. Their mass conversion negotiated by a headman in 1532 was very obviously a political act, a bid for a stronger independence under Portuguese tutelage. The attacks from Muslim seamen only intensified as a result. Francis Xavier's decision to make them the targets of his first Asian mission worked to strengthen their image as a newly Christianized people who depended on Portuguese support for their liberation from temporal iniquities. Nor was their sense of loyalty to the missionaries and to the faith itself feigned or trivial.[28] Undoubtedly, many converts, particularly those such as slaves who had so little invested in the status quo, converted for the most immediate and material of reasons. But the forces subsequently pulling them into a quasi- or at least pro-Portuguese identity were strong indeed. In some places converts assumed the conspicuous dress of the Portuguese and were thus marked out as different whatever their interior affiliations. This meant that evangelization could become another mode of political expansion, and the conversion of the Paravas in particular has been analysed as a strategic step whereby the Sea of Ceylon was transformed into a 'Portuguese lake'.[29]

If some South Asian rulers tended to see converts as a 'fifth column' this was then an understandable anxiety. Loyalties and revenues previously accruing to them were now being transferred to the Portuguese. The Raja of Cochin consistently

[25] SR, I: 61–2, 141. Reiterating five years later, he insisted that residents of all religions must remain his subjects. See also Silva Rego 1949: 114; Mundadan 1984: 358, which assumes the same for Cochin.

[26] C. R. de Silva 1994: 303–4.

[27] See Flores 1995; Bayly 1989: 321–40; Manickam 1983; McPherson 1998.

[28] SR, V: 49–53; *DI*, I: 126.

[29] Flores 1998: 179; Flores 1995.

made it clear that he was opposed to conversion among his subjects, particularly when this involved those of high status. This official ban on conversions was not lifted until 1560, but the raja had not managed to halt rapid conversions among the lower orders. By 1542, Lower Cochin was a large bustling town consisting of some 15,000 Christians.[30] Yet throughout this period, the Portuguese saw opposition to their faith in two forms, firstly in the ostracizing of converts, and secondly through the sequestering of their land and properties. One important question for us is how far these processes can be seen as deliberate policies designed to dissuade people from converting, and how far they resulted from a more organic and inevitable application of caste principles.

If this seems an obscure line of reflection, we should recall that there is now a great deal of debate about what caste was in pre-modern era South Asia, that is to say the extent to which it was formalized into a coherent, hegemonic, static and universally acknowledged system. As such this debate can be construed in terms of our traditionalism–historicism dichotomy. Just as with ethnic identity or religious continuity, post-Orientalist critiques dwell at length on the epistemic power of British imperial dominion. Sometimes, this is pursued to the extent of suggesting that before the classificatory projects of the nineteenth century, Indian caste practices did not strike outsiders as 'particularly striking, important, or fixed' – a position which seems difficult to sustain in the light of the Portuguese textual record from the sixteenth and seventeenth centuries.[31] When some of the first ethnological analyses begin to appear in the later sixteenth century, as in the reports of the Jesuit Visitor to the East, Alessandro Valignano, for example, we find the picture rather familiar. In 1575 he listed the obstacles to the mission in India (as opposed say, to the prospects in Japan), and says:

> The second obstacle, which is the most essential of them all, is a diabolical superstition to which they cling, of that division by birth which they call caste [*che essi chiamano caste*], in which they are so rooted that no argument can make them change, because all these people are divided into castes like the people of Israel, though in a much stranger way than they, because not only may they not intermarry, but they may not even touch one another, nor eat, nor pass together through a street. And these castes are further divided according to their occupations [*ancora divise in officii*] . . . and this must be done by all the members of the same caste and none of them may give it up or change it . . . If they touch one another or eat together, those of the higher caste are defiled in dealing with those of the lower castes and thus lose their caste . . . From this it follows that if a child loses his caste, the father treats him as an alien . . . This diabolical superstition is found in all places and is so strong that it is not overlooked even in the least detail . . .[32]

30 SR, I: 340; Mulakara 1986: 50. 31 Dirks 2001: 20.

32 *DI*, X: 180–1 (VP, II: 66–7). Valignano was most familiar with Malabar, the fishery coast, and Goa. See also the judgements of Diogo de Gonçalves in 1615, described by Rubiés 2000: 336. Queirós can only explain the inflexibility of South Asian social roles by suggesting that in the hot climate men would not labour unless forced into it by their *casta* (Queyroz: 18, and see 81 on the strange association between pride and cleanliness). Xavier (unpublished) is a nuanced study of a flourishing – if shifting, contested, unstable – caste system in early Portuguese Goa.

This is a truncated quotation, leaving out further appalled detailing of this tyrannical hierarchicalism. We ought to remember then, when Nicholas Dirks draws our attention to the way in which 'caste was increasingly identified as the structural mechanism for, and ideological apparatus sustaining, the hegemonic sway of heathen obstructionism' by mid-nineteenth-century Protestant missionaries, that Catholic missionaries had arrived at similar conclusions several centuries previously.[33] They could not fail to observe how their evangelical energies were thwarted and redirected by indigenous principles of purity and status: how difficult it seemed to convert the 'haughty' Brahmans, how opportunistically the lowest groups came to the pulpit, how fiendishly difficult it was to disentangle religious practice not only from politics but from the fibres of everyday life. Indeed this was precisely the dilemma which would later give rise to the radical missiology of de Nobili. At the same time, historicist critiques have performed a vital service in indicating to us the fluidity and instability of caste norms over space and time, and the way that they were continuously subject to manipulation and re-formulation by interested parties.[34]

It is not easy, however, to discern the exact nature of the Indian social processes at work from their trace in the businesslike Portuguese correspondence of the early sixteenth century. There are some indications that many converts were in some sense 'cast out' by their relatives and neighbours, although whether this was because of their perceived impurity and shamefulness or because of quite other impulses is difficult to tell at this stage. The claim of the Vicar-General, Miguel Vaz, in 1545 that 'when the people of the country become Christians, they lose all the help and support of their countrymen who hold them as enemies,' might suggest that conversion was seen as a political affront, although later comments indicate a more general opprobrium.[35] What evidence there is for the association between conversion and impurity in Malabar at this time mainly relates to Cochin: we hear that indigenous Catholics were not allowed to walk the streets of Upper Cochin, nor enter the residence of the raja, nor touch people of a more honourable status. In the Malabar kingdoms caste pollution seems to have been transmittable through atmospheric as well as physical contact.[36]

These letters have normally been interpreted as evidence that conversion to Christianity uniquely entailed a complete loss of any pre-existing caste status.[37] However, the great majority of Christian converts were of very low caste or untouchable status to begin with, belonging to the Irava and Mukkuvā peoples, and were thus already banned from all sacred precincts and procession routes. And

[33] Dirks 2001: 136. [34] See Dirks 2001: 13, and, from a different perspective, Bayly 1993: 30.

[35] Memorial on the Indian Mission, Évora, see VP: 123; echoed in SR, III: 319, 532–3; and SR, IV: 61–2. Also, from 1566, see VP, II: 5: 'Thus those who become Christians are abandoned by their gentile relatives.'

[36] Bayly, 1989: 248.

[37] Presumably because some letters imply that these purity issues afflicted Christian converts in general, which could be taken to include the few Nāyars and Panikkars who had converted (in 1514, SR, I: 225). See Barbosa 1918–21, II: 39, on Malabar Nāyars' high status.

a closer reading indicates that what our Portuguese clerics are really complaining about is the fact that the status of these converts was not raised after conversion – a situation that was so unpalatable because, intriguingly, this was apparently precisely what happened to converts to Islam.[38] In 1518, the vicar of Cochin tells us that,

in this land there is a great variety of kinds and nations of people [*generos e naçoees das gentes*], because there are here nayres [Nayars], bramenes [Brahmans], panicaees [Panikkars], who are the noble sorts. There are others who are called Iravas, of which the most part are Christians, and others, Macuas [Mukkuvās], who do not touch the aforementioned nobles. These lesser folk, making themselves moors, are in contact with and mingle with the nobles and walk along the streets of the king, but if they become Christians, they are not allowed to do this; *rather they are held in the esteem which they were in* [emphasis added].[39]

However, as the century wears on, the Portuguese evidence from Malabar and Goa becomes unambiguous on the capacity of conversion to destroy caste status. When set alongside the treatment of Saint Thomas Christians and Muslims, Catholic converts often suffered from a devastating form of discrimination. Why? One reason was the kind of conversion demanded by the Portuguese clergy, which would have entailed a thoroughgoing transformation of lifestyle, and thereby impinged on the purity regulations and ritual practices which expressed and maintained status identity. If the Saint Thomas Christians were not automatically considered pariahs, that is because this long-established community had secured itself a distinct and elevated niche precisely by accommodating local purity concerns.[40] More specifically, it has been suggested that Christian converts lost status owing to the practice of eating beef.[41] But why then did converts to Islam not routinely suffer social censure? The most fundamental reason appears to be a self-perpetuating associative logic: the more Christianity spread among the lower orders, the more it took on connotations of pollution. Again, it is Valignano who expresses this most clearly. He says that rulers do not want their subjects to convert,

due to a superstition prevailing among them that those of noble birth defile themselves [*s'imbrattino*] and lose their nobility and respect when they deal with those of lower birth. And as those we have baptized so far are all of lower birth, it follows they despise Christians. Hence thinking that on becoming Christians they will degrade themselves . . .[42]

Valignano goes on to observe that each caste 'has its own gods and temples to which those of another caste has no access', which ran counter to Christianity's

[38] First mentioned in 1514 (SR, I: 226). [39] SR, I: 343. See also CS: 330.

[40] See Bayly 1989: 251–2; Silva Rego 1949: 120; Mundadan 1984: 362. Susan Bayly (personal comm. 2004) has suggested that caste difference in relation to conversion may have been connected to Iberian Catholic ideas about 'blood, bodies, conception, divinity, and human relations with saints, God and holy sites'.

[41] Neill 1984: 114. On the importance of the cow as a subject of cultural antagonism in these early years, see SR, I: 75.

[42] *DI*, X: 180–1/VP, II: 66–7.

insistence on communal worship. The new religion would not fortify the social hierarchy as the old did, but rubbish it. There was then an 'organic' play of caste norms at work here, but its working out was not predetermined. At one point we find Portuguese commentators arguing that converts to Catholicism in other Malabar cites outside of Cochin, such as Calicut and Cannanore, suffered none of these indignities.[43] A deliberate policy of dissuasion on the part of the rajas of Cochin is certainly possible. We are thus drawn to the conclusion that strong caste principles were very much in evidence and exerting a profound influence over the ways in which Christianity was received or rejected right from the start, but they were sufficiently fluid to allow elites to interpret or manipulate them in response to political imperatives.

One reason why the Portuguese often emphasized the element of royal policy is that an anti-Christian disposition seemed brutally apparent in other measures, above all in the practice of immediately appropriating the 'lands and properties' of all those who converted to Christianity.[44] There is some vague evidence that this policy was pursued throughout Malabar, but, again, in the mid century we only have detailed evidence relating to the activities of the Raja of Cochin.[45] The raja's stance was not invulnerable to normal diplomatic pressures. In 1542 Viceroy Martim Afonso de Sousa forced his agreement in issuing a public provision to safeguard the property of converts. From this point on, then, the continuing despoliation of convert properties stands also as a reflection of the inefficiencies of the *Estado*. Two years later Vaz reported to his king that after issuing this proclamation the governor was never in a position to respond to appeals.[46] The sequestrations continued.

Caste and conversion in Sri Lanka

How did caste shape the social landscape of mission in Sri Lanka? It is immediately striking that in one regard Sri Lanka was no different to the mainland. Looking at conversion rates across this region in the mid sixteenth century one pattern stands out: the great success of evangelization among coastal peoples who made a livelihood from the sea, as fishermen or pearl-collectors.[47] This applies to the Malayālam-speaking Mukkuvās and Iravas of the Malabar ports, and there was also a concentration clustered around the Sea of Ceylon, chiefly consisting of the Paravas of the Indian littoral and the Karāvas of the facing Lankan seaboard.[48] Indeed one can see how the expansion of the mission in Sri Lanka was shaped by

[43] In 1522: SR, I: 437; in 1529, CS: 330.

[44] Garcês in CS: 330, refers to this policy being conducted by 'kings and lords'.

[45] Suggestions of it as a Malabar-wide policy in 1543 (SR, II: 329–30, and see SR, III: 319), and in 1548 (SR, IV: 6), where Cochin and possibly Cranganore and Param are implied. See too J. M. Correia 1998: 178, and Schurhammer 1973–82, II: 493.

[46] VP: 125, 139. King João III again urged his governor to 'detach the king . . . from such cruel brutality': SR, III: 318. The policy was still followed in the 1620s, Tavim 1997: 67.

[47] And indeed this holds true even beyond South Asia, see Boxer 1969: 82.

[48] Bayly 1989: 321; Flores 1998: 188; Roberts 1995: 18–26. On Xavier's work among the Tamil-speaking Mukkuvās of Travancore, see Schurhammer 1973–82, II: 460–76.

the Karāva communities, as the churches spread themselves along the coast rather than penetrating far into the hinterland. It is no surprise that the two largest mass baptisms in our period, in Mannar in the mid 1540s and in Kōṭṭe in 1556, occurred among these peoples.[49]

How can we explain this pattern? One salient feature is that all these communities, but particularly the Paravas and the Karāvas, were closely interconnected by ties of commerce and diplomacy, as Francis Xavier himself recognized.[50] Indeed our Portuguese sources indicate that significant numbers of Paravas had crossed over to live or work in Sri Lanka.[51] From a much longer chronological perspective, Michael Roberts concludes that 'in sum then, the Portuguese, the Portuguese language, Catholicism, the Parava, the Karayar, the Karāva and possibly others (e.g. Mukkuvās, Vaggai, Pattanavans), all these descriptive terms embody intimate connections in the patterns of cultural relations, cultural diffusion, migration and trade along the coasts of the southern part of peninsular India and the island of Sri Lanka from the sixteenth century onwards.'[52]

Given that the conversion of the Parava has attracted a good deal of theoretical enquiry, can we simply apply elucidations of their motivations to their Sri Lankan counterparts across the straits? The geopolitical position of peoples such as the Paravas (addressed above, p. 90) is obviously fundamental here: on the margins of the great land-based powers, yet at the centre of the increasingly fought-over economic and strategic networks of the maritime world, they were in need of powerful naval protection. The same could surely be said for the Karāvas or Karayars of Mannar and the north of Sri Lanka, whose association with pearl fishing and trade likewise drew the unwanted attentions of the Māppiḷas, and the brutal interventions of regional hegemons (in this case Caṇkili).

The Karāva communities along the south-west coast of Kōṭṭe would also have been among the first groups to sense the change in the wind. It was their world that the growing Portuguese dominance of the Sea of Ceylon impinged upon; to borrow again the words of Nunes Barreto, they converted 'because they see that the Portuguese are powerful and are masters of the sea.'[53] A response was required. In 1556 the Karāva leaders showed that they, like their counterparts in India, could take the initiative in orchestrating baptisms *en masse*, indicating a pre-existent sense of communal identity, organization and autonomy – which conversion would act to enhance.[54] On the other hand, there is nothing to suggest that they suffered particularly from their vassalage to Bhuvanekabāhu, or indeed that they were somehow removed from his authority. Their evangelization took place in the Kōṭṭe heartland, under the nose of their sovereign.

[49] See below, pp. 104 and 171; and C. R. de Silva 1998: 106. In fact, the converts of Mannar may have not been Karāvas, but a closely related group which was spread across both sides of the Palk straits, the Karayars: see VP: 49, and Schurhammer 1973–82, II: 460. Both groups are referred to by Portuguese sources as 'Careas'.

[50] See VP: 51–4, 114, 125, 137, Flores 1998: 74; Flores 1994: 126.

[51] VP: 323, 346.

[52] Roberts 1995: 31.

[53] *DI*, VI: 677.

[54] See below, p. 171, for queries as to what extent there really was a mass conversion in 1556.

Equally as intriguing is the *cultural* position of all these groups on the margins of the great traditions of Brahmanic Hinduism in India and Buddhism in Sri Lanka. But what precisely do we mean by 'on the margins'? There are two quite different propositions here. First, marginality can refer to a low status within an overarching social structure, so that the group members are all too aware of their exclusion from the religious and social life of others. As fishermen, the peoples in question may have felt disadvantaged by Indic principles about the taking of life: local 'tyrannies' can be socio-cultural as well as political. Mass conversion was then an attempt to leapfrog this traditional hierarchy altogether by acquiring a new communal identity.

Yet Susan Bayly has questioned some of the assumptions behind this kind of explanation: it is not easy, for example, to establish the Paravas as being burdened or motivated by consciousness of a uniformly lowly identity.[55] It may be better to see the Paravas as marginal in the second sense of the term, which is to say that they remained somewhat outside of the ambit of Brahmanic discourses. Bayly, for example, emphasizes the extent to which the socio-religious character of the dry lands of South India beyond Malabar was comparatively 'unfinished', or in a state of flux. In this environment, the Parava could build a caste identity shaped not by recourse to some Brahmanic principle of purity, but through communal veneration. Perhaps a similar argument could be advanced for the shadowy Hindu communities of the northern and eastern coasts of Sri Lanka.[56] However, the 'conversion-as-escape-mechanism' thesis is more plausibly relevant to the Iravas and Mukkuvās of Malabar proper, for whom the Portuguese sources register an unmistakably low status.[57]

How would all this apply to the Karāvas of Kōṭṭe? We need to step back for a moment here, in order to gain a perspective on the particularities of Lankan caste. While in the Brahmanized parts of India surrounding the Portuguese settlements, social and religious identities were thoroughly intertwined, this was not the case in Sri Lanka. Lankan states used caste as one means of organizing land and labour. It was not religious sanction but 'inveterate custom . . . the power of government departments, the dominance of the nobles and the authority of the law courts' that supported caste discipline.[58] If, in this particular sense, caste identities take on a more secular guise, they were nonetheless profoundly important and

55 Bayly 1989.

56 See below, pp. 158–9. There was, for example, a significant community of Mukkuvās living in Batticaloa by the early seventeenth century, see Miranda: 178–9.

57 The contrast between this situation and that analysed by Eaton 1997: 117–19, is discussed in Strathern unpublished.

58 Dewaraja 1988: 64; Malalgoda 1976: 45; B. Ryan 1993: 12–13. This requires many nuances and qualifications, as in Roberts 1995: 36–74. The most sophisticated recent discussion of Lankan caste is Rogers 2004b, which illuminates it as one aspect of South Asian regional variation rather than as a fundamentally different 'system'. On the other hand, the different role played by the religious factors explored here contrasts strikingly with areas such as the Malabar Coast where Brahmanic influence was strong.

subject to intricate hierarchicalization. There was apparently no one indigenous term equivalent to today's 'caste', although *jātiya* and *kula* may have been used, but the world evoked in the *Sītāvaka Haṭana* (1585) is not altogether unfamiliar.[59] For example, when the poet describes the great 1550s defection to Sītāvaka, we hear of various noble families bestowed with land rights, but the groups such as *baḍalā* and *ācāriya* are ordered to live in separate villages. The low status of such labouring and artisan groups is indicated by the rude endings to their names (*-a*), and the need for their residential and social separation.[60]

In the seventeenth century, outsiders such as Ribeiro, Queirós and Robert Knox were struck by the rigidity of the systems they describe. Knox (who, if we are concerned to examine the power dynamics between observer and observed, was a prisoner of the mid-seventeenth-century Kandyan kingdom rather than an administrator) was at pains to discriminate between this system and wealth-rankings or government *per se*:

> Among these People there are divers and sundry Casts or degrees of Quality, which is not according to their Riches or Places of Honour the King promotes them to, but according to their Descent and Blood. And whatsoever this Honour is, be it higher or lower, it remains Hereditary from Generation to Generation. They abhor to eat or drink, or intermarry with any of Inferior Quality to themselves.[61]

A valuable and detailed list of castes follows. Sinhalese arrangements were also distinctive by virtue of the fact that the highest caste, the Goyigamas, were also numerically the largest and there were comparatively few cultural markers distinguishing them from the lower-status groups. There is some evidence of practices that indicate strong anxieties over pollution, regarding food preparation and consumption for example, particularly in Queirós' account. But we have to beware of his 'Asiatic' or 'Hindustanic' perspective which routinely led him to blur or confuse distinctions between India and Sri Lanka, and between unassimilated immigrants and Sinhalese.[62]

This is a generalized, static picture, when we have seen how Kōṭṭe was caught up in currents of change coming from the subcontinent. It is true that by the sixteenth century Kōṭṭe was undergoing its own limited version of Brahmanization. One does see, for example, caste principles infiltrating the *saṃgha*.[63] Ilangasinha has even suggested that this alienated the lower castes on the seaboard to the extent that they were left without religious facilities and were thus more open to evangelization. Yet it is unlikely that the Karāvas saw themselves as Buddhist to begin with. Many

59 See also verse 826 discussed below, p. 179. 60 *SH*, verse 417.

61 And further: 'thus by Marrying constantly each rank within itself, the Descent and Dignity thereof is preserved forever, and whether Family be high or low it never alters,' Knox: 199–200. Compare with Ribeiro: 28–30, 50–1, and Queyroz: 81–7, 96–9, 147, and 1014–23 – which gives a fascinating lascarin perspective on caste functions and deserves much more theoretical attention.

62 One of Queyroz' sources was Sá de Miranda who had extensive personal experience of the island. See Miranda: 49, 55, and compare 178–9, on the seven low castes, with Queyroz: 19–21.

63 Ilangasinha 1992: 82–90, 124–5. Miranda: 183, clearly refers to nobility as a monastic prerequisite.

of them were recent immigrants to Sri Lanka or had yet retained some distinctive cultural traits from the mainland.[64]

How would they have been perceived by the Sinhalese Buddhists? Were perceptions of caste occupations informed by the Buddhist precept of non-violence (*ahiṃsa*), rendering fishing or hunting as inherently polluting? This was a major preoccupation of the treatise, *Janavaṃsa*, but its fifteenth-century provenance has been questioned, and a historicist reading of it might suggest that its very stridency as to the inferiority of Karāvas indicates their unwillingness to accept any such denigration.[65] In the mid sixteenth century, they were only beginning to become bound to the social and ritual life of the hinterland.[66] At the same time, what little evidence we do have for Karāva association with the central power of Kōṭṭe indicates that such 'integration' need not come at the cost of their collective self-esteem. In Chapter One we saw that some of the Karāvas were not simply migratory fishermen but had been invited in as mercenaries to defend the kingdom from raiding Mukkuvās, and had been rewarded with land in return.[67] In their role as militia commanders, Karāva caste headmen could gain considerable status; it was indeed one such headman who organized the conversion of 1556.[68] In conclusion it is as plausible to see their conversion as a reflection of a pre-existing cultural independence as it is to see it as a desperate attempt to escape cultural subjugation.

Yet what of those who were fully part of the Kōṭṭe social order, indeed were right at its apex in the royal city?[69] For the other perceptible conversion trend of Bhuvanekabāhu's reign concerns the elite. When the Kōṭṭe princes fled to Goa they attracted many nobles to cross over and baptize in their wake.[70] Their mother, Bhuvanekabāhu's secondary queen Padmā, was also highly favourable to the mission, and may have represented a pro-Christian faction at court.[71] Gonzaga tells us that a number of noble courtiers converted during Bhuvanekabāhu's reign. This does not seem unlikely once we consider the success enjoyed by the two Jesuits who arrived just after the king's death in 1551. Dias tells us that they baptized 'a leading person and the lord of many people. The man belongs to the best race [*casta*] and blood of the country since after the king there is no higher race.'[72] This led naturally to the conversion of friends and relatives, culminating in a public celebration of the baptism of a noble woman.

[64] Raghavan 1961: 31; Pieris 1983–92, I. 145–6; B. Ryan 1993: 12.

[65] Kannangara 1993: 139–40 (my thanks to John Rogers for this); C. R. de Silva 1995: 48.

[66] Roberts 1995: 62–8, emphasizes the integration and denigration of the Karāvas over centuries. See Nevill: Or. 6606(156.II), for a seventeenth-century poem denigrating Karāva status. On the possible lack of social 'enmeshment' of the Karāvas see Raghavan 1961: 32; B. Ryan 1993: 105, Roberts 1995: 48.

[67] Raghavan 1961: 15, and above, p. 000.

[68] Roberts 1995: 50–1, on the military careers of some of these.

[69] The way in which conversion hit both the very top and the bottom of the Kōṭṭe social hierarchy is underlined by the *Rājāvaliya*: 76; both groups are thereby derided for their sexual and political submission.

[70] VP: 105, 121. [71] VP: 76, 89, and see 208.

[72] SV: 644, and further elite interest: VP: 322–4, 331–4.

The explanation for this incipient success – which would shortly have huge consequences for the fate of Kōṭṭe – surely lies in the fact that the Sinhalese caste system was largely non-Brahmanized; there was no immediate mechanism whereby religious conversion would affect one's perceived purity or status.[73] In the mid seventeenth century, Robert Knox noted that in the Kandyan court all Christians 'whether white or black' were treated as equal to the Goyigamas (farmers).[74] In the mid sixteenth century it appears that there were also no inevitable presumptions on the part of wider society that conversion entailed a loss of caste status.[75] But by the 1580s, after decades of religious conflict, it appears that arguments to that effect could be advanced: the *Sītāvaka Haṭana* does seek to establish that the high castes were bringing themselves into disrepute by conversion, and that the Portuguese had thereby disrupted traditional arrangements, fragmenting or perhaps even destroying castes.[76] Moreover, we shall see (below, Chapter Eight) Bhuvanekabāhu expressing an approach to the conversion of fellow princes that was in keeping with the South Indian model. But his attitudes towards the conversion of his subjects were somewhat different. The early disturbances of our period, when the convert communities were small and still nominally under indigenous rule, serve to highlight the distinctive tone of Sinhalese caste: they turned not on the theological status or purity of the convert, but on his or her responsibilities as a subject.

Bhuvanekabāhu's religious policy: the question of property rights

Notwithstanding the small but worrying inroads made by Christianity into the Kōṭṭe court, the dilemmas of religious policy faced by Bhuvanekabāhu were not unusual. The range of issues addressed by the 1541 memorial indicates that the contract of vassalage to which Bhuvanekabāhu had submitted was brief or vague. The subsequent decrees of 1543 therefore acted as the equivalent to the longer treaties established with the Malabar allies. Up to that point, then, it would seem as if there had been no explicit extension of extra-territoriality to Sinhalese converts. But from the picture of convert behaviour presented in the memorial it appears that baptism was seen as bestowing a very literal entitlement to throw off all temporal burdens.

The fact that Bhuvanekabāhu felt obliged to ask Lisbon for a decree to establish that converts were still liable for services and taxes has been taken as a stark indication of how much authority he had lost even amongst his own subjects.[77]

[73] B. Ryan 1993: 12–13, and 105, on how the division of the Karāva into Christian and Buddhist elements has not given rise to any lasting caste schism.

[74] Dewaraja 1988: 59; B. Ryan 1993: 60. It is true that the two principal Hindu officers of the court, the Paṇḍita and the Chief Chamberlain, would also convert shortly. Yet at issue here was their status in the eyes of Kōṭṭe society.

[75] There is a crucial exception to this point, namely monarchs themselves.

[76] *SH*, verses 373, 516–17 (quoted below, p. 182). This theme of caste disruption was taken up by the *Rājāvaliya*: 76–7, in the following century, and later in Young and Senanayaka 1998: 11, 19, 87, 214, 218–19.

[77] VP: 32; Da Silva Cosme 1986: 3.

Yet we have seen how insidious was the assumption in the Portuguese East that converts were not properly or entirely the subjects of local kings. Perhaps the cosmopolitan inhabitants of Colombo had become conscious of the situation in places such as Cochin and Kollam where converts could escape local law. In this context, Bhuvanekabāhu's policy was comparatively robust, seeking to make that assumption legally void before it became established in practice. However, the forces pulling converts into a quasi-Portuguese identity were apparent in Sri Lanka as early as 1522 when Caração reported that in the battle over the Colombo fort the local Christians had flocked to the side of the Portuguese, supporting them in the siege and tending to their wounds.[78] Sri Lanka was one place where converts were made visually distinctive by wearing full Portuguese dress or cap, or by growing a long beard.[79] Moreover, as a close reading of the 1541 memorial suggests, the anomalous benefits of extra-territoriality enjoyed by the Portuguese were all too attractive: converts were lured into imitating *casado* practices.[80] The decrees issued by King João III in 1543 did not address the issue of jurisdiction in a general sense, but they did confirm Bhuvanekabāhu's authority in every specific instance, including the right to all dues and taxes.[81]

We know, however, what became of those decrees. Even before the embassy returned, Bhuvanekabāhu had been taking matters into his own hands: just like his Malabar counterparts, he had begun to sequester the properties and land of anyone who converted. We know this because Gonzaga's narrative presents it as one of the major issues to be resolved by the friars when they were granted an audience with the king in 1543.[82] They complained to him about two 'laws', the first apparently passed by his predecessors 'according to which the king succeeds to the inheritance of their deceased subjects', the second, 'by which [he] confiscates all the possessions of [his] subjects, especially the rich ones, who are converted to the Christian Faith'. The friars wanted converts to be exempt from both, to be able to retain their properties in their lifetime and to exercise the privilege of passing them on to inheritors.

Martim Afonso de Sousa's injunction against these practices in 1544 was directed at Bhuvanekabāhu as well as at the Raja of Cochin. But it had little effect. This was illustrated when a noble of Bhuvanekabāhu's household took the governor at his word by appealing to him after he was despoiled following his conversion.[83] The governor issued an order for the property to be restored but it was ignored. Bhuvanekabāhu was in no way underhand about this policy. It was one of the key issues to be addressed by Duarte Barbudo's embassy in September of 1545. In the missionaries' eyes it was a simple and brutal policy of coercion designed to dissuade people from converting while swelling the royal coffers.[84]

How could such a policy be defended? Bhuvanekabāhu's explanation was cogent and strong:

[78] Caração: 163; C. R. de Silva 1994: 317, points to later evidence.
[79] VP: 71, 108. [80] VP: 16–17. [81] VP: 17, 32.
[82] VP: 40–1. [83] VP: 208, and see also 125. [84] VP: 208.

With regard to lands granted to people [*as terras de mercê*], I wish to explain to you their nature. From ancient times up till now, kings gave these lands to whom they pleased, and having given them, they could take them back if the tenants became crippled or aged, and incapable of mounting guard at their palaces, or of going to war, or disobedient in any way. But I am unable to do so when they become Christians for I cannot even venture to speak to them. By which, I have no jurisdiction over them and for this reason I take away the lands from them as soon as they become Christians.[85]

The explanation for this policy thus lies in the intermeshing customs concerning subject obligations and land tenure. In fact, the system was extremely complicated, much more so than these words of Bhuvanekabāhu suggest.[86] While it is no longer accepted that royal titles such as *bhūpati* ('lord of the earth') indicate that the king enjoyed sole ownership of the land, his authority over it was unquestionably immense. The basic assumption was that subjects were obliged to perform services for their kings in return for their use of land.[87] Certainly by the Kandyan period, and perhaps as early as the thirteenth century, this 'king's work' was referred to as *rājakāriya*.[88] We know that a more general term for service, *mehe*, was used during the reign of Senāsammata Vikramabāhu (1469–1511).[89] It seems that all subjects were liable to be called up to serve in the militia or for public construction works.[90] For many of the lower castes in particular, the nature of their service was determined by caste. This was organized via a 'departmental administration' that operated in tandem with the territorial administration.

Some lands were more difficult for the king to alienate: *paravēṇi* lands tended to carry smaller obligations, and since they were heritable they could become strongly associated with a particular family. *Divel* lands, on the other hand, were only held while the subject was able and willing to provide stipulated services to the crown.[91] The latter seems to be exactly what is conveyed by Bhuvanekabāhu's words. Were then his policies directed only at Christians holding *divel* lands, withdrawing their fiefs as he would do *post hoc* for any unfaithful *divel*-holder? It would seem not. His phrasing in this passage indicates that he would appropriate the properties of *anyone* as soon as they became Christian.

The legalistic perspective of our European sources can be a hindrance here. Gonzaga asserts that Bhuvanekabāhu had passed a property-stripping 'law', but in fact his actions were normative in this regard. The Gaḍalādeniya inscription

85 SV: 196 (VP: 96–7).

86 C. R. de Silva 1995: 43–6; Siriweera 1971, 1972, which cast doubt on the applicability of the concept of 'ownership' here; M. U. de Silva 1994: 2–7; Dewaraja 1988: 196–261. Yalman 1997 emphasizes land service as a fundamental structure of South Indian and Lankan society.

87 As Gunasekera 1978: 125, points out, this was a normative rather than articulated principle. Knox: 139, comments: 'the country being wholly his, the king farms out his land, not for money, but service.'

88 Siriweera 2002: 72, 88.

89 Gunasekera 1978: 125.

90 Siriweera 1972: 27.

91 It is recognized that these terms, particularly perhaps the generic *paravēṇi*, may have been used differently over the centuries. Their usage here follows Siriweera 1972: 19–26; and C. R. de Silva 1995: 44. See Raghavan 1961: 18–19, for the *paravēṇi* lands granted to the Karāva mercenaries in 1508, and Ribeiro: 27, for a mid-seventeenth-century understanding of *paravēṇi*.

(*c*. 1467–9), for example, makes it clear that the confiscation of all kinds of land was a royal prerogative, particularly where subjects were found guilty of serious crimes such as treason.[92] Indeed, the whole point of Bhuvanekabāhu's letter of 1545 is that Christians were being treasonous by defying his authority in all sorts of ways. When Gonzaga also refers to the law by which the king succeeds to the inheritance of deceased subjects, this should be taken as referring to the preponderance of the king's authority at the point of the subject's death. This expressed itself in a number of ways: through the direct reversion to the crown of all *divel* lands, all abandoned lands, and all lands without heirs; and, where there were heirs entitled to the usufruct of land, through the imposition of death duty, *marāla*.[93] Bhuvanekabāhu tells us that some Sinhalese were converting only a few days before they died in order to evade these obligations. The confiscation of land was, then, a general solution to a general problem: converts were simply not abiding by the laws of the land. This would be disturbing even where the king's own revenues were not directly affected. For example, many temples enjoyed the surpluses from large stretches of land that were allotted to them with a special exemption from providing royal services. Evidence from the later Kandyan period shows that Muslims could be efficiently integrated into this *vihāra* system by performing services for the temple in the manner of their Sinhalese neighbours.[94] One cannot imagine our converts – or their Portuguese godparents for that matter – following suit.

But it was the pre-emptive and blanket nature of the policy that allowed it to be perceived as a tool of religious persecution. After all, what happened to converts who did continue as faithful subjects? The missionary leader Vila do Conde claimed that they all did: 'for all the chief guards ever since we have been here, and I myself, have made them do everything that they were obliged to; this is but an excuse, because he has nothing else to say. In truth, it grieves him that they should convert and he hates them for this reason.'[95] But he was surely distorting the facts, wilfully or unconsciously, as his desperation demanded.[96]

The gap between the perspectives of the Portuguese and that of the Kōṭṭe court has been narrowed but not yet closed. Perhaps all that remains is a failure of cross-cultural communication? But the communication was not so bad. The Governor João de Castro explained to King João III that 'according to the laws of the kingdom, the king was the heir of all the properties of his subjects.'[97] Heritability seems to have been the hallmark of ownership for the Portuguese, and its apparent absence in Ceylon was one of the few aspects of Sinhalese culture that were appreciated to be radically different and worthy of comment in the first half of the sixteenth century. This emerges from a fascinating document, the *Livro que trata das Cousas da Índia e do Japão*, a survey of the Indian territories

92 *EZ*, IV: 15; see also Dewaraja 1988: 223.
93 *EZ*, IV: 12, 15.
94 Dewaraja 1988: 180; Roberts 2001: 84.
95 SV: 224 (VP: 118).
96 He is implicitly contradicted by the stance taken by Duarte Barbudo and João de Castro and the cynicism of Padrão: VP: 192, 234.
97 VP: 192.

commissioned by the Governor Garcia de Sá at the start of his office in 1548. The author of the report on Ceylon was the highly experienced ex-factor António de Pessoa, who tells us that the fertile land on the island was relatively unproductive because 'the people of the area do not have properties because all belongs to the king.'[98] João de Barros may well have had Pessoa's report to hand, for we find the same argument in the *Decadas*.[99] This sort of argument would play a major role in the image of the 'Oriental despot' burnished by later European writers – we see here its empirical origins.[100] Therefore, we are faced not so much with a failure of understanding as a clash of values. The missionary perspective is the more puzzling: acknowledging that Bhuvanekabāhu's powers over land at the point of death were entirely within indigenous law, they still pressed for them to be suspended when it came to converts. In Chapter Six we shall make sense of this.

The missionaries were failing to acknowledge the jurisdictional anxieties of the indigenous princes, but they were probably correct in perceiving the policy of sequestering convert properties to be one part of a broader attempt to obstruct the progress of Christianity. We know that the ambassador Barbudo had managed to make Bhuvanekabāhu agree that he would not obstruct the mission in any way and even issue a decree allowing Christians to pass on their lands to inheritors.[101] But, the essential point is that this would be conditional on his convert subjects recognizing his true authority.[102] With such a proviso the decree could not but become a dead letter. Even after Bhuvanekabāhu's death, court officials continued to see the necessity of his policies.[103]

The seriousness of the Christian challenge was then widely recognized within and beyond Sri Lanka. The fact that in the 1540s both Bhuvanekabāhu and the Raja of Cochin vigorously pursued the same policy is surely significant. It may be that the two rulers were in communication and that what we see here is evidence of a common anti-Christian strategy. But the notion that they had both merely arrived at the obvious solution to the same dilemma is equally compelling. Both kings were insistent that missionary desires to carve out a new and favoured social space for converts should not be allowed to subvert traditional principles. If we allow an insight to travel from the Sinhalese material to the South Indian, it is also possible that the raja's confiscation of convert property was in part an attempt to protect his

[98] Pessoa 1960: 39.

[99] Barros: 35–6: 'And if its kings did not constitute themselves the heirs of their vassals, taking from them all the property that they possess at the hour of their death, of which, if they choose, they give some things to the children, it would be much more fruitful and well supplied; but through fear of this they do not care to cultivate anything,' in turn echoed by Queyroz: 98. See Xavier 2003: ch. 4, for later Portuguese documents making similar analyses of Goan practices.

[100] See Chapter Six.

[101] VP: 192. Gonzaga tells us that Bhuvanekabāhu issued decrees in 1543, but he probably has the 1545 decree in mind, see VP: 40.

[102] Bhuvanekabāhu wrote that he would carry out this promise, 'so long as they will carry out the decrees issued for my sake by the King of Portugal', VP: 98, 192.

[103] VP: 298, 336.

traditional rights over the disposal of land.[104] This is not the place for a thorough comparison of Malabar and Sinhalese tenure systems, but it does seem as if they had in common the principle that the usage of land entailed obligations of service and that both systems were sufficiently complex to render the establishment of 'ownership' analytically problematic.[105] No doubt in Malabar as in Sri Lanka this conflicted with the moral sentiments of the Portuguese and the material aspirations of converts. We ought to reflect on a central contrast too. When set alongside the legal concessions made by the rajas of Malabar, Bhuvanekabāhu's stance appears uncompromising. He pushed for converts to remain entirely within his jurisdiction and for them to receive no privileges without his permission. Otherwise, it would seem to him that his subjects 'only become Christians in order to take men away from my people'.[106]

Bhuvanekabāhu's religious policy: resistance

It was a similar intuition that lay behind a major incident in Jaffna that would send shock waves beyond Goa and Lisbon: King Caṇkili's massacre of 600 converts on the island of Mannar. In a letter that was copied and dispersed throughout Europe and read out at the Council of Trent, Francis Xavier denounced this deed as an act of tyranny requiring immediate justice.[107] He had good reason to be personally troubled. In Manappad in August 1544, he had received a delegation from the inhabitants of Mannar directly requesting that he come to baptize them.[108] The Karayār Mannarites had demanded Xavier's presence and called upon Portuguese protection and support just like their Karayār, Parava or Mukkuvā counterparts along the fishery coast of South India. In his place Xavier had sent a secular priest.

Queirós, typically and implausibly, suggests that religious resistance *per se* was a principal motivation for Caṇkili's massacre.[109] Did the officials of the *Estado da Índia* assume that the Mannarites who converted in October of 1544 came under their jurisdiction? Certainly Miguel Vaz asserted to the Portuguese king that 'they [belong to] your highness; they pay tribute to you so that you defend them.'[110] It is

[104] The raja excuses himself by saying that he 'would do as his ancestors had done' (SR, II: 329). This might mean by continuing as a 'Hindu', but the context suggests he is referring to powers over property. According to Schurhammer's chronology, this raja would be Rāma Varma (1503–45). Since there were no Christians before his reign, he would be talking about protecting pre-existing laws. However, others see an accession to the throne in 1537, see Tavim 1997: 102.

[105] Mathew 1989: 55–61. Queyroz: 91–2/*Conquista*: 70–1, claimed that in all Asian societies 'all land belongs to the Crown, not only in the supreme dominion but in direct (dominion) and even the usufruct. There is no vassal who has any heritage of his own that he can bequeath to his children.' This principle allowed Queyroz to argue that Dharmapāla could dispose of all the land in Sri Lanka just as he wished. Queyroz: 92, seems to be derived from Indian information.

[106] SV: 195, is more puzzling than this, but the sense of VP's translation (95) seems correct in the context.

[107] Schurhammer and Wicki 1944–5, I: 267; Quéré 1984: 170.

[108] Schurhammer 1973–82, II: 444–6, 471–3.

[109] Queyroz: 243, characteristically claims that the conversion produced an uprising by the '*jedacas* or priests of that heathendom', who persuaded Caṇkili on his course of action.

[110] SV: 249 (VP: 125).

not surprising then that Caṇkili perceived their loyalties had altered.[111] This was not so far-fetched if we consider the sustained Portuguese attempts to Christianize the strategically crucial and financially lucrative coastal lands of the Palk straits.[112] If the people of Mannar were acting in association with other fishery-folk across the seas, at the level of high politics Caṇkili may have proceeded in step with the Vijayanagar Nāyaks.[113] The manner in which religious affiliation sharpened or even generated political opposition was easily symbolized for him in the figure of his brother and rival who promised to convert in return for Portuguese support. The year before, only a large sum paid as tribute to Martim Afonso de Sousa had diverted Portuguese intervention on his brother's behalf.[114]

Just a few months later Bhuvanekabāhu also stooped to murder. His reign had begun with parricide and would proceed with the assassination of his son, Prince Jugo Baṇḍāra, in the last weeks of 1544.[115] This was an action almost as bold as Caṇkili's and scarcely less damaging to the progress of Christianity in the island, for Jugo had pretensions to the throne of Kōṭṭe and was willing to convert in order to claim it with Portuguese assistance. This event has been subsequently subsumed under the holy nimbus of Xaveriana and our view of it is now somewhat misted up. The branching oral traditions that came to surround the historical Xavier must have given rise to the peculiar turn that Queirós' narrative takes at this time.[116] He gives us two stories, both following the same pattern of the martyrdom of a princely neophyte, one in Kandy and the other in Trincomalee. This is in fact the story of Jugo told twice over, each just divergent enough to deceive Queirós and suitably embellished with further miracles, conversions and tyrannies. Yet the essential elements of these stories were already there in the report by our ultimate contemporary source and central protagonist in the affair, André de Sousa. The problem for the historian is that his immediate interests coincided so neatly with the narrative logic of martyrology. Finding triumph in death, Sousa had reason enough to represent the sad end to his plotting as a holy and mysterious beginning.

As is now well recognized, Jugo's motivations were primarily political: he was making a rather desperate bid for significance after his claims to the throne had been so conclusively sidelined by the installation of Dharmapāla as heir-apparent.[117] This was appreciated by more sceptical elements in Goa, particularly the Jesuits, as was Sousa's mendacity in hailing him a martyr.[118] After Jugo's death it had been the king's sister who had asked the surviving princes if they wanted to be Christians and then asked Sousa to take them to Goa.[119] This can be contrasted

[111] Queyroz: 247, gives Xavier a fictional speech explicitly making this point.
[112] Flores 1998: 194, and see above, p. 90.
[113] Queyroz: 243, 283; and Pathmanathan 1982: 38–46. [114] VP: 146–7; Correia: 323.
[115] Reported by Xavier early in 1545, see VP: 55.
[116] Queyroz: 244–6, which highlights Queyroz' use of unknown oral and martyrological traditions and the ways they distort his narrative.
[117] This is emphasized by the *Alakeśvarayuddhaya*: 33, reporting that Vīdiyē Baṇḍāra (Dharmapāla's father) was ordered to carry out the assassination. Bourdon 1936: 17–21, has a detailed but overly-credulous narrative.
[118] VP: 92. [119] VP: 93.

with Sousa's account, in which his own initiative assumes centre stage: it was he who had proselytized to Jugo; the prince had responded to his spiritual vision and had converted, only wanting the ritual of baptism itself.[120] Sousa then arranged his burial where he notes that:

> God performed there many miracles on the occasion of his death, for the earth trembled, and a cross the size of a mast was seen in the sky, and another cross was formed by the opening of the ground where the body had been cremated. When the king heard of it, he ordered that opening to be filled up; but after they had filled it up, the earth was soon found open again. Therefore, many became Christians and I, with my own hands, made more than two hundred of them.

Subsequently, he had converted Jugo's younger brother and cousin and smuggled them to safety. On the issue of Jugo's spiritual status, the ecclesiastics in Lisbon remained sceptical that he had been truly instructed in Christian doctrine before his death.[121] Sousa's eyewitness account ought to be seen alongside other indications of his opportunistic and self-aggrandizing character. His ambitions required Sri Lanka to be portrayed as a providential island of gloriously holy deeds. However petty its origins, this vision would only grow in importance. However sceptical they may have been of Sousa's claims in other respects, Xavier and his Jesuit brothers did not doubt that such miracles had occurred.

What stands out in conclusion is that only a year or so after the magnificent return of the Lisbon embassy, Bhuvanekabāhu was feeling so embattled that he was prepared to risk an action that would be unavoidably construed as antagonistic by the Portuguese. Now he was vulnerable to the accusation that he was simply and deeply anti-Christian, and that is how Francis Xavier described him in January 1545.[122] To be sure, his feelings on this matter now affected the tenor and conduct of his court.[123] The tempo had been raised by a more potent threat to his authority than the unruliness of the converts in Colombo: the Christianizing strategies of rivals in Kandy and in Kōṭṭe itself. When Vila do Conde reports that Bhuvanekabāhu was refusing to let a single convert into the palace while Muslims and all manner of pagans were granted admission, one immediately thinks of the controversies in Malabar. But whereas there the rajas of Cochin had recourse to a mechanism of purity in establishing such exclusions, Bhuvanekabāhu seems to have been simply projecting his disfavour: the explanation which he put to Duarte Barbudo was that 'through them [the converts] his kingdom would be taken away'.[124] This is excellent evidence that Bhuvanekabāhu's overriding objection to Christianity was precisely that it generated a 'fifth column'.

[120] VP: 109–11. Correia: 324, particularly useful for these years, states to the contrary that the princes 'had become Christians through the counsel of some friars, who had taken up their abode there in a little hut'. See also Andrada (*Crónica*) 1976: 890. Thanks to the research of VP: 45, n. 2, we can dismiss the idea (first introduced in Queyroz: 236) that any royal princes were entrusted to Franciscan education.

[121] VP: 126. [122] VP: 52.

[123] Broadly conveyed by Gonzaga's narrative (VP: 46–7), which is yet unreliable in detail.

[124] SV: 224 (VP: 118).

The king's fears were no more delusional or paranoid than Caṇkili's, for Bhuvanekabāhu now faced the looming presence of the princes in Goa. It is a mark of Francis Xavier's influence that the governor, Martim Afonso de Sousa, was persuaded to launch two expeditions. One was aimed at installing one of the Koṭṭe princes who had been baptized Prince João in the lands belonging to the dead Prince Jugo, while ensuring him access to a seaport in Kōṭṭe and attempting to convert Bhuvanekabāhu. Another was designed to install Caṇkili's brother in Jaffna.[125] The first was postponed owing to the sudden apparition of the Turkish threat while the second ran aground us a result of Caṇkili's chance capture of a cargo ship that he could ransom off to the Portuguese. Then, in the summer of 1545, the threat became greater still. Some noble inhabitants of Jaffna had journeyed to Goa to ask that Prince João become their ruler. The governor began to prepare for a mission that would depose Caṇkili and replace him with the Sinhalese prince. But André de Sousa, who was clearly the mind behind the ambitions and missives of the fugitive princes, wrote directly to King João III and his brother Prince Henrique, outlining a far more flamboyant scheme.

The missionary vision of a great new Christian space in the East, a place in which temporal obstacles would be dissolved to the extent that it would be all but impossible not to be Christian, could now be established as political reality.[126] Prince João's territorial reach would be greatly magnified through his instatement as the heir to throne of Kōṭṭe, but he would also initially assume extra-territorial powers by having 'jurisdiction over all the Christians of Cape Comorin and inland, both in civil and criminal matters'.[127] But then 'all the Christians should come to live in my territory, while now they are all scattered over the kingdoms of the gentiles, and justice is administered to them just as for others.' Sri Lanka would become the holy land of the orient, the solution to the basic missionary dilemma of how to nurture the faith amidst the diabolical temporalities of heathendom.

For Bhuvanekabāhu, who already saw some members of his court fleeing to the princes in Goa, this could only signify the end of his rule and the end of his hopes for his grandson Dharmapāla. Naturally this had consequences for his religious policy in general. Just as in sixteenth-century England fears of an internal Catholic conspiracy fed off the very real prospect of an external Spanish threat, so in mid-sixteenth century Kōṭṭe Bhuvanekabāhu was exercising his authority in his courtroom because he was powerless over the sinister events across the water in Goa. Not that Bhuvanekabāhu had to look abroad to see Christian perfidy rearing its head. It was the King of Kandy's success in luring the Portuguese to his kingdom on the promise of baptism that ultimately must have pushed Bhuvanekabāhu and Māyādunnē into that strange alliance of 1545–6.[128] Their plan was obviously a desperate one: to wipe out the Christianizing pretender and use his mountainous

125 See Xavier's letters in VP: 53–60, 77–8, 89–93, 97, 101–21.

126 VP: 101–3.

127 VP: 101. The plan was also to give Luís the princely lands belonging to Jugo.

128 This alliance must be the explanation for the puzzling occurrence of both Bhuvanekabāhu's and Māyādunnē's signatures at the bottom of the Ganēgoḍa Sannasa (*EZ*, III: 63–4), in 1546–7. But then how to explain the apparently Christian cross inscribed above Māyādunnē's signature?

territories as a redoubt from which to hold off the expected Christian invasion of the lowlands. According to André de Sousa, this was an anti-Christian league in domestic as well as diplomatic terms: 'we had information that the king had entered into an agreement with his brother to forbid people becoming Christian in Ceilão.'[129]

Sousa's assertion fits in well with the observations of other Portuguese in quite different positions. Duarte Teixeira, an old resident of the court of Kōṭṭe, confirmed that Bhuvanekabāhu and Māyādunnē had shown 'great contempt for the Portuguese and ill-treat the Christians, with the result that these all give up their Faith and lay aside the cap by which they are distinguished'.[130] Another *casado* gave a more grisly report, which (if true) would indicate the scale of the threat that this small conversion movement was imagined to present: 'both inflict many cruelties on the Christians. They impaled one along the road; they have others taken to Ceitavaqa [Sītāvaka] and there they have them stretched out on a shield and hammered. In this way they execute them.'[131] It is likely that the most terrible persecutions were at the instigation of Māyādunnē.[132] But has the violence of Bhuvanekabāhu's persecutions been embellished by the anger of the missionaries?

The principal reason to suspect this is the mildness of the stance taken by the ambassador Duarte Barbudo. In 1545, Martim Afonso de Sousa's planned expedition to Sri Lanka had been thwarted yet again, this time by the termination of his office and the arrival of his replacement João de Castro. Castro, on the instructions of King João III himself, then dispatched Barbudo to investigate anew the problematic issues concerning Bhuvanekabāhu and his religious policy. The disproportionately large number of letters that we have for the autumn of this year reflect the fact that all parties were desperate to persuade the new governor of their case in the wake of the embassy. This is when Vila do Conde's letter denying any convert malpractice by the converts was written, along with the *casado* reports of bloody persecutions and also Bhuvanekabāhu's skilful defence.[133] While the king's opposition to the mission was conceded explicitly by both sides, it is clear that the ambassador came away with an impression quite different to the harsh denunciations of some of his countrymen. Although the governor continued to back the proposal of the princes' installation in Jaffna, Barbudo's report in 1545 and the embassy of de Ayora in 1546 had convinced him that Bhuvanekabāhu's complaints were genuine, and that it was rather the 'importunate urging' of the friars that

129 VP: 113. These are very similar to the words put into Prince João's mouth (107), who had earlier asserted that Bhuvanekabāhu 'wishes to defend [his sect] with arms', VP: 105.

130 VP: 71. 131 VP: 122.

132 Simão de Coimbra described him (VP: 200) as that 'great persecutor of our holy Christian faith', but the distorting effects of his pro-Kandy bias are evident in his claims that Christians were being captured and sacrificed to false gods. That the Sītāvakan kings did use impaling as punishment for treason emerges from *SH*, verse 603.

133 The use of conversion theology by Bhuvanekabāhu's letter-writers mirrors that made by João III himself in 1533: compare VP: 95, with SR, II: 238–40.

was at fault.[134] Castro turned to Bhuvanekabāhu's history of generous Christian patronage in order to support the implicit argument that temporal complexities rather then theological battles were at the heart of the problem.[135] Thus thwarted, the friars began to rumour that Duarte Barbudo had been bribed in Ceylon. This was the cause of what must have been a major breach between the governor and the Franciscan community. We even find Castro wondering to his son whether the 'cawings' of the friars would lead to his arrest when he eventually returned to Portugal.[136]

According to the friar Simão de Coimbra, Bhuvanekabāhu continued to wage war on the Christian faith well into 1546 to the point of openly destroying Christian crosses. Missionary work, we are told, had therefore ground to a halt.[137] This emphasis is only to be expected once we recall that Coimbra was the most enthusiastic friar in the Kandyan affair and that he had a strong interest in painting Jayavīra as the Christian alternative to the King of Kōṭṭe. Coimbra was right about one thing: Bhuvanekabāhu was doing his utmost to dissuade the King of Kandy and the various lesser princes of the interior from converting and thereby winning Portuguese support. The reality of the King of Kandy's predicament approximated to neither the propaganda of Coimbra nor the fears of Bhuvanekabāhu. Indeed, the two kings faced the same dilemma.

The chronicle sources come into their own at this point, detailing the all-too-familiar problems of succession at the Kandyan court.[138] Jayavīra also had a young son and heir who feared that he would be passed over and was intriguing with the Portuguese. The mission of 1546 revealed that this prince, Karaliyaddē Baṇḍāra, was much more willing than his father to accede to baptism, and Coimbra hinted that he might carry the best hopes for the future. So Jayavīra had his own Christian menace at court and Bhuvanekabāhu's urgent letters quickly educated him as to the wider problems associated with evangelization. As described by the friar Padrão, his religious policy in 1546 was the same in spirit if not in detail as that of his Kōṭṭe or Sītāvaka counterparts: 'he does not want anyone in his territory except slaves to become Christians; and if anyone becomes a Christian secretly he immediately sells them into slavery.'[139]

From this point on we are caught in the same historiographical dilemma that detained us above in Chapter Four. Our sources separate into two opposing camps flatly contradicting each other and leaving us wondering whether the disingenuousness lies with a presumptuous Portuguese community or a devious king. By 1547, many Portuguese in Sri Lanka had united into such a strongly anti-Bhuvanekabāhu faction that their reports inspire suspicion. The *casados* claimed that:

[134] VP: 134–5, 191–5.
[135] Castro was influenced here by Bhuvanekabāhu's letter, supported by de Ayora, in which the same argument was made: VP: 182.
[136] SV: 440–1. [137] VP: 206–8.
[138] For the family history, see *Alakeśvarayuddhaya*: 36–7; *Rājāvaliya*: 78; Couto: 133–4.
[139] VP: 187.

He works against the Christians in ways that are hard to imagine. He persecutes so much those who become Christians here that no one now dares convert. On the other hand, those who already are Christians have for many days no longer dared to profess their religion. Because of the numerous persecutions which he and his followers inflict upon them, they go to the pagodas as they did before.[140]

The missionaries were so frustrated by the situation in Kōṭṭe that they actively sided with Māyādunnē, choosing to believe his diplomatic noises concerning Christianity rather than recalling his enthusiasm for impaling Christians a year or so before.[141] Outside Sri Lanka the impression among many religious was simply that Christians were being persecuted there by both their king and by the Portuguese captains.[142] In particular, this was the lament of Francis Xavier, who urged his king to take drastic measures against Portuguese officials and to give up on the alliance with that 'great enemy of God' Bhuvanekabāhu.[143]

Bhuvanekabāhu complained that far from persecuting Christians it was he who was the victim.[144] The key to this divergence of perspectives is to recognize that the jurisdiction issue had never been resolved. The tone of the Portuguese letters in the latter part of the 1540s gives the impression that the Christians were suffering in new and terrible ways. But this bitter tone was almost certainly the result of the hardening of Portuguese opposition to the king and the fact that Bhuvanekabāhu had been so successful in blocking the baptism of the King of Kandy. The unspecified 'persecutions' probably refer simply to the continuation of the policy of property-stripping. On this issue Bhuvanekabāhu was sometimes open and at other times less so. The friars, on the other hand, never acknowledged the problems caused by avaricious converts. To some extent this reflects the zeal and intemperance of the *piedoso* Franciscans in Sri Lanka. Their Observant Custodian in Cochin, António do Casal, came to a more balanced and seemingly more accurate assessment of the state of affairs. His letter of 1549 implied that although Bhuvanekabāhu could not be said to favour Christianity, the fact that he allowed the friars to preach and build churches and schools meant that he was not such a diabolical foe.[145]

An interesting example of how the reputation of religious tyrant could be generated is presented by the case of the razing of the church in Devinuvara ('Dondra') in 1550.[146] The king's refusal to punish the local people who had pulled down the church there was taken by the friars and the newly arrived Viceroy Afonso de Noronha as general evidence of his anti-Christian guilt. We know that the missionary responsible for erecting the church had been acting without the permission of Bhuvanekabāhu or even of any ecclesiastical authorities, and that the church

140 SV: 494 (VP: 238).

141 See VP: 232; Couto: 131; and particularly Correia: 362, for an interesting account of how the friars supported Māyādunnē's propaganda against Bhuvanekabāhu regarding the failed Kandy expedition. VP: 227–8, 237, reveals Vila do Conde's depressed state of mind at this time.

142 For example, the Dominican Bermúdez in VP: 246.

143 VP: 257–8.

144 VP: 182, 249–50.

145 VP: 256.

146 See the accounts by Noronha (VP: 266) and the Paṇḍita, (VP: 278). The Paṇḍita also pointed out that Bhuvanekabāhu had left all other churches unmolested, which only highlights the importance of Upulvan, see below, pp. 187–8.

had been constructed on the grounds of 'the chief *paguode* of Ceilao': indeed, one in which the protector-god Upulvan had his centre. Noronha dismissed these as 'cold excuses', but it does not take much imagination to see that they would have been serious affronts to Bhuvanekabāhu's authority and the sensibilities of the local population.

The behaviour of the converts to Christianity was a phenomenon unparalleled in Sinhalese history. What was new was the radical and comprehensive conception of religious conversion, which could easily be interpreted as a sloughing off of all former identities and loyalties. These propensities were given weight by the Portuguese commitment to the notion of the *padroado*, the protection of all Christians in the East. Disaffected or opportunistic elements in Sinhalese society were quite able to grasp these ideas and their power; in this case it was the indigenous peoples rather than the Europeans who proved themselves particularly adept at 'mastering the signs'. It was only in the 1540s, however, that Bhuvanekabāhu began to appreciate the full implications of this. It is not surprising then that his religious policy changed and nor is it surprising that many of his vassals and rivals seemed so much warmer in response to missionary overtures. For it was only really in Kōṭṭe and Colombo that the consequences of evangelization were being played out in the flesh.

Elsewhere in the *Estado da Índia* there were many other rulers undergoing the same tribulations. The effective extension of extra-territoriality to converts leached Portuguese authority into native communities that were nominally independent. We do not need to conclude that Christianity was then simply a Trojan horse, rolling along the coasts of South Asia and divesting itself of its hidden contents, military and political agents. The equation of spiritual and temporal responsibility brought otherwise unwanted burdens to Portuguese officials, which – if Xavier and like-minded clerics can be believed – many were all too keen to shrug off.

In dealing with these problems, Bhuvanekabāhu was not the pusillanimous figure of the *Rājāvaliya*. Contrary to the impression that may be obtained from some of the contemporary Portuguese commentators, nor was he unusual in his opposition to evangelism. If we compare his situation with that of the Raja of Cochin, it is initially noteworthy that the raja's anti-Christian policies seemed to come at a lower diplomatic cost. This might be the result of his status as an ally rather than a vassal. The Portuguese kings made it clear that one of the principal ways in which they could be 'served' was through the inculcation of Christianity.[147] The kings of Kōṭṭe and of Cochin both used the language of service to the Portuguese Crown, but for Bhuvanekabāhu it may ultimately have carried a greater weight of obligation. There are two more concrete reasons. Firstly, Bhuvanekabāhu was the victim of greatly inflated hopes. The misunderstanding resulting from the embassy of 1542, whether deliberate or accidental, meant that the friars' experience of the Sri Lankan mission would inevitably be one of miserable frustration. It also meant

[147] See, for example, Noronha, in VP: 266–7.

that the 1543 decrees intended to regulate relations would always be vulnerable to the accusation that they were illegitimate.

Secondly, in some ways Bhuvanekabāhu's religious policy was more daring than that of his counterparts across the sea. The Raja of Cochin's opposition to the conversion of high castes was very disturbing to the Portuguese, but he did allow a great city of predominantly low-caste converts to establish itself in Lower Cochin, whereas Bhuvanekabāhu's objections concerned all varieties of people who converted, and over none of them would he concede jurisdiction. His policies of stripping the properties of those who converted and actively dissuading rival princes to convert were a frank and diplomatically dangerous reassertion of his authority. If their aim was to dam the flow of conversions then they must be judged a success: by the time he died it was generally acknowledged that the Sri Lankan mission had foundered on the rocks of temporal opposition.[148]

[148] VP: 245–7. The new impetus created by the arrival of the Jesuits in 1551 does not seem to have had lasting results, see 342.

6
Missionary mentality

The concept of conversion

In Sri Lanka today, the Portuguese mission is rarely referred to unaccompanied by the phrase 'forced conversions'. Yet, for most of the sixteenth century while missionaries laboured under the heathen sovereignty of Bhuvanekabāhu or the fatally circumscribed one of Dharmapāla, this is an issue of little concern for the historian.[1] In more subtle ways, however, the missionaries surely did allow themselves to become the conduits for the worldly business of Portuguese imperialism. How could they have connived at the game of 'theological diplomacy' by which baptism was reduced to a cheap political token? How could they have assumed so blindly that Portuguese mores and laws must follow where the Holy Spirit led? If this chapter ranges some way beyond Sri Lanka to provide a context, it does so to restore some of the particularity and complexity to the missionary sensibility.

It was an obvious way to dissolve all the problems and hostility detailed in the last chapter: convert the ruler, and his jurisdictional independence would cease to matter. His people would inevitably follow suit. There was every reason to expect this, as it had been a constant of Christian history since the defining conversion of the Roman emperor Constantine in the early fourth century. In the earliest days of the Portuguese 'discoveries' it had been exemplified by the great success of the conversion of the King of Congo in 1491, and much more recently, the initial mass conversion of the Indian Paravas had been conducted in negotiation with a few headmen.[2] In the first years missionary letters routinely weighed up royal neophytes in terms of the thousands or millions of souls under their charge.[3]

But we shall see, as many contemporaries did, that rulers were only likely to submit to baptism as a condition of political advantage. For many Catholic writers in modern Sri Lanka this stands as another example of the tragically misguided nature of the Portuguese mission.[4] One could simply point to the inevitable failure of the human will to enact theological ideals. But the truth is that the theological

[1] The issue of 'forced conversions' was settled by Boxer 1960–1, but even 'pressured conversions' only became significant after the 1590s conquest of the lowlands.

[2] Thomaz 1993: 118; Thornton 1984: 147–67; Bayly 1989: 325–6.

[3] See Simão de Coimbra's comments in VP: 198. There were, however, those who were sceptical about the top-down model: SR, III: 303.

[4] See, for example, Don Peter 1978: 9, 25.

principles were themselves ambiguous. It is in the New World, with its vast tracts under direct rule, that the debate was pursued with the most explicitness and urgency. There mass coerced conversions were a real possibility, and some, often citing the parable of the banquet in Luke (14:16–24) – 'compel them to come in' – saw them as legitimate.[5] The most famous opponent of forced conversions and mass baptisms was Bartolomé de Las Casas. Writing from Mexico 1538–40, he argued that the contemporary Church was bound to follow the missionary methods that Christ had established for his twelve apostles: the kingdom of God had to be preached with love and by means of rational and peaceful persuasion.

In the *Estado da Índia* the philosophical depths of the conversion controversy were plumbed less often but the dilemmas remained: how important is the motivation, the sincerity, and the doctrinal comprehension of the candidate for baptism? Plainly these features belonged to an *ideal* candidate but there was considerable ambiguity and controversy about whether a *suitable* candidate had to measure up in this way. A strong tradition in Christian thought held that conversion was ultimately the work of God's grace. Consequently, what conversion is and how it happens retained an inherent element of mystery.

Immediately one becomes immersed in some of the deepest paradoxes of Christianity: how does one resolve the timeless omnipotence of God with human free will and how do the two interact in the process of salvation? What is faith? Does it arise from intuition or from intellect; from an assent to authority – scriptural or institutional – or an assent to reason? The relative importance of the will or the intellect in approaching God was an enduring theme from the Church fathers through to the medieval scholastics. Broadly speaking, Saint Augustine had been pessimistic about the role of human reason, in line with Ephesians (2:8) 'You have been saved through faith, and this is not your own doing; it is the gift of God.'[6] Of course, these debates about the nature of salvation and predestination were at the centre of Reformation controversy. In responding to the Protestant imagery of mighty God and helpless man, the Catholic Church had to define its position with care. The Council of Trent had to steer between a Pelagian extreme (the belief that everything depends on human effort) and a Protestant one (the belief that everything depends on God).[7] Its first sitting (1545–6) announced in its decree of justification that faith was an unmerited act of grace, but that it also included some assent to revealed truths.[8] The First Ecclesiastical Council of Goa, addressing itself directly to the comportment of the eastern mission, asserted in 1567, '. . . no one can come to Faith unless he is drawn by the heavenly Father with gratuitous love and prevenient grace.'[9]

[5] Phelan 1970: 7–11; Boxer 1978: 99. See MacCormack 1985: 445, for how the voluntarist principle (associated with the role of the intellect) and the legitimacy of certain kinds of coercion (associated with the role of acquiescence) were uneasily combined in the decrees of the first council of Lima in 1551–2.

[6] McBrien 1994: 32; Pelikan 1984: 62. [7] McBrien 1984: 806.

[8] McBrien 1984: 36. [9] VP, II: 33. See also Boxer 1960–1: 79.

The Catholic Church indicated that there was a bare minimum of the Christian message that had to be imparted to make conversion legitimate. One Franciscan document from early sixteenth-century Mexico held that candidates must understand and accept the following: a single omnipotent God, eternal, all-good and all-knowing, the creator of everything; the holy virgin; the immortality of the soul; the demons and their perfidies.[10] However, the Catholic position, even after the Tridentine decrees, still allowed great latitude of interpretation. Indeed, the Catholic insistence on the immanence of God in creation could make any qualms about the candidate's precise mental state seem trivial. It was difficult to second-guess Providence; it could be channelled by the unlikeliest of vehicles. The Council of Trent would affirm that the sacraments (mass, absolution, baptism) all conferred grace as 'the visible form of an invisible grace' regardless of how much understanding or sincerity there was on the part of the priest or the recipient. It is easy then to see how missionaries could place so much trust in the transformative power of baptism, as if the ritual itself made one a Christian. Post-baptismal teaching did not make one Christian; rather it had the function of turning people from bad Christians into good ones. Conversion could be seen as a long, even a life-long, process involving a continual refinement of understanding and devotion.[11] If baptism alone could stop souls from going to hell this was surely justification enough for mass baptisms of hundreds or thousands at a time.[12]

What manner of official guidance was offered to missionaries navigating their way through such choppy conceptual waters? Forming a picture of distinctively Portuguese intellectual currents at this time is rather difficult. The only Portuguese text to deal explicitly and systematically with the question of methods of conversion in the manner of the Salamanca theorists in Spain is Manuel de Nóbrega's *Diálogo de Conversão do Gentió*, written after the author's first three or four years as Provincial of the Jesuit mission in Brazil in 1556–7.[13] But what is immediately clear is that there was often a dissonance between the idealistic guidelines and principles stressed by the authorities in Lisbon and the perspectives of the missionaries who were testing and exploiting the conceptual ambiguities on the ground. The views of the former can be found expressed in the proceedings of councils of *letrados* and churchmen that were called upon to lend theological and legal legitimacy to royal policy. While in Spain such *junta*s were famously discussing the nature and rights of the Amerindian subjects, one of the first such dilemmas to arise from Portuguese Asia was the problem of slaves who appeared to be using conversion as a way of gaining liberty.[14] King João referred the issue to a council who recommended that any slave who asked for baptism was first to be examined by priests for three or four days to see if he wanted to convert out of 'devotion and determined will'.[15]

[10] Ricard 1966: 84. [11] J. D. Ryan 1997.

[12] Master Diogo de Borba's reply to the charge of hasty conversion methods, *DI*, I: 13–14.

[13] Nóbrega had studied at the University of Salamanca, where Francisco de Vitoria and Domingo do Soto taught, before transferring to Coimbra: Beozzo 1993.

[14] On the Spanish *juntas*: Pagden 1986: 27–33.

[15] SR, II: 238: '. . . se com devoção e vontade determinada se querião tornar christãos'.

This process, which placed a strong importance on the sincerity of the convert, was to be undertaken 'even though it may be prejudicial to the merchants'.[16] In 1568, the First Council of Goa would explicitly recommend that missionaries should pay close attention to the motives of anyone who asked for baptism, denying all those who betrayed cynical purposes.[17]

In our time-frame, the most impressive example comes from the report by a quorum of the Church elite in Lisbon who had met to discuss the problems of the Indian mission in 1545.[18] The year before, King Caṇkili of Jaffna (1519–61) had ordered the murder of some 600 or so recently converted inhabitants of Mannar, and many urged the governor to mount an expedition to punish or kill the king.[19] However, a number of these learned prelates in Lisbon argued that the first duty of the Portuguese mission should be to preach to Caṇkili. If he repented and allowed conversion to commence then, 'the Portuguese should not make war against him, notwithstanding the fact that he had killed those Christians, since it does not seem as if the Faith has been explicitly explained to the said king, and how his sect was false.'[20] The report goes on to comment on the problem of whether the Portuguese should continue to uphold Bhuvanekabāhu despite his murder of Jugo. They conclude in his favour by denying that Jugo could have been a Christian in any real sense, something that only follows once the faith has been divulged by 'persons of exemplary lives and doctrine'. These comments by the highest-ranking clergy in Portugal demonstrate a consistent emphasis on the role of intellectual persuasion.

As the 1540s progressed one comes to hear more voices objecting to 'lax' approaches to conversion in India itself, partly because of the arrival of men with a higher standard of learning, but also as a response to the disillusionment that followed the conjuncture of baptism requests in the early years of the decade. Diego Bermúdez, who was the first Vicar-General of the Dominican province of India, was one of the most perceptive and intransigent observers. Like Bartolomé de Las Casas, his Dominican counterpart in Spanish America, Bermúdez refused to accept the alliance of imperial and spiritual interests. For Las Casas this alliance fed off territorial conquest. For Bermúdez, labouring in the *Estado da Índia*, it was most apparent in the game of diplomatic conversions. By the time Bermúdez arrived in India, it was clear that this is what the appeals by the princes from Kandy and the Maldives amounted to: 'all foolishness and filth' as he put it.[21]

Turning now to our band of missionaries coming to Sri Lanka in 1543, can we see anything in their traditions of reformed Franciscanism that would tend to emphasize one kind of approach? One can perceive a certain emphasis on the

16 SR, II: 240. 17 VP, II: 37.

18 VP: 125–7; SV: 261–6 (full version). They included the Augustinian Bishop of Coimbra, João Soares, the Dominican bishop of São Tomé, Bernado da Cruz, and the Provincial of the Franciscans.

19 See VP: 50, 53–4, and above, p. 104.

20 SV: 263–4. At this level too there was disagreement, for some argued that it was legitimate to overthrow Caṇkili.

21 VP: 281–4.

relative unimportance of the cognitive aspects of religious life in favour of the implicit knowledge of God shown by ordinary people.[22] This is apparent, for example, in the attitudes of the Franciscan mission to New Spain in 1524. For our purposes, it is important that this mission was drawn from the province of San Gabriel, the Spanish sister to the Portuguese province of Piedade, which was another arm of the movement initiated by Juan de Guadalupe. The leader of the mission, Martín de Valencia, had even spent a few years in the Chapter-house of Piedade in Vila Viçosa in Portugal.[23] This emphasizes a point that seems to be under-appreciated in the existing scholarship, that there was extensive exchange between Spanish and Portuguese mendicant reform movements, which naturally indicates shared ideas and values.[24] The friars of San Gabriel were generally willing to accept the passionate desire to become Christian evident among many of the native Americans at face value and had few qualms about conducting mass baptisms.[25]

It is certainly true that Vila do Conde's mission did not generally place great emphasis on pre-baptismal instruction. Indeed Bhuvanekabāhu himself complained sharply about this and requested that they make a candidate wait for at least nine days before performing a baptism![26] However, what strikes one about our mission is not so much a common understanding of conversion as the lack of one. This is revealed through a case-study of the King of Kandy's fitful dalliance with Christianity, as perceived by two friars, António Padrão in the 'strict' corner and Simão de Coimbra in the 'cynical' one. Padrão was more senior: he had been sent to India in 1528 as a commissary, returning to Portugal in 1531, and it is probable that he was then sent out to Sri Lanka as part of the original Franciscan mission in 1543.[27] Perhaps even more than João de Vila do Conde, Padrão was given to severe chastisement as a method of evangelism.[28] He was then chosen as the missionary accompaniment to André de Sousa's expedition to Kandy in 1546, an appointment destined to end in unhappiness, for Padrão's standards were never likely to be met in the highlands of Sri Lanka. Arriving in Kandy, Padrão discovered that the king had already been secretly baptized by Francisco de Monteprandone a month or so before.[29] Padrão quickly concluded that it was all a sham, presenting the king as a willing tool of the designs of the secular adventurer Nuno Álvares Pereira.[30] For António Padrão this made the expedition redundant, or, worse, a farce.

When André de Sousa and Padrão reached Sri Lanka they were joined by another friar, Simão de Coimbra, whose subsequent reports of the situation were entirely at odds with Padrão's. They may have travelled upcountry together but neither friar mentions the other in his reports. It seems that their theological differences

[22] BA 47-VIII-5, 47–63. [23] Monforte 1751: 287.

[24] The *piedosos* or *capuchos* are paradigmatic in this regard, constantly moving between the Alentejo and Estremadura, see Strathern 2004: 855–64.

[25] As in the writings of Toribio de Benavente. Martín de Valencia apparently baptized 16,000 souls in just two towns: Monforte 1751: 302; Clendinnen 1987; Brading 1991: 102–10.

[26] VP: 95. Jesuits and various Church fathers thought likewise: *DI*, I: 13–14.

[27] As VP: 37, n. 1 argues. [28] See VP: 66–7. [29] VP: 171. [30] VP: 187.

caused ruptures on the ground that the friars refrained from openly mentioning in their correspondence.[31] For Simão de Coimbra was unrelentingly positive about the affair, presenting the King of Kandy as a genuine candidate for baptism and a wonderful opportunity for the mission and the *Estado*. He also enthusiastically pressed the case of the king's son and heir and of other Lankan rulers who had tendered requests.

How could these two Franciscans have arrived at such different conclusions? Coimbra employs the language of sincerity readily enough, commenting of the crown prince that he is 'as much a Christian in heart and mind, as any other who received it'.[32] However, Coimbra was surely fully aware of all the murky secular currents swirling around at the bottom of this affair. The document supposedly by the King of Kandy that he transcribes in his letter is very clearly the work of Nuno Álvares Pereira, with whom the friar had formed a peculiar understanding.[33] Whence this disingenuousness? A simple answer is that his own personal glory was tied up with the expedition. Who would want to ruin the marvellous news of a royal baptism? This was a powerful reason for the distortion of the facts on the ground.[34] But there is more to it than that. Underlying Coimbra's approach is a particular conception of mission policy. Referring to the conversions that would follow a visit to the island by the Governor, he says, 'Let not Your Highness think that it would not be good if this was done by force, for we do not expect anything from these first Christians who are the parents and are old: rather we look to their children and in those who will come afterwards.'[35] Via this argument, the state of mind of the 'convert' himself is deemed more or less irrelevant. This first generation will be spiritual waste, so to speak, Christian by virtue of baptism perhaps, but at the same time not really Christian at all. One must look to their children and grandchildren.

Coimbra was not making a novel argument. It had already been articulated by the Apostolic Commissary to the East in 1522.[36] It would also form the grand conclusion of the Jesuit Manuel de Nóbrega's work on the Brazil mission written in 1556–7, the only Portuguese theoretical statement on conversion surviving from this early period. Having been severely disillusioned as to the convertibility of the Amerindians, Nóbrega argued that they would have to be forced into Christianity. Naturally this would result in an empty and hypocritical travesty of faith, but this would be a price worth paying for a true faith among subsequent generations.[37] Therefore we see, not for the first time, an ideological tendency associated with the Jesuits and Counter-Reformation foreshadowed in the Franciscan experience. All this drew strength from a general belief that Catholicism was best inculcated from childhood, which helps to explain the importance placed on the establishment of

[31] But Vila do Conde refers to them in VP: 190. [32] VP: 209–10.

[33] Coimbra admits that 'the king does nothing except as he [Pereira] tells him', VP: 213, and see 132.

[34] As other missionaries realized: VP: 283; Correia-Afonso 1969: 16.

[35] SV: 427 (VP: 207). [36] Boxer 1978: 97.

[37] Beozzo 1993: 583–7. See too Thomaz 1993: 122. According to Botelho, by 1552 many friars were advocating the use of forced conversions in India: SR, V: 108.

schools. According to Paulo de Trindade it was in fact royal policy to focus on the children.[38] Certainly in Kōṭṭe we hear of children learning the doctrine and officiating at services by 1546.[39] While men like Bermúdez were enraged by the disappointments of the 1540s, other clergymen wearily acquiesced to the Coimbra style of argument.[40]

And this meant that they were able to lubricate the functioning of 'theological diplomacy', to join in the games set up by secular contact-men. In the first instance it was such secular types who represented the meaning of conversion to the indigenous kings. Sometimes the most visible cleavage of mentality was not between Portuguese and Sinhalese, but between the more or less theologically high-minded Portuguese. Neither of the adventurers, André de Sousa and Nuno Álvares Pereira, express concern over theological issues in their letters, feeling little compulsion to justify the pressured baptism of five Kandyan *mudaliyārs*, for example.[41] The Viceroy Afonso de Noronha (1551–4) seems to have equated conversion with pacification.[42] By contrast, another viceroy, and a more learned one, João de Castro, could come close to contradicting the practice of mission and even its principle: the conversion of Bhuvanekabāhu was 'the work of God, which will come when it serves him, and not by the force and the importunate urging of friars. . . .'[43]

If in the minds of irritated secular officials the idea of Providence could become a justification for inaction, for our *piedosos* it was an inspiration for evangelical fervour and an invitation to see the divine hand in the most unpromising situations. The gust of hope on which João de Vila do Conde and his men sailed into Sri Lanka probably derived from the obvious providential omens surrounding the embassy of 1543. After long months at sea thinking of the awaiting glory it must have seemed the cruellest of blows to discover that Bhuvanekabāhu had no intention of converting. The actions of both Vila do Conde and António Padrão are explicable in this way: their anger and frustration when Bhuvanekabāhu refused to play his role in the providential drama, their subsequent chiding which did so much damage to relations between the Portuguese and Kōṭṭe, and, above all, their swift shift of attention to the King of Kandy and the other requesters of baptism. From our perspective, their ability to summon up optimism about the Kandyan appeal can seem surprising. Did Padrão really think that the King of Kandy would be waiting there with the light of revelation shining through his eyes? Did he expect that God would find his agent in a man such as André de Sousa?

If the Holy Spirit was abroad, why not? Millenarianism had flourished in the Franciscan order since its inception.[44] The principal 'spiritual' Franciscans at King Manuel's court had been avid proponents of Joachimist prophecy. Such beliefs are clearly apparent in the statement given by the Minister-General to the Twelve Friars setting out on their mission to Mexico, which proclaimed that they were

[38] Trindade, I: 61; compare Clendinnen 1982. [39] VP: 193, 256: at least 3 schools by 1549.
[40] Comments of the Franciscan Custodian, João Noe, in 1551: see VP: 311.
[41] VP: 153. [42] VP: 269. [43] SV: 411 (VP: 192, 195).
[44] Muldoon 1979: 36–7. Subrahmanyam 1997: 747–50, 2005a: 133

making the last preaching of their gospel on the eve of the end of the world.[45] Although with the accession of King João III, millenarian visions ceased to animate Portuguese imperial policy in the same way, they remained influential among pan-Iberian Reformed Franciscanism. One wonders if the rigorous life of penitence followed by the *piedosos* would have given further encouragement to this kind of interpretation: mortification and spiritual exercise being technologies – much like certain Buddhist methods of meditation – designed to lift one's perception from the mundane.[46]

But such visions can crumble at the touch of reality. For a number of years, Vila do Conde asked for permission to give up and return to Portugal.[47] Much of his career in Sri Lanka was a rather sad oscillation between hope and despair. His approach to conversion was correspondingly fluctuating. At times he displayed an aversion to cynical motivations and a passion for instruction.[48] At others, he acquiesced to obviously political bargains.[49] As for his part in the 1543 disputation, it was its theatricality and the frisson of martyrdom that appealed to the friar.[50]

Civility

We have seen that as subjects became Christian they could draw Portuguese jurisdiction in behind them; equally, Portugueseness was somehow drawn into their identity. This was most clearly symbolized by the taking of a Portuguese name at the point of baptism and in the adoption of Portuguese apparel. For many Catholic clergy today this was one of the most regrettable features of the Portuguese mission, undermining any attempt to create a truly Sri Lankan Church. How did such conceptual linkages come about? It was widely assumed that Christian morality and dogma could be transmitted most efficiently when a certain minimum of civil society was in place. In King Duarte of Portugal's (1433–8) letter to Pope Eugenius in 1436 we hear perhaps for the first time the argument that the conquest of a non-European land was necessary so that its locals could be brought up to the level of civilization necessary to receive the gospel.[51] Over a century later in Brazil Manuel de Nóbrega despaired of converting Amerindians who, lacking any form of kingship and therefore a sense of secular adoration, could not be expected to have a capacity for spiritual adoration either.[52] Once again it was in the New World, with its instantly exotic indigenous peoples, and its immediately compelling dilemmas

[45] Phelan 1970: 23. Motolinia argued that the Joachite 'Sixth Age' of the world was now well advanced and little time remained to convert the Indians before the Last Judgement. See Brading 1991: 103–9, 126.

[46] Certainly the lives of the influential *piedosos* Francisco de Gatha and Martín de Valencia suggest this: Lisboa (*Crónicas*) 2001, III: 255. On Valencia's prophetic visions of vast missionary success: Monforte 1751: 299–300.

[47] VP: 244–6. [48] VP: 228. Also see his comments in SV: 451.

[49] As regards a ruler on the Fishery Coast, in 1547 (SV: 455–9), or the Raja of Tanor (SR, IV: 568).

[50] Gonzaga in VP: 36–47. For more on the debate see Strathern 1998, and unpublished.

[51] Muldoon 1979: 121–9.

[52] One of the interlocutors argues thus in Nóbrega's *Diálogo*: see Beozzo 1993: 576, and Sturm 1985.

of moral and legal responsibility, that such issues were thrown into starkest relief. The *encomienda* system employed by the Spanish to settle the indigenous there embodied the principle of 'enforced acculturation'.[53]

But the situation was quite different in the East. It would be wrong to assume that the Sinhalese were perceived as barbarous or even ontologically problematic in the manner of some of the New World peoples. In the surviving Portuguese correspondence from sixteenth-century Sri Lanka, civility does not appear as a critical norm in shaping assessments of and policies towards the locals. To be sure, our sources rarely stretch to ethnological or theoretical enquiries, but it is also clear that there were few areas of life in which the Sinhalese were obviously uncivilized by European norms. Most significantly, the society of the south-western seaboard of Sri Lanka partook of the cosmopolitan world of seaborne commerce and communication. Whatever ambiguities and curiosities of state power might reveal themselves to the observant European, the natural stratification of society, the machinery of government, and the establishment of literacy were all readily apparent.[54] The island's material culture was in many ways highly impressive. Queirós would summarize its people as 'noble, cultured and by no means barbarous'.[55]

Indeed one mark of civility was religion itself, and the Portuguese certainly recognized that they were encountering a religious life that was reasonably sophisticated – and indeed analogous to Christianity – in its outward or institutional forms.[56] Far from requiring some programme of mental or cultural cultivation, some drawing out of inhibited capacities, there was a feeling that the inhabitants of the island were ripe for conversion.[57] This did not make them any the less heathen; on the contrary, later theorists would consider the sophistication of heathen cults an index of satanic intervention.[58] Nevertheless, if Sri Lanka was relatively civilized, why couldn't converts simply purge their lives of such diabolical elements while retaining the acceptable, even admirable, forms of secular life? Why did they have to live in new communities huddled against the walls of Portuguese settlements?

Both in the East and in the New World, missionaries were assuming and developing a holistic appreciation of such matters, a recognition that religious ideas and practices did not constitute a separate realm from other aspects of society but were an intrinsic element of a whole way of life. Conversion was seen to be most successful as a process of de-socialization and re-socialization that required the daily company of other Christians.[59] In one sense this proceeds from the monotheistic conception of religious adherence as involving a total transformation of the self, a creation of a new identity, and what else but European trappings could be used as the visible markers and proclamations of that identity? Yet this is also a practical response to the predicaments of the mission field. Very early on we find some Portuguese noticing that those converts who returned to their old communities soon lost their Christian identity. Hence King João III was advised in the

[53] Pagden 1986: 34–7. [54] On these criteria see Pagden 1986: 77, 130, 163. [55] Queyroz: 298.
[56] Strathern 2002: ch. 6.3. [57] VP: 13, 286. [58] Pagden 1986: 178. [59] SR, I: 226, 353.

late 1540s that 'after they become Christians, they should have no dealings, nor live with their gentile relatives lest they should go back to what they were' – an argument particularly germane to South Asia.[60] If the missionaries were, at this stage, prone to rule out any attempt to accommodate their new theological message to old ways of life, it was partly because it seemed that indigenous society had already deemed it impossible.[61]

Whatever the relative civility of Sri Lanka, it did not follow then that it was reasonable to expect Christians to thrive within its particular political, legal and social structures. European Christendom was held to have realized and embodied the principles of natural law most perfectly. And there were at least two – related – issues through which Sinhalese society was vulnerable to accusations of barbarity: the 'absolutist' conduct of its monarch; and the perceived injustice of its norms regarding property and inheritance. In truth, the first of these was not a common characterization of Bhuvanekabāhu, whose power often seemed so fragmentary and fragile. But if we take another look at the letter giving voice to the settlers' complaints of 1547, we find that it seeks to insinuate the barbarity of Bhuvanekabāhu by invoking images of tyranny.[62] Tyranny is rulership defined by the barbarian qualities of lawlessness and unrestrained avarice.[63] The settlers describe the king as a foe of true religion; as one who perverts the principles of rational communication; and as one given to sodomy, a powerful marker of primitivism.[64]

> The sin of sodomy is so prevalent in this kingdom of Cota that it makes us very afraid to live here. And if one of the principal men of the kingdom is questioned about if they are not ashamed to do a thing so ugly and dirty, to this they respond that they do everything that they see their king doing, because that is the custom among them.[65]

These observations may carry a faint echo of more learned understandings of the nature of barbarian society: its subjects are not free to perceive how such practices contravene natural law; their customarily slavish imitation of their ruler ensures that their moral reasoning is obscured by his personal depravity. At any rate, the thrust of their appeal to the viceroy was: we are a small island of godliness adrift in a terrifying sea of barbarity, 'tyrannized by this heathen king'.[66] This little propaganda offensive may have had some impact in the short term – for it was at about this time that Goa's opinion towards Bhuvanekabāhu took a serious fall – but

[60] VP: 254, and 421.

[61] Later in the century, the separation of the religious from the social/cultural formed the foundation of Nobili-style accommodationism.

[62] In Sri Lanka, this was an unusual ploy at this time, but contemporary Jesuits in the Congo came to similar conclusions about the ManiCongo (king), as a symbol for all that was licentious or chaotic among his subjects: Almeida 2004: 865–88. Again, it is the sexual and marital practices which are most shocking and which seem to stimulate a nascent political stereotype akin to the 'Oriental Despotism *avant la lettre*' that Subrahmanyam 2005b: 14, sees animating Portuguese observations of the Indian Sultanates at this time.

[63] And only barbarians, being servile by nature and lacking any form of social contract with their rulers, could be expected to put up with it: Pagden 1986: 19, 131, 166.

[64] Pagden 1986: 177.

[65] SV: 495 (VP: 239) and Gonzaga's horror in VP: 38.

[66] SV: 496.

in the long term it failed to adhere to its target. It was not the overweening or ruthless aspects to his rule that would survive into posterity, but an inverse quality, equally redolent of barbarity: his effete incapacity to rule others.

The more significant issue of civility for the Portuguese, for it arose not simply as a momentarily useful device for a few malcontents but as a more deeply and widely felt sense of puzzlement and disgust, was the different nexus of norms governing property, succession and inheritance in indigenous society. After all, the origins of civil society were located in the family.[67] This is why our missionaries supported so vigorously the claims of converts who were clearly motivated by temporal advantages, and which obviously undermined indigenous law. Such incentives were also a part of official missionary policy in these years, intended to counteract the stubborn temporal facts militating against proselytization outside the territorial conquests of the Portuguese empire.[68] Beyond the deliberate machinations of heathen rulers, the missionaries saw themselves as struggling against the implacable weight of tradition.

Besides, indigenous law was reprehensible. The absence of legally protected private property rights would become one of the defining features of the image of 'oriental despotism' constructed by many European travellers and thinkers from the late sixteenth century onwards.[69] What our consideration of the sources in Chapter Five revealed is how early and immediately European observers were struck by the preoponderance of royal authority over land. In the first analytical report on Sri Lanka, by Caração in 1522, the author seems to assert that the population would rise up against the king at the first provocation. This is assumed as the natural result of a system in which the king receives the properties of the dead.[70] In Gonzaga's account of the 1543 exchanges, the friars find the local property 'laws' to be 'directly against all justice and every law of nations'.[71] They did not offend Christian morality *per se*, but contradicted a fundamental natural law enshrined in mainstream European legal theory: that the king may not lay claim to absolute dominion over the private property of his subjects.

By violating this principle Bhuvanekabāhu could easily be represented as a tyrant by definition, and Christians could not be expected to put up with such tyranny. Moreover, an important strand within canon law stated that infidels should not have to either, and that violations of natural law by a heathen ruler allowed the authorization of his deposition by Christian forces.[72] As it happened, the *letrados* in Lisbon did not come to this radical conclusion, but rather recognized the legitimate dominion of Bhuvanekabāhu and the integrity of the Sinhalese right of succession.[73] Yet all this meant that the missionaries were liable to interpret the

[67] See, for example, Afonso de Albuquerque's remarks on Malabar descent and succession practices in 1514, which have much in common with Spanish jurists' analyses of Amerindian barbarism ('they did not have letters nor principles nor law'), SR, I: 226–9.

[68] VP: 342; SV: 235; SR, III: 532–3, and António do Porto in 1548 in SR, IV: 61–2, arguing that alms would merely compensate for the shame and destitution that resulted from conversion.

[69] Rubiés 2005. [70] Caração: 167. [71] VP: 40.

[72] See Muldoon 1979: 8–10. [73] VP: 125–7.

grasping behaviour of converts as the expression of natural instinct and a right they held as Christians. The friars were pushing here for the application of the principle of the 'personality of law': if Christians were not to be officially placed under the Portuguese jurisdiction then at least their different status should be recognized by indigenous law.[74] In their eyes, consequent blurring of the distinction between mission fields within and without Portuguese control was all to the good.

If the feature of some Amerindian societies that was so perplexing for Europeans was their disregard for personal property, in Malabar and Sri Lanka it was the fact that property could not be passed on to one's offspring, or only under peculiar limitations or regulations, which disturbed European onlookers. From the assumed indivisibility of worldly and spiritual rectitude would follow the Lusitanization of converts and the erosion of native sovereignty.

What of that image of the 'oriental despot' that was just beginning to be assembled? Despotism is what happens when tyrannical rule becomes a legal system of government.[75] Rājasiṃha I (1581–93) and Vimaladharmasūriya I (1591–1604) may be portrayed as tyrants but this is quite different: a violation of indigenous or universal norms of kingship such as proper succession and ethical governance. In the same decade that Queirós completed his *Conquista*, John Locke (1632–1704) was drawing on Robert Knox's account of Kandy as an example of the perils of 'absolute monarchy'.[76] However, in the sixteenth and early seventeenth century, Sinhalese kingship would have resisted assimilation to a proto-theory of oriental despotism in at least one way. Its people were blatantly unservile – they left their mark as resisters of oppressive government or military conquest, not slaves to them. And we shall see that Rājasiṃha's reputation probably owed much to an indigenous sentiment premised upon discourses that were – in a deeply ironic subversion of later Western stereotypes – more insistent on cosmic monarchical responsibility and moral contractualism than Christendom ever was.

[74] Hence Gonzaga (VP: 41) has it that the friars argue for the decrees so that 'your people may have the same law as the Portuguese and all the other Christians'.

[75] The Jesuit Giovanni Botero (*c.* 1544–1617) helped advance that image of Eastern polities in the 1590s: Rubiés 2005.

[76] Locke 1964: 92; Rubiés 2005: 125.

7

The Buddhism of the Sinhalese

Having investigated the institutional and intellectual background of the Christian missionaries, what can we say about the religious world they encountered? From a traditionalist viewpoint, Sri Lanka has simply been Buddhist since the early Anurādhapura kings converted in the third century BC. It is hardly in doubt that Buddhism had achieved a certain religious hegemony on the island by early in the first millennium AD; that Sri Lankan rulers quickly became great patrons of Buddhist monastic orders, learning and art. But this leaves a lot of room for historicist critiques to get to work, posing questions about what it meant to be 'Buddhist' before the modern era, and especially the myriad ways in which 'doctrinal' Theravāda Buddhism was combined with a great range of other beliefs and practices that evolved on the island, sometimes in response to the so-called Mahāyāna Buddhist traditions or, more often, produced in creative response to the varied religiosities of South India.[1]

This religious openness is a result of the basic metaphysics of Buddhist thought. To return to the terminology of the Axial Age, if all such traditions share an appreciation of the superiority and otherness of the transcendent, what is striking and unique about Buddhist thought is that the transcendent is so much more rarefied, abstract and impeccably ineffable than in Christian theology. Theravāda Buddhism does of course have a soteriological goal. It is simply that nirvana (or in pāli *nibbāna*) is never defined except in negative terms, as liberation from the world of suffering. Liberation can only be achieved through the understanding and practice of Buddha's teachings, the *dhamma*. This denotes a supramundane orientation (*lōkōttara*). Everything else is mundane (*laukika*).[2] What Western observers might assume to be the essence of religion, the world of 'supernatural' beings and forces, is subsumed into the mundane. Since deities do not have the power to effect liberation, indeed are considered to be still in need of liberation themselves, they can only be appealed to for immediate or mundane ends and so are, in that sense, *laukika*. While the Sinhala Buddhist pantheon absorbed all manner of deities, the metaphysical significance of those gods was therefore transformed and degraded

[1] For a sense of variety see Gombrich 1988; F. Reynolds 1987; Hallisey 1988.

[2] This distinction is particularly articulated in Holt 1991: 19–26, who nevertheless dislikes the language of this- and other-worldliness, which I retain for its emphasis on soteriological commonalities.

and they were associated with new stories and attributes. The subordination of these gods to the Buddhist *dhamma* is symbolically expressed by the notion that they had received warrants from the *dēvati dēva*, the 'god above the gods', Buddha himself.

These categories are not entirely stable or all-determinative: they have an exceedingly complex interplay in philosophical texts and the devotional practices of everyday life. Indeed, Holt argues that the most successful and long-lived deities in Sinhalese Buddhism were those that did manage to acquire some sort of *lōkōttara* relevance. Not that they came to acquire salvational powers *per se*, but they were somehow associated with the myths and symbols of the soteriological project. This might mean that they were conceived of as a *bodhisattva*, an incarnation of a past or future Buddha, or that they were held to function as protectors of the *sāsana* (Buddhist 'religion').

This model of assimilation, as described by Holt and others, succeeds in mediating between traditionalist and historicist approaches to Sinhala Buddhism, which often appears to be at once conservative and mutable, defensive and tolerant. Naturally, it does not sum up all the various forms of religious interaction that would have occurred over centuries of migration and contact with other peoples.[3] Sometimes new religious forms were attacked outright and sometimes they retained an integrity that would tug Sinhalese religiosity in new directions.

The Hinduization of Sri Lanka and the institutional health of Buddhism in the mid sixteenth century

In the introduction we referred hurriedly to the different ways that monotheistic and Indic traditions bridged over the chasm they envisaged between the transcendent and the mundane. In institutional terms the crucial difference was this: in Buddhism, the *saṃgha* or monastic community are both priests and monks, which is to say, both the guardians or interpreters of the transcendent as well as exemplary embodiments of it. In Christianity, on the other hand, the monastic function was separated from the secular structure of the Church. Relatively free from the duty to represent otherworldly perfection in itself, the Church could thereby develop as a more this-worldly nexus of power independent from the state. By contrast, the *saṃgha* would remain much more dependent on its 'gift-giving' relationship with monarchs.[4]

Certainly by our period, the *saṃgha* was entrenched in Sinhalese society, connected to the centres of state power through extensive royal patronage and to local village life through the provision of educational and spiritual services to the lay community, for which it received alms and status in return. In common with all such traditions of 'religious virtuosi', its history was characterized by a constant slipping away from otherworldly orientations, periodically reversed by

[3] See B. Smith 1987: 27; Stewart 1999: 57; Walters 1995.
[4] Eisenstadt 1986: 16, and Silber 1995: 123–4.

movements of reform. Ilangasinha's valuable study of *Buddhism in Medieval Sri Lanka* argues that the *saṃgha* entered into a state of deepening decline from the late fifteenth to the late sixteenth century.[5] He sees this as largely due to a deteriorating relationship with the state, as monarchs failed to bestow adequate patronage on the *saṃgha* or regulate it, being themselves beset by political instability and warfare. After the exceptionally long and munificent reign of Parākramabāhu VI (r. 1411–67), Jaffna and Kandy seceded and rulers were routinely faced with rebellions and struggles for succession. With Bhuvanekabāhu's reign, the intervention of the Portuguese brought the internecine conflict to a higher pitch, and after his death the island was plunged into semi-permanent warfare. Ilangasinha also avers that the increasing influence of Brahmans and South Indian culture at the Kōṭṭe court was 'Hinduizing' the upper strata to the extent that the status of Buddhism suffered as a result. We shall address this last point first.

Kōṭṭe is sometimes described as subject to a cumulative process of 'Hinduization'.[6] The great Hindu empire of Vijayanagar enforced its overlordship over Sri Lanka with periodic invasions in the fourteenth and fifteenth centuries until the last one was effectively repulsed by Parākramabāhu VI in 1432.[7] Yet the atmosphere at the court of Parākramabāhu VI was highly cosmopolitan and held Tamil culture in great esteem. An exceptionally eclectic approach to religious traditions is revealed in the flourishing poetry of the era, the *Kōkila Sandēsa*, or the *Oruvula Sandēsa*, for example, or the extremely diverse interests and devotional practices of its leading literary figure and monastic *thēra*, Srī Rāhula of Toṭagamuva.[8] There had long been very close links between Sinhalese and South Indian royal families.[9]

Parākramabāhu was succeeded by Prince Sapumal, probably Malayāli by birth, who had been regent of Jaffna.[10] When he ascended to the throne as Bhuvanekabāhu VI (1469–77), Srī Rāhula lost his pre-eminence and Vīdāgama Maitreya was appointed as *rājaguru* (royal adviser). In this capacity he made a number of polemical attacks on Brahmanic influences filtering into popular religion – but he would be the last *bhikkhu rājaguru*.[11] At the same time, Bhuvanekabāhu continued to maintain lively contacts with the mainland, bringing over large numbers of immigrants and endowing them with lands and titles. Malayāli and Tamil migrants could take up elite positions as in the northern *vanniyār* region ruling over Sinhalese cultivators; Karāvas were given land in return for military service.[12] The honorific *baṇḍāra*, sported by many of the Sinhalese protagonists of this book, probably derives from immigrant Tamil *pantārams*, officiants at Saivite temples.[13] Vijayabāhu VI

5 Ilangasinha 1992: 123–8. C. R. de Silva 1998, 1995: 31–6, takes a more positive viewpoint.

6 Ilangasinha 1992: 218–19; Paranavitana 1959–60: 767; Pathmanathan 1982: 54. See discussion in Holt 2004: 32–61.

7 See above, p. 65.

8 C. H. B. Reynolds 1970: 283–317; Ilangasinha 1992: 149, on the *Oruvula Sandēśa*, which shows that the king had two Vaisnava Brahmans as his chief *purōhitas*.

9 Raghavan 1961: 2; Somaratna 1991: 20.

10 Holt 1991: 116, and see Couto: 69.

11 Ilangasinha 1992: 124.

12 D. De Silva 1996; Roberts 2001: 83.

13 Dewaraja 1988: 55. Also on Indian and Brahmanical immigration, Tambiah 1992: 144–54; Gunawardana 1990: 64.

(1513–21) had a South Indian captain of his bodyguard and chamberlain, and two Vaisnava Brahmans as *purōhitas* or 'chaplains'.[14] From very early on Sinhalese kings had cultivated a ceremonial system that was drawn from Brahmanical texts and officiated by Brahmans.[15] Temples and shrines sprung up to service these high-ranking Hindus.

In Chapter One we referred to evidence suggesting that Bhuvanekabāhu VII continued to encourage these migrations.[16] Indeed, it seems that an important development of the Gajabāhu myth occurred in the mid sixteenth century in order to offer an explanation or charter for significant numbers of Karāva settlers.[17] This trend is given independent corroboration by the Portuguese sources' insistence on the Kōṭṭe king's reliance on Indian mercenaries.[18] Therefore, there were probably large numbers of South Indians settled in the south-west, particularly clustered around and servicing the Kōṭṭe court, who were not yet fully assimilated into a Sinhalese or Buddhist culture. The continuing presence of this prominent Hindu community may help to account for a peculiar feature of Fernão de Queirós' ethnological overview of Sri Lanka, namely its fluctuating ambiguity as to whether the island was really part of 'Hindustan', or a distinct cultural unit.[19]

All the Sinhalese kingdoms appear to have relied on Brahmans as ambassadors in the sixteenth century, which, of course, includes Bhuvanekabāhu's powerful *purōhita*, Śrī Rāmaraksa Paṇḍita, who represented the king himself in the embassy to Lisbon.[20] He enjoyed the close advisory role that would have been discharged by a Buddhist *rājaguru* in previous eras. A Jesuit would later refer to him as 'a person very learned among these gentiles with regard to their beliefs of the *pagodes*'. A Brahman is thus presented as a religious authority for the Sinhalese.[21] When our Portuguese sources do describe Sinhalese holy men they always refer to *brahmanas* (Brahmans) or *jogues* (yogis) as well as *changatares* (*saṃghatthēras*).[22] It should not surprise us then to learn that Tamil was approaching the status of an official court language. Bhuvanekabāhu's letters to the Portuguese were naturally

[14] Pathmanathan 1982: 47.

[15] Paranavitana 1959–60: 768, Ariyapala 1968: 57, 98, 182; Pillay 1963: 141; Raghavan 1964: 53.

[16] Nevill: Or. 6606(77, III) *Kaňdurē Baṇḍāravaliya* and Or. 6606(50) *Kīravälle Rajamula*. The latter has portions allegedly recorded in 1501, 1527 and later about the Kīravälle family who held office under the Sītāvaka and Kandy kings. The family tree has a 'Kaňdurē Baṇḍāra' as a founding figure type but (contrary to Somaratna 1991: 27) it does not seem to tally with details in the *Kaňdurē Baṇḍāravaliya*. K. D. Somadasa's notes to the Nevill catalogue (p. 95) tell us that the Kaňdurē Baṇḍāra of the Kīravälle family was the minister who was killed in 1521. Also on this family see *Rājāvaliya*: 68–71; Or. 6606(132) *Kaňdurē Baṇḍāragē Nīti-Pota: Kīravälle Rajamula* (2); Or. 6606(152) *Kaňdurē Baṇḍāragē*. These family oral traditions associating Bhuvanekabāhu VII with the arrival of South Indian nobility suggest that he may be the king 'Bhuveka' referred to in another such family oral tradition, the *Malala Katāva* (Or. 6606 (150.III)).

[17] Obeyesekere 1984: 264–374, points to this development first arising in the *Rājaratnākaraya*. See too D. De Silva 1996: 180.

[18] See above, p. 32. A later *tombo* recorded that in Mādampe, 5 out of 13 local chieftains had the name of Perumāl, see C. R. de Silva 1971: 26.

[19] Hinduism is as prominent as Buddhism in his survey. See above, p. 97, on caste.

[20] VP: 61 80, 86. [21] VP: 28.

[22] VP: 61, 324, 334–5; and Gonzaga's account taken from notes drawn up in the 1580s: 38.

composed with the aid of an interpreter and scribe. In order to authenticate them Bhuvanekabāhu wrote his signature in Sinhalese ('Svasti Srī'), but preceded it by a confirmation in Tamil (to the following effect, 'accept this statement as true since it has been written at my command').[23]

Yet do we need to see this high point of Brahmanical or South Indian influence as necessarily fatal for the institutional health of Buddhism or the weight of *bhikkhus* at court? The archaeological evidence tells us little: there were at least two monastic sites within the walls of Inner Kōṭṭe – Srī Rāhula's house close by the palace, and the dwelling of the Saṃgharāja Vanaratna – but we do not know their exact periods of occupation or use.[24] Our spartan textual evidence does offer some hints that the *saṃgha* maintained its political relevance.[25] The *Alakeśvarayuddhaya* informs us that Bhuvanekabāhu and his two brothers had taken refuge in a Buddhist temple before they overthrew their father in 1521.[26] It is Queirós once more who gives us the strongest evidence. This may partly reflect his polemical agenda in which Buddhism is presented as a force necessarily and implacably opposed to the spiritual and temporal designs of the Portuguese empire, but his sources are too rich to be discounted here. He alone tells us that Buddhist monks were used to broker peace between Bhuvanekabāhu and Māyādunnē in 1537, and that it was the eloquence of one senior monk named 'Budavançe' (Buddhavaṃsa) which persuaded the King of Kōṭṭe to accept Vīdiyē Baṇḍāra as his son-in-law.[27] However that may be, the notion that the forms of Hindu influence described above presented a profound threat to the *saṃgha* is hardly one that can be assumed *a priori*, and therefore seems unwarranted in the absence of a satisfactory historical record.[28] For all the religious diversity observed by our Jesuits, the *bhikkhus* are yet identified as their principal counterparts.[29]

It seems more straightforward to concede that the political instability following Parākramabāhu VI meant that the kings of Kōṭṭe were less able to act as guardians of the Theravāda monastic order. However, a historicist caution would alert us to the fact that this argument is uneasily close to the narrative logic of the *vaṃsas*, which aimed at emphasizing the interdependence of monarch and monk, a perspective from which the political and the religious histories of the island appear to be smoothly coterminous.[30] On the other hand, we have already indicated a societal logic behind this literary one, which is usefully emphasized by Ivana Silber's work comparing Theravāda and Catholic forms of monasticism. She argues that the *saṃgha*, unlike its Christian counterparts, lacked a truly hierarchical organizational

23 VP: 185, 186, 251–3, 260–2. In Parākramabāhu VI's time (1411–67) a Tamil form of calculating regnal dates was used: see Pathmanathan 1982: 55.

24 Map 1, nos. 7 and 11. Also in Outer Kōṭṭe a Buddha shrine, no. 15.

25 C. R. de Silva 1995: 34 and C. R. de Silva 1998: 196, make many of the same points.

26 *Alakeśvarayuddhaya*: 30; *Rājāvaliya*: 71–2.

27 Queyroz: 214, 221. The *Palkum̆bura Sannasa* maintains that Bhuvanekabāhu had a brother who was a *bhikkhu* and may have wielded a certain amount of influence at court: Lawrie 1896–8: 687.

28 Compare Lü Tai of Sukhotai (*c.* 1347–74), who combined a reformist's zeal for Sinhalese-style Theravādin kingship with 'an increased interest in all things Hindu, Andaya 1978: 10, 13.

29 VP: 334–5.

30 See Blackburn 2001: 6–9.

structure that could enforce its own regulations by wielding secular instruments of discipline, thereby ensuring that it remained dependent on the authority of the king to fulfil this role.[31] To Silber's analysis one could add that in Theravāda Buddhism the transcendent cannot function as an active force or godhead to be drawn upon as a source of mystical personal experience by monastic leaders. There could be no equivalent to the reform movements such as the *piedosos*, springing from the visions of Juan de Guadalupe.

With the arrival of the *piedosos* in Sri Lanka are we then witnessing a virtuoso institution revivified by a particularly monotheistic form of spiritual reform coming into contact with a counterpart that was sunk into a particularly Theravādin form of stagnation? The fact is that once again the evidence for royal patronage of the *saṃgha* post-Parākramabāhu VI is just too slender to elicit any such broad conclusions. The *Rājaratnākaraya* blandly commends them all but gives us no such details concerning the kings that followed up to and including Bhuvanekabāhu VII.[32] At least this might suggest that none of these kings had created a reputation for damaging Buddhism.

Other sources tell us that Bhuvanekabāhu VI extended considerable munificence towards the temple at Kälaṇiya, constructed a new casket for the Tooth Relic, and received an important deputation of monks from Burma in search of higher ordination.[33] Dharma Parākramabāhu IX (1489–1513) also funded a great restoration of the Kälaṇiya temple in 1508, while Vijayabāhu VI was responsible for restoring a *pirivena* attached to the Kappāgoḍa monastery in Kägalla district. However, this leaves the reign of Vīra Parākramabāhu VIII (1477–89) with no evidence at all.[34] It is not therefore a great shock to find that the evidence concerning Bhuvanekabāhu's patronage is equally insubstantial and questionable. All we have is an eighteenth-century *ola* referring to either Bhuvanekabāhu VI or VII as the founder of the Kadigamuva temple in Galaboḍa-pattuva according to which in the seventh year of his reign he brought over Buddhist monks from abroad to help repair the 'sixteen holy places'.[35]

Such patronage was but one facet of the king's role as guardian of the *saṃgha*; he was also required to provide leadership, to ensure that it maintained its organizational structure and standards of discipline. But how can one measure the 'health' of the *saṃgha* in this period? A basic measure is whether there were enough monks who were qualified to perform the *upasampadā*, the ceremony of higher ordination. In the eighteenth century, for example, *bhikkhus* disappeared from Sri Lanka altogether with only *sāmanēras* (unordained monks) and *gaṇinnānses* (novices or pseudo-monks) occupying the monasteries and hardly living a life in

[31] Apart from the essentially 'otherworldly' orientation of the *saṃgha*, Silber 1995: 202, suggests that this was principally because Theravāda societies lacked forceful examples of institutional formalization, legalization and centralization that monasticism could take as its model.

[32] *Rājaratnākaraya*: 47. Compare with *Cūḷavaṃsa*, II: 219–20.

[33] Ilangasinha 1992: 111–15; Upham 1833: 113; Bell 1904: 83; Walters 1996: 56–8.

[34] Save an association in popular tradition with the Galagama and Algama monasteries, see Ilangasinha 1992: 112.

[35] Bell 1904: 40–1; Mirando 1985: 25. Given that the next king mentioned is Vimaladharmasūriya (1591–1604), the ascription to Bhuvanekabāhu VII is plausible.

accordance with the ten precepts.[36] In Bhuvanekabāhu's time this was certainly not the case. The word used by our Portuguese sources to refer to Buddhist monks is *changuatar*, that is *saṃghatthēra*, or elder *bhikkhu*. Another measure would be evidence of flourishing centres of Buddhist learning and monastic leadership. Ilangasinha suggests that the Raja Mahāvihāraya, the 'King's Monastery' at Kōṭṭe, disappears from sight in Bhuvanekabāhu's reign, but this may well be the 'community of monks' that the *Rājāvaliya* tell us abandoned Kōṭṭe after Dharmapāla's conversion.[37] It is true that we hear very little of the two monastic groupings, the *vanavāsī* ('forest-dwellers') and *grāmavāsī* ('village-dwellers'), apart from a reference in the *Rājaratnākaraya*.[38]

Royal acts of purification are often taken as primary evidence for standards of discipline. But how should we interpret them? If we take Senāsammata Vikramabāhu of Kandy, for example, who purged the *saṃgha* of its more lax and disreputable elements according to the *Rājaratnākaraya*, does this indicate that the *saṃgha* was particularly corrupt in this period or simply that the king, as an upstart, was particularly desirous to establish his Buddhist credentials?[39] Similarly, we cannot assume that the absence of evidence for purifications, as in Bhuvanekabāhu's reign, indicates a certain lack of interest or a failure to arrest an inevitable decline.

In order to demonstrate how dangerous it is to interpret the trickling out of our Sinhalese evidence as the trickling out of the well-spring of Lankan Buddhism itself, we can turn to the tantalizing observations of our European sources. The high esteem accorded to Sinhalese monks, both domestically and abroad, is asserted in Gonzaga's account of the 1540s.[40] The Jesuit pair Morais and Dias who arrived on the island in 1551 did not remark on neglect or decay among the religious buildings of Kōṭṭe, but rather marvelled at their ubiquity and sumptuousness.[41] The two Jesuits were equally impressed by the disciplined life of these *bhikkhus* who lived apart from the people in secluded monasteries.[42] As Jesuits they had the highest appreciation of both spiritual dedication and hierarchical obedience:

36 *Gaṇinnānse* was originally simply a term of respect and it is difficult to know when it came to indicate unordained monks. Queyroz: 114 employs *changatare* (*saṃghatthēra*) and *ganez* (*gaṇinnānse*) interchangeably. Higher ordination must be carried out by at least five monks who have been fully ordained for at least ten years, Blackburn 2001: 51.

37 Ilangasinha 1992: 61–2, suggests that the influence of Catholic missionaries eroded its power in Bhuvanekabāhu's time. However, we saw in Chapter Five that the influence of the missionaries in the court at this time is highly questionable. See Map 1, no. 16 for the location of the *Raja Mahāvihāraya Pohoyagē* in Outer Kōṭṭe.

38 *Rājaratnākaraya*: 55. As for the institutions known as *muḷas*, the last known reference to them occurs within Bhuvanekabāhu's brother's name of Seneviratmuḷa *mahāsāmi*, in the *Palkum̆bura Sannasa*: Lawrie 1896–8: 687; Ilangasinha 1992: 74. Beyond issues of the *sannasa*'s authenticity, it is difficult to know what kind of enduring institutional presence that title signified at this time.

39 *Rājaratnākaraya*: 57/Upham 1833: 137; Ilangasinha 1992: 115, 127. See also Collins 1998: 69.

40 VP: 46, repeated by Trindade, III: 33. As noted in the Introduction, n. 62, Gonzaga's report derived from Gaspar de Lisboa's memorial. This in turn may have drawn upon notes by Vila do Conde.

41 VP: 324–5 (Morais), and 334 (Dias), refer to *pagodes*, i.e temples or shrines, as opposed to monastic buildings. However, it is likely that they are referring to Buddhist *vihāras*. C. R. de Silva's study (1998: 106) of Portuguese *tombos* has revealed evidence that a number of monastic institutions were maintaining very healthy finances late into the sixteenth century.

42 VP: 324.

> These [*saṃghatthēras*] are sustained by alms which they beg from door to door, and when they go begging they have not to speak to anybody. They attach great importance to the serenity of their countenance, and of their sense and dress, and from their deportment it seems they are very submissive to their prelate and very patient. They say that they carefully keep themselves chaste and they pointed one out to me who had been disrobed because he had been found with a woman. They take no food from midday onwards, but till midday they may eat as often as they like. They go with one shoulder uncovered, while all the rest of the body is covered. On the shoulder they wear a kind of stole made of many pieces of cloth. They go with face and head shaven.[43]

All of these points demonstrate the continuing predominance of the *vinaya* rules concerning diet, clothing, sexual relations and material possessions. We even have evidence of a disrobing. Equally important is Morais' description of a *bhikkhu* who seems to have been living an ascetic lifestyle. He is referred to as 'a well known *changatar* who resides here, who never leaves his dwelling, whom all obey and whom they hold as a holy man'. Later accumulative sources such as Queirós' *Conquista* generally confirm this picture, dwelling on the adherence to discipline in eating, meditation, discipline and poverty: 'and with this kind of life they consider themselves as saints.'[44] Lastly, we should also be wary of assuming that royal patronage and regulation of the *saṃgha* can stand as an absolute index of the general vitality of Buddhism. On a local level, the monasteries had struck deep roots into village life. Although the wars with Sītāvaka and Kandy would have made religious patronage often difficult, particularly in the 1540s, we shall argue that the real damage to institutional Buddhism was surely done with the upheavals and persecutions that followed Bhuvanekabāhu's death in 1551.[45]

Religiosity

Interpretations of the Buddhist–Catholic encounter in Sri Lanka have tended to acknowledge that, in terms of religious *practice*, the two religions shared much common ground, including the making of vows or appeals to intercessory figures, the veneration of relics and images, ritual offerings, ceremonial processions and pilgrimages.[46] This may have played a role in facilitating the Christianization of the 'loyal' aristocracy of Kōṭṭe later in the century. But the most crucial 'conversion moments' in the earlier period concerned elites in regions where there was as yet no real Catholic ritual life to be observed. How then would Christian *ideas* have been received? To approach this we need to get a purchase on the interior

[43] SV: 649 (VP: 335).

[44] Queyroz: 115. This jars with his later assertion (140) that Sinhalese monks contrasted badly with their Japanese counterparts, a typical incoherence resulting from his collage of different sources. Furthermore, having previously commented on the stubbornness of Theravāda peoples in refusing to convert, Queirós had an interest in presenting the Sinhalese monks as being less of an obstacle. Compare Miranda: 183.

[45] See Chapter Nine.

[46] Don Peter 1978: 98–112; Malalgoda 1976: 33. See, however, Holt 1996: 5, n. 5, for a critique of the British-era trope associating Catholic and Buddhist ritualism.

religious life of the sixteenth-century Sinhalese while remaining humble in the face of scholarly warnings as to our ignorance on the meaning of the Buddhist life in the pre-modern era.[47] While the world religions such as Buddhism offer the most remarkable examples of enduring mental structures in human history, historicist critiques have reminded us how much change and variation a 2,000-year past should yield.[48] Sadly, the evidence available for our period is not very helpful. Certainly, one faces the dilemma of the *longue durée* in Sri Lankan history in its starkest form once one tries to peer through institutional history to the history of mentalities that lies beneath. We must be content with generalities.

We have seen how Buddhist metaphysics enabled the Sinhalese both to tolerate other religious forms and incorporate them into their own religious lives. They were too part of a wider Indic religious culture that Michael Carrithers has described as 'polytropic', which is to say that it elicits a certain form of devotional behaviour that outgrows all the prunings of orthodoxy or cognitive constraint.[49] As a result they were liable to slip into modes of religious behaviour that might implicitly conflict with some aspects of Theravāda doctrine. Of particular note is the influence of Saivite and Vaisnava *bhakti* (devotionalism). This was probably associated with an emergent Buddhology, a tendency to see the Buddha as a god-like being, or even to imagine in Mahāyānic style that his various incarnations (*bodhisattvas*) had salvific power.[50] In this way, against the tidy distinctions made at the beginning of this chapter, Buddhism did allow the transcendent to become immanent in the world through Buddhist relics and statues and so on.[51] It was this shared sacralization of earthly forms that enabled the sense of congruence with Catholic ritual. Although it is unlikely that Theravāda soteriology was conclusively undermined by these influences, it did take on more complex and ambiguous forms as deities acquired a greater *lōkōttara* relevance and attracted more intense forms of devotion.[52]

The concept of the *bodhisattva* reaches a little closer to Christianity. As Queirós complained:

> The fact is that the Devil has forestalled everything. When we preach to the heathens of hither India, they reply that they also have a Trinity, and that their Vixnu [Viṣnu] incarnated himself times out of number; if we preach to those of further India and Ceylon (for this sect has disappeared from many parts of India, wherein it began), they reply that their Buddum [Buddha] or their Fô or their Xaka [Śakra] also took the shape of a man, though he was an eternal being.[53]

47 Blackburn 2001: 8.
48 See Collins 1998 on the enduring structure of the *Pāli imaginaire*, and Rogers 1994, on religious heterogeneity and change.
49 Carrithers 2000: 852. 50 B. Smith 1987: 265, Blackburn 2001: 26.
51 See Collins 1998: 23.
52 Holt 1991. Incidentally, Holt (personal comm. 8 May 2001) tells me that he has found no references to the Mahāyāna *per se* after the 1470s. See Ilangasinha 1992: 59–61, on the development of the doctrine of the three bodies of Buddha, elaborated in the sole work on the *dhamma* from the fifteenth century, the *Saddharmaratnākaraya*, and Walters 2000: 131, on similarities between the theology of Śiva and of Avalokiteśvara.
53 Queyroz: 141.

Hindu ideas allow for a more comprehensive elucidation of transcendent immanence, and it was through such theistic modes, particularly *bhakti*, rather than *nibbānic* Buddhism that a bridgehead of understanding with Christianity could most easily be formed. One of the recurrent images from the history of evangelism in India is that of missionary alarm at the ease with which local people made parallels between the gospel and their Hindu teachings.[54] In particular the Christian notion of God taking a bodily form to enter into history could be interpreted, and often was, as another re-telling of the stories of the incarnations of Viṣnu.[55] Regardless of whether Sinhala Buddhists pursued an orthodox form of Buddhism or engaged in a very free and polytropic religious life, many of them would have been well aware that other people had quite different relationships with the world of gods. The idea that a god might bring salvation may have been disputed but it was unlikely to have been incomprehensible to the elites at the royal seats of Kōṭṭe, Sītāvaka and Kandy.

If Sinhala Buddhists had a route into comprehending Christian soteriology, did they thereby understand the implications of assuming a Christian identity? At this point the image of ceaseless fluidity needs to be qualified. Whatever shifting contents may be enclosed by these identities, the boundaries themselves – between say, being Buddhist or a follower of one of the 'Hindu' traditions – could still matter a great deal. In this sense one can speak of a pre-Christian notion of religious *conversion*, as long as one does not assume an easy equivalence with its Christian counterpart. There were those who would define religious boundaries in Sri Lanka, seeking to insulate *nibbānic* Buddhism from Hindu devotionalist passions.[56] The wars with the Cōḷas from the ninth to thirteenth century had served to politicize religious affiliation, pitting the aggressive Saivism of the Pandyan imperial court against the Buddhism of the Sinhalese kings. It is not surprising, then, to find that this coincides with attempts by the Mahāvihāra to create a more homogeneous and defined Buddhist laity, one educated and drawn into a wider range of Buddhist practices.[57] Hallisey even points to the fear of Hell being employed to induce conformity, which offers an obvious point of analogy with Christianity.[58] Hierarchs wrote denunciations of the insidious influence of *bhakti* or ridiculed the behaviour of Saivite ascetics, notably in the fifteenth-century texts *Saddharmālaṃkāraya*, *Saddharmaratnāvaliya*, and *Buduguṇānalaṃkāraya*.[59]

The latter, written *c.* 1470, reveals a world of religious competition between opposing Saivites, Vaisnavas, devotees of Agni, Buddhists and Jains.[60] The great

[54] Rubiés 2000: 333, on a revealing comment by the missionary Antonio Rubino, *c.* 1608.

[55] I owe this point and the next sentence to John Holt, (personal comm. 8 May 2001), who also suggests that the cults of Kriṣna and the goddess might allow some to field the cults of Jesus and Mary. For more on Hindu bridgeheads to understanding Christ, see Young 1989: 75. Young and Senanayaka 1998: 5, 88, 168, remind us that the term *avatāra* has different – worldly – connotations in Sinhala.

[56] On this typical 'ambivalence' in attitudes towards Hindu influence, generating antipathy at moments of great receptiveness, see Holt 2004: 29–59.

[57] Hallisey 1988: 192; Gunawardana 1990: 60.

[58] Hallisey 1988: 201.

[59] Hallisey 1988: 179–84; Ilangasinha 1992: 12–14; Gunawardana 2000: 60–4.

[60] C. H. Reynolds 1970: 269–73. Compare with Malalgoda 1976: 34, on inter-religious debates in early eighteenth-century Kandy.

educational centres – the *pirivenas* – that flourished in Parākramabāhu VI's reign would have prepared their students for inter-religious debate through the comparative study of Brahmanic texts.[61] As befits a flourishing transcendentalist tradition, the more educated monks would have been well aware of the sheer variety of mistaken metaphysical possibilities.[62] We can say then that Sinhalese Buddhists could have recourse to something like a conception of heresy, if by that we mean a conception of false and even dangerous doctrines that require vigorous denunciation.[63] The suggestion that it was not until the Christian challenges of the nineteenth century that Buddhism was configured as a 'religion' (or 'a deployable ideological entity') can therefore mask a long and vibrant history of theological opposition.[64]

By the mid sixteenth century, a range of Sinhala terms had been pressed into service to capture the new religious world, and they served fairly well. The Sinhalese Christian author of one portion of the *Alakeśvarayuddhaya* used the term *samaya* as a rough correlate for 'religion'.[65] Hence a Kōṭṭe officer can be described as coming 'to the divine religion of our Jesus Christ, the Lord of Lords' (*dēvāti dēvavu apagē jesus kristu dēvasamayamehi*), followed by other nobles who established themselves as of the Christian religion (*kristiāni samayamehi*).[66] The non-Christian author of the *Sītāvaka Haṭana* (1585) used the venerable term *sāsana*, in a sense which is also roughly translatable as 'religion', particularly in its institutional aspect.[67] The poet also arrives at phrases for conversion (*kulavaddanavā*), and baptism (*paṭa bäňda*), which make religious change analogous to (or constitutive of) shifts in social status.[68]

However, there was no independent central coercive dogma-defining institution equivalent to that of the Christian Church.[69] Moreover, many arenas of life and thought which the monotheistic faiths deemed religious and therefore in need of regulation, were, for Buddhists, mundane affairs irrelevant to the business of salvation. So the particular conceptualization of conversion common to the monotheistic religions – as the process of sloughing off all past habits and identities and

[61] We know also that the *Brahmajāla Sūtta*, which discusses a wide range of metaphysical positions as a list of 62 false beliefs, was taught at the Käragala monastery of the *vanavāsī* sect in Parākramabāhu VI's time, see Mirando 1985: 10.

[62] The comments of Jesuits (SV: 649) notwithstanding. See Strathern (unpublished) for more.

[63] The *Pūjāvaliya* refers to non-believers as *mithyādruṣṭi*, the possibly dubious *Sitāvaka Rājasiṃha Rājja Kālaya* uses the term *mithyādruṣṭika* for the Portuguese (see Amarasinghe 1998: 7); see too Malalgoda 1997: 77; Collins 1998: 21–2.

[64] See Roberts 2004: 6–7; Malalgoda 1997.

[65] In Strathern 2006a, I argue that this portion of the *Alakeśvarayuddhaya* was composed in 1557, the text updated in the 1560s and 1590s. See Malalgoda 1997: 74–7 for some discussion of *samaya*.

[66] *Alakeśvarayuddhaya*: 37. C. R. de Silva 1994: 319, says that a deliberate copying error may have transformed *kristu samaya* (Christian faith) into *kristu samayama* (Christian farce), but also records a comment by Goonewardena to the effect that that *samayama* need not have pejorative connotations in this context. Whatever the case, it is clear that the original author was referring to Christianity with the greatest respect, referring to the religion as 'divine' and Christ as 'Lord of Lords'.

[67] *SH*: verses 250–2; it is followed here by the *Rājāvaliya*: 74–5; not in *Alakeśvarayuddhaya*.

[68] *SH*: verses 368–9. *Paṭa bäňda* is used in verse 449 to refer to the bestowal of a title such as *mudali*.

[69] This seems to be another consequence of the comparative lack of interest in the mundane world as a soteriological arena. Note *comparative*, as this point will be qualified later. See Eisenstadt 1986: 238.

acquiring a new persona – was also new.[70] To that extent there remained a significant conceptual breach between the exclusivism of Christianity and the kinds of religious identities possible in Sri Lanka. This is surely behind Queirós' confused lament of the Sinhalese for their soteriological uncertainty, 'they hold that one can go to Heaven by many ways.'[71] It is only left to remark on the possibility that some Sinhalese might have developed a consciousness of a more tightly drawn and exclusive religious identity through contact with the previous seafaring group to take control of Sri Lanka's oceanic trade, the Muslims.[72]

If these reflections give us an *a priori* sense of the possibilities of comprehension, we also need to consider the role played by exposure to Christian teaching on the ground. For now, we can posit three broad responses: First, where Christian teachings were essentially comprehended they could be brought into conflict with the logic of the *dhamma* in which the only way to achieve ultimate salvation is through the 'eight-fold path' and not through the worship of the gods. It is possible – although unlikely in the absence of a thoroughgoing Christianization of society – that the *dhamma* might come off the worse and be rejected in favour of the new teachings. On the other hand, the Christian teachings could be easily assimilated to other theist heresies encountered in the past and so disposed of. A fascinating collection of stories from the mid eighteenth century recently published as *The Carpenter-Heretic* (after a story about a demonic low-caste polluting Jesus Christ of the same name) is superb evidence of the way in which refutations of Christianity could draw upon and become part of a broader, older discourse about heresy. Although these stories sometime evince a shaky grasp of the details of doctrinal Buddhism, indicating their popular or lay origins, their rejection of the new theism is based upon a firm adherence to the soteriological underpinnings of Buddhism: it is the notion of a creator divinity with salvific powers that is fundamentally repulsive.[73]

Secondly, if Christianity is perceived as another theist sect, this need not be accompanied by an appreciation of the extent to which conversion to Christianity required the establishment of a highly visible and exclusive form of religious identity. Given that the former principle was prefigured in Sinhalese experience and the latter was largely not, this is potentially a very large category. Nevertheless, we shall see that in areas where Portuguese and missionary influence was strong (particularly at the royal courts) the notion of conversion as identity-transformation could be readily expressed and grasped through the symbols of Lusitanization. In the casket made to commemorate Dharmapāla's baptism of 1557, the transformative power of conversion may be figured in a dual representation of Dharmapāla's wife, once in Sinhalese and once in Christian dress: before and after shots as it were[74] (Plate 8).

[70] Reid 1988–93, II: 140. [71] Queyroz: 700.
[72] Although it does not seem as if Islam was proselytized in Sri Lanka. See Schurhammer 1973–82, II: 414, n. 54. There was at least one mosque in Colombo: C. R. de Silva 1998: 106.
[73] Young and Senanayaka 1998. [74] Jaffer and Schwabe 1999: 8–9.

Plate 8: Top view of lid of c. *1557, 'Robinson' casket, Victoria and Albert Museum, London.*
Jaffer and Schwabe 1999 date the casket to 1557, commemorating the conversion of Dharmapala and the accession of King Sebastião to the throne of Portugal. Notice the two female heads, in European and Sinhalese dress.

Thirdly, the Christian deity might be interpreted as little different to all the others in the Buddhist pantheon, as a god of this world rather than a source of salvation. One imagines this as either deriving from a superficial exposure to Christian dogma, or from a creative appropriation and transformation of it. The frustration of Christian missionaries in later centuries testifies to the unwillingness of many Sinhalese to engage with Christianity in quite the terms expected of them.[75] And it is important to remember throughout the following chapters that even those who came to oppose Christianity most virulently would have few qualms about accepting the notion that the god of the Christians did, at least in some form, exist.

[75] Malalgoda 1976: 210; Scott 1994: 165. A 1630s Portuguese MS (Perera 1930: 19): 'He pretended to become a Christian as all the Sinhalese do, but remained an idolater, sacrificing to Buudum.'

III

The temporal and the spiritual

8
The religious obligations of kingship

A king has to be set apart from his fellow men – estranged, exalted, sacralized – and yet because of this can represent and touch them all. His power is unique but is uniquely constrained by the ritual and behavioural prescriptions that sustain his uniqueness. Within this genre there are, naturally, variations. For example, monarchical systems typically afford some sort of acknowledgement of the popular will. In Portuguese political thought this had been articulated in the principle of *pactum subjectionis* and symbolized in the investiture ceremony, which was not the coronation of the king but his public acclamation.[1] This is broadly analogous to the rites of popular ratification in re-founded Kandy, in which representatives of the four principal caste-groups took turns in admonishing the king at the *abhiṣēka* or consecration.[2]

However, in Portugal the rite had become little more than a ceremonial device whereas in Sri Lanka the act of acclamation expressed loyalties that could not be taken for granted.[3] Here then, the sense of contract between sovereign and subjects (or at least his principal vassals) was alive and dynamic. It was not to be found in 'contractualist' or 'pluralist' institutions of government such as the tax-raising assemblies that we find in Europe, but was expressed through the greater conditionality of subjecthood itself.[4] One virtue of Tambiah's language of the 'galactic polity' is that it distances us from European or modern concepts of the state by illuminating the political volatility that resulted.

From a European perspective, Lankan kingship was subject to rather alien deification, and a rather alien vulnerability. The person of the king was vulnerable – to conspiracy, assassination or abandonment by his subjects. The institution of kingship was also vulnerable – to the adoption of royal titles and trappings by lesser rulers. In the same way, Sinhalese kings could appear as tyrants when they wielded their tremendous powers over land, yet in other ways their administrative reach appeared to fizzle out long before their sovereignty did. The continuing control of

[1] Thomaz 1985: 528–9. Hence Francisco de Vitoria and the Portuguese jurist Pedro Simões argued that popular election was a legitimate title of dominion acquisition: Saldanha 1997: 236–7.
[2] On Kandyan Kingship and its limits, see Dewaraja 1988, particularly 262, 197–210; Dewaraja 1995: 453–69; Goonewardena 1977. John Davy described a mock-election in the early nineteenth century.
[3] I owe this comparison to Biedermann 2005a: 317.
[4] See Roberts 1984 on the absence of a comparable feudal notion of reciprocity.

manpower was the key. For 'manpower' or 'the people' we can usually imagine 'the nobility'. Indeed, it is their *de facto* power that may explain the proliferation and elaboration of principles of royal legitimacy: these were means of cutting horizontal slashes through the sliding scale of political hierarchy. Thus the exclusivity of royal ancestry was insisted upon, while the imagery of the *cakravarti* was deployed to distinguish high kingship from the various relatives in lesser courts.[5] To the extent that the operation of succession and ancestral rules held firm, they offered a check to the fluidity of the 'galactic' system. There is a certain isomorphism between these structures of the Sinhalese state and the religious conceptions of kingship which we shall explore in this chapter. Both promoted a specific and limited form of contractualism.

The suggestion that if Sinhalese kings were anxious about undertaking baptism it was because they feared alienating their subjects, as if they would thereby be breaking some sort of religious contract with their people, is very old. In Queirós' *Conquista* this empathetic reasoning becomes a recurrent motif, a frustrating example of the way in which temporal concerns obstruct the work of the Holy Spirit.[6] P. E. Pieris affirmed that the Sinhalese populace would only stomach a Buddhist king.[7] Perhaps all too appealing to twentieth-century sensibilities, it has now become a routine, if hardly domineering, conceptual presence.[8] Nor will this book seek to overturn it. It will, however examine the argument more thoroughly, teasing apart its filaments, testing their strength, and appraising their place in a wider civilizational context. It does this in the light of the traditionalist versus historicist dilemmas outlined in the Introduction. At its heart lies a question of the historical relevance of an allegedly fundamental ideological structure. Did the *vaṃsa* ideology of virtuous Buddhist kingship survive into epochs for which our evidence-base somewhat shades away? If so, did it have a life in the consciousness of the wider population or was it reduced to a dead rhetorical gesture, a scholastic and monastic ideal? Were not other, more cosmopolitan discourses equally relevant?

The terms of this discussion may be controversial from another angle too. It is perhaps not very fashionable now to think in terms of the 'legitimization of power'. It smacks of a heavy-handed Marxian or functionalist approach; it may be taken to rob our historical agents of a more complex psychological relationship with the myths and symbols of their cultural heritage or to charge them with manipulative and deceitful strategizing.[9] But these are pitfalls that it is possible to acknowledge and avoid. The ideological apparatus surrounding kingship may serve to render

[5] Perhaps, the more institutionally vulnerable kingship became, the more cultural resources were channelled into its reification; but as such resources proliferated, the more upstarts could exploit them too.

[6] E.g. Queyroz: 261, 266. [7] Pieris 1983–92, I: 396–7.

[8] S. G. Perera 1951: 23; Abeyasinghe 1966: 11, 211; Don Peter 1978: 29; Ilangasinha 1992: 117; Quéré 1988a: 79.

[9] Fashionable in the 1970s (e.g. B. Smith 1978a), it has lately received much criticism: see Pollock, 1998: 44; Blackburn 2001: 103–4. Obeyesekere 1995a: 234, refers to religious patronage as a way of assuaging guilt for kings involved in violence.

more palatable the brute exercise of power, but it will also serve to insist that such power is not exercised brutishly. In 'practice theory' fashion, while elites may harness cultural forces to their own ends, those ends are in turn moulded by cultural forces.

We shall begin by showing how rulers in both Malabar and Lanka resisted conversion by claiming popular displeasure in the 1540s. After a survey of the religious status of Lankan kings over the historical long term, we shall consider the evidence relating to these traditions in the sixteenth century. But how do we square those conversions that *did* occur with our argument of 'transcendentalist intransigence'? The answer lies in the marginality of these princes, as understood in several distinct ways. Lastly, we shall return to Bhuvanekabāhu, and his policies in the face of such pressures.

The fear of popular opposition in Malabar and Sri lanka

Over the following chapters, the evidence for the resistance of Sinhalese rulers will mount up. But it is first of all important to note that many of their counterparts along the Malabar Coast appeared likewise to consider the baptismal waters as poison for their legitimacy. In our very first report of a conversation aimed at converting an Asian ruler, Afonso de Albuquerque claimed in 1514 that the Raja of Cochin assented to the reason of his arguments, but held back from baptism principally because his subjects would not suffer it.[10] Particularly interesting for us is the case of the Raja of Tanor, the ruler of a petty principality that included a Portuguese fortress.[11] Becoming friendly with the fortress commander, as well as a vicar and a Franciscan stationed there, the raja was encouraged to write a letter in late 1545 indicating that he would be willing to accept baptism if the governor would come to Tanor to provide support. He claimed that he could not convert outright owing to the hostility of the Nayars. When it transpired that the governor would be unable to come, the raja proposed that he receive baptism in secret. He would not in any way change his outward clothing or ceremonial comportment.[12] This was, in fact, the policy that he adopted, and it is broadly that which the King of Kandy had attempted within a more truncated timescale. In March or April of 1546 while André de Sousa was still trudging up to his highland kingdom, Jayavīra received Christianity 'secretly and by night'.[13] In all outward respects, nothing had changed.

We do not need to imagine that their requests for baptism had been 'sincere'. Whether the intention was to accept baptism and keep the fact secret or to just promise baptism and never go through with it, reference to the offended sensibilities

[10] SR, I: 229. Many historians (e.g. Schurhammer 1973–82, II: 493) have taken this as a frank and straightforward narrative. Earle 1990, explores its rhetorical wiles more carefully. Here, Albuquerque failed in his mission, but acquits himself of intellectual or diplomatic inadequacies, for the raja's cowardice was to blame.

[11] SR, III: 284–317; IV: 347–55; Schurhammer 1973–82, III: 309–10; Neill 1984: 159.

[12] SR, IV: 567–8. [13] VP: 152.

of the people was clearly a very useful diplomatic tool. One could thereby imply, I am a loyal and even pious ally, but my hands are tied. The cases of the King of Kandy and the Raja of Tanor both inspired debate among the Portuguese as to their sincerity and whether a clandestine faith was theologically justified.[14] It is a mark of how seriously such issues were taken that the case of the Raja of Tanor, a relatively insignificant principality, was made the subject of a lengthy council meeting held by the Governor João de Castro in 1546. This produced some eighteen documents giving the testimonies and opinions of various individuals and bodies.[15] These discussions represent a major precursor of the rites controversies that would erupt in Malabar and China in following centuries. In wearing the sacred thread of the Brahman and observing caste regulations, were men such as the Raja of Tanor maintaining purely secular customs or engaging in heathen abominations?

One of the justifications for secret conversions deployed by the *piedoso* bishop, Juan de Albuquerque, was that the Raja of Tanor would be like Saint Sebastian, retaining conventional dress so that he might mix freely among his kind and thereby bring souls to God unhindered before publicly revealing his faith.[16] Yet the conduct of neither king could remotely bear such an analogy. The case of the Raja of Tanor seemed the more promising: after years of conversations with the clerics at the fortress and the dispatch of expertly pious epistles, he did eventually journey to Goa where he was received with great honour to make a public proclamation of his faith. But on his return to Tanor the raja not only personally disowned Christianity, but roused opposition against it.[17]

Therefore, throughout all the following discussions, we need to be sensible of the fact that reference to the disposition of 'the people' had become a rhetorical touchstone that served diverse and often contradictory political ends. For Portuguese missionaries and adventurers, sometimes an optimistic view was useful (that the conversion of a prince equalled the conversion of his people), and sometimes a pessimistic view (that the prince had been successfully convinced but the stubbornness of his people held him back). Both devices also had their uses for indigenous South Asians. This is encapsulated very neatly in a letter by Viceroy Afonso de Noronha from early 1552. The new king Dharmapāla had proposed that Noronha take hostage a very young son of the dead Bhuvanekabāhu and have him baptized as a guarantee of their promises. But then 'once more they changed their minds. They declared that the kinsmen of the prince on the mother's side had run away with the prince, saying that if the child had become a Christian, they would not agree to accept him in the country as king.'[18] In response Noronha effectively kidnapped two leading Kōṭṭe officials. Dharmapāla then sent word to say that they would find the prince and hand him over, 'and that once the child had become a Christian, he also and his own country would embrace the Christian faith': the

[14] See above, p. 000, on differences between Simão de Coimbra and António Padrão
[15] SR, III: 284–314. [16] SR, IV: 353–4.
[17] VP: 283, 305; SR, V: 96; Neill 1984: 159. [18] VP: 307.

analytical premises have been entirely overturned. There was clearly a debate within the ruling elite of Kōṭṭe whether to appease or defy Noronha. The most politic way to express that debate to the Portuguese was by reference to optimistic or pessimistic views of the popular reaction.

This ought not to preclude us from concluding that the pessimistic perspective was much closer to the truth of the matter. The varying fortunes of the Raja of Tanor indicate that his fear of public retaliation was hardly fantastical. Nor was the King of Kandy's, when he warned the friar Coimbra that his baptism must be kept secret, 'so that his [people] would not kill him'.[19] On the arrival of the Portuguese expedition in 1546, Jayavīra revealed his conversion and the country broke out into rioting and uproar. Coimbra suggested that this was the result of a general restlessness in a time of war compounded by the slanders of Bhuvanekabāhu.[20] But the captain André de Sousa tells us explicitly that the revolts resulted directly from the proclamation of faith and that in order to pacify the situation Jayavīra immediately gave out that he was not really Christian at all but only intended to deceive the Portuguese.[21] This was successful. The position of the Chief of Batticaloa was also assailed when he considered converting later that year.[22]

Buddhist and Indic representations of kingship over the long term

What lay behind such popular displeasure? Its very existence seems to frustrate the model of the pre-modern state in which power is legitimated from above.[23] It is indeed a critical novelty of modern nationalism that the common mass is conceived as the source of authority. But in our period we see at least this one way in which subjects could act as arbitrators of their rulers.

The conversion of a ruler would not inevitably incur such dangers in other parts of the world. In the Introduction, it was suggested that it would tend to do so in societies with established transcendentalist traditions. In an important sense then, the behaviour of our Buddhists can be compared to that of Christians, Muslims and perhaps Hindus. Yet, this is true on a very abstract level only, and we must now proceed to draw some distinctions between these obviously different interpretations and institutionalizations of the transcendentalist urge. Since we have already noticed a pattern common to both Hindu and Buddhist rulers, ought we to explain it by reference to a general 'Indic' understanding of the relationship

19 SV: 421 (VP: 201). This is echoed by Couto: 126, where Māyādunnē warns the king that 'his own subjects would try to kill him in order not to be governed by men of a different law.'

20 VP: 202.

21 VP: 152–3. Furthermore, if the prince and princess of Kandy had been baptized 'the people of the whole country would have risen in revolt'.

22 Coimbra in VP: 212: 'Finally as he was about to become Christian, there broke out a war against him, which an aunt of his began to wage against him at the time. He told me that I well saw how things stood, and consequently he was not able to become a Christian then . . .' Likewise see VP: 283, for the case of a Maldivian prince in 1551.

23 This is a feature of Nissan and Stirrat's (1990: 24) model. Kapferer 1998: 70, argues that 'hierocracy and democracy exist in complementarity in Buddhist notions of the ideal king'.

between political and religious authority? One could argue that the Indic traditions represent a particularly emphatic encapsulation of the Axial Age principle by which mundane power is theoretically subject to the norms of the supramundane. Both Buddhist and Brahmanic textual traditions place great emphasis on the virtue of the king as the source of order, the religious champion of his subjects and the guardian of their spiritual and temporal welfare. And Lankan courts borrowed readily from both traditions in their fashioning of kingship.

But are our brush-strokes still too broad? What if the Malabar and Lankan rajas resisted conversion for subtly different reasons? For some have seen the Buddhist tradition as offering a quite separate and radical perspective on politics. Such is contended by Tambiah, who argues that one can discern a recognizable Buddhist political ideology in the earliest Pāli scriptures.[24] There we find an 'elective and contractual theory of kingship' expressed in a myth about the origins of kingship.[25] The primordial king was Mahāsammata, the 'great elect' because he has been chosen by the people to restore order to the world in return for a share of their rice. This story appears to express a principle reminiscent of the political theory of Thomas Hobbes (1588–1679), which argued for the necessity of an absolute sovereign figure determined by consent in order to lift men out of the brutish state of nature and into society.[26] In India, the reign of Aśōka (*c.* 268–239 BC) offered to future Theravāda monarchs a paradigm of righteous Buddhist rule.[27]

In Sri Lanka, what emerges most strongly from the literary record is the intertwining of the destinies of king and *sāsana*.[28] The king ought to act as the fountainhead of Buddhism throughout his kingdom. He cannot simply patronize the *saṃgha*, he must take responsibility for its continuing vitality and discipline and govern according to a set of almost monastic norms enshrined in the ten royal principles or *dasarājadhamma*.[29] In this way he would provide the temporal conditions in which the search for salvation could take place. As Tambiah has famously put it, he would be both 'World Conqueror' and 'World Renouncer'. Among Tambiah's many complex arguments surrounding Buddhist kingship in 'galactic polities' is the suggestion that the paradox of the 'traditional co-existence of divine kingship and political insurrection' in Theravāda kingdoms is partly a result of this sacred accountability.[30]

It was in the tenth century that it was first asserted that the Buddha had ordained that only *bodhisattva*s would become kings of Lanka, a Theravādin reworking of a

[24] Tambiah 1976: 52, 167; and Ariyasena 1987: 105–8, emphasize the idiosyncratic power of Buddhist traditions to legitimize and de-legitimize kingship. H. Seneviratne 1987: 152, Obeyesekere 1979: 635, and Collins 1998: 466, stress commonalities and intermixtures of Buddhist and Brahamanic traditions.

[25] Tambiah 1976: 9–18. See the discussion of the *Aggañña Sutta* of the *Dīgha Nikāya* in Ariyasena 1987: 102. Collins 1998: 448–58, prefers to emphasize its humour and ambiguities, and resists ascribing a comprehensive social theory to such texts.

[26] Hobbes 1991.

[27] Tambiah 1987: 201, on the Buddhist borrowing of the *cakravarti* concept.

[28] B. Smith 1978a: 78. [29] Ariyapala 1968: 47.

[30] Tambiah 1976: 523, and 122; Silber 1995: 100.

Mahāyānist idea.[31] It was thenceforth a pervasive ingredient of royal imagery, and one that followed easily from asserting lineage from Mahāsammata, and therefore Buddha himself.[32] It has been argued that by the twelfth century, kings who appeared to have abandoned Buddhism – such as Vikramabāhu I (r. 1111–1132) and Gajabāhu II (r. 1132–53) – would be denied full royal titles.[33] The twelfth century, which seems crucial for the development of so many of the grand themes of Lankan history, was, however, a paradoxical crucible, forging its legacies through an amalgam of massive Indian-Hindu influence and conspicuous attempts to define Lankan civilization through and against it. Cōḷa imperialism left a powerful imprint on the Sinhalese kings who reclaimed power in its wake, who turned to the patronage of Saivism in order to pronounce their fitness to rule to the wider world. To what extent this involved an explicit abjuration of Buddhism is another question; it would be safer to say that Gajabāhu II in particular did enough to lay himself open to charges of heresy by the orthodox-minded.[34]

Then, however, came the pivotal reigns of Parākramabāhu (1153–86) and Niśśanka Malla (1187–96), the consolidation of Mahāvihāran dominance, and the first *argument* that the king must be a Buddhist. Niśśanka Malla, of Kālinga blood himself yet determined to resist the claims of Cōḷa and Tamil princes, sought to excise his rivals by explicitly defining Lankan kingship through adherence to Buddhism.[35] The reign of the 'heretic' Māgha (r. 1215–36), who actually persecuted Buddhism, burning texts and forcing the people to adopt 'wrong views', appears to have cemented this understanding rather than undermined it, for his was a marauding rule imposed from without. On the illegitimacy of his rule, its transgression of the indigenous norms of just kingship, the Pāli and Sinhala texts are uniquely strident.[36] Given that the popularization and localization of Buddhism in Sri Lanka were firmly under way from the beginning of the millennium, such moral-political discourses may well have permeated down to a substantial body of the society, which could now be encouraged to imagine itself as a community with a karmic destiny dependent on that of its ruler.[37] Perhaps the most valuable text for our purposes is the thirteenth-century *Pūjāvaliya*, written in strikingly demotic Sinhalese. Obeyesekere gives the following translation:

> Just as the demons could not find permanence here, neither can this land become a place of residence for non-believers (*mityādrusṭi gatavungē vāsaya*). If any non-believer becomes a king of Sri Lanka by force at any time, that dynasty will not last owing to the special influence of the Buddha. Because this Lanka is rightfully those of kings who have right views [Buddhists], their rightful dynastic tenure (*kula pravēṇiya*) will absolutely prevail.

[31] Inscription of Mahinda IV (956–72) in *EZ*, I: 240. See Walters 2000: 130–2; Gunawardana 1978.
[32] *Mahāsammata* origin: *Mahāvaṃsa*, ed. Geiger 1993: 10; Ariyapala 1968: 52; Dewaraja 1988: 262.
[33] Kiribamune 1978.
[34] *Cūḷavaṃsa*: 70, 53–5. Gunawardana 1990: 64, 1979: 204. Liyanagamage 1968: 36, warns that the *Cūḷavaṃsa*'s assertion of heresy-promotion could be a pretext to justify Parākramabāhu's conquest of Rajaraṭa.
[35] Gunawardana 1990: 65. [36] Liyanagamage 1968: 110–32.
[37] Hallisey 2003: 701 quotes a pertinent Niśśanka Malla inscription and a fifteenth-century poem. See the essays in Holt et al. 2003.

For these various reasons the kings of Sri Lanka are drawn by a natural love of mind to the Buddha and will establish the *sāsana* without delay or neglect and protect the wheel of the law and the wheel of doctrine and reign so that the rightful dynastic tenure will be preserved.[38]

It is not surprising, then, to find one study of dynastic change in fourteenth-century Sri Lanka proposing that the moral-religious responsibility of rulers constituted 'the essence of politics' in Sri Lanka, and that the downfall of the powerful Alagakkōnāra family was partly due to their failure to discharge it appropriately.[39] But the best evidence for how deeply kingship bore the impress of Buddhism is to be found in the Kandyan era, with its combination of indigenous texts and European reports.[40] The Kandyan monarchs conform to the model of early modern South East Asian Theravāda kings in being both increasingly distant from their subjects in ritual terms and conceptually bound to them as a coherent moral community.[41] The comprehensiveness of that imagined community can be seen in the different classes represented in the Perahära procession. Their claims on the conduct of the monarch were vividly portrayed in the wall-paintings that could be found in many eighteenth-century Kandyan temples depicting the popular *Sutasomsa Jātaka*. One of its central themes: that kings who violated Buddhist moral codes could expect to be driven out by their subjects.[42]

Such is to dwell on rather 'traditionalist' preoccupations. To the 'historicist', this account might seem to cleave uncomfortably close to the agenda of our monastic sources, in which political disarray and the degeneration from orthodoxy are two sides of the same coin. Tambiah, in particular, has received criticism from scholars who argue that his model eviscerates the various evolutions and appropriations of Buddhist thought in different times and places.[43] It is, moreover, an exceedingly slippery question how far the injunction to be Buddhist and a patron of Buddhism can be equated with an assertion of religious identity as a monotheist might understand it.

It is crucial to bear in mind that the Buddhist responsibilities of the king did not exclude him from offering vigorous patronage to other religious groups. If the Kōṭṭe emperor wanted to claim overlordship over the increasingly variegated communities on the island, it followed that he would be drawn to attending to their religious needs, patronizing various Hindu and latterly Islamic and Christian

[38] Obeyesekere 1995b: 234; C. H. Reynolds 1970: 168–92. Roberts 2004: 24–5, suggests that the *Pūjāvaliya*, written in simple Sinhala, was used for recitation and discussion by lay people at ceremonies.

[39] Kulasuriya 1976: 154 .

[40] One Dutch observer, 1680s: 'People also say that those who are going to be crowned must swear an oath to do everything good, to duly maintain the religion of the Buddha . . .' Goonewardena 1977: 10, 23). There is broad agreement here: Rogers 1994: 15; Gunawardana 1990: 69; H. Seneviratne 1997: 8–10; Dewaraja 1988: 162; Malalgoda 1976: 12. See also the eighteenth-century Nevill: Or. 6603(65).

[41] Lieberman 2003: 36.

[42] See Dewaraja 1988: 200. Further evidence of living contractualism: Roberts 1984: 213, 2004: 45; Gunasekera 1978: 131–3; H. Seneviratne 1978: 94–7.

[43] See H. Seneviratne, Reynolds, Carrithers, Keyes (all 1987).

institutions as well. The theatrics of Sinhalese kings were clearly intended for broader consumption than the indigenous moral community: neighbouring South Indian dynasties and their emissaries above all, with their cosmopolitan language of *kṣatriya* kingship; the Hindu attendants at court; the larger unassimilated groups of immigrants from India such as mercenaries and traders and *vanniyār* clans. Sri Lankan kings could not afford to ignore the cults of divine royalty on the mainland. King Niśśanka Malla, while articulating the adherence to Buddhism, also claimed, 'though kings appear in human form, they are human divinities (*naradēvatā*) and must, therefore, be regarded as gods.'[44] In the Gampola and Kōṭṭe periods we see a growing tendency to allude to the king as an avatar or even as Rāma, Viṣnu, or (Viṣnu's Buddhist counterpart) Upulvan, *per se*.[45] Mapping the heavenly hierarchy onto the worldly, the king was also associated with the Lord of the Gods Indra or his indigenized counterpart Śakra.[46] For a Portuguese commentator such as João de Barros, it was the conflation of divine and worldly hierarchies that was most characteristic of South Asian society in general.[47]

This means that while Theravāda contractualism fits nicely into our Axial Age terms of analysis, we also have to deal with monarchical images that may undermine them. While the Axial Age logic is supposed to precipitate a 'secular' and 'accountable' conception of kingship, the capacious energies of Indic religious culture allowed a much greater accommodation of pre-/non-transcendentalist themes than monotheism.[48] In parts of Africa and Polynesia we see kingship as a ritual device for securing well-being for the community in the face of the otherwise uncontrollable threats ranged against it. We can call this 'sacred kingship'. 'Divine kingship' occurred when the centralized states of major agrarian civilizations elaborated a cosmological drama played out by priests and kings – the latter now being elevated to a more distant form of godhood. Only in those civilizations that underwent an Axial Age did 'righteous kingship' emerge.[49] Hinduism and Buddhism retained elements of all three. Thus 'sacred kingship' is observable in the persisting belief that the conduct of the king was mystically connected to the welfare of his kingdom as a whole.[50] The king could even be held responsible for natural disasters. We see this transposed into the mode of 'divine kingship' by the Śakran discourse of the king as a god-like being who was the seat of microcosmic and macrocosmic order. If the primary form of action here is ritual, 'righteous

[44] *EZ*, II: 121. [45] John Holt, personal comm. 8 May 2001; Holt 2004: ch. 2.

[46] See Holt 1996: 20.

[47] Barros: 44–5. Yalman 1997 has argued that a form of divine kingship drawing on the resources of a common social and tenurial system was a fundamental feature of both South Indian and Sri Lankan society.

[48] Eisenstadt 1986: 300. 'Secular' only in a very particular sense. Of course, different notions of divinity itself were operating here, the Indic category being more attainable and worldly than its monotheistic counterpart, see C. R. de Silva 1995: 25, and Rubiés 2000: 233.

[49] I am conscious of over-summarizing here, but hope to substantiate these analytical terms in a work-in-progress. Meanwhile, Strathern (2007b) gives a few more details.

[50] Tambiah 1976: 50, describes this as the 'multiplier effect'. See also Ariyapala 1968: 45–6; Collins 1998: 461–4, on this 'blend [of] magic with morality'.

kingship' then lent this an ethical-soteriological overlay. Now, the karmic progress of all the king's subjects depended on his virtue.[51]

These elements were massaged into a reasonably coherent scheme. Divinizing conceptions, for example, were generally subordinated to a Theravāda cosmology and soteriology: kings and gods were both kept in their place. Yet tensions persisted too and the inherent or accomplished qualities of the *dēvarāja* or the *bodhisattva* may have pulled against the contractualist connotations of the *dhammarāja* image. Duncan suggests something similar in his reading of Kandyan royal architecture as exhibiting some tension between its Aśōkan and Śakran aspects.[52] We should consider these as etic distinctions, and not emic incompatibilities: the evidence for contractualism may be strongest in the Kandyan period, but so too is the evidence for the divine magnificence of kings.[53] Nevertheless, these points are worth noting for the sake of our comparative framework, which emphasizes the particular resistant properties of 'righteous kingship' (the Aśōkan mode).[54] As an aside, one wonders too, whether there is a connection between the greater vulnerability of Lankan kingship as compared with Portuguese, and its retention in some form of these other ('older') elements of kingship ideology by which the king's servitude to society is emphasized.

The sixteenth-century context

Thus far we have skipped over the sixteenth century. With what particular inflections and idioms was the language of sacred kingship spoken in our period? We can start with the space in which it was broadcast. The physical environment of the Kōṭṭe court was chiefly the heritage of the exceptional reign of Parākramabāhu IV (1411–67). The chief temple of Kōṭṭe, the ritual centre of the city, was the Daḷadā Māligāva.[55] It was a three-storey building located within the palace precinct at the end of the royal street, announcing the king's guardianship of the Buddhist Tooth Relic (Map 1, no. 5).[56] The immense importance of the Tooth Relic for the legitimization of the monarchy is one of our rare certainties, and in later chapters we shall see the vital role it played in the power struggles of the later sixteenth century.[57] No wonder it was so closely associated with the unifying vision of *cakravarti*-ship: only one king could have it, after all. One can see the relic to be a verification of the living power of specifically Buddhist discourses, their symbolic

[51] B. Smith 1978c: 62; H. Seneviratne 1978: 94–7.
[52] Duncan: 1990: 38–40; Dewaraja 1988: 262.
[53] Knox: 125; Roberts 2004: 44–52; Dewaraja 1988: 265.
[54] Nevertheless the god-king image offers its own form of resistance to conversion, through the threat of ritual infelicity, even if as part of a generally less resilient (because less ethicized) civilizational structure: See Strathern (2007b).
[55] *Cūḷavaṃsa*, II: 215–16; E. Perera 1910: 17; Siriweera 1993/5: 13–14. See Viterbo 1904, for a list of the objects which were found in the palace and temple precinct by Noronha in 1551.
[56] This must be the 'pagoda' referred to as within Dharmapāla's palace in 1551, VP: 300. Described in *SH*, verse 19. See also Geiger 1960: 215, 254.
[57] Widely acknowledged: Flores 1998: 89; C. R. de Silva 1998: 106; H. Seneviratne 1978: 17; Herath 1994.

concretization.[58] However, such objects can also acquire a generic power that lifts them out of such specific webs of meaning.

The Daḷadā Māligāva housed in its four corners shrines to the gods, Nātha, Saman, Viṣnu and Śiva, and this reflects the highly syncretistic or incorporative tendency which characterizes the religious architecture of Kōṭṭe in general.[59] When the kings of Kōṭṭe and Kandy claimed guardianship over Adam's Peak (Sumanakūṭa), they were associating themselves with a truly cosmopolitan site of sacredness. It was indeed one of the most important holy sites in Asia and easily the most famous feature of Lanka for centuries before the Portuguese arrival. The presiding deity of the mountain was Saman, and he was one of the four protector deities to whom the founder of Kōṭṭe, Alakeśvara, had constructed temples in the city walls.[60] Adam's Peak was endowed with sacredness by people of all faiths, Buddhists, Hindus, Muslims, and latterly Christians too, who each attached their own significance to the mysterious depression at its summit.[61] That Saman remained of vital importance for the Sītāvakan kings is evident from their royal pilgrimages to Adam's Peak. It is only matched by the Kataragama abode of Skanda in this regard, with whom the Sītāvakan kings apparently entered into a particularly profound relationship.[62] Unsurprisingly, Skanda was a god of war, and another of the guardian deities. He was also associated with the historical king Mahasen. The *Sälaḷihini Sandēśa* described his temple, the Mahasen Mahā Pāya (Great Palace of Mahasen) rising out of the southern side of Kōṭṭe like 'a blazing orb': a splendid example of the post-mortem ascension of mortal kings to divinity.[63] The third guardian deity was Upulvan, but only the fourth, Vibhīṣaṇa, has an identified temple among the surviving ruins.[64]

All this reminds us that the argument between Sinhalese and Christian languages of sacred political power was most visibly expressed in the changing nature of the capital city. This is where the distinction between specifically Buddhist-contractualist and generally Indic-divinizing discourses appears rather irrelevant, because the rites and trappings of kingship can generate authority quite apart from the particular theologies they gesture to. If one aspect of righteous rule was simply the dutiful performance of such rites – rites which may have actually constituted as well as expressed the quasi-divine attributes of kingship – the radical implications of conversion are immediately apparent.[65] When Kōṭṭe was Christianized in

58 See Tambiah 1976: 97.

59 E. Perera 1910: 16; Schurhammer 1973–82, II: 419.

60 Saman was identified with Lakṣmana the brother of Rāma, Ilangasinha 1992: 201–7; Flores 1998: 86.

61 Barros: 36–7; Ilangasinha 1992: 185–8.

62 *SH*: verses 165–74, 210–43, 290, 458–60, 590, 702.

63 E. Perera 1910: 15. Not only kings, but heroic types. Queyroz: 209, has it that the people of Kōṭṭe had raised shrines to two Portuguese men who had died fending off the Māppiḷa attack in 1524.

64 Map 1, no. 19. Close by is a temple to the Hindu goddess of education and Brahma's consort, Sarasvatī, no. 20. No other ruins have been identified with particular gods. The chief excavator of Kōṭṭe, Douglas Ranasinghe, told me that in his opinion the ruins displayed an overwhelmingly 'Hindu' tendency (interview, Colombo, Feb. 2000).

65 The daily routine of Parākramabāhu II (1236–70), for example, in S. Paranavitana 1959–60: 727.

the 1550s and abandoned in 1565, Dharmapāla would have been stripped of the most concrete signs of royalty that had surrounded his forebears. Kōṭṭe may have been built as a microcosm of the heavens in the manner of South East Asian and Kandyan capitals, so that as it suffered the order of the cosmos itself would have been figuratively torn apart.[66]

The flourishing of Tamil cultural and religious forms in Kōṭṭe has already been emphasized here, and it is especially important that by the time Bhuvanekabāhu set up his court, the *purōhita* was afforded a central role. As the official primarily responsible for the conduct of the sacred ceremonies of royalty, he may have emphasized the more 'Hindu' aspects of the king's representation at court. The remaining scraps of evidence from Bhuvanekabāhu's reign emphasize above all his association with Śakra, the king of the Gods, who is sometimes referred to by his Hindu name, as in the *sannasa* of Bhuvanekabāhu's tenth year which describes him as sitting 'in glory like Indra upon his throne under the *makara torana* and the white canopy, encircled by his ministers in the Citra Kūta Hall in Jayavardhana Kōṭṭe.'[67] We can see what this looks like in the representation of Bhuvanekabāhu's coronation from the Munich casket of *c.* 1543 (Plate 1).[68] If Bhuvanekabāhu is Śakra-esque in this image, his posture is that of a Buddha; certainly he holds one of the five emblems of Buddha in his hand, a lotus flower.[69] The ivory carvings on an earlier casket, which betray very little Portuguese influence in their stylization, are largely devoted to the Hindu epic the *Rāmāyana*, and there Bhuvanekabāhu appears riding an elephant and bearing the eye of wisdom: the attributes of Indra.[70] Once again the Sītāvakan imagery appears little different, to judge by the *Sītāvaka Haṭana*, in which the Śakra analogy is played upon to the point of tedium. The heavens are given a political geography and hierarchy that mirrors the kingdom on earth, or vice versa one might say. Rājasiṃha's men compare him to the Śakra who united the celestial city and cast the demons (*asuras*) off Mount Meru.

If kings were endowed with a sacred mystique merely by analogy or association, more concrete connections could be asserted through lineage. It is entirely orthodox for Bhuvanekabāhu VII's *sannas* to claim derivation from the lines of the Mahāsammata, Manu.[71] Explicit claims of *bodhisattva* status are less apparent, although there is possibly an obscure reference in the *Kandy Nātha Dēvāle* inscription of 1543.[72] In Chapter Five we saw how caste principles structured the conversion process in the coastal cities of Malabar, making baptism attractive to

66 Duncan 1990.

67 Pieris 1910–12: 272. This follows the form of the Päpiliyāna inscription of Parākramabāhu VI in Müller 1883: 138.

68 The *makara torana* and the white parasol of state are apparent above the emperor on the Lion Throne.

69 P. H. De Silva 1975: 72, evokes Śakra; Coutinho 1972 refers to Buddha and Siva; Jaffer and Schwabe 1999: 7, refer to the lotus flower.

70 Jaffer and Schwabe 1999: 5.

71 *EZ*, III: 247. Somaratna 1975: 222–4, argues that the epithets listed by Queyroz: 195–6, and 'translated' by Pieris 1983–92, I: 54, are fictitious.

72 *EZ*, IV: 34, 269. Jayavīra Mahā Väḍavuntäna: 'one who comes and remains'. We do not find the epithet 'bosat' (*bodhisattva*) in use, although Parākramabāhu VI's Oruvala Sannasa had it (*EZ*, III: 68).

low-status groups while threatening to deprive high castes of their exalted position, and that this was not the case for Sri Lanka. However, the Lankan royal families claimed a status, as *kṣatriyas* of the *sūryavaṃsa* caste, held by no others on the island, one which invoked Indian origins.[73] The historical record has left us only one description of a letter written by Bhuvanekabāhu that was not addressed to the Portuguese. It was sent to the King of Kandy in 1546 and argued that he 'could not believe that a king so great and of such high race [*casta*] and so judicious should wish to dishonour himself and commit so serious a mistake as to become a Christian, and that from being a king he would become an outcaste [*parea* or pariah]'.[74] This suggests that for Sinhalese *royalty* caste status was sacralized and therefore potentially a central obstacle to conversion, although we should not consider this an immutable principle.[75]

Sometimes these different strands of religious tradition were perceived as pulling in different ways, generating tension and open debate in the body politic.[76] But the various borrowings from (or shared traditions with) Hindu culture need not have undermined the particular sense of moral contingency cultivated by the Buddhist legacy. If the *Sītāvaka Haṭana* seems enamoured with Śakran imagery, then we need only recall how closely associated Śakra is with the myth of the Buddhist consecration of Lanka, how obviously he has been subordinated to Buddha. Its Mount Merun *dēvas* listen to *baṇa* on *Pōya* day, just like all other right-thinking creatures.[77] Equally the implications of the Mahāsammata invocation are not easily categorized. As a glamorous ancestor, he may be taken to reinforce the inherent (not contingent) authority of royalty. The version of the *Rājāvaliya* chanted to Azevedo in the 1580s emphasized Mahāsammata's distinction as the father of the solar dynasty, and that only in Lanka was the direct line of descent from this first king truly preserved.[78] But the symbolism of Mahāsammata's own origination in popular election references the notion of contingent (not inherent) authority.[79]

[73] *SH*: verse 449, on dynasty of the sun; *Alakeśvarayuddhaya*: 21, on Parākramabāhu VI's lineage; Couto: 100; Miranda: 163; Queyroz: 6; a letter by Karaliyaddē Baṇḍāra in 1546 likened himself to the sun (VP: 208).

[74] Simão de Coimbra to João de Castro, Goa, 18 Dec. 1546: SV: 426 (VP: 206). Coimbra's comments on Bhuvanekabāhu must be treated with suspicion, but they are also asserted by N. A. Pereira's letter of 29 May 1546, in SV: 368 (VP: 164), which reported that Bhuvanekabāhu 'cannot believe that this is true of one with blood so great as his and being a kinsman of the sun [i.e of the solar dynasty] of which there is none more legitimate [*ligitimo*] in the land'. The *casado* Fernandes later commented on 'how the King of Cota [Kōṭṭe] and the other kings of this island despised him when they heard of it [the baptism]' (VP: 175–6). And see comments in Queyroz: 321, that the Sinhalese considered Dharmapāla 'undeserving of the Kingdom by reason of him becoming a Christian, which, in their opinion, was an infamy unworthy of a Prince of the race of the Sun'.

[75] See Yalman 1997: 141. But *SH*, verses 517, 874, for all its revulsion for conversion, yet allows the baptized Dharmapāla his nobility, his epithets of august and pure lineage.

[76] Remember Vīdāgama Maitreya's scathing attacks on Saivite and Vaisnava worship in the late fifteenth century, see Ilangasinha 1992: 214–15

[77] *SH*, verse 668. [78] Azevedo: 242/Couto: 101.

[79] Its contractualist sense has been somewhat obscured by its Christian mediation. The election of the *Mahāsammata* is, however, expressed in *Rājāvaliya*: 4, which was in turn drawing on re-tellings of the myth in Sinhalese texts such as the *Pūjāvaliya*.

The Mahāsammatan and Śakran images both work to promote the vision of the *cakravarti* as the fount of all order, and it is this vision that is most consistently expressed by the *Sītāvaka Haṭana*. The king is the fount of prosperity too, comparable thus to a paddy field or a heavenly tree of bounty.[80] Harmony, justice, prosperity and virtue are all somehow equated, just as the king's exemplification of these qualities is merged with their general prevalence among his subjects: the king must embody them in order to transmit them. The legitimacy of the ruler is thereby made contingent on the continuing welfare of the ruled. There seems to be a suggestion of this in Bhuvanekabāhu's description of the Portuguese as 'the men who ruin my country and make themselves kings of it without being able to bring prosperity to it'.[81]

The *Sītāvaka Haṭana* is not insistently Buddhist. That is neither its object nor its authorial milieu. It is a useful reminder of a more secular martial ethos less troubled by the familiar concerns of the monastic texts. But its grounding in a conspicuously lay, even crude, Buddhist sensibility emerges here and there, as when the Buddha who banished the demons (*yakun*) is asked to watch over Rājasiṃha or when the inevitability of Māyādunnē's death is softened by noting that even he who had 'become Buddha to Lanka' had met this fate.[82] There is also a reference to 'the island of Lanka called *dhamma*'.[83]

Particularly pertinent are its attempts to exalt Sītāvaka by calling into question the legitimacy of rival or 'enemy' kings. When Vīdiyē Baṇḍāra treacherously murders his host, Edirimansūriya, the ruler of the Seven Kōraḷēs, the poet comments: 'to acquire the country he did this harm, so that the virtues of compassion (*meth gunas*) would not carry forth in *Siri Laka*.'[84] Thus his personal vice is couched in terms of societal virtue: Rājasiṃha has to restore it, transmitting an ethical lesson and a threat by tom-tom. The child king Dharmapāla is not explicitly blamed for his baptism; he is the symptom of a disease spread by his predecessor. The manner of Bhuvanekabāhu's death, effected by a Portuguese bullet, was irresistible to the karmic imagination:

> Thus he reaped the results of his past karma in its full force
>
> Injustices fell upon society
> The religion (*sāsana*) was destroyed
> The Portuguese left [Portugal for here]
> Because of Bāhu Bhuvaneka
>
> The prosperity (*siri*) of the island of Lanka was made barren.
> The society was made barren.
> The nobility (*udaraya*) of the high-born children
> And the temples were destroyed.[85]

[80] *SH*, verses 26–7, 332.
[81] VP: 136. B. Smith 1978d: 73: the king's role as provider is not just a ritualistic conceit but 'a serious political commitment, which is breached at the monarch's peril'.
[82] *SH*, verses 1002, 1009. [83] *SH*, verse 998, assuming that *dahan* = *dhamma*.
[84] *SH*, verse 848. Analogously with his treatment of Bhuvanekabāhu, the poet asserts that Vīdiyē Baṇḍāra karmically paid for this crime with his own death.
[85] *SH*, verses 350–2.

This short passage clearly inflamed the *Rājāvaliya* author, who elaborated and repeated its theme a number of times, thus injecting a passionate judgementalism into a narrative otherwise reliant on the frustratingly neutral *Alakeśvarayuddhaya*.[86] Because of his 'foolish deed' of allowing Dharmapāla to come under Portuguese influence, let it be known that 'Bhuvanekabāhu caused harm to the people who would be born in future Sri Lanka and . . . to the Buddhist religion (*Buddha sāsana*) as well.'[87] This draws out a latent communal understanding of soteriology, by which the actions of a king reverberate through the karmic fates of his subjects, bringing misfortune not just upon himself, but upon all his people, the whole island, the religion itself. By that time, the late seventeenth century, the sufferings of the people of Lanka under Portuguese dominion could be related not just to the political chains of cause and effect issuing from the mistakes of long-dead rulers, but the karmic consequences of their religious improprieties as well.

When Bhuvanekabāhu was growing up, the anti-Brahmanical campaigns of Vīdāgama Maitreya were under way. His poem *Buduguṇānalaṃkāraya*, from the 1470s, emphasized the importance of the monarch's adherence to *dasarājadhamma* for the welfare of the whole realm.[88] Meanwhile in Kandy, the Alutnuvara slab inscription from Senāsammata Vikramabāhu's reign (1469–1511) offered a very blunt assertion of the moral contingency of kingship: allegiance could only be depended upon until 'a mistaken [course of action] might be adopted by any lordship of the royal family, small or great, including His Majesty'.[89] Nor is the *Rājaratnākaraya*, written in mid-sixteenth-century Kandy, overly subtle. It begins with a re-telling of the *Mahāvaṃsa* story of the Buddha's three visits to Sri Lanka, his expulsion of the *yakās* or demons, and his consecration of the island as a guardian of his *dhamma*.[90] In a departure from the *Mahāvaṃsa* (or perhaps an extension of its logic) and strongly echoing the *Pūjāvaliya*, it then asserts that only those dynasties of kings who are worshippers of the Triple Gem will survive in Lanka, and that if a king of a different religion should ascend the throne he would be driven from it by force.[91] Clearly this text reflects the agenda of a monastic elder concerned with ensuring patronage and support for the *saṃgha*. Yet its contemporary provenance, unambiguous argument, Sinhala mediation and obvious intention for royal consumption lend it substantial evidential weight. It is possible that it derives from the 1540s, precisely the time when Jayavīra was flirting with the Christian missions. The *Rājaratnākaraya* may be reminding the king of

[86] The *Alakeśvarayuddhaya* contrasts with both the *SH* and the *Rājāvaliya* in not registering religious/cultural antagonism, see Strathern 2006a.

[87] *Rājāvaliya*: 75. The *Rājāvaliya* begins by evoking an ancient world in which kings are admonished by their spiritual advisers or even subject to summary karmic justice – vanishing through the trapdoors to hell – for unethical behaviour.

[88] Ilangasinha 1992: 23; Roberts 2004: 45.

[89] *EZ*, IV: 269.

[90] *Rājaratnākaraya*: 1–6/Upham 1833: 1–3.

[91] In the first part of the *Rājaratnākaraya*, a Pāli quotation is followed by a Sinhala commentary, which is where these statements occur. As testimony to the continuing vitality of *vaṃsa* motifs, this hypothetical expulsion of a heathen king is compared to the Buddha's expulsion of the *yakṣas*. Senāsammata is also compared with Duṭugämunu, see *Rājaratnākaraya*: 54/Upham 1833: 127.

what the consequences of conversion might be as contrasted with the glorious fate of good patrons of Buddhism.

The decision to be baptized: aspects of marginality

But where does agency fit into all this structure? Having heaped up all these weighty traditions that would appear to militate against conversion, it now becomes difficult to see how they could be disregarded. For, in some cases, disregarded they were. Particularly in the 1540s, and again in the 1590s, a number of elites appeared ready to submit to baptism. Many of them were *vanniyār* chieftains of the extensive if fragmented dominions in the north and east of the island, who periodically swore allegiance to either Kōṭṭe or Kandy but maintained a practical independence.[92] They emerge only rarely and briefly from the historical silence. As soon as Portuguese relations began to develop with Kandy it seems that other princes began to press their cases with the Portuguese. In 1545, Nuno Álvares Pereira reported that the chiefs of Trincomalee, an important seat of power in the east and a well-known port town, were willing to baptize along with 3,000 persons.[93] Also pursuing an alliance and baptism through his mother stationed at the Kandyan court was the ruler of the Seven Kōralēs. He stands apart from the *vanniyār* neophytes in that his lands were nominally part of Kōṭṭe proper, taking up a great part of the north-west of the island.[94]

When André de Sousa's expedition reached Kandy in the summer of 1546 more ambassadors from the Seven Kōralēs, Batticaloa and Trincomalee greeted the friar Simão de Coimbra, all expressing their willingness to convert.[95] Jayavīra himself may have resorted to all sorts of devices to stall his public baptism, but his increasingly disaffected son dispatched an *ola* expressing a more passionate desire.[96] On his return from Kandy, Coimbra visited Batticaloa, the other major port and political centre on the eastern coast, and a similar pattern emerged there: the chief claimed that he too was willing to convert along with his people, but while he could not do so just now he would have his son and heir baptized as Luís.[97] In 1547, António Moniz Barreto's expedition disembarked at Batticaloa and was reportedly greeted by a great show of local fervour for Christianity. Wending his way through the rugged terrain up to Kandy, he managed to convert promises into baptismal success, acknowledging the conversion of several rulers of territories further inland from the east coast: Bintänna, Vellassa and 'Cauralle'

92 Barros: 37, avers that there were nine different kingdoms on the island, of which four were on the eastern side: Yāla (*Iaula*), Vellassa (*Vilacem*), Batticaloa (*Batecalou*) and Trincomalee (*Triquinámale*). These are better thought of as *vanniyār* chieftancies whose borders and interrelationships are difficult to ascertain. For example, Coimbra tells us that the prince of Batticaloa was heir to Yāla (VP: 62). Of these four, Trincomalee and Batticaloa seem to be the most important while contemporary letters also refer to Bintänna (220, 229). Vellassa and Bintänna were further inland and closer to Kandy, see Queyroz: 62–3 (who describes them as 'Vidanas' of Kandy in a later period).

93 VP: 62.

94 VP: 62, 71.

95 VP: 154, confirmed by 148.

96 VP: 208–9.

97 VP: 211–13. This was also the period when Caṇkili's elder brother was asking for baptism: see VP: 147.

(Kōralē?).[98] In other words, by the end of 1547, swathes of Sri Lanka were under the nominal rule of men who had either professed Christianity or expressed a conditional willingness to do so. The explanation for their enthusiasm lies in their marginality, albeit a marginality as understood in a number of different ways. These same principles would underlie many of the elite conversions of the 1590s too.

On the margins of Portuguese culture. Recall that Lankan traditions did not call for exclusivity: the introduction of a new cult need only present a problem insofar as it damaged the status of the old. We have laid the foundations for our explanation here in Chapter Seven, which suggested three broad interpretations of Christianity that Sinhala Buddhists might arrive at depending on the extent of their exposure to Christianity. In the second category of comprehension the exclusive claims of Christianity are not recognized. In the third category the implications of soteriological theism are unappreciated: the Christian god is seen as equivalent to other *dēvas* and thereby comfortably assimilated into the Sinhala Buddhist pantheon.

What kind of understanding of Christianity and the business of conversion would these rulers have entertained? And how much power did missionaries have to dictate religious behaviour? On these resting stops en route to Kandy it is difficult to imagine that much of what was radically different about the Christian message made its way past the translators and into the contemplations of the petty princelings. In Coimbra's description of his meeting with the chief of Batticaloa it is precisely the this-worldly power of the Christian transcendent that is brought to the fore:

> As soon as the king saw me, he rendered me great honour and entertained me. I was carrying a Cross in my hand; he asked me what that object was. Regarding that, I replied to him what the Lord inspired me, and I also told him that it was the device of the arms of Your Highness, while relating to him the magnificence of the power of Your Highness, with various other matters at which he was much astonished. Then he told me that since the King of Camde [Kandy] had become a Christian, he also wished to embrace the faith together with his son.[99]

This was the god who had given the Portuguese their world empire rather than the one that offered an utterly new form of salvation and the negation of *dhamma*.

The most notorious and troublesome candidate for baptism in the 1540s, Jayavīra, the King of Kandy, must have received very little exposure by the time he made his offer. In contrast to the Raja of Tanor who had sustained contact with clerics, we know that Jayavīra was advised solely by the adventurer Nuno Álvares Pereira, for perhaps three years before any missionaries arrived in his highland kingdom. Sometimes the King of Kandy claimed that he was altogether unaware of the promises to baptize made in his name.[100] Whether this was a ruse or not, it is clear that the significance of baptism had not been effectively conveyed to him: everything suggests that Pereira represented the rite as a symbol of the

[98] VP: 220–1, 229. [99] VP: 211–12; SV: 431. [100] VP: 187, 223.

political relationship of vassalage, a superficial gloss on a basically secular contract.[101] This interpretation may have been supported by indigenous assumptions about the relationship between political subordination and theological accommodation. Jonathan Walters has recently argued that the political hegemony of the empire of Vijayanagar over Kōṭṭe in the fourteenth and fifteenth centuries was given theological expression through the introduction of Vibhīṣaṇa as one of the four guardian deities of Lanka.[102] If genuflecting to a new deity was a natural corollary of submitting to a new overlord, the implications for the Kandyan case are obvious enough.

With the arrival the first friar, Francisco de Monteprandone, Jayavīra would have received a better inkling of what was entailed. Nine days later he was baptized in secret.[103] By this point he could have attained to our second category, of 'semi-comprehension'. Whether or not it was grasped that the Christian God was a source of salvation, the extent to which conversion required a highly visible and exclusive form of religious identity remained unappreciated. António Padrão tells us that the king's movements did not show any trace of Christian intention: 'he does not believe in God; he refuses to be instructed; he does not want to see a Cross . . . the King visits his *pagodes* [temples] as before.'[104] The friar was proved right by the king's disdainful response to the mission of António Moniz Barreto the following year.[105] It had become clear by then that Jayavīra had had little else but diplomatic strategies in mind. Once the Kōṭṭe–Sītāvaka axis had been dissolved he could afford to be high-handed. Barreto confirmed that the king 'had had many pagan images made but none Christian'.[106] Unlike Bhuvanekabāhu, Jayavīra had not had the opportunity to see the social implications of baptism acted out before him by his subjects. Whatever his subsequent deceits, his policy probably had its origin in a misapprehension.

On the margins of Sinhalese Buddhism? The question mark signals the tentativeness of this suggestion, which was first raised in Chapter Eight, that the chiefs of the eastern *vanni* districts were in some sense also on the margins of Buddhism, and that they belonged rather to the world of maritime Hindu converts. The *vanniyār* regions were the location of many relatively recent arrivals from South India who often assumed aristocratic roles, and it is plausible that Hindu practices and cults had a particular hold there. Trincomalee would later become a major Saivite centre, and Queirós tells us of the Mukkuvās of the Batticaloa region, 'in religion they are different from the Chingalas and are more like those of Jaffnapatão.'[107] These two major port towns maintained lively relations with the seafaring communities of the

101 VP: 188. Only when the factory project was definitively defunct did Pereira begin to advertise Kandy's desire to convert. See VP: 207, on Jayavīra's confusion on the Portuguese arrival.
102 Walters 1991–2.
103 VP: 159–60. Couto: 124–5; Trindade, III: 60; Queyroz: 257–8, are mistaken in claiming that the first friars into Kandy were Pascoal and Gonçalo, who probably arrived in 1547.
104 Nov. 1546, VP: 187–8, 171–3.
105 As he reiterates in 1547, 'here there is no king or ruler who seeks that faith sincerely. All is deceit', VP: 234.
106 VP: 221.
107 Queyroz: 65–6, 19.

fishery and Coromandel coasts. The way in which headmen or chieftains took the initiative in asking for baptism and claimed that they were speaking for a large but presumably cohesive body of people, which they numbered in the thousands, very much resembles the conversion of the Paravas in 1532 or the Karāvas in 1557. The links between Trincomalee and the mainland were revealed in 1552 when a group of men from that area arrived among the Christian Paravas presenting a young boy for baptism.[108] The boy was the heir to the Trincomalee lands. A dispute had broken out among the leading men as to who should be his guardian, and his uncle had led a faction to rouse support on the fishery coast, taking the boy with them. What is interesting is that 1,000 Paravas then joined their party and crossed the sea in an attempt to install the prince in his Lankan lands. That attempt failed, but the Christian uncle came to rule the land jointly shortly afterwards.[109]

On the margins of Sacred Monarchy. The apparent problem with which we set up this discussion rests to some extent on a sleight-of-hand that elides the distinction between 'king' and 'ruler'. Most of our neophytes are best described as 'chieftains' rather than the heirs to legitimate monarchical traditions – notwithstanding our Portuguese sources which refer to them as 'princes' or 'kings'. They would have been unable to claim *kṣatriya* status, royal blood or trappings, the 64 royal ornaments, a traditional seat of power and so on. They had not been consecrated or acclaimed or sworn on oath to conduct themselves according to the *dasarājadhamma*. Their authority was therefore less magnificent and less awesome, but also less contingent on visible demonstrations of piety. In this respect they are poorly served by the 'galactic polity' vision of satellites imitating regal splendour. Better served by it is the case of Kandy. Its founder Senāsammata Vikramabāhu could claim the requisite dynastic and caste ancestry of a true monarch and had always represented himself in this way, attempting to mint coins in defiance of Kōṭṭe overlordship.[110] He thereby assumed the weight of sacred imagery that Buddhist kingship entailed. In fact, perhaps largely because of the survival of the *Rājaratnākaraya*, we have more evidence for Kandyan patronage of Buddhist projects and institutions than we do for Bhuvanekabāhu.[111] Unlike his father, Jayavīra seems to have forgone the title of *cakravarti*, but such modesty did not much diminish his sense of sovereignty.[112] As for the Seven Kōralēs, it had been the seat of Sakalakalāvallaba, a son of Vīra Parākramabāhu VIII, and it is likely that his royal-blood offspring were left in place. But it could not have approached Kandy in its claims to monarchical or sacred status.

108 VP: 285–8, 309; SR, V: 96–8.

109 The Christianized prince was then kept as an heir-in-waiting. Another faction arrived in Goa from Trincomalee in 1555 requesting baptism and missionaries to return with them, see VP: 346.

110 See Somaratna 1975: 190–202, for a superbly detailed account of the first Kandyan kings.

111 Jayavīra is possibly the ruler whose great patronage of Buddhism is described in the *Cūḷavaṃsa*, II: 220–3, and *Rājaratnākaraya*, 46–60/ Upham 1833: 125–38, which also refers to his ancestry from the Kōṭṭe line – but states that he was established as king in Kandy by acclamation.

112 *EZ*, IV: 19, 33.

On the margins of the game-board. Of course, we also have to descend from the sacred to give mere political factors their due. For the lesser players on the island one of the most significant spurs to baptism was anticipation: if a central player seemed about to baptize it was natural to fear that those who remained unconverted would come off badly. Referring to the people of Vellassa, António Moniz Barreto commented that 'all these became Christians as they live near the King of Camde [Kandy] and are afraid that, if they remain pagans . . . he might destroy them and take their lands and give them to the Christians of Camde' – which, incidentally, betrays an instinctive understanding of the connection between religious and political loyalties.[113] They were vulnerable both to the exercise of power and to changes in the criteria by which its exercise was legitimized. It was the major figures who were more able to rewrite the rules of political legitimacy, while lesser rulers could only sense that wholesale change was in the winds. At the same time, the atmosphere was charged with competition. Those who looked closest to conversion quickly inspired the jealousy and suspicions of other rulers. While some ruling parties in the Trincomalee region strove to establish a close association with the Portuguese, there was also a manifestly hostile faction who fought for independence from Kandyan overlordship and tried to obstruct its developing relations with the Portuguese. The *Kandy Nātha Dēvāle* inscription of 1543 refers to an uprising in the region in which the Portuguese were involved, which was put down by Kandyan troops.[114] These Portuguese were mutineers from a party of men who had put in to Trincomalee and been blocked from reaching Kandy by a 'bandit' who held power there.[115] Again in 1546, when news of the baptism of Jayavīra leaked out, a 'prince' of Trincomalee supported by other chiefs pinned back and attacked the expedition led by the *casado* Miguel Fernandes, which was attempting to journey upcountry.[116] It is possible that elites recently arrived from South India were adding to the diplomatic strife in this region.[117]

Marginal figures at the centre. There were of course Christianizing pretenders within the true royal capitals and who did have real contact with missionaries. These figures were marginal in only the most straightforward of senses: they happened not to be in power and they had little to lose through a disruption of the status quo.

[113] VP: 221. [114] *EZ*, IV: 27–33. [115] VP: 80–2; Abeyasinghe 1973: 16. [116] VP: 177.

[117] If the information in the *Kandurē Baṇḍāravaliya* (Nevill: Or. 6606(77.III)) has its basis in the events of Bhuvanekabāhu VIIs's reign then a new construction could be placed on the events of the 1540s. We could suggest that much of this eastern swathe of the island and particularly Bintänna and Vellassa had been seized by members of the Kaňdurē Baṇḍāra family recently arrived from the Malabar coast. Four of these brothers had rebelled against the King of Kōṭṭe. Their chief was Herat Baṇḍāra who became enshrined in *väddā* tradition as Kiṁbu-obbe of the fortress rock of Kokāgala in lower Bintänna. The Portuguese were then encountering lands caught up in the turmoil of a relatively recent acquisition of power by South Indian nobles who were prepared to mount newly vigorous claims to independence. It is possible that in the mid-1540s this opposition to the king took the form of appeals to the Portuguese, appeals that included the offer of baptism. In general the King of Kandy seems to have had more authority over this region, but Bhuvanekabāhu was possibly capitalizing on discord between Kandy and these new figures by using the lever of marriage alliance, as the *Kaňdurē Baṇḍāravaliya* narrative might suggest. We know that, at this time, Bhuvanekabāhu managed to mollify the King of Kandy using the same method, arranging for the marriage of the latter's daughter with Dharmapāla, see VP: 164–5, 222, 224, 266.

In these cases considerations of popular legitimacy were simply deferred. They might ultimately be dealt with in two ways. First, they could simply be ignored if one envisaged a rule largely propped up by Portuguese military might. Second, the power of the Portuguese could be seen as transforming the social order as effectively as the political order, enabling popular legitimacy to be construed in Christian terms.

The reasoning of the Kōṭṭe princes preparing for their triumphant return from Goa rested on both principles. While they were not placed under the tutorship of João de Vila do Conde as has often been claimed, they do seem to have had extensive contact with the clerics at the Kōṭṭe court.[118] They seem to have been infected by the passionate optimism of the friars and the self-interested optimism of André de Sousa who predicted that mass conversions were just around the corner. Such dreams, somewhat shaky and implausible when expressed in the humble confines of Portuguese Colombo, must have assumed a greater solidity when they were related amidst the pomp of Goa. In fact, a sojourn in the *Estado's* capital was a good way of changing minds: the spiritual and temporal power of the Portuguese was made concrete and visible and perhaps seemingly inevitable.[119] The basic calculations of the 'marginals at the centre' are also a feature of our Indian material. In both Malabar and Sri Lanka, the complexities and contestability of succession meant that there were always relatives for the Portuguese to do business with.[120]

Bhuvanekabāhu, the holy Heathen

At the centre of the centre, of course, we find Bhuvanekabāhu. By now we should be able to appreciate that what the Portuguese found so frustrating – that the most authoritative king and the one closest to Christian society was also the most resistant to conversion – makes a great deal of sense. Like many rulers throughout history, Bhuvanekabāhu was intrigued by Christianity as the defining feature of the new civilization that produced his vigorous allies. He had had many friendly conversations with the Franciscans since the 1520s and during the 1540s missionaries became a fixture of court life.[121] Even by 1528 an officer in Cochin could report that 'he is so much inclined towards us and our customs that we may hope soon he will become a Christian.'[122] Bhuvanekabāhu continued to visit the church in Colombo (which he had endowed) several times in the 1540s.[123] In contrast to the situation in Kandy, there was already a small conversion movement in Kōṭṭe and the king was under more sustained and serious pressure from the

118 See above, p. 106, n. 120. 119 SR, IV: 354–5.

120 The Raja of Cochin's uncle was willing to be a puppet of Afonso de Albuquerque in order to gain the throne: SR, I: 228–31.

121 Queyroz: 212–13, 235; VP: 182, 193; Trindade, III: 24–5.

122 Flores, Doc: 349. By 1541, both the Viceroy Martim Afonso de Sousa and Francis Xavier thought Bhuvanekabāhu was ripe for conversion, see VP: 13.

123 VP: 193.

Portuguese. According to Gonzaga, he was presented with a very tempting offer in 1543, namely that one friar would return to Lisbon and act as his agent in Lisbon in return for his baptism.[124] Aware as he was of the importance of such direct channels of communication, he turned it down.

But we now know that his very proximity to Christianity, his first-hand experience of the way in which it transformed the loyalties and identities of his subjects, would also have engendered his antagonism towards it. As the heir to the imperial *cakravarti* tradition, the sacred imagery surrounding his rule was intensively developed in a way matched by no other ruler on the island. What we should not do, however, is translate this particular consciousness of the august and ancient nature of his royal lineage, his rarefied status and onerous responsibilities into a single overriding emotion shaping his decision not to convert, namely, the fear of popular rebellion. That, indeed, is precisely what Queirós does, whose interpretations will be addressed in the next chapter. What was Bhuvanekabāhu's policy, then?[125]

His stance was consistent, very frankly expressed, and had the distinct air of being informed by more than political calculation. During Barbudo's embassy of 1545, Bhuvanekabāhu asserted that he would always be a friend of the King of Portugal but that he would never give up his religion.[126] His follow-up letter stated that 'no one calls anyone father except his own. I am unable to believe in any other god besides my own.'[127] He never allowed his guardianship of religious institutions to be impugned. When the Kōṭṭe–Portuguese army entered Sītāvaka in 1550, Bhuvanekabāhu ordered that guards be placed to protect all the holy places in the city.[128] That same year comes evidence of the importance of cult of Upulvan: he refused to punish those who pulled down a church that had been built on the site of its temple at Devinuvara.[129] 'They say he died a great pagan,' wrote Queirós.[130]

Bhuvanekabāhu's letters tightly twinned confessions of religious disavowal with professions of friendship. He and his advisers were well aware of the threat to his reputation in Goa and Lisbon posed by his refusal to convert. How could he retain his alliance in these circumstances? Bhuvanekabāhu perhaps dissimulated on only one point: the promise to receive baptism made by his ambassador at the 1542 embassy. His claim that he had never issued such instructions to the ambassador is lent some support by his blatantly heathen self-representation on the *c.* 1543 casket, but we will never know for sure what happened.[131] It seems a variant of the 'letters, what letters?' device utilized by the King of Kandy, who professed innocence about

124 VP: 40.

125 See Strathern (unpublished), for what the 1543 disputation reveals on this issue. Along with his two brothers he had taken refuge among the monks during the palace intrigue of 1520–1 (*Rājāvaliya*: 71), and he had a *bhikkhu* brother (p. 131, n. 38 above).

126 Reiterated in a letter to João III of 1548, and by João de Castro. André de Sousa dubiously claimed that Bhuvanekabāhu said that he would 'rather become a Muslim than a Christian': VP: 66, 130, 191, 249.

127 VP: 98. 128 Couto: 139. 129 VP: 266, 278. 130 Queyroz: 296.

131 For a cynical view, see VP: 164.

everything Nuno Álvares Pereira had written in his name.[132] But the key stratagem behind the 1542 embassy and its request for missionaries could be described as the 'holy heathen act'. The tone of the good god-fearing vassal that his letters evince may be the result of his Portuguese secretaries massaging their materials into the form most agreeable to the recipients. This obviously applies to various conventional Christian phrases and signings-off, which were used by Māyādunnē, Bhuvanekabāhu and Malabar rajas too.[133] But Bhuvanekabāhu formed close relationships with his scribes and interpreters, who became extremely loyal to him, and much of himself seems to have made it into his letters.[134] The language of these letters destroys the Christian particularity of 'God', who sometimes becomes an entity that both sides acknowledge and sometimes functions as a short-hand for distinguishing religions: 'my God' versus 'your God'. This ambiguity was perfect for blurring the stark category of paganism.[135] For modern readers, the most delectable expression of holy heathenism occurred when Bhuvanekabāhu took it upon himself to give a lesson to the Portuguese in Christian theology, advising them in 1542 that converts should only convert out of 'love of God' rather then for material gain. In 1548 we see a very neat trick. He says on the subject of his conversion that 'since this is the work of God, it cannot be effected by force; God will himself determine when it is to his greater service.'[136] The Christian doctrine of Providence is used to deflect the urgent claims of the friars. The governor himself found this rather persuasive.[137]

[132] VP: 187, 223. The Raja of Cochin resorted to this defence too: SR, I: 228–9.

[133] SV: 198, 478; VP: 48, 135, 186; Flores, Doc: 340–2; SR, I: 62–3.

[134] The scribes and translators would have drafted them according to conventions suitable for Portuguese officialdom. But one notes the frankness, sometimes to the point of rudeness, of these letters, their succinct explanations of indigenous custom (VP: 96–7), their humour ('wandering in the forest', 136), the fact that they contain expressions similar to those reportedly used by Bhuvanekabāhu elsewhere; the firmness with which they press his case.

[135] VP: 182, 249. [136] VP: 249.

[137] VP: 192. The Raja of Cochin used this trick in 1598, see Letter IV in Tavim 1997.

9

The consequences of royal conversion in Kōṭṭe and Sītāvaka

With hindsight, Bhuvanekabāhu's reign can be likened to the brewing of a storm, an uneasy containment of forces both Portuguese and Sinhalese that would be released with his death in 1551. History becomes more turbulent in the aftermath. What follows in the next two chapters is not an attempt to provide a narrative of the later sixteenth century, but a pursuit of the two principal themes of Part Three: sacred legitimacy, and also the problem of identity – ethnic, political and religious – which begins to stake its claim to our attention.

Fernão De Queirós: hindsight and insight

When it comes to the intangible and elusive qualities of identity and legitimacy, the judgements and interpretations of our primary sources are liable to exert an unusually strong influence. This is particularly the case for Queirós, on whose vast text we become increasingly dependent as the century progresses, contemporary correspondence dwindles and Couto lapses into the silence of his lost ninth decade. Queirós' retrospective does more than any other source to provide explicit evidence for traditionalist understandings. These passed, with surprisingly little embellishment, into Pieris' writings, and from there into the mainstream of historiography. Yet, Queirós' text issued from Goa, decades after the expulsion of the Portuguese from the island, and was freighted with a ponderous and complex rhetorical agenda.

All our later European writers can be read as the heirs to a post-Reformation world in which the relationship between state authority and religious fidelity was fraught and theorized: what status has sovereignty when exercised by a heretic?[1] Over the course of the sixteenth century, Europe had been plunged into the 'wars of religion', in which the hand of theological controversies could be seen in popular uprisings and high politics alike, in runaway massacres and dynastic crises. This ideological inheritance is most obvious in the speech which Queirós gives to the *bhikkhu* during the great set-piece debate of 1543.[2] The monk is made to begin by

[1] See Bodin 1992: 110–26 (bk. II, Ch. 5 of *Six Livres de la République*, 1576).
[2] Queyroz: 238–40. Strathern 2005 explores the intellectual context in which Queirós could imagine that Eastern religions were fundamentally similar to Christianity.

appealing to classical nations (Spartans, Athenians, Egyptians) that had warded off foreign presences,

> . . . because as they only try to violate native rites by foreign customs, good sense prompted them to oppose dangerous novelties; and there can be no greater [novelty] than those which cause the diversity of sects, because of the great popular uproars which result therefrom, and because of the great dangers which ensue from the disunion of minds in a Realm, which must acknowledge the same head and be governed on the same principles and by the same laws. And it may be that the variety of the nations that have come to Ceylon has partially perverted the renowned sect of Buddum, for at its commencement it was, according to our documents, greatly different. And though all here present know this truth, it will be necessary to make it known to this Portuguese Padre, so that he may realize that the Chingalaz are also men of reason and culture.

Here we have the hermeneutic dilemma of the *Conquista* perfectly expressed: Queirós at once thoroughly Europeanizing his subjects, so that the Sinhalese are presented as opponents operating according to essentially similar principles, as if *cuius regio, eius religio* ('whose territory, his religion', a doctrine revitalized at the Peace of Augsburg, 1555) was recognized by them also; and yet, also articulating something which seems loosely authentic to a strain of Theravāda thinking, as if this Portuguese clergyman had in mind the anti-Brahmanical outpourings of Vīdāgama Maitreya.[3]

The *Conquista* is beset too by anxieties particular to Asia. By the late seventeenth century, it had become a matter of great frustration to Portuguese churchmen that 150 years of proselytization in Asia had failed to result in the great top-down conversion movements that had been anticipated. This conundrum leaked into Queirós' writings in all sorts of ways. The most magnificent example he gives is that of the previous emperor of China (Shunzhi 1644–61) who, 'though perfectly convinced of the falsity of his sect and of the truth of the law of Christ', even at the extremity of his imminent death was dissuaded from baptism by 'political and human considerations'.[4]

Queirós is also concerned to defend the Portuguese record of conversions in Asia against unflattering comparisons with the Spanish successes in the New World. He gives three – cogent – excuses. The third is 'because the Idolaters and their Princes are fanatical and most obstinate in their blindness, and those who follow the law of Buddum . . . seem to be doomed men . . .'[5] Buddhists may be particularly obstreperous, with their infuriating respect for their own monastics, but all the idolaters of the East are strangely resistant.[6] Queirós then explicitly addresses the reasons why the princes of Ceylon failed to convert, suggesting that it is because the island played host to *both* 'the two common sects with which the Devil keeps the eastern heathendom in thrall', i.e. the vedic cult of the Brahmans, and the

[3] On this fifteenth-century hierarch, see above, p. 155.
[4] Queyroz: 463, and see 286–7. Shunzhi had developed close relations with the Jesuit Johann Adam Schall von Bell and seriously considered conversion (Hsia 1998: 190.).
[5] Queyroz: 660. [6] Queyroz: 115, 141, 700.

teachings of the Buddha. The land is held in heathendom by a diabolical pincer movement, between two traditions each with an awkward pride in their antiquity. And thus in these lands princes are liable to face popular displeasure if they converted.[7]

Nevertheless, for all of this, Queirós' analysis rests on a keen insight: Asian rulers failed to convert partly because of the societal resilience of Indic traditions, and also because of the way these traditions encouraged a particular relationship between the ruler and his subjects. Naturally, his interpretation stops well short of where it needs to, but in one sense Queirós was right to indicate that the 'heathen' Sinhalese would find it difficult to stomach a Christian king.[8] But readers should be aware that in the *Conquista* this insight hardens into a governing stereotype that intrudes upon his narrative crudely. This is why we resisted the temptation to call upon his enticingly explicit evidence regarding Bhuvanekabāhu's interior reasoning. On the occasion of the 1543 debate he portrays Bhuvanekabāhu as being pulled back from the brink of conversion through a craven fear of his people's reaction – but in Gonzaga's more reliable account this is not an issue at all.[9]

Another and even more peculiar invented speech is put into the mouth of Bhuvanekabāhu when addressing Francis Xavier a few years later. The king, who we know was in fact being condemned for his hardening stance towards converts in this period, is made to give a little discourse on the follies of Buddhism.[10] This is then a peculiarly persistent and fictitiously developed trope for Bhuvanekabāhu.[11] The explanation lies in Queirós' feeling that religious and political loyalties are intrinsically bound together. As an enduring ally of the Portuguese and yet a resolute pagan, Bhuvanekabāhu sat awkwardly athwart Queirós' battle-lines. Queirós' solution was to attribute to Bhuvanekabāhu one overriding characteristic: weakness. He is given a passive role, while it is his subjects who are the active force.

Yet, the *Conquista* is far from monological; it is much too ramshackle and sprawling an edifice for that. Queiros' missionary defensiveness was cross-cut by another agenda, which was to emphasize that Sri Lanka could have been – could still become – a truly Christian land if only the progress of the faith had not been tainted by the baser elements of imperialism. Hence he has to give contingency its due and acknowledge sources of monarchical legitimacy beyond the customary religious commitments. He argues that in the tumult of the 1590s, the Sinhalese could have been induced to follow an indigenous Christian prince, but not a Portuguese power nakedly intent on avaricious conquest. As a result when the plan leaked out that the Portuguese were going to set up one of their number on the Kandyan throne, 'that great change succeeded in alienating the minds of a nation that ill-endured its own government [and was] unyielding to a foreign one . . . uniting the whole

[7] Queyroz: 699–702, compares the King of Kandy to Ethiopian kings.

[8] Queyroz: 522–3, 708, and elsewhere. [9] Queyroz: 242.

[10] Queyroz: 266–7. 'I see that the religion of Buddum contains errors as intolerable as they are incompatible with reason . . . [But] I am unable to receive baptism at once, for the least suspicion that they should have of me in this regard would be enough to ruin the whole of my realm.'

[11] See the 'second disputation', in Queyroz: 258–261, discussed in Strathern unpublished.

Island against the Portuguese nation without hesitating to accept a subject for King, provided he was an Apuami or Chingala gentleman.'[12] Queirós acknowledges that Sinhalese royal legitimacy is also nourished by ancestral claims and indigenist sentiment. One might expect such an assumption of the instinctual repugnance of foreign rule from a Portuguese who had grown up under Castilian monarchy during the 'Union of Crowns' (1580–1640). Moreover, the text, littered as it is with erudite references, is also informed by classical models of history that require the empathetic ennobling of the enemy. And as we watch Queirós flexing the muscles of humanist rhetoric through the Tacitean oratory of Sinhalese leaders, we can see how treacherously empathy can obscure cultural difference.[13]

But again, it would be wrong to see his interpretations as a mere product of textual logic or a reflex Eurocentrism; they were grounded in bitter experience. By the time he was writing, the Sinhalese were known as the instigators of the fiercest and most long-lived resistance to the Portuguese anywhere. It is hardly surprising then that they are portrayed as a brave nation intolerant of foreign dominion and with a deep-seated hatred of the Portuguese.[14] Sometimes Queirós' tendency to present spiritual and temporal conflict as isomorphic, as if the island were one vast religious battleground, can overwhelm his ethnological understandings, so that he makes Caṇkili, the Hindu King of Jaffna, party to a pact to defend the 'law of Buddum', for example.[15] Elsewhere I have explained this in terms of Queirós' need to defend a precarious dialogical position on religious similarity/difference in Jesuit circles, and his overwhelming preoccupation with the mystical-prophetic vision of Ceylon's place in a divine providential scheme.[16] However, as we progress further into the sixteenth and particularly seventeenth century, it becomes clearer how much of this sensibility Queirós has imbibed from his Portuguese sources on the island, and, in turn, how much their feelings reflect the very facts of life there. Political struggle had become unmistakably associated with religious and cultural conflict. To consider the *Conquista* as merely a European text is to overlook not only its Goan genesis, but its deep roots in Colombo sources whose identities become more difficult to locate by the compass points of 'Portuguese' or 'Sinhalese'.

Dharmapāla, Vidīyē Baṇḍāra and the consequences of conversion

The collapse of Kōṭṭe after Bhuvanekabāhu's death in Kälaṇiya in 1551 reveals how important he had been to the continuing resilience of the kingdom.[17] The issue

[12] Queyroz: 478. [13] Queyroz: 334–5, 762–4.

[14] Queyroz: 286, 508, 540. Yet, once again, we must watch out for the extension of this seventeenth-century perspective to earlier eras, particularly when it provides a ready-made – and sometimes anachronistic – motivational logic for the mid-sixteenth-century actors: Queyroz: 296, 306.

[15] Queyroz: 262. This is because Buddhism is seen as the principal enemy. The Portuguese rush into battle under the banner of St James; the Sinhalese under 'Buddhum' (Queyroz: 340).

[16] Strathern 2005. Part of Queirós' almost-glorification of Sinhalese opposition derives from his belief that they had been animated by God against the Portuguese for his own purposes: Queyroz: 355.

[17] For a detailed narrative of these years, see Couto: 141–79; Queyroz: 296–347; *Rājāvaliya*: 77–82; C. R. de Silva 1995: 83–92; Quéré 1988a; Lopes: 1967.

of the succession would no longer be denied: while Dharmapāla was proclaimed as king in Kōṭṭe, Māyādunnē pressed his claims and threatened the capital anew. But the impact of the new Viceroy Afonso de Noronha (1550–4), determined to introduce a more brusque style of imperialism, was equally decisive. Indeed, it is likely that Bhuvanekabāhu himself had been the first casualty of this new intrusiveness.[18] When Noronha arrived on the island towards the end of 1551 he was accompanied by 3,000 men, easily the biggest Portuguese force yet seen on the island. This readiness to deploy military might on an unprecedented scale was combined with a decision to re-fortify the Colombo settlement. Noronha's interventionist policy would seem like a throwback to an Albuquerquian vision of empire if it were not for its volatile short-termism.[19] Moreover, the viceroy came prepared to match temporal with spiritual dominion, bringing with him the Bishop of Goa, Juan de Albuquerque, the Superior of the Franciscans, João Noé, the Vicar-General of the Dominicans, Diego Bermúdez, and two Jesuits.[20] This formidable phalanx of ecclesiastical personnel indicates Kōṭṭe's priority status for the Asian mission. It also conforms to a more general pattern across the Portuguese East: the tightening of spiritual attitudes that was causing trouble even in the viceroyal capital of Goa.[21]

Intense pressure was thus brought to bear upon the young king to convert. For the time being, it was withstood. His advisers made a direct connection between his religious allegiance and wider political stability. In advising Noronha that Dharmapāla could not be converted until Māyādunnē was defeated, the Kōṭṭe courtiers were no doubt striking a bargain. But when we hear that the ex-factor António Pessoa had advised the viceroy that conversion was impossible since 'the greater part of the people had gone over to Madune [Māyādunnē]', and that such considerations would have to wait until the country was pacified, it seems there is much more at play than dissimulation.[22] Shortly afterwards the king again refused, saying that he 'could not become Christian because the people would not come to him'.[23]

Dharmapāla eventually acquiesced to baptism in late 1556 or early 1557, and his case stands as the clearest indicator we have of how high the price could be set for breaching the obligations transcendentalist religion incurs. The latter half of the sixteenth-century is characterized by a great shift in power from Kōṭṭe to Sītāvaka. This reflected a transferral of manpower as much as any imbalance of military and financial acumen. In a political culture of contingent, even volatile loyalties, the comparative claims of kings to legitimate authority could be decisive. But a close examination of the sources reveals that for many of his subjects the critical moment in which that authority was lost occurred with his accession itself in late 1551. For them it was not the adoption of Christian rites *per se* that was inflammatory, but the threatened abandonment of old ones.

[18] On his assassination, see above, p. 75. [19] VP: 269; Couto: 154. [20] VP: 285–6, 298, 311.

[21] The description of people fleeing Goa, and of dwindling revenues and trade, in SR: V: 297, could describe Kōṭṭe or Colombo during the same year of 1552, which is cited here in a list of places at war.

[22] VP: 297. [23] VP: 303, 331.

Here, Dharmapāla fell victim not so much to an evolution of Portuguese imperial vision or an influx of evangelical energy as to the most sordid and personal of imperatives: Noronha's desire to seize the royal treasure of Kōṭṭe, which he suspected was far larger than Bhuvanekabāhu had made out.[24] Finding very little, he set out on a quest for it, torturing the royal eunuchs in a vain effort to reveal its hiding-place. Vīdiyē Baṇḍāra as regent then acquiesced to the plunder of the '*pagoda* which was in his palace', most probably a reference to the Temple of the Tooth.[25] Noronha's anodyne account skims lightly over this episode, but details provided by Couto and Queirós suggest that it was acceded to in an atmosphere of violence and intimidation.[26] It is possible that the handing over of the temple was actually the first step towards a public announcement of Dharmapāla's conversion.[27]

These were disastrous miscalculations. Noronha tells us that:

> Then the king and his father informed me that all the people of the city of Cota [Kōṭṭe] and even from the rest of the country had fled, and that all or the majority of the captains had gone over to Madune [Māyādunnē]. This was true, for although my son Dom Fernando had taken the precaution to watch the city . . . , it had not been possible to find means to prevent them going. And it was said that all this was due to the fact that the pagoda was going to be turned into a church and that the king was becoming a Christian.[28]

So serious was the situation that Noronha was forced to hand back the temple. Still the people did not immediately return. Our most important indigenous source, the *Sītāvaka Haṭana*, presents the Kōṭṭe nobility as being sundered in two. The 'pure noble people' (*sudana dana pirisidu*) transferred their allegiance to the Sītāvaka Raja who continued to reign like the pure moon (*pirisidu sañda*).[29] This was a major bureaucratic event. The long list of named individuals and the land rights awarded them, as well as the allocation of residences for lower-status groups, must derive from court records made at the time. Now, the *Sītāvaka Haṭana* presents this as the moment of Dharmapāla's conversion (*kulavaddā*), but it is clearly describing the events of 1551. This represents the sort of chronological slippage one might expect from hindsight of some thirty years, but it derives from an understandable conflation of the critical moment for Dharmapāla's loss of religious legitimacy (1551) and the moment of its symbolic expression or culmination (1556/7).

The poet is engaged in a more artful blurring of the facts when he represents Māyādunnē as the sole beneficiary of this movement of men. In fact, it was Vīdiyē Baṇḍāra whose campaigns articulated most clearly the popular revulsion against these sacrileges. And this is surely one reason why he draws so much of the *Sītāvaka Haṭana*'s sting. As Kōṭṭe's 'internal' answer to Dharmapāla's perfidy, he competed with Sītāvaka as the true guardian of traditional liberties and practices. It is a perverse acknowledgement of his appeal that he should attract so much

[24] VP: 285, 291–2. [25] VP: 330. [26] Couto: 150–1; and Queyroz: 300–1.
[27] VP: 301, where Dharmapāla kisses the cross. [28] VP: 301.
[29] *SH*, verses 370–4. My thanks to Nilmini Dissanayake, Nihal Kiriella, Padmasiri Kulasekera, Sandadas Coperahewa, and Rohini Paranavitana for all their help in translating this work for me.

of the poet's attention (roughly verses 520–950) and scorn – more even than the Portuguese themselves.

As Bhuvanekabāhu's son-in-law and commander of his military forces, Vīdiyē Baṇḍāra had been a key figure in the pro-Portuguese Kōṭṭe court of the 1530s and 1540s. Subsequently, as regent bearing the title *raja*, there was no one more tied to the traditions of the imperial centre than he.[30] He had been willing to cut all sorts of deals with Afonso de Noronha in order to keep Kōṭṭe sovereignty intact, including promising his own conversion in return for the Portuguese disposal of Māyādunnē.[31] In these circumstances Noronha's abrasive style was particularly destructive. Suspicious of Vīdiyē Baṇḍāra's abilities and ambitions while he was out of the country, he ordered his arrest.[32] In 1552, this was finally accomplished but not without public outcry.[33] In an attempt to win his release he converted to Catholicism. According to Couto, this only served to anger the Captain Duarte de Eça, who intensified his punishment. Vīdiyē Baṇḍāra's enterprising wife then engineered his escape from prison, and he embarked on his first spree of violence against the Church.[34] There appears to have been a short period in which he was ready to be reconciled with his son, but he then embarked on an intense military campaign that was unmistakably informed by a hatred of the Portuguese and their faith.[35]

He apostatized with a vengeance: in his sweep up the coastal belt south of Colombo he targeted Christian churches, burnt them down, martyred Franciscans, and forced converts to give up their new identity.[36] Beyond an alliance with the Prince of the Seven Kōralēs, the quick success of his campaign indicates that he drew on considerable popular support, and Trindade's assertion that Māyādunnē supported him at this early stage is also plausible.[37] If he did indeed hold the Tooth Relic, the gravity of his threat becomes even more explicable.[38] From his headquarters at Pälañda, he directed attacks at Kōṭṭe with such vigour that Māyādunnē began to consider him a dangerous rival. In April 1555, the new Captain of Colombo, Afonso Pereira de Lacerda, entered into a pact of alliance with the Sītāvaka leader in order to defeat Vīdiyē. The latter's response was to wage more war against the Christian establishments of the south. This was not simply a Buddhist campaign.

[30] *Rājāvaliya*: 77. [31] VP: 300, 306. [32] VP: 304–8; Couto: 157–62.

[33] Baṇḍāra's wife 'stirred up the greater part of the people of Cota', according to Couto: 159.

[34] VP: 337; Couto: 161. In December 1552, people were returning to paganism out of fear of Vīdiyē Baṇḍāra. Queyroz' (302–15) chronology seems muddled in suggesting that Vīdiyē was already waging an anti-Christian campaign *before* his arrest, but the level of narrative detail indicates the use of an otherwise unknown *casado* oral tradition concerned with the career of Vīdiyē Baṇḍāra. The statement (315) that he was released through the mine-digging services of the Pallara ('palaraz') men indicates that this may be a fairly reliable strand of oral tradition – compare *Alakeśvarayuddhaya*: 36 – and is not to be found in Couto. *Rājāvaliya*: 77, adds that Vīdiyē assumed the title of '*Tuttarāyankanada Ēkā-anganvīra*', which is difficult to translate – perhaps 'hero of the village training ground' – but is heroic rather than regal (my thanks to Rohini Paranavitana and K. N. O. Dharmadasa for this).

[35] Couto: 160–2. [36] VP: 342; Queyroz: 316.

[37] Trindade, III: 92–3; Couto: 170. The assertion of Queyroz: 321, that the Sinhalese joined Vīdiyē 'in order to have a native king who kept the law of the Buddum', may be authorial inference.

[38] Queyroz: 314.

According to the report of one horrified missionary, the previously Hindu Paravas who had converted were ordered to 'shave their beard[s] and apply ashes on their forehead[s] and become pagans again'.[39] There were mass apostasies.

There was a personal history to this new force. According to his son and our Portuguese sources, Vīdiyē's resentment at his ill-treatment while in prison was its principal inspiration.[40] Undoubtedly the overweening element to the Portuguese presence had been brought to a new pitch by the latest wave of officials. But there is more to it than this. Vīdiyē would have had extensive experience of Christianity before and after his conversion. His actions can be seen as bearing the mark of the aggressive ideology he fought against. In this, as in so many other ways, he stands as the first example of a recognizable type whom we shall meet many times from the 1590s onwards: the Lusitanized aristocrat who rebels and takes up the symbols of indigenous identity. Vīdiyē Baṇḍāra was thus the first rebel apostate. Like those of many later leaders, his campaigns also followed a resonant humbling of the Portuguese in the field. In his case, the first great defeat of Portuguese armed might on Lankan soil in the debacle of the 1550 expedition to Kandy would have still been fresh in the mind.[41] He was not defeated until Māyādunnē was brought on side in 1555 by a treaty that granted the bulk of Kōṭṭe lands to Sītāvaka. When Māyādunnē, once again reneging on his vassalage, resumed war with the Portuguese in 1557, he could now do so as the most powerful Sinhalese ruler on the island.

The destruction of Vīdiyē Baṇḍāra was the most important reason why Dharmapāla could now entertain the prospect of baptism. This was facilitated by the growth of the small Christian-leaning movement in the Kōṭṭe court, which now encompassed the top two figures in government. The chaplain and ambassador Śrī Rāmarakṣa Paṇḍita, a man who described himself as 'gentile and Brahman' in January 1551, had undergone baptism while staying in Goa in late 1552. His godfather was the viceroy himself, whose name he then took.[42] He had been among the most Lusitanized of Kōṭṭe men, but one suspects that Noronha's heavy-handed tactics were again involved. The conversion of the chamberlain – then acting as regent – followed the same pattern: he too was baptized after being taken as a hostage to Goa in 1555.[43] In early 1556, thousands of the Karāva people in the coastal districts to the north and south of Colombo converted en masse. It is possible, as C. R. de Silva has suggested, that these were mainly people who had recently apostatized and were now returning to the fold.[44] But this was a moment of hope for the mission as the new Captain-General of Ceylon, Afonso Pereira (1555–9), and the Guardian of the Franciscans in Colombo, Pedro de Belém, swiftly moved to rebuild the church.[45]

[39] VP: 346, 342. [40] VP, II: 55. [41] VP: 265; Queyroz: 274. [42] VP: 278, 305, 327–8, 338.

[43] Trindade, III: 92–3; *Alakeśvarayuddhaya*: 35. On his religious life, VP: 306, 330

[44] C. R. de Silva 1998: 108; Quéré 1988 b: 165–70; Roberts 1995: 30. VP: 348–9, n. 3, estimates the number of converts as 3,000, in contrast to inflated reports of 70,000, see VP: 356; Trindade, III: 134; Queyroz: 326.

[45] VP: 354–5.

When all this culminated in the prize that the Eastern mission had been holding out for and Dharmapāla finally consented to become João, the chronicler Trindade took the opportunity to reiterate his faith in the top-down conversion model. There was rejoicing in Portugal at the news, 'for they understood that, since he had accepted the Faith, his subjects too would accept it, because ordinarily the people follow the example of those who rule them. In fact this is what happened.'[46] Undoubtedly, the mission did receive a boost and several leading men of Kōṭṭe felt compelled to accept baptism.[47] But Trindade ought rather to have invoked the opposing missionary trope of awkward custom.

However, the only source to give explicit information as to the popular reaction is the *Conquista*. This tells us that in June of 1557, monks re-entered the capital and spread the word to revolt.[48] Soon enough the Captain, Diogo de Melo, and Dharmapāla were pinned back to the palace. The Captain of Colombo arrived the next day to find the city quiet, but as a punishment all the monks (referred to here as 'yogis') were rounded up and thirty of them were killed. Revolt erupted again, Māyādunnē stepped in to lure the disaffected populace to come over to him, and many did so. Queirós' text seems to have preserved memories of a genuine popular movement at the time of most heightened religious sensitivity. It stands as an excellent demonstration of the way in which a transcendentalist clerisy – the *saṃgha* – could articulate and foment broad sentiments against elite conversion.

But Queirós might be overplaying the wider consequences of the baptism itself.[49] Naturally, he saw that rite as the definitive act by which one moved from one heavily defined religious community to another. As such, he imagined it must have constituted the critical blow. In reality, that had been struck in 1551. If the baptism itself inspired further revolt among the remaining inhabitants of Kōṭṭe, it was partly again through its consequences for the Temple of the Tooth. Dharmapāla signed a document diverting its revenues and those of all other 'heathen' temples to the Fransiscans.[50] The *Daḷadā Māligāva* was transformed into the Church of the Holy Saviour. The Tooth Relic was whisked away. Kōṭṭe itself was abandoned in 1565, as the Portuguese retreated to Colombo. Now there was little of the pre-Christian apparatus to sustain Dharmapāla's monarchy, and even the Portuguese officials conceded that his new dwellings were hardly commensurate with royal glamour.[51]

46 Trindade, III: 39–43. See also VP: 352, n. 1, and 357, n. 1; Queyroz: 327–30, Ferguson's notes in Couto, 172–3; *Rājāvaliya*, 77; Gonzaga 1603: 1204; Ribeiro: 13.
47 VP: 359. *Alakeśvarayuddhaya*: 37/*Rājāvaliya*: 76.
48 Queyroz: 337–8. It is not unusual that this does not appear in our contemporary letters given that there are so few for the period Jan. 1557–Feb. 1559.
49 Queyroz: 321–4, 344.
50 Including the great temple at Kälaṇiya, Queyroz: 330–1; Trindade, III: 48; VP, II:: 117.
51 Couto: 240–1, 415, 421, *Rājāvaliya*: 85; IAN/TT, Maço 107, Doc. 51, Letter of Simão de Brito de Castro to the Cardinal Archduke, 7 Dec. 1588.

It is a strange fact and a dreadful irony that once they converted, kings often lost status in the eyes of the Portuguese too.[52] We do then have to pause to acknowledge the complex jumble of factors behind Dharmapāla's impotence. In 1574, he wrote an extraordinary letter bemoaning his fate to Pope Gregory XIII:

> After I had become a convert to the most holy Catholic Faith, the fathers tried to constrain the nobles who still remained hardened and obstinate in their false paganism; but as they saw me with little power, with few subjects, and without kingdom and treasures, they abandoned me and went their way; from this arose many wars.[53]

There is just a suggestion here that, temporal concerns being otherwise, Kōṭṭe could have persisted as a viable Christian state. Increasingly impoverished, Dharmapāla lost the redistributive powers that were so vital to Lankan leadership. Holed up in Colombo, he was often at the mercy of Portuguese officers who abused his finances and refused to accord him regal respect.[54] Since the 1530s, the Kōṭṭe kings had always enjoyed a superior relationship with their royal counterparts in Lisbon and Madrid rather than with the Portuguese officers in Colombo. Royal letters commended his status as a Christian king and worried about his finances, but even they eventually came to echo the feeling that 'he had no understanding of how to govern either himself or his vassals.'[55]

We shall see that some of the symbolic capital of the *cakravarti*-ship remained intact, allowing the Kōṭṭe line, even *sans* Kōṭṭe city, to enjoy a brief resurgence in the unusual context of the early 1590s. Dharmapāla's titles and ancestry still held some appeal to the lesser rulers who would come to render obeisance. But if the idea of Kōṭṭe survived in some form, it seems that for many decades and in the eyes of many Sinhalese he was not fit to wear its crown. His religious capitulation undermined the semblance of independent indigenous authority that Bhuvanekabāhu had sought to uphold. In 1589 a friar articulated his predicament succinctly: the Christian king had been 'deprived of his kingdom and the great honour and credit that heathen kings receive in these parts'.[56]

52 The Jesuit Nunes Barreto, 1566: 'We see by experience that all the kings who have become Christians are less honoured and favoured than when they were gentiles. The King of Ceylon became a Christian, and while before he was a great lord, now he is practically deprived of his kingdom just because he has received baptism,' see VP, II: 5, and compare with complaints of the Raja of Tanor in 1549 in SR, IV: 567–8.

53 VP, II: 55–6.

54 In 1574, Dharmapāla complained (VP: ii. 54–7) of domineering Portuguese officers, which spurred Valignano's complaints of 1575 (VP, II: 68, 72). See too VP, II: 88, on his shrunken dominions, and IAN/TT, Maço 107, Doc. 51 (cited above), on how his diplomatic activity was obstructed. As for his poverty, which detracted from his royal presence according to Rodrigo da Cunha in 1589, and Portuguese interference in his finances, see Lopes 1962: 141–2; VP, II: 104–5; *APO*: 486. See AGS-SP, Códice 1551, 229 (from 1589), on the poverty of a relative despoiled by Rājasiṃha.

55 *APO*: 816, and on his affairs in general: 75, 180–1, 254, 309, 445, 486, 730, 860; AHU, Códice 281, royal letters of 1590, 1593, fols. 74–74v, 80v, 234.

56 Lopes 1962: 141–2.

Māyādunnē: a national-spiritual champion?

Māyādunnē enjoys something of a reputation as the leader of 'national' and spiritual resistance to this day.[57] If Bhuvanekabāhu's 'foolish' friendliness began the sorry story of foreign domination, his great foe Māyādunnē can be seen as a foresighted defender of independence. Behind this one discerns the vivid characterizations of Fernão de Queirós. In one of his Tacitean imaginings of the Sītāvakan camp, we are told of a council convened by Māyādunnē in order to decide upon the legitimacy of his claims to the emperorship.[58] The argument is proposed *inter alia* that Dharmapāla had lost any rights to the throne when he abandoned Buddhism. A minority opposition then argue that there was no actual law to that effect. This is a little puzzling until one realizes that Queirós must have been keenly aware of the complex legal wrangling that had surrounded Dharmapāla's donation of sovereignty to the King of Portugal in 1580. Portugal's justification for the conquest of Ceylon, the righteousness of which the *Conquista* insisted upon, rested on Dharmapāla's legitimacy.[59] Then we are told of a renegade who had joined the Sītāvaka camp, one Afonso Rasquinho, who

> having apostatized from the Faith tried to prove that João [Dharmapāla] had ceased to be King from the time he received baptism, for just as when Catholic princes become heretics, they lose the throne or state of which they were lords, in the same way if one who is pagan becomes a Christian, he incurs the same penalty, and with greater reason, because the guilt is greater: a law and theology quite worthy of a renegade.[60]

Queirós represents this as a mendacious argument: he needs there to be no *legal* reason why conversion would render Dharmapāla's illegitimate, precisely because he has dwelt repetitively on indigenous *feelings* that this was so. It remains a confounding piece of evidence. If – in its odd particularity – it deserves any credence, then Sītāvakan rhetoric was being influenced by renegades and adventurers and the European legalisms or constructions of religious identity they carried with them. At any rate, we are told that Māyādunnē is convinced and prepares for war. During these preparations the mysterious figure of Buddhavaṃsa ('Budavance') arrives. He is drawn to Māyādunnē and, in a rousing speech of patriotism and piety, hails him for fighting 'because he fears that in the course of time this Kingdom will go to strangers, and that the religion of Buddum will be altogether displaced by that of Christ'.[61] This speech reeks of a fictitious dramatization of Queirós' own preoccupations.[62]

57 Mirando 1985: 25–6; Quéré 1988b: 170–3; Bourdon 1936: 64; Flores 1998: 193; Ilangasinha 1992: 117; C. R. de Silva 1995: 88. The influence of Pieris 1983–92: 151, 396, is perhaps at work here.

58 Queyroz: 334–5.

59 Saldanha 1993. Clearly, the issue had been raised as to whether Dharmapāla's conversion nullified his sovereignty.

60 Queyroz: 335. 61 Queyroz: 336.

62 It was perhaps Queirós' way of introducing or explaining the Buddhist revolt in Kōṭṭe, June 1557, which does have the ring of truth and would have been witnessed by many Portuguese.

Queirós' stereotype of Māyādunnē is not, however, absurd. He had provided violent opposition to conversions in the 1540s.[63] In 1551, religious warfare had been brought right into the heart of Sītāvaka when Noronha invaded the city and ordered all the temples to be burned down.[64] It is also plausible that 1557 was the key moment for the formulation of a religious policy in opposition to Dharmapāla's – because of the latter's baptism, to be sure, but also and perhaps more importantly because Vīdiyē Baṇḍāra could no longer claim that role.[65] The religious anger and rallying cries that his campaigns invoked could now be exploited by Sītāvakan forces as they marched to besiege Kōṭṭe. It is likely that Māyādunnē's appeal to these sentiments gained weight by his acquisition of the Tooth-Relic – or at least *a* tooth-relic.[66] A strong Sinhalese oral tradition, surviving in a number of diverse *ola* manuscripts in the Nevill and *Saparagamuvē Pärani Liyavili* collections, tell us of a monk, one Diyavaḍana-nilame of Hiripitiya, who had a dream in which he heard the words 'clean the tooth'.[67] Under threat as it was from the Portuguese, the monk interpreted this as an injunction to escape with the tooth to Sītāvaka. Further Sinhalese sources at least confirm that Māyādunnē had a tooth installed at a shrine in Delgamuva. The *Rājāvaliya*, which does not appear to have drawn on the same strand of oral tradition, tells us that the community of monks dwelling in Kōṭṭe fled to Sītāvaka and the hill country in *c.* 1552.[68] They may have absconded with the relic during the negotiations over the royal treasure. In general terms, the regrouping of monks fleeing from Kōṭṭe in Sītāvaka makes a lot of sense.

But we should distinguish between the tenor of Māyādunnē's propaganda and his personal motivations. It was his aggression against his brother that had necessitated Portuguese involvement in Kōṭṭe in the first place. And what comes through most strongly is his opportunism. Just as politically he had become a vassal and an ally of the Portuguese when it suited him, so in the religious sphere he was not above coming to an agreement with António Moniz Barreto in 1547 'regarding the spread of the Christian religion'.[69] As the 1550s wore on, however, such compromises became increasingly untenable.

[63] See above, p. 108. [64] VP: 304; Couto: 152.

[65] Nevill: Or. 6606(106–7), refers to Māyādunnē as a protector of Buddhism, but is probably late. Or. 6605(3) and Or. 6609(147) are religious works copied in 1559 and 1569 respectively, indicating continuing patronage of Buddhist textual production.

[66] According to Queyroz: 364–5 (and see also Couto: 176, 191–2), Vīdiyē took the Tooth Relic to Jaffna as one of the 'treasures' when he fled Kōṭṭe. This was then the item discovered by the Viceroy Constantino de Bragança during his expedition to Jaffna in 1560 and subsequently destroyed. However, it is possible that Vīdiyē passed the relic to monks for safekeeping before his death, who then took it to Sītāvaka with the conversion of Dharmapāla (Queyroz: 314, 333).

[67] Nevill: Or. 6606(3) *Daḷadā Sirita*; Or. 6606(34) *Daḷadā Puvata*; Or. 6606(106–7). On documents in *Saparagamuvē Pärani Liyavili* (Nanavimala 1946) see Ilangasinha 1992: 185. Sub-portions of these texts may date to the early seventeenth century, reflecting perhaps a Kandyan need for a coherent story affirming the survival and authenticity of the current tooth.

[68] *Rājāvaliya*: 76 (but not in the *Alakeśvarayuddhaya*).

[69] VP: 236.

Blessed Lanka: the Sītāvakan political imagination

Never mind that his *de jure* rule only came in 1581–93, from the early 1560s onwards Rājasiṃha I became the most formidable opponent the Portuguese ever faced on the island. For almost thirty years, Portuguese authority was pinned back to the immediate environs of Colombo.[70] The Venetian merchant Cesare Federici who visited the island in the 1570s reported that that Rājasiṃha, having 'made the whole soldiery favourable to himself', had dominated the island for the last thirteen years as 'a great tyrant'.[71] After his annexation of Kandy in 1582, his mastery was a simple fact, acknowledged by a survey report of the East for that year, which evoked an image of inherent ceaseless war between past and present kings of Ceylon and the embattled toe-hold of Colombo.[72] Rājasiṃha besieged it many times, desperate for a monopoly on the imperial title that only the extinguishment of Dharmapāla could bring. The shift of the Sinhalese reputation from a pacific people to a stubbornly militiarized force was well under way.

Nor was Rājasiṃha merely a warrior. In the later sixteenth century, Sītāvaka began to exhibit a few of the characteristics of the 'early modern' state form that was flourishing in other parts of Asia contending with the arrival of Christian and Muslim seaborne powers.[73] Just like other rulers rising to prominence in these newly intensified military and commercial struggles, Rājasiṃha sought to harness the new technologies to his advantage and develop a naval force that could, at times, stand up to the Portuguese; to exploit and develop the trade in high-profit goods such as cinnamon and pepper; and to form strategic understandings with neighbours, the princes of Malabar or the Nāyakkars of the Coromandel, extending his anti-Portuguese alliances as far as Aceh and engaging the Portuguese in the subtler arts of diplomacy.[74] Sītāvaka, then, had typically cosmopolitan aspirations, and continued to draw in foreign specialists to high-status positions, whether South Indians or indeed Portuguese.[75]

But cosmopolitanism and erratic xenophobia are not mutually exclusive. With the production of the *Sītāvaka Haṭana* in *c*. 1585, we see the earliest extant example of a genre that would come to fruition in the middle of the next century, the *haṭana* or war poem.[76] As with the subsequent *haṭana*s, this was secular idiomatic poetry

70 Couto: 233
71 Trans. by Ferguson in Couto: 242–3, n. 4; *Livro das Cidades* . . . in Luz 1953: 75.
72 *Livro das Cidades* . . . in Luz 1953: 75. By this time, three-quarters of the principal Malabar cities had at some point turned against the Portuguese.
73 See Strathern forthcoming c for an in- depth consideration of how Sri Lanka might fit into models of 'early modernity'.
74 Queyroz: 425, 429, 440; Couto: 266; *APO*: 207, 216–17; VP, II: 72; C. R. de Silva 1995: 92–3, 97, 103.
75 Couto: 339, 290: in the 1587 siege, Rājasiṃha had 400 bombardiers, including Javanese and Kaffirs, but the greater part were Portuguese. The latter were therefore both vilified and recruited.
76 *SH*. This section owes an intellectual debt to Roberts 2004, which first used the *haṭanas* as a source for identity. Please note the possibility raised in the Introduction that the *SH* is later than its advertised date of 1585.

intended to rouse men to action in a common cause. At its most basic, that cause is loyalty to the Sītāvakan kings, but it also takes in a sense of the guardianship of the Sinhalese cultural heritage.[77] There is little sense of such a community as 'the people of Sītāvaka'.[78] The term 'Sinhala' is used by the poet, but not as a touchstone.[79] It is possible that this is because Rājasiṃha's court was so oriented to drawing in diverse cultural groups that it sought to emphasize a more Lankan or indigenist sentiment. But we have cautioned against slotting group identities into exclusive dichotomies of resistance or integration. It is more likely that Sinhalaness is simply taken for granted; is not explicitly exalted because it is implicitly acknowledged.

Sometimes it is explicitly acknowledged. The occasional differentiation between the Sinhalas and the Tamils is effected by recourse to ancient wars and insulting epithets, as in the reference to Duṭugämunu's feats in breaking the 'savage Tamils' (*säḍi demaḷun*).[80] This differentiation is lent a territorial dimension when we are told of the King of Jaffna's displeasure at hearing of the arrival in this country (*meraṭa*) of Vīdiyē Baṇḍāra – he who had caused so many disturbances in 'Sinhala country' (*siṃhala raṭa*). The subsequent verses are particularly revealing. Recall that this Vīdiyē has been the most traduced figure in the poem. And that at this point (both when these events were taking place, and when the poem itself was composed), the Jaffna king was at peace with his southern neighbours and was here obliging them by dispatching this awkward rebel. But there now occurs a curious twist in perspective. We are presented with the enemy uncivilized Tamils (*rupu demaḷu vanasara*) advancing upon the beautiful Vīdiyē and decapitating him. Meanwhile some princes in his retinue, who had complexions like that of Śakra, had been wreaking sexual havoc among the Jaffna women: these potent princes were cornered and killed by the unfavoured Tamils (*novasaru demaḷu*) – leaving the women mourning.[81]

The representation of the Portuguese also suggests how they could be seen as an antitype to indigenous virtues. The *raison d'être* of Sītāvakan power as a scourge of the Portuguese is evident in the vow undertaken by Māyādunnē that he will give over Lanka to Kataragama if he is provided with a son who will vanquish them.[82] The epithets awarded to the Portuguese conjure up unethical power: they are cruel, fierce (*napuru, ruduru*), frightening. They are beset by disgusting appetites for arrack, opium, and flesh (*geri mas*, beef, but which carries an untranslatable

77 See above, p. 154, for its comments on the destruction of Buddhism.

78 There is no mention of the Sītāvaka *sēnā*.

79 Sinhala *sēnā/senaga* (people or army): verses 347, 498, 507, 510, 871, 1021. Both the Kōṭṭe kings and the Sītāvakan kings can call on them. Occasionally, when the Portuguese are the foremost enemies, the Sītāvakan forces are equated with the Sinhala *sēnā*: verse 507.

80 Verse 447. Michael Roberts 2004: 133, suggests 'fierce', 'filthy' as translations of *säḍi*.

81 Verses 937–52. The Tamils may be 'enemies' here only from Vīdiyē's perspective, not necessarily from the perspective of all Sinhalese. *Novasaru* is presented as the antonym of the *saru* (fertile, potent) princes. The fierceness of the Tamils is emphasized in these verses.

82 *SH*: verse 238.

sense of distaste).[83] The cosmopolitan armies assembled by the Kōṭṭe–Portuguese allowed the poet to indulge in a more generic xenophobia:

> Accompanied by Vadakkara, Mukkaru, Doluvara, Kavisi and Uruvisi[84]
> The Portuguese who fought having come with vast foreign armies [*para senaga*]
> Were, without even a cloth at the waist, felled in the middle of the paddy fields and heads were cut and piled up
> Half-castes [*tuppahin*] of this country [*meraṭē*] who had joined to swell their bellies were caught and tied up.
>
> The Sinhalese soldiers who were in this country properly were set free in charity without being killed
> The half-castes who were inseparable in joining for the consumption of beef [*geri mas*]
> And who were deceiving the world by uttering falsehoods and by trickery and thereby swelling their bellies,
> All of them were condemned to a humble state by being giving in servitude to väddā chiefs.[85]

It is a comment on the typical incoherence of identity rhetoric that Rājasiṃha's armies were also stuffed with foreign bodies! For this passage illuminates the different orders of enemy in the Sītāvakan imagination, each endowed with a different moral status according to the degree and nature of their foreignness. Portuguese and overseas mercenaries are just slaughtered. The mixed-race of Lanka are evidently troubling to consider, a new sort of being generated by and embodying the Portuguese sins of greed and lust, bearing in their very selves a form of treachery. (The theme of greed here also serves to emphasize the mercenary nature of their allegiance.) These have to be humbled, their low status established by being given in servitude to the väddās. Last, we have the Sinhalas who had fought against the Sītāvakan kings. These may be enemies but of a different order; being 'rightful residents', they were merely sent away.[86]

The poet is conscious too of the way in which warfare not only issues from such group sentiments but ushers them into being, thrusting other solidarities momentarily into the background. The following verse is difficult to interpret, partly because of the vagueness of the term *jāti* (birth, kind, community etc). Given that the ethnic heterogeneity of the Sītāvakan armies is occluded by the

83 Verses 285, 362–4 (a disgusted listing of their provisions), 508–9, 515–17, 1020.

84 'Vadakkara' are probably *vadugai*, Telugu-speakers; *Alakeśvarayuddhaya*: 34, suggests they are Māppiḷas. 'Mukkaru' are Mukkuvās; Kavisi may mean black Africans, from 'Kaffir', although Paranavitana suggests 'Malays'. Amarasinghe 1998: 204–5, nn. 13–17, suggests that 'Doluvara' came from Kulu district (?) in South India, and 'Uruvisi' from Ormuz.

85 Verses 1107–8. *Tuppahin* can mean both those of mixed race and those of mixed culture (the Lusitanized). Here I have tried to retain its pejorative flavour. In the first line of 1108, '*meraṭa nisi koṭa hiṭiya siṃhala senaga*' could also mean 'those Sinhalese who conducted themselves reasonably', although Rohini Paranavitana suggested to me that it means 'the Sinhalese who lived permanently' or 'by descent'. 'Inseparable': *paṇaṭa paṇa*: would give their lives for each other.

86 The poem concludes (verse 1119) with a verse calling on foreign enemies (*para rupunaṭa*) to be dishonoured. See too Roberts 2004: 120.

poem, *jati* seems to refer to what we would think of today as caste. *Jāti* matters and yet can be transcended:

> People of different *jati*, statuses, lineages, names,
> Disregarding *jāti* divisons, pouncing with relish
> In the name of the *jāti* taking up arms, with arms in hand,
> The *jāti* uttering war-cries and attacking.[87]

It may be more accurate to describe the main concern of the imagery as not the struggle between the Sinhalese and their enemies, but the struggle between Lanka and her enemies. However, this is partly simply because the interests of the Sītāvakan kings and Lanka are conflated through the *cakravarti* title, and there seems to be a similar conflation of the Lankan with the Sinhala. All, in the poem's vision, are mustered into the same cause.

If the poem is a panegyric, its subject is Lanka (*Siri Laka* or *Lakdiva*) as much as any king of it. It appears again and again as the most vivid and natural political unit; as an entity to inspire love and devotion; as a bounteous, rich, fertile land of world-renown.[88] The way in which this image outshines any other political boundaries is revealed by the imprecision of the territorial terminology it leaves in its shadow. All units are lumped under the generic term *raṭa*, which is perhaps best translated as land(s), but signifies variously regions or places, chieftaincies, princely fiefdoms, Lankan society, or Lanka itself.[89] *Raja*s are based in cities (*nuvara*), not territories. Look at Map 2: is it not otherwise puzzling that the Kōṭṭe inheritance should be 'divided' among royal seats which remain so closely huddled together? There was certainly a 'king of the city of Sītāvaka', but the 'kingdom of Sītāvaka' is more a crutch for our own imaginations than it was a living reality in the minds of its inhabitants. There is no equivalent term in the poem.

The only occasion where Sītāvaka itself takes centre stage is the narration of its place-name myth.[90] When King Rāvaṇa ousted the pre-existing kings of Lanka, one had fled to the forests to become an ascetic (*tapasi*).[91] Rāvaṇa sent his men to kill him, demanding a pot of blood as proof of his death. But they colluded with the ascetic king who produced it instead from his thigh by spiritual exertion. It was then buried. Later, a farmer's plough turned up the pot and it was opened to reveal a baby girl. She was brought to the ascetic king and named Sītā (plough-line). The fabrication of a new royal seat evidently required ancient royal associations. If this is the Rāvaṇa familiar to us from Rāmāyana-derived mythology, then the story

[87] Verse 826, which is obscure, particularly the first line (*jāti tharan kula nām lat aya niti*, which could mean '*Jāti* chiefs, in possession of lineage names') and third.

[88] There are too many mentions to list, but see, for example, verses 5, 27, 165, 187, 238–40, 264, 322, 352, 517, 848, 999, 1005–11, 1117–19 1032.

[89] Indeed the only other territorial division of Lanka is the antique/anachronistic *trīsiṃhalā*, in verses 36, 880–6, 998.

[90] Many thanks to Rohini Paranavitana for drawing my attention to this section and producing a valuable summary of it.

[91] This indirect founding father is thus endowed with spiritual virtue, but it appears to be of 'Hindu' sort, perhaps because a pre-Vijayan/Buddhist history is imagined here.

would appear to be located in a pre-Vijayan world. Thus we are reminded of the fluidity and fecundity of origin myths at this time. However, while it may exude the expected whiff of blood and violence, this story is structurally very different to the Vijaya myth. It does not function as an account of the foundation of the socio-political community, of a people under a king. It operates at a different level: the origin of a particular kingdom, or the name of that kingdom, within an already existent civilization. Instead of a foreign prince bringing civilizing power by outwitting the indigenous folk, we have an indigenous king outwitting a powerful overlord . . .

Sītāvaka is merely a stepping-stone in the rest of the poem, whose overriding concern is to show how the Sītāvakan kings are the rightful heirs to the *cakravarti* title.[92] How it does this, how it legitimizes the claims of this rebellious younger brother in his parvenu capital, tells us a great deal about the particularities of sixteenth-century kingship. The poem begins by implicitly acknowledging Kōṭṭe's claim to pre-eminence. But it appears titles must be justified through *deeds* as acknowledged by *popular acclaim*, and the Kōṭṭe kings prove unworthy of their inheritance while Māyādunnē shows his mettle. Royal authority is a succession of steps rather than a throne ascended to once and for all, and there are three principal stages of Māyādunnē's ascension. First, he plays the lead role in righting the wrongs of disinheritance by gathering support from various regions before the march on Kōṭṭe in 1521.[93] Second, he is the lone leader mounting resistance to the Portuguese in the 1530s and 1540s. His pilgrimage to Kataragama in these years is extended into a tour of the island and its defining sites such as Adam's Peak. Wherever he goes he inspires love and awe: the masses flock to the *narañidu* (king of the people), pay him homage, worship at his feet.[94]

This attests to Michael Roberts' arguments as to how pilgrimage and travel-by-foot could cultivate a sense of community in a pre-modern society.[95] One can see Māyādunnē circumambulating the country as marking out its sacredness in the way a Buddhist encircles a *stūpa* – or at least signifying his proclamation of control.[96] In the poem he thus enacts what the Kandyan Äsala Perahära would later do symbolically.[97] If, in the first two stages, Māyādunnē tours the country, in the third stage the country comes to him, in the great defection of the 1550s which we considered above.

Rājasiṃha cannot simply inherit the hard-won authority of his father; he must embark upon his own ascension. His pursuit of Vīdiyē Baṇḍāra across hill and dale is made the occasion of a royal tour to mirror his father's, winning acclaim in

92 However, the term *cakravarti* is only mentioned once, verse 1010.

93 Verses 102–3.

94 In particular, verses 224–30. In verse 48, we are told that Vijayabāhu had been brought to be a king by the mass of people (*mahasenaga*).

95 Roberts 2004.

96 See Holt 1996: 31–3 on the practice of *pradakṣiṇā*, and the *Cūḷavaṃsa*'s descriptions of Kīrti Śrī Rājasiṃha's extensive pilgrimages.

97 In the Perahära, the Tooth Relic circumambulated the capital as a means of metaphorically taking possession of the kingdom: Duncan 1990:136.

battle and love from the people, and including a pilgrimage to Kataragama, thus completing the cycle and fulfilling the oath sworn by his father.[98] The second stage comes with his victories over the Portuguese and Kōṭṭe forces in the late 1550s at Denipitiya and elsewhere. This, according to the poem, is the occasion for the transfer of sovereignty proper: Māyādunnē officially hands over the allegiance of his principal vassals to his son.[99] The royal jewellery is laid upon him, the crown is donned, a golden sword placed in his hand and he is seated on the throne, until he resembles the vision of kingship that we see, for example, in Plate 6. In reality, his victory at the battle of Mullēriyāva in the early 1560s marked a further stage of his rise, and the actual transfer of the title did not occur until 1581. But for poetic reasons Rājasiṃha's eclipse of his father is conflated with his father's death.[100]

For the poet, these campaigns in the mid-1550s are significant not only as the occasion on which the young prince won his spurs but on which dynastic authority was reconstituted. Indeed, these verses reveal more eloquently than any Portuguese source the extent of the chaos unleashed by Vīdiyē Baṇḍāra's rebellion. As Rājasiṃha travels, he is not simply raising troops and revenue and installing garrisons, but dispensing justice and order – insofar as morality in general is identified with the functioning of central authority. He is set on punishing people who had been 'creating disturbances' and 'building forts'.[101] These do not seem to be only supporters of Vīdiyē Baṇḍāra or Kōṭṭe, but purely local leaders attempting to provide some sort of local security. The political convulsions following Bhuvanekabāhu's death had created confusion in the minds of local elites. Who was the most legitimate contender for power? Who was the most powerful contender for legitimacy?

Alternatively, Sītāvakan authority was not reconstituted from the chaos but newly built out of it. The assembling of a general league against Vīdiyē had allowed the establishment of new relations as well as the reaffirmation of old ones.[102] At its conclusion, the poem describes Māyādunnē gathering the various parties and enjoining them to come to his son's aid if any other king in Lanka should create disturbances in the future.[103] That this could not be taken for granted indicates the fragility of central authority, as does the role played by the liberal dispersal of the spoils of war. Heroic deeds, or simply loyalty, are rewarded with necklaces, wages, lands. One way, then, in which the military campaign could pacify the regions was by funnelling redistributive powers to the centre, a mechanism that Jayavīra Baṇḍāra would exploit to the full in the 1590s.[104]

Naturally, the representation of these campaigns is shaped by a poetic concern with the imagery of unity and harmony. The litany of place-names, from the highlands and lowlands, the east and the west, works to knit the country together

[98] Verses *c.* 580–830. [99] Verses 993–1007.
[100] See Strathern forthcoming a. This is not an entirely satisfactory solution to the apparent anachronism of the narrative here, but other solutions to this anachronism are more far-fetched still.
[101] E.g. verses 600–20. [102] Compare with Couto: 175 on a general league against Vīdiyē Baṇḍāra.
[103] Verses 893–5. [104] E.g. verses 1110, 1051.

linguistically.[105] What Rājasiṃha brings to each of these places, as to Lanka as a whole, is *eksath* or unity.[106] It is as if Lanka were an organism vulnerable to damage and disintegration and in need of healing. *Eksath*'s conceptual opposite is *avul* (disturbance), which is used to describe various phenomena that modern observers would probably seek to distinguish by terms such as rebellion, secession, not paying revenue, invasion, conquest. What all have in common is some sort of affront to the *cakravarti*'s authority.

The natural order is thus constantly assailed by threat, as the references to the struggle between the *dēvas* and *asuras* indicate – but note that threats can issue from within as well as without. Thus, at one point Vīdiyē Baṇḍāra is insulted in terms similar to those directed at the Portuguese: he and his men are motivated by greed, 'devouring the country' like monitor lizards, dogs, crows and other scavengers.[107] Indeed, this situation elicits the most obviously patriotic phrase in the poem. Men sign up to Rājasiṃha's campaign out of 'constant love for the country' (*nitara raṭa ālē*) to destroy this internal source of chaos.[108] The phrase reveals a collective sense of entitlement and attachment to Lanka, but in the poem that sense is configured by dynastic devotion. Loyalty to the king and to country are made one and the same: a feature perhaps of all monarchical societies.

'Loyalty to country' may seem to rely on a Eurocentric or anachronistic conflation of territory and society, but it is arguably true to the semantic range of *raṭa*. A Kōṭṭe–Portuguese incursion is described thus:

> The enemy army having thus arrived and entered the city of Kälaṇiya
> Attractive noble youths were given royal positions and names
> The viceroy having come to this country (*meraṭa*) from the pleasant and powerful city of Goa
> Destroying this country by converting several beings of beautiful lineage (*rusiru kula noyek sataṭa kulavaddā nahapu meraṭa*).
>
> [This viceroy] having become the ally of an attractive king of exalted character and unsullied noble lineage, intent on destroying the country [*raṭa*]
> He brought over fierce Portuguese [*pratikalun*]; not sent back, they remain in this Lanka to this day
> Removing the noble pride of children of noble birth, he destroyed pure lineages [*kula*]
> This viceroy is a high-born personage; he descended strongly upon this Lanka to destroy *Siri Laka*.[109]

In what sense is the 'land' destroyed here? Both verses twin this theme with the conversion of high-born men and the disruption of status, which suggests

[105] Verses 580s, including Sabaragamuva, Ūva, Badulla, Vellassa, Bintänna etc.

[106] Verses 682–5, 927–8. [107] Verse 830.

[108] Verse 865. The men are from the Four Kōraḷēs, but *raṭa* seems to mean Lanka here. The internal origin of this threat is not adduced in Roberts 2004: 120.

[109] Verses 516–17. Could 'given names' mean conversion? *Siri* could be rendered 'blessed' or 'prosperous'.

that the destruction of the 'land' is a metaphor for the destruction of a social system.

Rājasiṃha, on the other hand, will sustain the land. And in his tour of the regions, he is not just imposing himself on Lanka, but allowing Lanka – its fertile fields and forests teeming with wildlife, its beautiful women overflowing with milk – to seep into him. Perhaps, in the light of the discussion of anthropology in the introduction, one could say that if he re-creates the realm, the realm also makes him a king: his journey out into the margins and back again is a journey into civilized kingship.

There was, of course, a religious dimension to the political reification of Lanka. In João Garcês' letter of 1529, he recalls a conversation with the 'old king', who could be either Bhuvanekabāhu or his father.[110] The ruler observes that,

> God had dealt with him better than with all the kings of the world, which is to say his land was full of precious stones, the hills of elephants, and the mountains of cinnamon and the sea of pearls and that all this was because of our father Adam walking in it and his footprint is there, and one can tell that this is true by seeing that of all the mountains there it is the highest, and that all the others of all four quarters are inclined towards it, as are the trees and palms . . .

Garcês was privy to this kind of insight because of his intimate position as a translator, but his rendition reveals the fragility of theological translation in these early years. The king was certainly referring not to the Muslim/Christian Adam, but to Buddha.[111] In the *Mahāvaṃsa*, the Buddha leaves his footprint on the peak (Sumanakūṭa) while visiting Lanka to consecrate it as a most holy vehicle of the *dhamma*.[112] It is that specialness of Lanka, special by virtue of Buddhist grace, which the king may have been attempting to express.

In this light, the Portuguese trope of Ceylon as an earthly paradise is revealed as a borrowing from indigenous tradition: exploited by adventurers and missionaries to promote their own projects for the island and rendered into the language of Christian providentialism by the *casado* and convert community, but visibly rooted in a local Buddhist self-regard. This palimpsest of Eastern and Western political and religious fantasies could then be pressed into service as a charter for the conquest of Ceylon, or in Queirós' vision, its re-conquest.

Rājasiṃha and the Saivite turn

Rājasiṃha might seem a nice candidate for a national hero, yet he has a somewhat awkward place in nationalist memory by virtue of his notoriety as a convert to

110 CS: 329: 'ho Rej velho' could be a reference to Bhuvanekabāhu's age or to the 'past' king, Vijayabāhu VI.

111 Compare with Couto: 108–17. A similar 'providentialist' translation of an indigenous conception occurs in Albuquerque's report of his conversation with the Raja of Cochin ten or so years before, SR, I: 229.

112 *Mahāvaṃsa*, ed. Geiger 1993: 8–9.

Saivism. And what does this simple fact tell us about the obstacles to conversion in Indic societies? This is a much more complex issue than it appears, both in terms of semantics – defining what conversion might mean here – and source-criticism. Indeed, the following discussion will have to proceed some way into the intricacies of the evidence in order to ascertain what was going on here. If Rājasiṃha's sheer individual power allowed a certain triumph of agency over structure, it did not carry all before it, as we shall see.

We can begin by returning to the *Sītāvaka Haṭana*, given its origin in the critical years of the mid-1580s. As we have seen, the poet makes Rājasiṃha don the mantle of cultural guardianship that Māyādunnē had snatched up when Dharmapāla became a Christian. Hence it represents the defections of noble factions in the 1550s not as mere opportunistic struggles for status, but in terms of their fidelity to a wider common heritage. That heritage is Buddhist in a fundamental sense, as the references to the *sāsana* make evident.[113] But we have observed that in general this secular court panegyric is not preoccupied with Buddhism. Nor does it revel in anti-Christian imagery, in the way that the rebellions of the next decade would do. It does not provide us with any evidence that Rājasiṃha deliberately targeted churches in his attacks, for example. Indeed such evidence is very hard to come by, although it seems that Rājasiṃha insisted on apostasy for his Portuguese henchmen.[114]

Obviously, the poem does not suggest any official deprecation of Buddhism either.[115] Other texts confirm that for part of his reign Rājasiṃha was a good Buddhist patron. They record him hosting the Tooth Relic procession and the recitation of *pirit* at the Mahā Saman Dēvālaya in Ratnapura.[116] It is under Rājasiṃha that we see the emergence of the only major poet of the era, Alagiyavanna Mukavāṭi (or Mohoṭṭāla: magistrate), whose poetry of this time seems entirely conventional in its religiosity. He was also responsible for the first major works of Buddhist literary activity since the fifteenth century.[117] Alagiyavanna's *Sävul Sandēśaya*, which describes the voyage of a messenger from Sītāvaka to the god Saman, depicts a flourishing Tooth Relic temple at Delgamuva and ends with a prayer for the protection of Rājasiṃha and Buddhism.

However, the messenger cock of the *Sävul Sandēśaya* also alights to describe the Bärändi Kōvil in Sītāvaka, dedicated to the 'Bhairava' form of Śiva. The conjunction of Saivite and Buddhist references reminds us that many Sinhalese would

[113] See above, p. 154.

[114] Hence they would be not merely *aleventados* but *renegados*: Couto 339, Freyre 1630: fols. 14–15. The latter includes a story (probably *casado* tradition) that the bodies of Rājasiṃha's renegades who died in Kandy were left untouched by the carnivores, a sign of their abomination. See also the questionable Apologia of 1602 (VP, II: 212) on Rājasiṃha's 'hatred against the faith'.

[115] Further, Or. 6606(130, 131 *Vikramasiṃha Adikāram Varṇanāva*), from the mid-1580s, says that Rājasiṃha's military commander, Vikramasiṃha, was a patron of Buddhism, 'procuring books and relics for Siddhārta thēra'.

[116] *Cūḷavaṃsa*: 225; Ilangasinha 1992: 119, 185,

[117] Ilangasinha 1992: 21 119–20, on the *Kusajātakaya, Subhāṣitaya*.

have seen Saivite worship as quite compatible with their Buddhist aspirations.[118] Indeed, Śiva had become an accepted aspect of royal cult. On the rear of the *c.* 1543 casket, we find an image of Bhuvanekabāhu VII praying to Śiva, who is mounted on the sacred bull Nandi [Plate 3].[119] The Bärändi Kōvil had actually been constructed by Māyādunnē, at enormous expense, and was the chief temple in Sītāvaka by the time it was attacked in 1551.[120] Rājasiṃha does seem to have accelerated the arrival of South Indian Brahmans, merchants and soldiers, concerned, no doubt, to muster all possible resources in his struggle with the Portuguese. It seems that some Brahmans were given revenues from the Adam's Peak region, and they may have gained these at the expense of Buddhist foundations.[121] One such immigrant, the *Alakesvarayuddhaya* tells us, was a *sāḍhu* by the name of Ariṭṭa Kīvenḍu Perumāl who was given the post of Manamperuma Mohoṭṭāla: a figure we shall come to know very well.[122]

This in itself need indicate nothing more than the traditional cosmopolitanism and 'polytropic' spirituality of Sinhalese kings eager to promote their standing in the wider Indic world. But according to the *Cūḷavaṃsa*, Rājasiṃha proceeded to murder Māyādunnē in order to finally usurp the throne and asked the *saṃgha* to provide him with a means of cleansing himself of the sin of parricide; they denied him this and so he turned instead to the Saivites who would grant him absolution. Aflame with 'heresy', he set about persecuting Buddhism.[123] For a long time it has been recognized that this account looks suspiciously like a monastic cover-up of a more plausible reason for Rājasiṃha's antipathy to the *saṃgha*, namely their role in a conspiracy against him, which will be considered below. The parricide element

118 Ilangasinha 1992: 212–14, on attempts to incorporate Śiva into the Buddhist pantheon dating back to the twelfth century. Ilangasinha suggests that the bulk of evidence for Saivite institutions may primarily reflect Tamil usage, but proceeds to adduce evidence that some Buddhists were also taking to the cult.

119 Jaffer and Schwabe 1999: 6–7. Queyroz: 296, asserts that Bhuvanekabāhu was buried at Trincomalee, which was known primarily for its Saivite temple. Could this reflect, via the opaque byways of Queirós' oral sources, Saivite tendencies at Kōṭṭe?

120 Couto: 139, 152, describes it as the chief temple encountered by the Portuguese in 1550 and 1551, which contradicts the local tradition that Rājasiṃha built it when he converted to Saivism in order to redeem his parricide (Bell 1904: 62–5). However, it is possible that Couto (writing this decade in 1596) was using eyewitness accounts of Sītāvaka post-Rājasiṃha's Saivite turn to imagine the scene in the 1550s. Couto describes this temple as dedicated to Paramisura (i.e Parameśvara or Śiva) and as having strange architecture, which ties in with Bell's comments on the strongly Dravidian features of the surviving structure. See also Pieris 1913–14, I: 123, 221; Pathmanathan 1982: 52–4; J. Seneviratne 1913. In the account of the 'second disputation' in Queyroz: 258, the opponent is a Saivite Brahman who had converted to Buddhism.

121 Malalgoda 1999: 17–18, refers us to Knox's reference to pilgrims from the 'Other Coast' being given revenues by 'a former king'. Dewaraja 1988: 57, 68, refers to the donation of villages to Brahmans in Sabaragamuva, in a text (from 1586) in *Saparagamuvē Pärani Liyavili*; BL Or. 4964, fols 27–8. The *Kuṭṭāpitiya sannasa* from 1752 refers to the transfer of patronage to Saivites according to Gunawardana 1994: 216.

122 *Alakeśvarayuddhaya*: 41–3/*Rājāvaliya*: 88–9. Compare with Queyroz: 485, where Rājasiṃha smuggles in *vadugai* troops 'under the disguise of *jogues* [yogis]'.

123 *Cūḷavaṃsa*: 225–6. This story must have been current at least by the 1660s because we find a debased version of it in Baldaeus 1752: 604 (first published 1672).

has also been widely discredited given that Rājasiṃha had had the command of Sītāvaka for nearly twenty years by this time, and several sources make no mention of it.[124] However, this element cannot be entirely disregarded because it is present in our most contemporary sources, in particular Diogo do Couto.[125] Indeed, Couto is the most interesting and rich source we have for the internal dynamics of Rājasiṃha's reign – but just as with Queirós, his own sources of information and biases require some discussion.

Unlike Queirós, he was a contemporary to these events and wrote about them not long afterwards. The relevant passages were completed in 1600, but we know that there were some important Sinhalese informants in Goa in the 1580s, when Couto was already gathering material: Filipe, or Yamasiṃha, the heir to the Kandyan throne who had been expelled by Rājasiṃha's conquest, was taking refuge there along with his son João. It is very likely they were informants, directly or indirectly, for material on contemporary events in Ceylon.[126] One reason for this is the parricide story itself, because the only other sources to carry it are the Dutchmen Linschoten, who was also in Goa in the 1580s, and Spilbergen, who received it direct from Kandyan informants in 1602.[127] The conclusion here then is that (regardless of its accuracy) the parricide story we find in Couto has its origins in a contemporary Kandyan oral tradition profoundly hostile to Rājasiṃha. I shall argue below that Vimaladharmasūriya built his royal propaganda upon these regional sentiments: the new Kandy was to be Buddhism restored, as contrasted with the moral degradation under Rājasiṃha. The insistent depiction of Rājasiṃha as a tyrant and the visceral hatred of him which springs from the pages of Diogo do Couto is not only a European stereotype. Rather it represents a dovetailing of two traditions, deriving from the embattled Christian settlers and converts of Colombo on the one hand and the embattled Sinhalese highlanders on the other.

A double dose of bias, then, but we are also reminded of how closely placed his sources were. Couto and the Dutch writers are also the only sources to tell us that Rājasiṃha slaughtered various rivals to the succession, including his brother Palē Pandār, a.k.a. Tim̆biripola. This little fact receives some independent corroboration from a Portuguese land register of 1614, which records the latter's death in 1581.[128] Whatever the role of Māyādunnē in the manoeuvrings behind the throne, Rājasiṃha's transition from *de facto* to *de jure* rule was probably violently

[124] See C. R. de Silva 1995: 96–7, which offers a sensible discussion of this whole issue. *Rājāvaliya*: 82, Queyroz: 438, and Ribeiro make no mention of it, but are all late seventeenth-century sources, while the *Alakeśvarayuddhaya* has a hiatus for these decades.

[125] Linschoten: 78 (who left Goa in January 1589); Couto: 271–2, who also reported the tale that he was the son of a barber, for which see Spilbergen: 36. In the early 1570s, Federici (cited in Couto: 243) claimed that Rājasiṃha had usurped the throne.

[126] When Couto: 62, 101 claims to have heard these princes chant their chronicles, he is merely copying a sentence from Azevedo: 235–49, whom he commissioned in the late 1580s to prepare translations of the *Rājāvaliya*. See Schurhammer 1973–82, II: 612–16. Nonetheless, Couto may have had interviews with the princes himself, or Azevedo may have passed on more information than contained in his *Relação* (as Loureiro 1998: 229, implies). Prince Filipe of Sītāvaka, who arrived in the late 1590s, may also have been an informant of Couto (but not of Azevedo).

[127] Linschoten: 78; Spilbergen: 36. [128] C. R. de Silva 1995: 96.

contested rather than peacefully assumed.[129] In Couto's account, the court is routinely drenched in blood thereafter, as an increasingly paranoid Rājasiṃha snuffs out potential rivals and their families with as much desperation as a king in a Shakespearean tragedy.[130] His mounting tyranny no doubt transformed imagined conspiracies into real ones. Couto tells us that one of these involved some relatives in conjunction with the chief *saṃghatthēra* of Sītāvaka, and here we have the first clue of his conflict with the *saṃgha*.[131] The monk was stoned and cut to pieces. For those who want a political motivation for his religious policies, revenge against an institution plotting his demise ought to do.

As for his turning to Saivism, this could also be attributed to his strong consciousness of his reputation among South Indian rulers. We certainly know that he sought alliances with mainland princes, and Couto says 'he persuaded them that since they were heathens like himself, they should wish to aid him in that war against the Portuguese, and should come to his help for the honour of their idols.'[132] Furthermore, Holt has recently reflected on the – potentially huge – ramifications of the Portuguese destruction of the temple to Upulvan at Devinuvara in 1587. Holt argues that this god, 'whose power was intimately linked to the welfare of Lanka's religious culture and to the well-being . . . of the Sinhala political state', would have been discredited by this failure to resist the storming of the centre of his cult.[133] We can find support for this intuition in Couto's narrative, which describes Devinuvara as the greatest site of pilgrimage after Adam's peak, and the occasion of its downfall thus: as a Portuguese fleet was passing by the town, it was hit by a tremendous thunderstorm.[134] Thomé de Sousa noticed his lascarins whispering amongst themselves and was informed that 'these heathens were glad, because their pagoda had hastened to maintain his honour; and that knowing the Portuguese were going to insult him, he had sent that storm to chastise them.' Couto goes on to say that since over the years many Portuguese ships had been blown away in this fashion, the notion had developed that the god was keeping the Portuguese at bay, and the town had swelled as people came to live under his aegis. Indeed, this was why Thomé de Sousa swore to attack it, in order to disabuse them of that superstition: precisely to effect the 'disconfirmation' of its power. In the end, his men encountered no resistance at all.

If we recall, too, Bhuvanekabāhu's insistence on keeping Devinuvara (which his chaplain described as the 'chief *pagoda* of Ceilão') free of Christian presence

[129] One potential motive for Rājasiṃha to murder Māyādunnē: fear that the old king would exert some unwanted influence over the succession.

[130] Couto: 271–3, 277–8, 284–6.

[131] Couto: 284. C. R. de Silva 1995: 96, rightly says 'it is not known whether the opposition of the *saṃgha* was a cause or a result of Rājasiṃha's conversion to Saivism'.

[132] Couto: 348, 385.

[133] Holt: 2004, 2007. Therefore at some point over the next seventy years he became displaced from the fourfold formulation of guardian deities and was eclipsed by or absorbed into a Buddhicized cult of Viṣṇu. See too Paranavitana 1953; Ilangasinha 1992: 114, 198. Upulvan was presumably transformed in this way before 1638, because Miranda: 165, is the source for Queyroz's: 35, attribution of Devinuvara to Viṣṇu.

[134] Couto: 373–5; Queirós: 441.

in 1550, then the idea that the Upulvan cult had a particular role in representing – and manifesting – the political-cum-religious resistance of the Sinhalese to the Portuguese becomes compelling.[135] The cult may have taken on a similar significance for Rājasiṃha also. According to the *Alutnuvara Devirāja Sirita*, he gave dedications to the upcountry seat of Upulvan at Alutnuvara in 1559 and 1569, the decade in which he established his pre-eminence.[136] The awful demonstration of Upulvan's weakness came at a time when Rājasiṃha was dug in to his last siege of Colombo. Shortly afterwards, he withdrew his men and returned to Sītāvaka in order to celebrate a 'very great festival'.[137] Perhaps, he was forced then to look for protection from a new divine patron, and found it in Siva. That Rājasiṃha was strongly associated with Saivism at the point of his death is confirmed by the portion of the *Alakeśvarayuddhaya* apparently written shortly afterwards, which describes him as passing on to Kailāsana.[138]

But what evidence, apart from the retrospective monastic admonitions of the *Cūḷavaṃsa* – 'he became a (dead) tree-trunk in the cycle of rebirths, he adopted a false faith' – is there for a 'conversion' which entailed the abjuration of Buddhism?[139] Ilangasinha has assembled the evidence from Sinhala texts that he persecuted the *saṃgha* and transferred his patronage from the *bhikkhus* to Saivites. However, most of these references appear to be as late as the *Cūḷavaṃsa* itself.[140] At the very least, the widely accepted sources do indicate a Saivite aspect to Rājasiṃha's personal religiosity and a major clash with the *saṃgha*. The parlous state of the *saṃgha* by the end of the sixteenth century is certainly consistent with a disastrous loss of patronage in the preceding decade or so. It does seem then that there was more going on here than simply the continuation of multi-religious patronage or the inevitable tensions between throne and *saṃgha* that we see across the *Theravāda* world.[141]

135 See above, p. 110, VP: 278.
136 Nevill: Or. 6606(145), which also extols him as 'defender of the religion', see Ilangasinha 1992: 119. Upulvan is not a major presence in the *Sītāvaka Haṭana*, but he is one of the gods (as *Mahikat Devindu Pura Kisirālli Upulvan* – an interesting reference to Devinuvara two years before its destruction) called upon to bless Rājasiṃha at his coronation, see *SH*: verse 1003.
137 Couto: 380.
138 *Alakeśvarayuddhaya*: 43. The *Rājāvaliya*: 90, copies the relevant sentence on Rājasiṃha's death but tellingly leaves out this final clause. Mount Kailāsana was Śiva's Himalayan abode.
139 *Cūḷavaṃsa*: 226, and see Liyanagamage 1968: 119–32 for a useful discussion of the *Cūḷavaṃsa*'s language in dealing with another heretic king, Māgha.
140 Ilangasinha 1992: 121–4. *Senkaḍagala saila-sāsanavaṃsa* Or. 6606(128), is late eighteenth-century. A *sannasa* from that period (discussed in the notes to the earlier *Palkum̆bura Sannasa*, *EZ*, III: 241) refers to a *bhikkhu* who was forced to disrobe after Rājasiṃha's invasion of the highlands and went on to become Senarat's tutor (another clue to the heritage of the Buddhist resurgence in Kandy). The *Sulurājāvaliya* has a version of the *Cūḷavaṃsa* parricide/atonement story. This was finally compiled in 1821, but Nevill suggests that the relevant portion may have been first redacted towards the end of Senarat's reign, *c.* 1620. See Nevill's notes to Or. 6606(106 and 107). It is just possible then that the story belongs to that time. This leaves only the texts compiled in the *Saparagamuvē Päraṇi Liyavili*, which I have not been able to access or date. Ilangasinha also relies on the *Mandārampura-Puvata*, which is dealt with below as an 'unverified text'.
141 These are emphasized by Mirando 1985: 26–8.

But the evidence is not firm on how far this amounted to a 'conversion' equivalent to the exclusivist journey undertaken by Dharmapāla. Buddhist and Hindu practices had long lived side-by-side and in amongst one another. It is quite possible that Rājasiṃha maintained some of the Buddhist apparatus of kingship till the end of his reign, in particular the Tooth Relic, which had by this time acquired an unassailable legitimizing force that may have anyway transcended its specifically Buddhist associations.[142] It would, however, be equally remiss to overlook the Lankan traditions of religious antagonism, which had produced anti-Saivite invectives in the last century and would do so again in the eighteenth.[143] As he channelled more and more of his religious activity into his personal relationship with Śiva, Rājasiṃha would have laid himself open to accusations by *bhikkhus* and rivals that he had abandoned his Buddhist responsibilities and thereby damaged the karmic prospects of his subjects.

What connections might there be between his religious policy and his political standing? It is evident that the spiralling violence of his reign was fuelled by serious challenges to his authority, but it is naturally difficult to disentangle cause from effect: his strong-arm governance was enough by itself to render him unpopular. Moreover, we have emphasized that all Sinhalese rulers had to contend with powerful centrifugal tendencies. But we can say that the increasingly dark and troubled tenor of his reign is at least consistent with the loss of religious legitimacy. His standing in Kandy deteriorated. Shortly after claiming the throne, Rājasiṃha conquered the highland kingdom with the support of a section of the local nobility, led by Vīrasundara Baṇḍāra. By 1585, we find the same Vīrasundara Baṇḍāra being executed for conspiring to oust Rājasiṃha from the *udaraṭa*; only four years later the region rose in successful revolt under Dom Francisco Mudali.[144]

Given that Kandy had long proved troublesome for would-be *cakravarti*s, it is the evidence of internal unrest that is more significant. In 1585 Rājasiṃha suffered an assassination attempt by poisoning. Ailing and weak, he was forced to make a truce with the Portuguese, and attempted to send ambassadors to Goa.[145] Meanwhile some of his officers defected to Kōṭṭe.[146] In this context, the composition date (1585) of the *Sītāvaka Haṭana* takes on a new significance. Does the poem expend so much energy on destroying the reputation of Vīdiyē Baṇḍāra in order to remind Rājasiṃha's internal enemies of the dishonour attached to their infidelity?[147] A few years later, Linschoten reported of Rājasiṃha that he trusted in no man, for the Sinhalese 'are not his good friends, and yet they live in obedience under him, more

[142] This is indicated by the *Saparagamuvē Päraṇi Liyavili*: 36, according to Ilangasinha 1992: 122–3.
[143] See above, p. 134, on the *Saddharmālaṃkāraya*, *Saddharmaratnāvaliya*, and *Buduguṇānalaṃkāraya*.
[144] *Rājāvaliya*: 85–6. See below, p. 212. Francisco Rodrigues Silveira (Lobo 1887: 104) suggests that Rājasiṃha's taxation of Kandy was one source of ill-feeling.
[145] *APO*: 72. Queyroz: 444, refers to an assassination attempt and fear of rebellion in a narrative of 1592.
[146] Couto: 286.
[147] See above, and also *SH*: verse 847, on the disgust for the treacherous Irugul lineage.

through force and fear, than for love and good will'. If no one dared stir against him it was from fear of execution.[148] An English visitor described him as travelling in the middle of a bodyguard of 1,000 men, and banning precious-stone mining in case it gave his enemies further cause to drive him out of the country.[149] In 1591 Sotupāla Baṇḍāra led the Seven Kōraḷēs in revolt against him.[150] Rājasiṃha now suffered further military reverses: his aura of success, to which his royal authority owed so much, would have begun finally to dissipate. In 1592, Rājasiṃha executed one of his leading generals, Vikramasiṃha Mudali, for a defeat in battle, which led to further defections.[151] In 1593 he died from a bamboo splinter in his foot; it was later rumoured that poison or sorcery had been administered to speed death on its way.[152]

One hint that all this swirling opposition to Rājasiṃha had some moral or religious aspect to it comes to us, once again, by the slippery vehicle of Couto. To be sure, we must remain conscious of the way in which Couto's narrative mirrors the mentality of the Christian community walled up in Colombo, for whom Rājasiṃha was a nightmarish occult-wielding figure, as we shall see in the following chapter. Nevertheless Couto's lurid account may contain an echo of indigenous feelings in its representation of Rājasiṃha as a tyrant whose religious behaviour is transgressive or somehow unhealthy. After the first conspiracy he faced as king, Couto tells us that, 'the tyrant gave his vassals to understand that all that he did was by order of the gods, and that his idols counselled him; and in order to make them believe it he invented this method . . .' The method was to hide people within a shrine or temple, and then, after the performance of certain rituals, have them speak as if they were the summoned gods, listing the names of those suspected of conspiracy. Among those fingered by the cod-gods were some *bhikkhus* who were executed on the spot: 'a very abominable thing amongst them and in their law'.[153] During the siege of Colombo in 1587, Couto's narrative takes a strange turn, claiming that Rājasiṃha actually ordered the sacrifice of 500 children, beheading them in front of the idols in order to win victory.[154] Again we are told that Rājasiṃha employed the trick of the loquacious deities in order to manipulate his people, and with this

148 Linschoten: 78; Couto: 347. The Kandyan tradition is heavily evident in Baldaeus 1752: 601–3.

149 Ralph Fitch, visiting in 1589, in Foster 1921: 43.

150 Queyroz: 443; C. R. de Silva 1995: 101–2. Hence he requested peace again: *APO*: 426.

151 Couto: 273 (whose chronology is defective). An oral tradition incorporated into *Rājāvaliya*: 88–9, but not the *Alakeśvarayuddhaya*, has it that Vikramasiṃha was killed for allying with the Kōṭṭe–Portuguese in order to facilitate an attack on a rival general. This may derive from Nevill: Or. 6606(86) *Yav-Ra-sin-Rājāvaliya* and Or. 6606(130, 131) *Vikramasiṃha Adikāram Varṇanāva*.

152 AHU, Códice 281, fols. 323v–324, 328. The earliest reference to poisoning is in Spilbergen: 36; the most intriguing is *Rājāvaliya*: 90, which is oddly similar to Queyroz: 469, 707. Also see Trindade, III: 72. And just as Rājasiṃha increasingly instigated magical attacks so he increasingly felt assailed by them: Couto: 284.

153 Couto: 284–5. Couto's sources here may include the Sinhalese princes mentioned above (p. 186) or other defectors to Kōṭṭe, but we do know that the Portuguese had successfully implanted spies in Sītāvaka: Couto: 385. See too Loureiro 1998.

154 Couto: 290–1.

they held him for a saint and worshipped him; and so far did his folly go that he commanded many golden images to be made in his name, and ordered them to be distributed throughout all the kingdoms and to be placed among the idols, that adoration should be offered to them even as to these.

Whatever one makes of the factual content of these stories, it is more instructive to reflect on their themes and functions. They show Rājasiṃha as a man who has become enslaved by an obsession with the gods; how that obsession has led to evil and to conflict with the *saṃgha*; they show that the supernatural or divine powers he calls upon are fake, the product of human mendacity; they try to explain how a false or artificial form of worship could nevertheless be accepted by or even win popularity among (some of) his subjects. One can see how a Christian might need these stories. But equally, one can see how they might reflect the offended sensibility of more orthodox-minded Buddhists who became Couto's informants.

For all their debt to the psychology of Rājasiṃha's enemies, these stories may yet provide a clue to the psychology of the man himself. His whole life was shaped by warfare and the single unfulfilled aim of winning Colombo. Constantly playing for high stakes, assailed by threat, desperate for victory in the here-and-now, it is not surprising that he became ever more beholden to the insurance-policy enticements of deity-worship and astrology.[155] From a Theravādin perspective his religiosity was overwhelmed by the imperatives of *laukika*. Couto's account is also very explicit on the role of self-divinization in all this, and it is at least feasible that he bestowed his favour on the Saivite Brahmans because of their willingness to promote such imagery. His self-deification had apparently begun by 1585, because as the action of the *Sītāvaka Haṭana* reaches a climax Rājasiṃha takes on an epithet awarded to no other king: *dēvi*.[156] There is much here that is reminiscent of Alexander the Great: the megalomania and paranoia of a restlessly successful military leader, simultaneously overweening and insecure, striving to transcend conventional constraints on the inflation of his image while periodically sunk into despair at being unable to match his highest ambitions.[157] There is also an intriguing analogy to be pursued with the Toungoo king Nandabayin who ruled from Pegu (1581–99). Intent on driving his people to war, he attacked the *saṃgha*, the monks revolted, his legitimacy was squandered and the Toungoo empire fell as he died.[158]

His post-mortem deification was assured.[159] It was not alien to his people or to Buddhism for men to be raised to gods. Couto translated this into the Catholic

[155] Or that when his plans failed he became troubled by the notion that he had offended the gods: Couto 365. The importance of astrology in his court is suggested by the role of the astrologer's family after his death, see *Rājāvaliya*: 90.

[156] *SH*: verses 1027–8, 1055.

[157] Incidentally, Queyroz: 322 compares Rājasiṃha to both Caesar and Alexander.

[158] Of whom, a local chronicle commented, 'he neither respected the monks nor valued the life of his subjects', see Reid 1988–93, II: 282, and Guedes 1994: 213, and the letter of 1599 by Pimenta 2004: 184–6.

[159] See the local traditions described in Roberts 2004: 241, n. 66; Pieris 1983–92, II: 266.

language of sainthood, which might suggest a popular sympathy for his religiosity.[160] But in the Indic world, deification need not reflect one's popularity but one's prowess; it need not entail an endorsement of one's spiritual vision, but an acknowledgement of one's supernatural potency. This is why, for example, when the dreaded Portuguese general and temple-destroyer, Constantino de Sá de Noronha, was finally killed in 1630, his arch-enemy the King of Kandy was quick to lead the rituals addressing him as a deity.[161] Vīdiyē Baṇḍāra too was honoured by a temple where he died in Jaffna. Queirós understood that they were 'giving him worship not out of love but for fear of him'.[162] It was difficult to imagine that the awful power of such figures would simply dissipate on their death; it would need to be contained and propitiated. In the Sītāvakan stories that emerge in Couto's *decadas* we may hear the guilt and fears of those who had wished Rājasiṃha harm and wondered now how they would pay the price. Rājasiṃha the terrible: in life and in death.

A postscript on the unverified sources

Much of what has been advanced here in a cautious and piecemeal manner finds apparent support and amplification in what were described in the Introduction as the 'unverified sources'. Amalgamated, they present a story which ties up many a loose end and laces threads of meaning through otherwise disconnected events. They also give us some dates.[163] The story would run like this: in 1587, there was a conspiracy among the Kandyan *saṃgha* and nobility to oust Rājasiṃha's man and raise Konappu Baṇḍāra to the throne. Chief among the conspirators was the prominent *bhikkhu*, Devangala Ratanālaṃkāra, who tried to discredit Rājasiṃha by spreading the rumour that he had killed his father. This was the conspiracy that aroused Rājasiṃha's great anger against the *saṃgha*. While not perhaps instituting a general anti-*saṃgha* policy, he nevertheless inflicted great damage on it and turned his favour upon the Saivites in whom he felt he could place his trust. This met opposition by the common people and the nobility in both Kandy and Sītāvaka, who hid monks where they could and urged their king to abandon his false views. The chief *bhikkhu* of Māniyamgama Raja Mahāvihāraya, traditionally patronized by the Sītāvakan kings, wrote to Rājasiṃha urging him to abandon his purge. But he did not and his popularity dwindled. The Kandyan conspirators,

160 Couto: 291.

161 See Cruz and Flores 2007, with wonderfully explicit comments on this theme from the 1635 *Jornada de Uva*, and see in particular the comments of John Holt. I am also grateful to Holt for his elucidation of this theme in conversation.

162 Queyroz: 323.

163 I have constructed this synthesis using what Amarasinghe 1998 reports of the *Sitāvaka Rājasiṃha Rājja Kālaya*, the *Asgiriye Talpatha* and the documents associated with the Māniyamgama temple in Avissāvēlla. The *Mandārampura-Puvata* is much more widely known. While on many points these sources agree, it would not be scholarly to amalgamate them in this way if I were to rely on their evidence – but I shall not.

feeding off this displeasure, had their day when Konappu Baṇḍāra was acclaimed as Vimaladharmasūriya of Kandy in 1590.[164]

But if we turn over this neat and attractive patchwork to reveal the manner of its construction, we find it messy and complex, its constitutive parts yet to be untangled by thoroughgoing source-criticism. The origins, dating and interrelationships of these sources are all open to question.[165] Some of them may reflect the tense politics of religious identity under Kīrti Srī Rājasiṃha (1747–82) – or even much later sensibilities – in their emphasis on the destructiveness of Rājasiṃha's Saivite inclinations.[166] Such laborious unpicking cannot be undertaken here. Instead, these sources have been quarantined into this postscript where their potential can be advertised at the same time as their dubiousness is prevented from infecting the preceding arguments.

164 Konappu Baṇḍāra was by this time João D'Austria. One of the most puzzling or suspicious features of these sources is the way in which the Christian element of the Kandyan rebellion of 1589–90 has been entirely erased. See Chapter Ten. The normal accession date is 1591, but the Portuguese sources are not definitive in this regard.

165 See the Introduction.

166 On the eighteenth-century sentiments, see Young and Senanayaka 1998; Malalgoda 1999.

10
Christianity and Buddhism resurgent

The last chapter dwelt on the consequences of breaching traditional principles; this chapter will examine how tradition itself was shifting. We shall explore the mentality of the Portuguese, mixed-race and converted Sinhalese who lived in and around Catholic Colombo, a mentality that did so much to advance religious antagonism without entirely rejecting the pre-Christian past. The late 1580s and 1590s is a bewildering period, but it needs to be addressed here in order to understand how so many of the elite could suddenly find it acceptable to switch their loyalties to the aged Christian emperor in Colombo, Dharmapāla – and thereby facilitate the Portuguese conquest of the lowlands. And how did apparently Christian kings of the highland kingdom of Kandy command authority from the 1560s to the 1580s? Ultimately, however, Buddhist kingship was reasserted in Kandy with the rise to power of Vimaladharmasūriya I in the early 1590s. Lastly, we shall consider what the rebellions against Portuguese direct rule can tell us of identity politics in our period.

Catholic Colombo

During the rioting that followed Dharmapāla's baptism, the young king was wounded as stones rained down upon his palace, and Queirós tells us that he had already begun to read spiritual struggle into his predicament. When asked what could be the cause of such vehement opposition, Dharmapāla replied, 'what else should it be but the Devil?'[1] After the riot had died down, and the subsequent Sītāvakan siege had been weathered, Kōṭṭe announced itself as a truly Catholic city. In 1558, a thanksgiving procession now made its way through the streets, giving thanks to God for the reprieve, and holding aloft an image of Christ.[2] Many of Dharmapāla's subjects had defected: those who remained were signalling their willingness to throw in their lot with the Portuguese and the new religion.

That identification became clearer still when Kōṭṭe itself was abandoned in 1565. Dharmapāla's authority and that of the Portuguese contracted to the city of Colombo and its immediate environs for the best part of thirty years. But where they retrenched, they thrived in adversity. The Colombo *casado* and *morador* tradition

[1] Queyroz: 337. [2] Queyroz: 344.

has left us a mass of miraculous, martyrological, providential and prophetic material that survives in Couto's and Queirós' narratives. Animating these stories is the image of a Christian destiny for the island that would ultimately outshine any of the diabolical creeds ranged against it. There is a martial and mystical quality to Catholicism in these decades that owes much to the Franciscans, who enjoyed a monopoly on the Sri Lankan mission until the century itself expired.

There can be no doubting the ability of the friars to mould and sustain the mentality of the Colombo inhabitants facing out the constant threat of extinction. We hear, again and again, of the heroic deeds of friars risking all to minister to the dying or indeed to fight in the front line of battle themselves.[3] The saints were by their side too, the banners of Saint Lawrence, Saint Francis, Saint Thomas, Saint James and others walked proudly through the city.[4] Amongst them was Francis Xavier, hailed as a saint in Sri Lanka before he was beatified, whose physical bestowal of grace on the island was perhaps, for the converts, a substitute for the role of the Buddha's presence. His importance is reflected in the way his actual visits there were quickly multiplied by oral tradition.[5] More fecund still was the generation of stories about the Holy Virgin, who was ever at hand to put in a miraculous appearance, pausing a storm to allow a ship to reach port, or giving forth a blinding flash of light to scatter the enemy.[6]

Stalking this magical battleground were the ogres of the independent Sinhalese kings, Rājasiṃha and Vimaladharmasūriya, the King of Kandy. In Couto's account, Colombo is encircled not only by the armies of Sītāvaka but by the forces of the occult. He relates several occasions on which Rājasiṃha attempted to smuggle poisoners and sorcerers into the city. There is nothing implausible about this, given the various forms of magical activity that have flourished in Lanka then and now. Within the city, these activities seem to have been subsumed under the diabolist interpretations that were gaining ground in Europe and generating the surge in witchcraft trials there of the later sixteenth century.[7] Indeed, Couto's account reveals that in Colombo too investigative torture was playing its part in confirming and inflating the paranoid fantasies of its inhabitants.[8] It was only the powers of Christianity that shielded them.

Vimaladharmasūriya, a much less potent figure in modern historiography, was apparently regarded with horror by Colombo contemporaries appalled by his apostasy. Their need to see him punished is behind the little aperitif of hell he is depicted as suffering in the days before his death.[9] He fails to remember his baptismal rebirth even as he dies. At his cremation a wonderful thing happened: the fire failed to

[3] Beyond Paulo da Trindade's biased defence of the Franciscan mission, see Couto: 220, 325; VP: 430–3; Queyroz: 403, 415–17, 451.
[4] Queyroz: 343; 426 (on St James). [5] Strathern 2005.
[6] Queyroz: 613–14, 647–50, 667–85; Couto: 238, 346.
[7] Even if in Portugal actual executions were comparatively rare: Levack 1995: 188, 223.
[8] Couto: 343–9. One famous sorcerer was captured and revealed to be carrying a book and many intriguing magical accoutrements.
[9] Queyroz: 604, works up this suffering from 'some partly worn-out pages which are the last of Bento da Silva'.

consume his heart. For the pagans 'that fire had not the strength to consume such an invincible and valiant heart', a miracle about which 'they made many songs and verses, distributing it [the heart] among themselves as a marvel'.[10] Queirós naturally preferred an interpretation more amenable to the Catholic mind: that God wished to preserve that dark heart for the flames of hell. Clearly Queirós has preserved here a genuine Sinhalese oral tradition symbolizing Vimaladharmasūriya's feats of resistance, but his counter-point illustrates how the ground of the miraculous and the sacred was fought over at this time.

We find this same process of what might be called the 'substitution' approach to cultural warfare – akin to the way in which churches were assembled out of the rubble of heathen structures – elsewhere in Queirós' narrative.[11] The footprint atop Adam's peak is the shining example, which drew the energies of many Portuguese writers concerned to squeeze Christian feet into its contours.[12] If sacred geography could not be captured for Christianity, it had to be cognitively razed. One of Queirós' unacknowledged sources, the Portuguese captain Sá de Miranda, writing in 1638, strove to pour scorn on the 'monstrous falsehoods' written by the rebellious Sinhalese about Anurādhapura, the seat of ninety kings, the source of Buddhist traditions of inclusive ethical kingship.[13] The Catholic community sought to efface these stubborn accretions of non-Christian history through their visions of Lankan soil watered by the blood of martyrs and touched by the grace of the saints. Thus was signalled its special place in Providence. This sense of specialness was fed also by the pragmatic proposals of mission administrators such as Alessandro Valignano, who recommended the conquest of the island so that it could act as a safe haven for persecuted Christians in the region.[14] For the moment this was enacted only in miniature, on the Jesuit-dominated island of Mannar. Paravas from the opposite coast fled there in numbers, a foreshadowing of the Parava colonization programme extended to Sri Lanka proper in the seventeenth century.[15] Queirós' evocation of Lanka's providential destiny is shot through with regretful hindsight, but he was drawing too on the collective imagination of generations of *casados*, and this in turn was subtly inflected by the Buddhist past.

This was an ideology in which the core of the Sinhalese Kōṭṭe aristocracy who remained faithful to Dharmapāla, and the Sinhalese inhabitants of Colombo itself, genuinely participated.[16] Outside the city walls most of the masses seem to have been essentially pragmatic in their nominal allegiances, switching religious labels

[10] Queyroz: 605.

[11] Queyroz: 29–31, for example, is a Christian re-telling of a very old Sinhala story of Kälaṇi Tissa's murder of an *arhant*: Strathern 2005.

[12] Couto: 108–15; Miranda: 53, 153; and see Queyroz: 387–90, on the scheme to move the sepulchre of St Thomas from India to Sri Lanka, which was another way of presenting the island as the destined centre of Asiatic Christendom.

[13] Miranda: 171, which reflects more frustration in the face of Sinhala pride and indigenism, I would suggest, than a European superiority complex.

[14] VP, II: 71, 97, 119.

[15] Queyroz: 379, 394; Abeyasinghe 1966: 59–62, 193.

[16] We hear some of the names of these Christian aristocrats in Dharmapāla's deed of gift: VP, II: 91; Queyroz: 526; *Gavetas da Torre do Tombo* 1963: 610. Gonzaga 1603: 1208, refers, probably with

as they saw fit, some responding to the resurrection of the mission in the late 1550s then falling away with the subsequent sieges of Kōṭṭe.[17] But inside the city, the faith was becoming essential to an increasingly mixed-race population. As a generation of *casados* rooted themselves in the land, they developed a localized sensibility distinct from the imperial mechanisms of Goa, Lisbon and Madrid.[18] Sinhalese and Portuguese were sallying out together into the hinterland, fighting for their now mutual interests, or were walled up in the constant sieges: the hot-house conditions in which a sense of communal soteriological fate would flourish.

Meanwhile, the force of the Counter-Reformation was making itself felt in the *Estado* of the 1560s through the office of the first Archbishop of Goa, Gaspar de Leão Pereira (1560–8, 1571–6), and the Council of Goa, first held in 1567.[19] In previous decades there had been calls for programmes of pagan temple destruction within Portuguese-held territory, but the express pronouncement of the Council of Goa on the issue gave the policy a more general legitimacy.[20] From here on the activities of theological warfare were violently concrete. Whether surging out of Colombo in raiding counter-attacks, launching opportunistic naval sorties, or reclaiming areas of the south-west for their command, the Portuguese (and sometimes Kōṭṭe) forces destroyed Buddhist and Hindu sites at Kälaṇiya, Trincomalee, Madampe, Rayigama, Negumbo, Munnēśvaram and the Upulvan centre of Devinuvara.[21] Some of these places may also have had a strategic importance, but there was much more going on here than the application of military logic or the prosecution of ecclesiastical decree. It represents an ancient Christian urge to scourge the land of abominations, perhaps further stimulated by a reaction against Vīdiyē Baṇḍāra's destruction of churches. It is as if both sides instinctively understood how the other conflated political and religious legitimacy and projected it in sacred space. Such outrages were one aspect of the increasingly desperate war of morale that would be brought to a pitch with the conspicuous cruelties of Jerónimo de Azevedo's (Captain-General 1594–1612) campaigns.[22] Couto says of Devinuvara that 'for greater insult to the pagoda they slaughtered inside several cows, which is the most unclean thing that can be . . .'[23] A broader contestation of culture had become locked into political rivalry. When Jesuit scholarship finally arrived to the

exaggeration, to 12,000 native Christians in 1580s Colombo. Lobo 1887: 107, refers to the 'many Sinhalese Christians . . . exercised for a long time now against the heathens' who took part in the expedition to Kandy of 1593–4. Clues that not all the Kōṭṭe faithful converted come from Queyroz: 492 (Sinhala Kōṭṭe prisoners of Kandy mocking Christianity), and VP, II: 147 (where a leading family baptizes only in 1594).

17 VP, II: 5, 19, 88–90; Ribeiro: 52.

18 See Biedermann 2005a, which argues that the *cakravarti* aspirations of the Kōṭṭe nobility were the prime motor of Kōṭṭe–Portuguese activity before the late 1590s.

19 Queyroz: 381; VP: 360, II: 34–7, 94.

20 Early calls: *DPM*, VI: 80; SV: 229–60; SR, II: 293–305, III: 315–22; *DI*, I: 45; and see Monforte 1751: 300–2, and Xavier 2004. But from the 1560s there was a legal and ecclesiastical basis for the territorial expansion of Christianity, the establishment of mission centres and the seizing of temple revenues.

21 Amongst others: Queyroz: 424–7, 441, 487, 555, 614, 714; VP, II: 122, 304, 321; Couto: 369.

22 Cruelty in the 1590s: Abeyasinghe 1966: 33; Queyroz: 493, 534; Couto: 424.

23 Couto: 369.

island in the shape of instructions to Padre Eutico in 1606 to write a history of the island, he complained of how difficult this would be given that 'during the past wars all the books of the Chingalas were burnt'.[24]

For most of the sixteenth century there was, however, one simple fact that restricted the extension of cultural antagonism from particular religious battlefields to the whole of the pre-Christian heritage: the continuing existence of Dharmapāla as the native authority under which Portuguese power was advanced. If the Portuguese and the core of faithful aristocrats were going to restore their fortunes, it was crucial that they exploit whatever symbolic capital the overlordship still retained. One consequence of this was that the friars and the settlers had then to find some sort of acceptance of local norms and tastes. According to Jaffer and Schwabe, the iconography of the casket made to commemorate Dharmapāla's baptism of 1557 also references the accession to the throne of Portugal of the three-year-old prince Sebastião in the same year, twinning the two souls through Christian and Sinhalese motifs (Plate 9).[25] Both the birth of Sebastião's kingship, and the spiritual re-birth of Dharmapāla are expressed in the actual and spiritual birth of Christ. One eye-catching scene (Plate 10) depicts the dream of Jesse in which he prophesied that the saviour would descend from twelve kings of Israel.[26] This tentative Christian association of divinity and royal ancestry may have been an attempt to compensate for the loss of glamour that derived from royal blood lines traced back to the Buddha and Mahāsammata. The rebirth of conversion appears to have been expressed here through the use of the *kinnara* motif, which signifies the cycle of creation and could not but have carried overtones of the Buddhist concept of rebirth (Plate 9).[27]

This equation between the two royal houses is underscored by another casket, of controversial date.[28] Jaffer and Schwabe suggest the iconography of its lid (Plate 11) refers to the disappearance of the King Sebastião at the battle of El Ksar Kebir (in 1578), giving rise to the messianic hope that he would rise and return again as Portugal's saviour.[29] Whatever its date, the images of suffering martyrs, Saint John the Evangelist and Saint Sebastian (Plates 11, 12), must have resonated with the beleaguered Christians of Colombo. It is possible that the casket celebrates a concrete merging of the two dynasties, when an impoverished and siege-bound Dharmapāla bequeathed his sovereign titles to the Portuguese throne in a will drawn up in 1580. In the front panels (Plate 13) stand two warriors dressed in the Sinhalese manner and wearing royal tiaras and feathered headdresses. In between them are carved two identical representations of what may be Dharmapāla's coat-of-arms, which marries Portuguese blazoning with Sinhalese charges, including a

[24] VP, II: 253. [25] Jaffer and Schwabe 1999: 8–9.

[26] The scene was copied from a Book of Hours by Thielman Kerver in print from 1499 to at least 1546, and therefore stands as 'one of the first instances of the use of western print sources by Asian craftsmen' according to Jaffer 2004: 255.

[27] Jaffer and Schwabe 1999: 9–10.

[28] Nuno Vassalo e Silva (personal comm., 7 Feb. 2006) suggests that it may have been made closer in time to the 1557 casket above.

[29] Jaffer and Schwabe 1999: 10–12.

Plate 9: Rear of c. *1557 casket.*
The main panels contain scenes depicting the birth and infancy of Christ.

royal lion. The Kōṭṭe carvers of these images had been commissioned to portray popular biblical scenes (Plates 14, 15), but indigenous and Buddhist-Hindu motifs were still readily to hand.

Nor was the flow of influence entirely one way. A later text comments on 'how the natives of Ceylon dislike new customs, and the majority of us who serve therein have adopted their style and manner of life'.[30] The promiscuity of the Portuguese in their mixing with the Sinhalese was noted with some disapproval by the first Dutch observers.[31] The poetry of Alagiyavanna following his conversion early in the seventeenth century provides the best example of the potential for a harmonious meeting of cultures, in which a native talent for a more gentle method of symbolic substitution found expression.[32] The typical reference to the Triple Gem, for example, is replaced by one to the Triune God. The adornments of Sanskritic learning are retained so that the beings of Hindu mythology are invoked in much the same way that contemporary European poets (not least Camões) marshalled classical pagan motifs. Indeed, when we see the Portuguese general Constantino de Sá repeatedly compared to Śakra or Viṣṇu we ought to acknowledge the apparent liberation of thought and expression it indicates – and also think again about the

[30] As avers a character in the *Expedition to Uva* of 1635, see Perera 1930: 13. [31] Spilbergen: 37.
[32] *Kustantīnu Haṭana*, Or. 6606(156); VP, II: 355; Don Peter 1989. C. R. de Silva 1998: 111 (and 2000) refers to the rise of 'a counter ideology which glorified Christianity'.

Plate 10: Right end of c. *1557 casket.*
Depicts an interpretation of the dream of Jesse, which Jaffer and Schwabe tell us was copied from a Book of Hours printed by Thielman Kerver as early as 1499.

Plate 11: Top of c. *1578–80 casket, Museum für Indische Kunst, Berlin.*
Jaffer and Schwabe read the scenes on the front of the lid as depicting the life and death of King Sebastião, and the top panels of the lid as concerning St. Sebastião. Nuno Vassalo e Silva considers a date closer to the 1557 casket to be more likely. Given that it may have taken some time for the messianism surrounding Sebastião to have developed, if we wish to preserve Jaffer and Schwabe's reading of the iconography we could push the date further into the 1580s or 90s.

Plate 12: Left-end of c. *1578–80 casket.*
This depicts the legend of the boiling of St. John the Evangelist by the Romans.

subtle distinctions to be made between literary device and statement of belief in the divine analogies employed by our Buddhist-Hindu textual sources. Buddhism is neither entirely ignored nor attacked in the *Kustantīnu Haṭana*. King Senarat of Kandy (1605–35), for example, is simply allowed his belief in the protection of the Triple Gem.

By the time Alagiyavanna was converted (sometime between 1602 and 1612) the Christian community in Lanka had reason to feel much more secure,

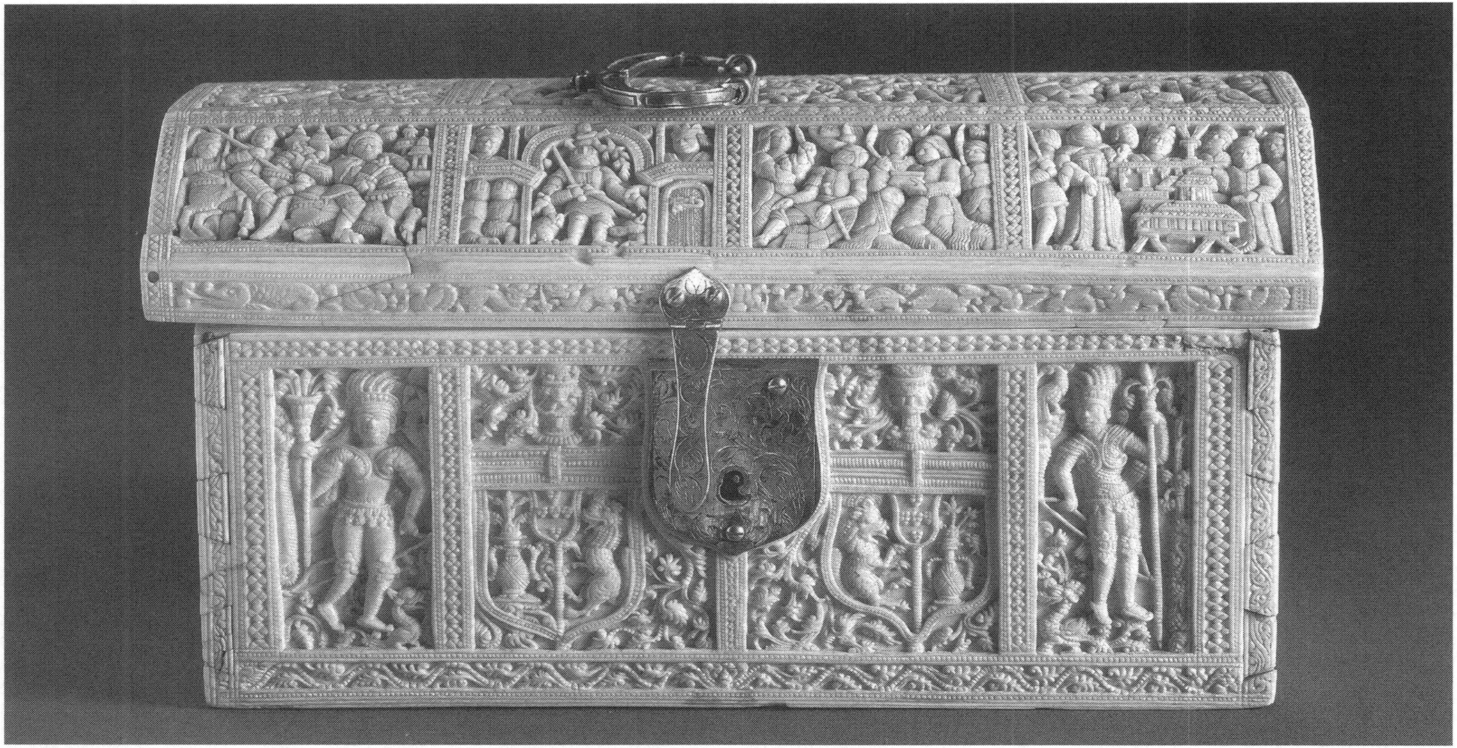

Plate 13: Front of c. *1578–80 casket.*
Note the two Sinhalese warriors standing in the end panels, and the coats-of-arms in the centre.

Plate 14: Rear of c. *1578–80 casket.*
Scenes from the life of Christ, for example, the nativity in the third panel.

Plate 15: Right end of c. *1578–80 casket.*
The Adoration of the Magi.

even vindicated in its providential dreams, certainly protected and increasingly enhanced by the Portuguese control over the lowlands. In all likelihood it was finally introduced to some of the sophistications of the Jesuit accommodationist approach to Asian culture initiated by the Jesuit Visitor Valignano as early as the 1570s and most famously cultivated by Roberto de Nobili (1577–1656) in India. The application of accommodationism in Lanka had been thwarted by the Franciscan monopoly of the island until that was broken in 1602. Yet even in the desperate atmosphere of the final decades of the sixteenth century, religious conversion was not always incompatible with the indigenist energies that we shall encounter in much of the rest of this chapter.

The chaotic 1590s: elite conversion and Portuguese conquest under indigenous authority

The 1590s were a pivotal moment for Sri Lanka: all sorts of futures suddenly seemed possible.[33] Contingency and complexity have to be our bywords here, as the principles or patterns of behaviour we have discerned thus far become subject to the unruly tides of *histoire événementielle*. The crisis was precipitated by traditional means: disputed succession. Rājasiṃha was already suffering from serious internal discontent, his dominion diminished by crucial rebellions in the Seven Kōraḷēs and Kandy, and when he died in 1593 he was not able to leave behind any legacy of stable authority. With the loss of his personal force, a power vacuum was revealed in which none of his potential successors could retain a foothold.[34] Sītāvaka collapsed. Into this space was wheeled the decrepit figurehead of Dharmapāla, barely masking the Portuguese engine propelling this Kōṭṭe resurgence, but able nonetheless to pull a number of Sinhalese leaders into his embrace. Within a year almost all its former territories had been restored to 'obedience'.

The remnant Kōṭṭe aristocracy no doubt saw this as their chance to assert once again the imperial titles that had been dead letters for so long, but local Portuguese officers and *casados* in Ceylon had been arguing the case for conquest for many years.[35] In the last decades of the century the *Estado* was assailed by a welter of similarly ambitious schemes for the conquest of lands in South East and East Asia, dreamt up by ambitious frontiersmen hoping to capitalize on a new enthusiasm for territorial dominion aroused by fascination with the Spanish model in the New World, the recent successes in the Philippines and the colonization of Brazil.[36] In Sri Lanka, Dharmapāla's startling bequest of his kingdom allowed these schemes to become reality. Recent research indicates that Lisbon–Madrid was still reluctant to take the petitions from Sri Lanka seriously in the late 1580s, but that from 1594 onwards a more insistent official policy of conquest started to emanate from the centre.[37]

Among the independent Sinhalese, alternative figures of dynastic authority were suddenly hard to come by, and into the breach stepped leaders pursuing their own ambition above all else, rising from sometimes unexpected social backgrounds to

[33] The island appears to share – whether by virtue of obscure conjunctural forces or simple coincidence – in the late sixteenth-century crisis that also afflicted the Theravāda states of mainland South East Asia, see Lieberman 2003: 81, and Strathern forthcoming c. In Lieberman's theory of Eurasian history, this is a period of disintegration between the administrative cycles of Pattern B and Pattern C.

[34] *APO*: 480; Queyroz: 469; *Rājāvaliya*: 90.

[35] See Biedermann 2005a.

[36] Flores 2001c: 69–72, 2001b: 18; Subrahmanyam 1990: 138–47, 2005*a*: 198. Also Rubiés 2003: 423; Abeyasinghe 1966: 40.

[37] Biedermann 2005a: 447–504.

win support through charisma, military prowess and the accumulation and dispensation of wealth, prepared to switch sides more than once, eager to second-guess the ebb and flow of fortune, and notably less beholden to any one court. In the increasingly militiarized mileu of these years, the loyalties of bands of fighting men to their unit leaders acquired an especial significance. We can think of many of our rebel leaders in this light, but their contribution to the 'chaos' of this decade will be deferred until the end of the chapter.

The chief exemplar here, and indeed the central figure behind the stunning reversal of power to the Portuguese, is Manamperuma Mohoṭṭāla, whom we met in the last chapter as a Saivite immigrant favourite of Rājasiṃha.[38] When Rājasiṃha died, Manamperuma was left clutching the reins of the Sītāvaka military, and he formed an alliance with Rājasiṃha's elder sister who was acting as Queen Regent on behalf of her five-year old grandson Nikapiṭiye Baṇḍāra.[39] However, he was then forced out of Sītāvaka and into league with Kōṭṭe.[40] What lay behind his defection? Queirós may well be correct to say that he had aroused the disfavour of the Queen Regent through seeking the hand of the young king's sister in a bid for royal status.[41] He now sought to get his hands on Sītāvaka by conquering it in the name of the emperor in Colombo. In the celebration of this new alliance he was accorded some sort of royal status. Queirós suggests this was promoted by the Portuguese Captain of Colombo, Pedro Homem Pereira, who gave him a *kabāya* (coat) sporting a regal device. This was eagerly grasped by Manamperuma, who held an investiture ceremony and adopted the name Jayavīra Baṇḍāra.[42]

Such symbols of authority were clearly still thirsted after by such freewheeling leaders, eager to make the transformation from warlords to kings. But they did not automatically confer authority. On the announcement of his royal status many of Jayavīra Baṇḍāra's captains deserted him in turn for the young king of Sītāvaka. Queirós says that they hated him because 'he was a foreigner, and the Chingalaz never had a King who in their judgement was not of the race of the Sun'.[43] A Queirósian intervention? But the importance of caste (lineage of the sun) in securing royal legitimacy is well substantiated.[44] And as for the matter of 'foreignness', it has left a trace in the most contemporary source we have, by the viceroy

[38] Queyroz: 483, implicitly comparing 1590s Sri Lanka with the rise of military professionalism during the Thirty Years War (1618–48) in Europe, aptly refers to him as the 'Wallenstein of Ceylon'. Albrecht von Wallenstein was another low-born figure who exploited the opportunities offered by a period of constant warfare to wield great political power as a specialist military leader.

[39] Rājasiṃha's eldest son Rajasūriya was briefly enthroned but then killed by Manamperuma according to *Rājāvaliya*: 90.

[40] *APO*: 486; Lobo 1887: 106.

[41] These years demonstrate the importance of queens for royal legitimacy – when other sources of it were in short supply. Queyroz: 477, describes Jayavīra as pursuing three princesses who had escaped to Denavaka, 'which was a prize Javira greatly esteemed, because it increased his pomp and state, which consists, for the most part, in having many wives and especially of such quality as these.'

[42] Queyroz: 471–2. *Rājāvaliya*: 92, says Dharmapāla gave him the honorary name.

[43] Queyroz: 473–4.

[44] Couto: 100, writing only two years after these events, and drawing on the reports of refugee Sinhala royalty, informs us that 'none could inherit the empire of Ceilão except those that came directly from that caste [of the sun], which the Chingalas hold to be divine.' See also above, p. 153, n. 73.

Mathias de Albuquerque. He tells us that the reason why Jayavīra Baṇḍāra betrayed Sītāvaka in the first place was 'since he was a foreigner and also because he knew that the natives had become envious of his position and were plotting to kill him'.[45] Unquestionably, his rapid rise had furnished him with rivals. As soon as his position of power became clear after Rājasiṃha died, two chief nobles had deserted to Kōṭṭe with 700 followers.[46]

Some may consider Albuquerque, as a European, a suspect interpreter of Sītāvakan sensibilities.[47] However, a passage of the *Rājāvaliya* suggests that cultural-religious antagonism had indeed contributed to the perennial frictions of court factionalism in Sītāvaka.[48] We are told that one of his rivals composed four-lined verses about him 'for the reason that he was having company with Fakirs', which were recited around the city and forced him to shift residence to Moravatta.[49] In this account, there was no quarrel with the Queen Regent; indeed, she summoned him back to the city. But then 'lads began to sing these verses, whenever he was seen.' This is when he defected. It seems that when Rājasiṃha died repressed elements saw the opportunity to fight back against the Saivites whom the old king had promoted, and they were not above picking away at group loyalties to do so.

Still, Jayavīra Baṇḍāra remained a popular and exceptional military commander and was able to live up to his promise to subdue the Sītāvakan lands, mustering recruitments from the territories he had defeated and combining with substantial Portuguese reinforcements to rout the remaining Sītāvakan troops at the battle of Hanvälla.[50] One key to his authority lies in the redistributive powers that his capture of the bulk of Sītāvakan royal treasure bestowed upon him.[51] He was a central figure too in the invasion of Kandy later that year, but then became implicated in a plot with Vimaladharmasūriya. His power was so great that when this was discovered the Captain-General hesitated before dealing with him.[52] Jayavīra was finally killed, but by then the lowlands had been restored to the Kōṭṭe throne and its Portuguese liege.

45 Translated in Abeyasinghe 1978–9: 90. For his *Vida* Albuquerque drew on the notes he made on his tenure, which he compiled in 1597 in the *Lembrança dos Galeões* . . . , see BL, Add. MS 28,432, fols. 124–31. There Jayavīra exits Sītāvaka 'por ser estrangeiro' (fol. 128v). This ties in with (or informs) the claim of Queyroz: 471, that merely for the presumption of reaching for the throne 'they tried to kill him' and were only hindered by a faction won over by large bribes.

46 When Jayavīra followed suit, one of them, Pannikār Mudaliyār, then switched back to Sītāvaka and became commander of its forces, and then switched back one more time to the Portuguese on the eve of the decisive battle of Hanvälla! Queyroz: 475; *Rājāvaliya*: 89.

47 It is possible, but unlikely, that Albuquerque misinterpreted his illegitimacy in caste terms as a matter of ethnicity.

48 *Rājāvaliya*, 91–2, drawing here on other sources than the *Alakesvarayuddhaya*.

49 Each verse ended with the word *kokkānama*, see Roberts 2004: 24, n. 22, for possible meanings.

50 Queyroz: 477: *Rājāvaliya*: 92.

51 *APO*: 61; Queyroz: 484; AHU, Códice 281, royal letter of 1596, fol. 396.

52 According to Queyroz: 483, he was manoeuvring for a prominent position within Kandy, which aligns with BL, Add. MS 28,423, fol. 129. *Rājāvaliya*: 93, and Ribeiro: 18, have it that he was innocently snared by a ruse by Vimaladharmasūriya; Francisco Rodrigues da Silveira (Lobo 1887: 110–11) claims that his rival Sinhalese captains framed him.

Jayavīra Baṇḍāra had been in a position to dictate the terms of alliance, but for lesser leaders a switch of allegiance often had to be underpinned by the assumption of a new religious identity. Once again the 1590s appear as a replay of the 1540s in that the penetration of Portuguese power deep into the interior intensified the play of 'theological diplomacy'. This is particularly pertinent to the rulers of semi-autonomous fiefdoms, perennially probing for opportunities to break free from the hegemony of monarchical centres and sniffing for a change in the wind. Religious identity was reduced to a badge of political allegiance that could be pinned on and cast off with little reference to one's conscience.[53] Perhaps the most critical conversion in the 1590s was that of the ruler of the Seven Kōraḷēs, Jotupāla Baṇḍāra. In 1591 he revolted against Rājasiṃha and swore allegiance to Dharmapāla. When he was driven out of his lands by his wrathful liege, he sought refuge among the Portuguese of Mannar and was baptized as Manuel.[54] Yet on Rājasiṃha's death he returned to become 'a great enemy of the Portuguese, as usually happens when one receives Baptism out of respect, force, or self-interest'.[55] It appears that in his absence the Seven Kōraḷēs had been allocated to another prince, who it appears went by the name of Vīdiyē Baṇḍāra. However, he too agreed to convert as António in 1594 in order to side with Jayavīra Baṇḍāra.[56]

In this decisive year, of course, there were many others who did likewise.[57] Nikapiṭiye Baṇḍāra, the child-king of Sītāvaka who had been dispossessed after the battle of Hanvälla (1594), was baptized as Filipe and ended up in Goa with the similarly dispossessed Christian prince of Kandy. These elites opted to play the game of theological diplomacy for all the reasons of marginality listed in Chapter Eight. Political marginality lies behind the most important conversions: these are men either already stripped of power or with little option but to acquiesce in a new status quo. In these tumultuous years, both leaders and their subjects were more likely to be concerned with protection than theological fidelity; with short-term survival than long-term legitimacy. For a spell in the 1590s the foundational relationship between king and *saṃgha* was suddenly nowhere to be seen: indeed it had been imperilled for several decades. It was not just that Rājasiṃha had deliberately dislodged that foundation stone in Sītāvaka, but that his bullying presence pushed other rulers into the arms of the Portuguese and the waters of the font. After his death, kings were anyway thin on the ground; the firmest claim

53 See Trindade, III: 66. Chiefs in Trincomalee had been very willing to receive baptism in the 1540s and 1550s and may have done so again when they became tributaries of the Portuguese in the 1570s, C. R. de Silva 1995: 92.

54 VP, II: 211. 55 Queyroz: 444.

56 This is my way of reconciling some confusing sources: Trindade, III: 60; Queyroz: 481. By the later 1590s Jotupāla Baṇḍāra was fighting for Kandy (Queyroz: 547, 575). By 1602, the prince of the Seven Kōraḷēs was Dom Luís, who was Vimaladharmasūriya's brother according to Spilbergen: 43.

57 Including: the Prince of Ūva trying (unsuccessfully) to forestall his execution on being captured; a relative of Jayavīra attempting to win Portuguese favour at the expense of his kinsman; the families of Kōṭṭe commanders who had held out until then, and a *väddā* queen. Queyroz: 482–4; Trindade, III: 61; VP, II: 211.

to royal status emanated from Christian Kōṭṭe. The religious traditions of Lankan kingship were in meltdown.

It is in this light that we should see the resurrection of Dharmapāla as an emblem of native authority under which Portuguese dominion could be advanced: a major reverse.[58] Within Colombo, a new generation of Kōṭṭe nobility may have grown up who had only known Christian monarchy, but, beyond this core, Dharmapāla's abjuration of the religious traditions of state had damaged his legitimacy for the last four decades. Now that such traditions were everywhere in disarray he could reclaim some authority through his representation of another kind of link to the past: his unbroken line of regal ancestry and possession of the *cakravarti* title.[59]

Even in the last years of his life, Dharmapāla sought to make his authority as real as it was emblematic, to rule in true partnership with the Portuguese. In 1594 he requested – to no avail – that Philip II set out a proper delimitation of powers between himself and the Captains of Colombo, and authorize the creation of a supreme council comprising of a Portuguese *fidalgo*, a friar, and 'a man chosen by the natives of my kingdom'.[60] In reality, his personal standing was fragile. With Jayavīra Baṇḍāra's death, the first revolts began to break out and he was sent into an impotent rage when he found that he could not even enforce the punishment of a revealed traitor to his throne: he claimed that the new Captain-General Jerónimo de Azevedo (1594–1612) had been given advance warning of Edirillē Rāla's revolt in 1595 but had been bribed to keep quiet about it.[61]

Nevertheless, even when Dharmapāla died in May 1597, that mere semblance of partnership could not quite be allowed to die with him. What we see in the ensuing legal elaborations of the transition of sovereignty from Kōṭṭe to Portugal is a merging of the Portuguese principle of *pactum subjectionis* with the Sinhalese equivalent, namely, the acknowledgement of the will of the people through the acclamation or consecration of the monarch.[62] The primary legal principle for the Portuguese remained Dhamarpāla's right to dispose of his sovereignty in this way, as he exercised in his deed of gift of 1580. But in that deed we find the will of 'the people' of Ceylon supposedly represented by the *mudaliyārs* in attendance, and its ratification in 1583 catered for traditional procedures: while Christians present swore on the Bible, the 'heathens' swore in their temples.[63] And

[58] In 1595–6, Jerónimo de Azevedo was accompanied by Dharmapāla 'in order to make himself more acceptable to the natives', as Queyroz: 495–6, has it, and see Abeyasinghe 1995: 124.

[59] The importance of Dharmapāla's authority in the mid-1590s is reflected in the language of the *Rājāvaliya*: 94–5, which is concerned to emphasize indigenous agency.

[60] *APO*, III: 733–6, and see 857.

[61] *APO*, III: 857–8. This recapitulates an outraged letter by the Colombo Franciscan Guardian of 1596, complaining that Dharmapāla could not challenge Portuguese abuses (such as the theft of his land) because he was afraid of being poisoned (as he had been in 1574)! This may reflect Dharmapāla's declining status under the newly domineering conquistadorism of Azevedo, but it is also consistent with earlier portrayals of the king's status in 1574 and 1589: see above, p. 173, n. 54.

[62] See above, p. 141.

[63] *Gavetas da Torre do Tombo* 1963: 50; BL Add. MS 20,861, a royal letter of 1584, fol. 2v; Queyroz: 526; VP, II: 87–92. Clearly, the ceremony was designed to cater for the as yet unconverted masses residing outside of Kōṭṭe control.

when that deed was invoked by Jerónimo de Azevedo two days after Dharmapāla's death to proclaim Philip II as the successor, he made sure to hold an assembly of the leading Sinhalese officers from the court and the provinces. This assembly then elected certain persons to swear the oath of allegiance to the new king on behalf of them all.[64] Most importantly, Abeyasinghe has drawn our attention to the way in which the captains-general of Ceylon based at Malvāna assumed much of the paraphernalia of the Kōṭṭe kings, travelling in palanquins, greeted by the prostrations of their subjects, addressed as *deviyo* (deity), and, until at least 1606, holding the *däkum* or homage ceremony to which the leading men were obliged to come and pay their dues.[65]

The clothes of political legitimacy could be cut from a range of different fabrics – if of diminishing quality. Once religious propriety had been forfeited, then native dynastic authority could be gathered for the job, and when this too had passed away, the mantle of the Kōṭṭe dynasty could be used to enshroud the ceremonial behaviour of the Portuguese captains-general. That a Christian and then even a Portuguese officer could win at least some acquiescence in this way shows us how dynastic and titular continuity could surpass ethnic or cultural principles in shaping the loyalties of Sinhalese in this era. But the rest of the chapter will emphasize the limits that must be placed on that argument, for the traditional forms of royal authority were not in fact so easily hollowed out.

The Christian interlude in Kandy

From the extremely murky history of later sixteenth-century Kandy we receive only flashes of the fragile 'Christian' rule of Karaliyaddē (1552–82).[66] This was the prince who had made overtures to André de Sousa's mission in 1546.[67] Exciting his father Jayavīra's jealousy, he was forced to flee to Ūva, taking with him a Franciscan friar.[68] He issued another siren call to Jorge de Castro's expedition in 1550, which was diverted from the pursuit of Māyādunnē to make its way once

[64] Queyroz: 529; Couto: 413–15. According to a 1636 document in Queyroz: 1009–22, there had been a general assembly at Malvāna in which the *mudaliyārs* and nobles of the island opted to keep their own laws as the basis for colonial government. Abeyasinghe 1964 argues that this was a comforting myth arising from memories of the more negligible ritual in Colombo, but Biedermann 2005a: 485–93, suggests that it may have its origins in a real assembly designed to secure the acceptance of Portuguese rule.

[65] Abeyasinghe 1966: 76–7. See too Queyroz: 1008; Ribeiro: 26, 45; VP, II: 378.

[66] Quéré 1987; VP, II: 6; Couto: 133–4; Trindade, III: 70–2; Queyroz: 438–9, 704–5.

[67] While Coimbra enthused in ludicrous tones over the prince, António de Padrão remained entirely cynical, see VP: 188.

[68] Couto: 128, 133–4: the king imprisoned two friars during the Barreto debacle, who were later released at the behest of Karaliyaddē. These may have been Pascoal and Gonzalo, who had arrived in 1547. The most reliable sources here are Couto and the Paṇḍita's letter of 1551 (VP: 272–80); Afonso de Noronha's account (VP: 263–70) requires caution. See too Perniola's notes in VP, III: 101–2. Trindade, III: 63–4 and Queyroz: 257–8, 701–7 are rather confused (for example, 702–3 appears to be a misapplication of Gonzaga's account of 1543 Kōṭṭe to Kandy). Couto, whose source here may have been Yamasiṃha, tells us that the quarrel originated in Jayavīra's decision to replace him as heir with another son. But *Rājāvaliya*: 78, describes a different dynastic quarrel.

again into the highlands. In fact, the events and dizzying diplomacy surrounding this expedition are much more complicated than that. In brief, a putative joint Portuguese–Kōṭṭe invasion of Kandy returned Jayavīra to his old tactic of offering his baptism, and Castro was moved to resolve the situation once and for all. En route to the highlands his men were ambushed and suffered heavily. The Kandyans had inflicted the first major defeat of a European force on Lankan soil.

Jayavīra could not crow for long. Within a couple of years, Karaliyaddē had succeeded in usurping him. But it was not until a decade later that Karaliyaddē finally received baptism, and it is clear that this was part of a deal by which he gained a permanent bodyguard of thirty Portuguese soldiers and the opportunity to combine with much larger Portuguese forces to defend his borders against Māyādunnē or Rājasiṃha, who was rising to pre-eminence in the early 1560s.[69] This strategic alliance between Kōṭṭe and Kandy need not have expressed a genuine shared religiosity. In 1566 the King of Kandy claimed to have possession of the Tooth Relic in an attempt to outbid Kōṭṭe in winning the favour of an embassy from King Bayinnaug of Burma (r. 1551–81).[70] He may well have continued to discharge his public Buddhist-Hindu responsibilities then, dissimulating no less than his father. An observer in the 1570s reported that 'it was said that he lived secretly as a Christian.'[71] Perhaps this sort of ambiguity as to his religious allegiance helped him to continue to rule until 1582.

He had his enemies, however, and in 1582 Rājasiṃha's invasion of Kandy was supported by a faction led by the nobleman Vīrasundara Baṇḍāra. Karaliyaddē Baṇḍāra fled to Trincomalee, attempting and failing to win support from the *vanni* chiefs there.[72] The religious policy of Vīrasundara Baṇḍāra, whom Rājasiṃha installed as a sub-ruler of Kandy, remains unclear. In any case, he was soon assassinated after moving to oust Rājasiṃha from the highlands in 1585.

The main reason for imagining that there was at least one faction of the higher Kandyan nobility who had made a more open or permanent identification with Christianity is that a subsequent revolt against Rājasiṃha in 1589/90 was led by a Christian with royal blood, Francisco Mudali. He was acclaimed as king in Kandy, and after six months he called on another Christian prince to replace him on the throne.[73] This was Yamasiṃha Baṇḍāra, a nephew of Karaliyaddē Baṇḍāra, who had fled to Goa after the 1582 invasion. After some time in Goa, he was baptized as Filipe, receiving instruction from the friars, and in 1588 he was sent to Mannar to await an opportunity to press his claims. Yamasiṃha now became a tantalizing possibility in Portuguese discussions about how to expand

[69] This had become the standard 'price' of baptism in the 1540s. VP: 270; Couto: 234; Queyroz: 707; Trindade, III: 54–6.

[70] Couto: 252–3. In 1566, a Jesuit reported that 'the king of Candea is already a Christian with some of the leading persons of his kingdom' (VP, II: 7).

[71] See Ferguson's n. 4 to Couto: 242; C. R. de Silva 1998: 116. The *Palkuṁbura Sannasa* (*EZ*, III: 241) says that Bhuvanekabāhu VII's *bhikkhu* brother left Kōṭṭe after the latter's death and found patronage in Kandy, as later did his nephew.

[72] Queyroz: 438–9.

[73] Rodrigo da Cunha, 29 Nov. 1589, in Lopes 1962: 141–2; Trindade, III: 69–76; Queyroz: 439, 705–7.

their influence on the island.[74] When the call finally came he set off for Kandy accompanied by a substantial Portuguese and lascarin force. He was well received and acclaimed king in late 1589.[75]

These events indicate that many Kandyans were prepared to accept Christian leadership, but this was probably contingent on forthcoming support from the Portuguese. That is to say, they were making the same bargain – baptism for military aid – that had appealed to marginal rulers since the 1540s. It is noteworthy that Yamasiṃha, despite being such a close relative of Karaliyaddē, had not actually been baptized until he had taken refuge among the Portuguese. He was then, characteristically, removed from power at the point of baptism.[76] Equally characteristic is the way in which he was Christianized during his years in Goa and Mannar. His case needs to be seen in the context of a Portuguese policy to expose the young princes and heirs of indigenous royal families to a Catholic education. Apart from the princes of Kōṭṭe (João and Luís) who died in Goa in 1546, we have already referred to the son of Bhuvanekabāhu (João) who was taken away in 1552 at the age of five and the prince of Trincomalee (Afonso), his companion in the Jesuit college of Saint Paul.[77] We shall hear more below about Nikapiṭiye Baṇḍāra (Filipe), the heir to Sītāvaka, who was captured and baptized in 1594.[78] Most of these kings-in-waiting settled down to a sedate ecclesiastical life, none of them to return in glory. Yamasiṃha is then a rare example of the policy bearing fruit.

He was no cipher, however: he clearly had strong personal political ambitions, if his persistent petitions to the Crown are anything to go by. Hence it is no surprise to find the governor Manuel de Sousa Coutinho (1588–91) expressing serious doubts as to the authenticity of his Christianity.[79] Nevertheless he was ready to bequeath his kingdom to Portugal in the event that neither he nor his son should leave heirs, and on being acclaimed king he allowed a vigorous missionary effort to take its course. Queirós can tell us of the consequences: within a matter of months, Yamasiṃha was dead,

> not without suspicions of being helped by poison, because, though the Chingalaz abominate this treachery, as the majority of his lieges were heathens and the King a Christian, there could not be wanting those who found an excuse for this sin. On the following day Prince

[74] *APO*: 187, 203, 255. Biedermann 2005a: 405–17. Hence we should take the Captain of Mannar's, claim that Yamasiṃha would have the clear support of the Lankan population with a large pinch of salt, see João de Melo to Filipe I, Mannar, 28 Dec. 1588, AGS-SP, cod. 1551, fols. 539, 549.

[75] AHU, Códice 281, royal letter of 1592 (fol. 209). AGS-SP, cod. 1551, nos. 158 (letter of 28 Dec. 1588), 220 (Dec. 1589), 226 (Nov. 1589).

[76] The two exceptions, Dharmapāla and Karaliyaddē, who converted whilst on the throne, had both been exposed to Christianity during their youth and a time of political crisis.

[77] See above, pp. 108, 144, and, for Prince João, who would live an honoured life as a Jesuit in Goa till his death in 1587: VP: 283, 306–10, 341, 345, 391; Trindade, III: 60; Couto: 155; Queyroz: 304–5, 328, 706–7; Ribeiro: 23. On Prince Afonso: VP: 285–8, 309, 341, 345, 372; VP, II: 23, n. 1 (his death in Goa, 1568); SR, V: 96–8.

[78] He was educated in the college at Bardez and then travelled to Lisbon, dying in a monastery in Coimbra in 1608. Trindade, III: 61, 73–6; VP, II: 211; Queyroz: 477, 706–8. There are further lesser examples: Queyroz: 377; VP, II: 255–6, 275.

[79] *APO*: 255.

D. João, the son, was sworn and acclaimed King of Candea. But some of the great men, seeing that he lacked the protection of the Portuguese and despising him because he was a boy and a Christian, revolted against him . . .[80]

Yamasiṃha's young son João escaped with his grandmother and friars to become another Sinhalese scion lost to the safety of Luso-indic society.[81] If there was a group of Kandyan nobles who were willing to come to terms with Christianity in return for independence from Rājasiṃha, there was also apparently an important faction who were not. Once the bargain became less compelling, once Rājasiṃha was expelled and Portuguese support revealed as less than awesome, once nominal Christianity was replaced by stone churches and real conversions, the voice of the latter faction rose to the fore.

Vimaladharmasūriya: the apostate king

That faction found its leader in a man who had arrived in the highland kingdom of Kandy with the expeditionary force from Colombo; indeed, a man who had spent the last ten years fighting for the Portuguese, married a Portuguese orphan in Goa and been baptized as João de Áustria.[82] But on claiming the throne of Kandy he apostatized and assumed the name Vimaladharmasūriya I (1591–1604), drawing on newly empowered Buddhist and indigenist sensibilities. His first act was to expel the Portuguese from the kingdom. They did not give up on their hope of a Christian ruler in Kandy, but rather sought to pursue it through the vehicle of Karaliyaddē's daughter, Kusumāsanadēvi, or Catarina, who had been residing in Mannar. In September–October 1594, the Capain-General Pero Lopes de Sousa led a large expeditionary force, further swelled by the thousands of lascarins under the command of Jayavīra Baṇḍāra, into the highlands. Vimaladharmasūriya was forced to abandon the city of Kandy and retreat to the hills.[83] All the main political centres of the island were now under Kōṭṭe–Portuguese control. But it was at this juncture that the Portuguese deviated for the first time from their policy of exerting influence through native rulers.[84]

It was decided to place Catarina on the throne with a Portuguese noble named Francisco da Silva for a husband. This was clearly a step too far for the Kandyans. Queirós, again:

80 Queyroz: 708, which seems to be closely based on Trindade, III: 71–4; also *APO*: 370; Queyroz: 445. Francisco Rodrigues Silveira (Lobo 1887: 105) claims that João D'Austria orchestrated the poisoning, echoed later by Biker, I: 221, 227.

81 VP, II: 211.

82 *Rājāvaliya*: 86; Couto: 294; Queyroz: 439; Linschoten, I: 78; Ferguson 1928: 167. His baptismal name, ironically, was taken from the Habsburg prince Don Juan de Austria (1547–78), who had spearheaded the Christian alliance against the Muslim Ottomans at the Battle of Lepanto in 1571.

83 Queyroz: 445, 480–2; Trinidade, III: 95; *Rājāvaliya*: 93; Ribeiro: 14–20; Spilbergen: 37–8.

84 See Biedermann 2005a on the shift of policy as indirect dominion was replaced by a Castilian emphasis on direct territorial control.

> The General placed Portuguese to guard the Princess, not allowing any Chingalaz to speak to her, lest they should attempt any rebellion, from which they concluded that the war was not being made in her name, as was given out and as they believed in the beginning, and this was the principal reason why the kingdom did not come into obedience, the inhabitants retiring to the hills to seek help from the rebel [Vimaladharmasūriya].[85]

This was compounded when the Portuguese murdered Jayavīra Baṇḍāra, which induced the mass of auxiliary troops to desert.[86] It would seem then that the Portuguese had achieved a measure of acceptance among both the Sinhalese lascarin forces and the people of Kandy through their invocation of 'indigenous' military leadership (Jayavīra Baṇḍāra) and indigenous dynastic authority (Catarina).[87] But once the former was lost and the latter suspected of being disingenuous, their apparent position of strength crumbled with astonishing rapidity. Faced with a general revolt, Pero Lopes de Sousa was forced to withdraw his men to Colombo. Vimaladharmasūriya seized the initiative and cut them off, giving battle at Dantūrē in October 1594, and inflicting on the Portuguese their largest defeat yet on the island. The whole force was either killed or captured.[88]

Eight years afterwards, Spilbergen explained Vimaladharmasūriya's initial rise to leadership by the facts that he 'had the soldiers in his control and was also much liked by the *Singales* as he too was a Sinhalese. . . .'[89] He was 'one of us'; the Portuguese captain was not. This also highlights his power base in the military. He was proclaimed king by 'the armies having made consultations' according to the *Rājāvaliya*.[90] The victory at Dantūrē was decisive for the establishment of his authority: it consolidated his martial prowess in glorious fashion, and his marital prowess too, allowing him to take the young princess Catarina as his wife. This was particularly important considering that Vimaladharmasūriya conspicuously lacked any real royal pedigree.[91] His consort now gave him that crucial connection to a *kṣatriya* dynasty.

There was one further bastion with which he shored up his legitimacy, and that was his religious policy, which was orthodox and beneficent enough to win praise

[85] Queyroz: 483.

[86] Queyroz: 485–7. 8,000 of the 9,000 deserted. The only loyal lascarins were those from the two major Christian centres, Colombo and Mannar. See too Silveira (Lobo 1887: 112).

[87] Jayavīra was therefore at once vulnerable to attacks on his foreignness, and yet also capable of representing a form of indigenous leadership when contrasted with the Portuguese, reflecting perhaps the long-term incorporation of Indian immigrants within Sinhalese society, their greater willingness to Sinhalacize and his prior position at the Sītāvaka court.

[88] Queyroz: 487–90; Ribeiro: 20; VP, II: 155; Spilbergen: 38.

[89] Spilbergen: 37.

[90] *Rājāvaliya*: 88; Ribeiro: 14: he assumed the title 'Defender of the Kingdoms', intriguingly echoed by the contemporary language of De Weert in Ferguson 1928: 117; Baldaeus 1752: 603. The importance of martial prowess to his continuing legitimacy seems to be behind the story in *Rājāvaliya*: 88, that he had won fame through defeating an errant captain (Gajabāhu) while he was in Goa. The sketch of his coat-of-arms published with Spilbergen's text of the 1604/5 edition (see Spilbergen: pl. 9) shows the king holding a sword aloft in a similar manner to the martial Kōṭṭe image of *c.* 1547, see Plate 6 here.

[91] Abeyasinghe 1966: 15–16; Queyroz: 489; Ribeiro: 21. His sons therefore claimed their right to the throne through their mother. Portuguese documents stressed the 'plebeian' origins of this '*mudaliyār*': Lobo 1887: 105; Biker, I: 226.

from later *vaṃsa*-writers.[92] The most noteworthy features of it are the reinstatement of the Tooth Relic, which apparently appeared in Delgamuva and was transported to a new temple in Kandy, and the cultivation of relations with the kings of Arakan (in present-day Burma), which resulted in the re-establishment of higher ordination. He seems to have been particularly keen to ordain 'sons of good family', perhaps in an attempt to bind the nobility to his religious project. This extended to his own brother, who became a *bhikkhu* and would later rule as Senarat (1604–35), a particularly strong indicator of his desire to re-found the Kandyan dynasty as inherently Buddhist.[93]

Arakan (or Mrauk-U) benefited from the exchange by receiving Lankan texts.[94] These maritime Theravādin relations were observed by the Portuguese with some alarm: the factual kernel of the ordination ceremony developed a mythic husk in which the staunchly Buddhist Sinhalese were imagined as receiving support from an international hierarchy strategically orchestrated by the *mahaterunnānse* of Arakan. The latter was thereby rendered a pagan equivalent of the Catholic Pope.[95] Again, the evidence of the Dutch visitors is very valuable. Spilbergen tells us that Vimaladharmasūriya made a pilgrimage to Adam's peak, and then set up a model of the footprint in Kandy.[96] He also used the offerings made by other pilgrims, many arriving from far overseas, to help finance an extensive programme of temple building and repair. Spilbergen was mightily impressed with the 'many and costly pagodas, which had more than four or five thousand figures'.[97] Buddhist vitality was also to be found in outlying centres, if we consider Spilbergen's description of the town of Bintänna: its dagoba, its processions, its people prostrate in worship, its monks 'highly respected and free from all kinds of labour'.[98]

All this signalled a return to a more traditional Buddhist model of kingship, just when that model might appear to have been all but extinguished. We have seen how the conflicts of the past three or four decades had churned up the ground of political and religious legitimacy. The *saṃgha* had been without any major royal protector for at least a generation, increasingly incapable, one might think, of appealing to their role as the moral guardians of the Sinhalese. Leadership was more often provided by military freebooters comparatively detached from the mores of wider society. It was as if all the elements of rulership had been thrown into the air.

[92] *Cūḷavaṃsa*: 227–9: he 'freed the whole kingdom of Lanka from all oppression'; Ilangasinha 1992: 84, 127; Nevill: Or. 6606(145).

[93] This also emerges from clues in Queyroz (565, in which Vimaladharmasūriya places himself under a Bo tree, 571, 605). Also see Holt 2007 on an image of Vimaladharmasūriya wearing a royal chapeau with a Buddha figure in its frontal crest, and holding a lotus, evoking the symbolism of the *bodhisattva*.

[94] Godakumbura 1966: 154; Raymond 1995: 481.

[95] Queyroz: 237, 257, fictitiously amplified from the reference in Miranda: 183. The Sinhalese Christian Botelho had identified the *mahaterrunānse* in Kandy as an equivalent to the Pope in 1633: Cruz and Flores 2007.

[96] Spilbergen: 44; Bree 1603 in Ferguson 1928: 166.

[97] Spilbergen: 31.

[98] Modern-day Alutnuvara. Remember that the ruler of Bintänna had requested baptism in the 1540s! (see above, p. 156).

But when they finally settled it was into the largely traditional and familiar contours of Kandyan kingship, structures of the long term persisting underneath the surface swirl of events. It is possible that Vimaladharmasūriya's actual rise to the throne was assisted by the *saṃgha*.[99] He had begun life as Konappu Baṇḍāra, the son of Vīrasundara Baṇḍāra, and as such had been forced to flee Kandy when his father's uprising had been put down. On his return, it is likely that he drew support from those who had previously supported his father, and these were men who had sought to overthrow both the Catholic Karaliyaddē and the Saivite-leaning Rājasiṃha. Certainly, the imagery of his subsequent reign can be read as a rebuff to both those visions of kingship.[100] Yet his Lusitanization had not been a shallow pretence to be cast off on ascending the throne. Spilbergen is as forthcoming on the Portuguese aesthetics of the court as he is on its 'heathen' religiosity. He found the whole royal family to be 'dressed in the Christian manner', intimates that the king's two brothers were known by their baptismal names, and comments that the king 'has had all new buildings to be constructed according to the Christian style'.[101]

We learn too that a version of the 'personality of law' principle prevailed, by which the many 'Moors, Turks and other heathens' who lived among the Sinhalese were governed by their own special laws.[102] Indeed, Vimaladharmasūriya came to rely heavily on foreign troops, just as his Kōṭṭe predecessors had done, drawing on Telugu soldiers from South India and Portuguese renegades as well as various Muslim groups.[103] It is not surprising then that Spilbergen found Brahmans in Kandy in large numbers. This is all by way of emphasizing the point that a return to a more traditional model of kingship ought not to be equated with indiscriminate xenophobia or parochialism. On the contrary, it meant catering for the religious tastes of the various specialist foreign groups that he sought to draw into his service, as rulers throughout Asia understood in the early modern period.

Spilbergen was clearly impressed by this partially 'Westernized' Buddhist king whom he felt he had left half-convinced of his heathen errors. After all, he had exhibited curiosity about the Dutch brand of Christianity, and appeared pleased when a young man named Matsberger consented to remain behind to educate him further and function as his secretary. In one theological debate, the Dutch general remarked on the punishment in the after-life that awaits the sinner. Vimaladharmasūriya 'understood this very well' and responded, 'it is all true, for as a man sows, so shall he reap.' The latter phrase, of course, could just as easily

99 Ilangasinha 1992: 122–4; Queyroz: 569; Bell 1904: 88, on the role of the chief monk of Devanagala. The 'unverified texts' discussed in Chapter Nine are very firm on this point.

100 One 'unverified source', the *Mandārampura-Puvata*, claims that Vimaladharmasūriya fought Saivite forces brought over by Rājasiṃha (C. R. de Silva 2000: 289).

101 Spilbergen: 30–2, 39, 43. Remember, however, that Spilbergen may be attempting to cast Vimaladharmasūriya in an attractive light.

102 Spilbergen: 42.

103 Spilbergen: 38: most of his soldiers 'were recruited from foreign nations'. He sought help from the Nāyak of Madura and the King of Meliapor, providing *vadugai* troops: Queyroz: 552, 595; Couto: 427; Abeyasinghe 1966: 36, 43; Wickremesekera 2004: 54, 58–62.

express the Buddhist concept of karma: Vimaladharmasūriya may have been after commonalities here.[104] In common with many other European attendants at Lankan courts, Spilbergen mistook intellectual tolerance for Christian leanings. This may have influenced him to report that '*Dona Catharina* visits no pagodas. *Dom Ioan* the King does it mostly to please the Singales.'[105] In this account, Vimaladharmasūriya bears no great personal animosity towards Christianity. Both his baptism in the 1580s and his subsequent apostasy were political necessities; his own theological predilections were not at issue. What were relevant, apparently, were the sentiments of his subjects.

This point becomes all the more pertinent as we consider the evidence that in other contexts his behaviour was guided by anti-Christian symbolism. The crucial case here is his treatment of the Portuguese prisoners whom he captured at the battle of Dantūrē. And the crucial fact: that he tried to force his prisoners to apostatize just as he had done. . . . We have to tread carefully here, given our earlier comments on how the image of Vimaladharmasūriya as the violent apostate is over-determined by the narrative logic of our Portuguese sources.[106] As a royal letter from Lisbon in 1595 put it, he must have known that spurning his baptism would make him 'a greater enemy of this state than Rājasiṃha ever was'.[107] Behind the chronicle accounts lie *casado* sources such as Lomba, for whom the aftermath of Dantūrē – with substantial numbers of Portuguese at the mercy of a vengeful Sinhalese king for the first time – must have been terrifying, and Franciscan sources such as Negrão and Trindade who were always concerned to elaborate the martyrdom and suffering of their brethren in Sri Lanka.[108] They all needed to see their ordeal as part of a struggle against religious, diabolical opposition, as opposed to mere political resistance.

But, in this instance, it would appear that their nightmares had fed off the facts of the matter. Trindade's account seems to be derived from a Franciscan apologia written only eight years after Dantūrē.[109] All the salient points are there. It claims that Vimaladharmasūriya promised to reward his Christian prisoners if they would 'apostatize and abandon the Faith of Christ'. But, strengthened by the friars, 'many Portuguese did not abandon their Faith or have their ears pierced, which in India is a symbol of heathens, undergoing death by torture instead.'[110] Vimaladharmasūriya

104 Spilbergen: 31. Earlier, Vimaladharmasūriya had asked 'whether our God was eternal', perhaps probing a point of difference with Buddhist thought in which deities are bound by *saṃsara*.

105 Spilbergen: 44. Prefaced by: 'Yea, they often confess that their gods are of no value,' which may reflect the mundane (*laukika*) status of Sinhalese Buddhist deities when set alongside the quest for salvation (*lōkōttara*).

106 A further reason for Queyroz: 472–3, to dwell on the apostasy and tyranny of Vimaladharmasūriya was to provide legal justification for the attempted policy of assassination.

107 *APO*: 479, 504.

108 Queyroz: 490–2. Stock martyrological motifs abound here. The difference between the *casado* and Franciscan traditions may explain why in the *Conquista*, it is the captains who receive martyrdom by refusing to apostatize and chastising the king, while in Trindade that role is played by the friars.

109 VP, II: 204–22.

110 Lopes 1967: 65 (VP, II: 214). See too VP, II: 135, n. 2. Also present is the claim that Vimaladharmasūriya had been publicly admonished by his old teacher at the College of Colombo,

was not acting here in a fit of blind rage. Mindful of diplomatic considerations, he treated one of the captives, the Jesuit António Schipano, quite differently and dispatched him as an ambassador to Colombo.[111] The Franciscans may have contributed to their brutal treatment through their characteristically unbending zeal: they had a simple passion for martyrdom that their Jesuit counterparts were taught to avoid. Yet the gestures of religious antagonism in these events, the distinct abeyance of religious tolerance, cannot be denied. Friars were killed during the battle and after it; others were tortured, or disfigured by having their noses sliced off.[112] The Portuguese prisoners were forced to labour on the construction of temples – an abominable subjection for the devout – and other public works in Kandy.[113]

How do we reconcile all this with the apparent curiosity and regard for Christian culture that we find in Spilbergen's account of Vimaladharmasūriya? First, the king appears to have discriminated between the Dutch Reformed faith and Portuguese Catholicism. Second, it was precisely his personal background in Christianity that necessitated such a publicly unimpeachable reproach to it. This was the cultural logic of the apostate rebel, which we have witnessed already in Vīdiyē Baṇḍāra, and shall see in many more below. The rejection of both the Christian experiment of 1590–1 and Portuguese power was spelled out in such ostentatious acts of disfigurement. In this way Vimaladharmasūriya fuelled the escalating use of extreme cruelty by both sides.[114] Third, this stands as an illustration of the way in which group sentiments are rarely played out according to neat dichotomies. In Spilbergen's account the king is both enduringly Lusitanized and possessed of an entirely authentic antagonism towards the Portuguese. A subsequent Dutch emissary to Kandy was killed when Vimaladharmasūriya discovered that he had not punished some captured Portuguese. For the king 'never trusted the Portuguese and considered that severe measures should always be taken to deal with them, for there is no King or nation who resist the Portuguese so inimically'.[115]

Let us examine more closely the issue of forced apostasy and consider what it tells us about the operation of religious boundaries in 1590s Kandy. The acts of conversion and apostasy mediate the transition from one group to another, and only become so highly charged where the distinction between two groups is considered highly meaningful. We can see this enhanced sense of 'groupishness' as either imported from Christianity or rather modified and enhanced through

a Franciscan commissary named Lucas. Trindade, III: 56, 96–9, refers to him as Fra. Lucas dos Santos, Commissary of Kandy, 'a great helper of mine' (and therefore perhaps biased in his report!), which would appear to be the same as the Fra. Lucas in the Apologia (212–13), and the Lucas de S. Francisco mentioned by Trindade, III: 186, as a commissary for Ceylon, 1591–4 (and see Lopes' n. 2).

111 VP, II: 177, 201. Compare with Vimaladharmasūriya's calculating treatment of Pedro de Christo in Trindade, III: 101; VP, II: 213.

112 Certificate of Dharmapāla in Trindade, III: 56; VP, II: 155 (a letter of 1595 on Franciscan deaths); Queyroz: 490.

113 Spilbergen: 39; Trinidade, III: 102; Queyroz: 492.

114 Trinidade, III: 102–4; *Rājāvaliya*: 94.

115 Spilbergen: 50; confirmed by De Weert in Ferguson 1928: 108–10.

contact with and opposition to it. But how would one define the group into which the unwilling apostates were to be forced? From the evidence of the apologia quoted above and other sources, the primary boundary marker – the anti-baptism, as it were – was the rite of ear-piercing. There is no evidence that this implied an acceptance of either a particular form of Hinduism or Buddhism *per se*, or even that it originally had any religious significance.[116] Indeed, ear-piercing was also a custom in parts of India, and by 1566 Jesuits with proto-accommodationist leanings were already having arguments with other missionaries about whether it constituted a secular or religious symbol.[117] But most missionaries at this time, and certainly the Franciscans in Sri Lanka, did not draw such distinctions, and rather sought to use secular cultural trappings as a way of expressing and reinforcing the total transformation of identity that conversion ought to entail. If converts had to give up their earrings on baptism, assuming them again would naturally signify their rejection of Christianity.

These acts then took on political implications. Couto tells us that after the youth Diogo Gonçalves was captured, 'Raju commanded his ears to be bored and that he be taught the customs of the Chingalas.'[118] Spilbergen comments on the similar case of Manuel Dias, who would rise to high office under Vimaladharmasūriya: 'he let his ears be clipped like all the other Portuguese who serve in *candy* and who must have their ears adorned according to the custom of the Sinhalese.'[119] It had become a means of binding Portuguese to royal service through conspicuous indigenization. Indeed, this ought to be seen in terms of the broader phenomenon of the renegade in Asia. Throughout the region one sees political defections expressed in religious and cultural terms. The defector was an inherently untrustworthy figure and such comprehensive transformations were demanded as a means of making them more beholden to the court they had appealed to. This politics of identity was particularly promoted by the rising monotheistic powers, for whom it was natural to tie together different strands of identity in this way, but it soon seeped into the behaviour at some Hindu and Buddhist courts too.[120]

It would therefore be more appropriate to describe the rite of ear-piercing as signifying the transition between Christian culture and indigenous culture rather than between Christianity and Buddhism.[121] This is not to displace the role of religion in these antagonisms – merely to redefine it – and nor does it force too much of a breach between Portuguese and Sinhalese understandings of what was

[116] See Queyroz: 22; Barbosa 1918–21, II: 110; Knox: 257. Queyroz: 554–5, describes how a native Goan Christian, Manuel Gomez, came to Ceylon and became a rebel leader by 'apostatizing from the Faith, bored his ears and let his beard grow and gave out that he was the son of a Bragmene, in order to be better esteemed'. Further, 'in order to show himself a good pagan' he burnt down churches in the Chilaw area.

[117] VP, II: 4. This was then another precursor of the rites controversies.

[118] Couto: 339, 358.

[119] Spilbergen: 29, 40; Queyroz: 522.

[120] Valignano in 1575 (VP, II: 74) asserted that Portuguese who defected regularly became renegades to both gentiles (Hindus and Buddhists) and Moors. Freyre 1630: fol. 14, presents it as generally a practice of Muslims rather than 'os gentios'.

[121] The hair-knot is another such marker judging by Queyroz: 491. We can see it worn in pictures in the Biblioteca Casanatense (See Matos 1985, Flores 1998) of Sinhala warriors and women.

going on in the Kandyan court after the battle of Dantūrē. The Portuguese prisoners were right to feel that Vimaladharmasūriya, the product of a Catholic education, knew very well what he was doing to his captives. And he was out to give them a taste of their own medicine.

Rebellion: a common cause?

He was not alone. Vimaladharmasūriya's behaviour needs to be understood within the context of an incipient rebellion that swept through many parts of the old Kōṭṭe lands after his victory at Dantūrē. Indeed, the rumble of rebellion rolled on for the next four or five decades, producing major revolts in 1594–6, 1603, 1616–17, and 1630–1, along with many other more minor acts of resistance. At several key junctures, Portuguese invasions of Kandy were thwarted by the mass defection of Sinhalese auxiliaries. For many inhabitants of Kōṭṭe, the desire for stability or mere survival had clearly become secondary to other concerns. There can be no question but that the increasingly naked Portuguese policy of conquest, exposed after their dealings in Kandy of 1594, and finally divested of any vestiges of native authority after Dharmapāla's death in 1597, had fomented an altogether new spirit of unruliness. What remain very much in question, however, are the sentiments and motivations behind this refusal to acquiesce in the new status quo. The extent to which the rebels were inspired by a repugnance of foreign rule or some sense of common identity that vaulted over all the myriad divisions of Sinhalese society, is matter of importance for the controversies surrounding the history of ethnic consciousness in Sri Lanka. How strong were the bonds between the inhabitants of previously separate kingdoms, between the followers of different and often competing military or feudal leaders, between upcountry and low-country sorts, between the various castes (particularly Goyigama and non-Goyigama), between the court and the periphery, between the literate and non-literate?[122]

The historicist perspective, which emphasizes the (spatial and temporal) discontinuity of consciousness, would incline us to question the influence of such bonds. The debate on 'Sinhalaness' has barely touched on the rebellions of the Portuguese era, but we can find an expression of this approach in Gunawardana's famous panoramic essay on the 'People of the Lion', where it is the many occasions in which native troops fought willingly on the side of the Portuguese and Dutch that are emphasized, and it is claimed that 'there are no instances of "the whole ethnic group" being united in an uprising against the foreign occupation . . .'[123] A more recent paper by John Rogers argues that in the Dutch period, the latter's misunderstandings 'shaped their perceptions of their subjects' loyalty in times of tension or war with Kandy. Sinhala-speaking Dutch subjects sometimes supported Kandy in such struggles. The Dutch often saw this as a natural consequence of

[122] See Rogers 2004a and Gunawardana 1990 for the most sophisticated historicizations of various identities in pre-modern Lanka.

[123] Gunawardana 1990: 68. His famous debate with Dharmadasa (1992) largely concerns an earlier period.

national identity, but it is likely that economic exploitation or resentment over the early Dutch religious policies was more important.'[124]

The chief historicist argument might be that central rule was always difficult to enforce in Sri Lanka: the galactic-political system typically generated breakaway movements which drained loyalties away from the centre. What we describe as 'rebellions' and 'defections' from the 1590s onwards, are simply a mutated version of such traditional fissiparous forces, strengthened by the resentments engendered by a newly oppressive and insensitive form of government. For our Portuguese sources are themselves replete with reflections on the great injustices, the colonial rapaciousness and indignities, that might have induced the afflicted Lankans to hate their imperial rulers.[125] But, the argument has thereby returned full circle, for these are surely the conditions in which one might expect some sense of solidarity among the indigenous people, and a widespread affection for Kandy, to flourish. And how would opposition to these new masters have mustered, legitimized and described itself?

If it is true that the act of opposition by itself need not indicate a common identity, the reverse logic, that acquiescence to foreign conquest indicates the lack of a common identity, is equally suspect and belied by many examples, even from the nineteenth and twentieth centuries when ethnic and national solidarities were at their most virile. The quarry we are after – a form of cultural or ethnic identity that might overarch regions previously claimed by competing kings – is more elusive still. We can get a little closer to it by considering: (1) the geography and chronology of these rebellions; (2) the symbolism of cultural antagonism they deploy; (3) the examples of co-operation between low-country rebels and the kingdom of Kandy; (4) how we should interpret the interpretations of our Portuguese sources.

The earliest rebellions were centred right at the heart of the kingdom of Kōṭṭe, in the basins of the Kälaṇi Gaṅga and Kalugaṅga.[126] These districts spreading out from Colombo were therefore also those with the most sustained exposure to Portuguese influence. But disquiet quickly spread to outlying areas such as the Seven Kōraḷēs and Mātara. As Portuguese control tightened over the core territories of Kōṭṭe by 1600, revolts began to issue from further afield, such as Balana in the Kandyan borders, and Badulla. In fact rebellions arose in all the main regions of 'greater Kōṭṭe' facing the threat or reality of Portuguese conquest. The fact that the first decade of Portuguese 'rule' was the most turbulent (producing four major rebellions) suggests that the mere idea of it had become distasteful to many

[124] Rogers 2004a: 631, which contrasts with Roberts 2004: 82–3. My thanks to John Rogers for our discussions on this issue.

[125] C. R. de Silva 1972, offers an excellent study of these issues of seventeenth-century governance. An anonymous memorandum of 1610 (Pato 1880–1935, II: 8–6) is particularly critical here, pointing to excessive taxation, harsh laws, iniquitous property policies, and the policy of destroying temples. See also the comments of Bocarro: 17, 58; Azevedo in 1614, in Abeyasinghe 1974: 43; Queyroz: 1023–49; Abeyasinghe 1966: 117.

[126] Abeyasinghe 1995: 129. Abeyasinghe 1966 remains the foundational study of these rebellions, and C. R. de Silva 1972 for post-1618 affairs.

Sinhalese, before the full burden of exploitative or incompetent colonial policies *per se* had been felt.

The first revolt was the product of the Dantūrē defeat. A leader with royal blood, Akaragama Appuhāmi, raised the standard in Sītāvaka and enlisted men with the help of some remaining royal treasure, and there were simultaneous revolts in Sabaragamuva and Mātara. Queirós may have been speaking loosely when he wrote that 'the whole country was in rebellion', but that is perhaps how it seemed to the beleaguered Portuguese captain at the time.[127] A still greater threat, however, would come from a lascarin commander who had been involved in suppressing Akaragama Appuhāmi's revolt, Edirillē Rāla or Domingos Correa to use his baptismal name.[128] His case is striking because he seems to have been raised within Catholic aristocratic society in Colombo. He was a literate, second-generation Christian with many Portuguese relatives by marriage and well-favoured with the high offices of interpreter to the king and then Vikramasiṃha (generalship). And yet in November 1595 he fled to Atulugama, followed by his brother Simão and his nephew João Fernandez, where he apostatized and took on a royal title.[129] Soon much of the lowlands were in revolt.[130]

He has entered history as one of the most violently iconoclastic of the Sinhalese rebels. Trindade's account, with all due recognition of its Franciscan penchant for martyrdom narratives, is particularly revealing of the subversive theatricality of his campaigns. With one friar,

> they stripped him of his habit; they pierced his ears and passed a chord through them. Then one of them put on the friar's habit and, in order to ridicule our Christian religion, took the missal from which the father used to say mass and went in front of him with the others as in a procession and pulling him with the cord through his the ears, saying *ora pro nobis*.[131]

Coming as he did from such impeccably Lusinatized origins, Edirillē Rāla prompted Queirós to the most explicit account we have of the cultural politics of the apostate rebel:

> And because the one and other infidelity [i.e. to God and to one's King] is wont to be equal in this matter and those who are traitors to God show more zeal and forwardness to the new Princes or to the new subjects, *in order to escape the suspicion which might be had of them*, there was no sacrilege which this apostate did not commit. He burnt Churches, profaned the ornaments, hacked sacred images and used the chalices for shameful purposes, cudgelled the priests, making mockery and derision of them. [italics added][132]

All of which is very eloquent on the way in which would-be leaders had to respond to more popular widespread expectations and sentiments. Edirillē Rāla himself may have been spurred by a typical aristocratic ambition or by an appalled revelation as to how thin the veneer of indigenous authority at Colombo actually was – he

[127] Queyroz: 486, 494. [128] Queyroz: 496–500. [129] Queyroz: 501.
[130] Queyroz: 508. Only Colombo and Galle remained faithful. [131] Trinidade, III: 106.
[132] Queyroz: 507–8; see also 587 which explicitly links mutilation and religious antagonism.

had been in a position to witness at first-hand how Dharmapāla was sidelined by Azevedo's bullying style.[133]

He was eventually captured by his rival, the Kōṭṭe commander Samarakōne (Fernando Mudaliyār) in May 1596, and killed shortly afterwards.[134] Queirós' account of his lengthy deathbed recantation and confession ought to be read as a reflection of the psychology of the outraged *casado* community, which found its voice in the fragmentary notes of Bento da Silva. Edirillē Rāla is made to take on all manner of vices, beyond his religious and political treachery, as if a range of horrors and evils could be contained within his person and thus made amenable to destruction in the ritual dismembering of his corpse.[135] But what most stands out is the convergence of symbolism between his campaigns and the concurrent conduct of Vimaladharmasūriya that we examined above: an anti-mass is performed, an anti-baptism; the cruelty is ratcheted up, noses are sliced off and ears are pierced as a way of destroying or reversing religious status.[136] It was those who most understood the sanctity of Christian rites who were most concerned to abuse them. Anti-Christian symbolism continued to surface in further revolts.[137]

Shared hatreds are one thing, shared political allegiance quite another. Any discussion of these rebellions has to proceed from a basic historicist reminder: the absence of unitary rule in sixteenth-century Sri Lanka. Furthermore, by the 1590s, often the most visible loyalties were to local chiefs or individual military commanders. As we consider how the behaviour of Sinhalese military units may reflect wider identities, it is worth bearing in mind that the process of continuous warfare can create very tight bonds between the fighting men themselves that can override any other other solidarities and which are focused on the person of their unit leader.[138] They become predisposed to follow their leader whither he takes them. It is then the calculations of such officers, their weighing up of personal opportunistic motivations against deeper emotional commitments, which became crucial in deciding whether a unit would stay loyal to the Portuguese, rebel against them or defect to Kandy. Therefore, such conjectures about identity that arise in this context must be seen as particularly germane to this 'officer class' – and a prosopographical study of their caste status, regional background, and extent of their Lusitanization would surely be revealing here.[139]

Edirillē Rāla may have died a rebel, but his brother Simão Correa was tempted to defect back to the Portuguese, and after surviving the Inquisition in Goa he married a Portuguese orphan and was appointed a *disāva* of the Seven Kōraḷēs. This

[133] On Edirillē as Machiavel see Queyroz: 476, 501. The latter describes his ascendance up the scale of titles. Also *APO*: 668.

[134] The rivalry with Samarakōne may have been what caused him to defect in the first place: *Rājāvaliya*: 94; VP, II: 164; *APO*: 819.

[135] Queyroz: 514–15. His quartered remains were buried in consecrated ground.

[136] Queyroz: 507; VP, II: 256.

[137] Queyroz: 539, 553, 712–13.

[138] Thanks to Alexander Watson for raising 'primary group' theory with me in conversation.

[139] If the evidence permits. For example, it may be that lascarin commanders were liable to defect/rebel out of frustration at the limits placed on their status advancement by the Portuguese elite.

elicited a response from the *Rājāvaliya* writers that indicates how much Buddhists and Christians would come to participate in a shared politics of apostasy:

The person by the name of Simankurerala, not paying heed to the four Devālās, and not paying any respect to the world-supreme religion (*sāsana*) of *Buddha*, was engaged in killing endless numbers of animals and doing sinful acts. By the power of the Guardian gods who had taken charge of protecting Sri Lanka, Simankurerala died of an inflammatory disorder of the body.[140]

Many times we have found the same abhorrence of religious treachery, and the same need to see it divinely punished, in our Portuguese sources.[141] And both sides imagined physical violence as a way of containing or scourging the chaos represented by the other.

Those who defied Portuguese rule were not doing so in the name of a single indigenous political structure pushed underground and now orchestrating a return to power. On many occasions, Kandy would co-operate so intensively with rebels that it might sometimes seem to be the above-ground tip of such a structure. The 1630 rebellion in particular convinced many Portuguese observers that the King of Kandy was the source of all the dissension in the land.[142] But Kandy's interests and those of the lowland rebels were not reliably identical. For the lowlanders, total expulsion of the Portuguese often seems to have been the objective; for the Kandyan monarchs, the preservation of their highland dominion was their first priority.[143] Hence Vimaladharmasūriya at three points in his reign (1594, 1598, and 1603/4) made offers of peace to the Portuguese. He could not always be relied on to pour his resources into rebel efforts.[144]

However, this does not mean that co-operation was only founded on strategic alignments of interest. The generic authority of the Sinhalese royal family was vital. Even in the earliest days of his reign, Vimaladharmasūriya's kingship was recognized by low-country rebels, who were drawn to him by his ability to endow them with status titles and high office.[145] When Edirillē Rāla fled to Kandy, it was to be made a sub-king; Vimaladharmasūriya married him to a daughter of the prince of the Seven Kōraḷēs and had him consecrated as 'King of Kōṭṭe and Sītāvaka' amidst great pomp.[146] They then joined forces to take the battle to Sabaragamuva. Particularly in the conflicts over the strategically crucial Four and Seven Kōraḷēs in the later 1590s, Kandyan involvement was so intense that it can be difficult to know

[140] *Rājāvaliya*: 96.
[141] See further VP, II: 256, 324; Queyroz: 532, 535, 601, 778; C. R. de Silva 2000: 288.
[142] Bocarro: 15–16. Queyroz: 1165, sees the King of Kandy as stoking rebellion; if he was removed, the 'Chingalaz' would be 'a people without a head'.
[143] As Abeyasinghe (1966: 21–4) pointed out. Abeyasinghe later (1995: 130, 148–50) came to see the connections between Vimaladharmasūriya and the low-country rebels as more meaningful.
[144] Further, Queyroz: 545, suggests that some of his vassals claimed they were not obliged to make war outside Kandy – an important indicator of regional sensibilities.
[145] Queyroz: 532, 541, 576.
[146] Queyroz: 509–10. The reference to the involvement of a chief *saṃghatthēra* here may be an interpolation.

where war ended and rebellion began.[147] The chronicles contain many references to the campaigns of sub-rulers such as the chief of Uva (Rājasiṃha) and the chief of Denavaka (Māyādunnē) in these regions – their very names indicating that the patriotic glorification of Sītāvakan resistance had already begun to be exploited by Kandy.[148] Vimaladharmasūriya's ability to raise morale among the rebels is also evident: rebels were spurred on by his victories and quietened by his reverses.[149]

More significant, however, are the defections which undermined the Portuguese attempts to invade Kandy in 1594, 1603 and 1630.[150] In fact, by illustrating the extent to which the Portuguese were dependent on the indigenous military officers, the *disāvas, āraccis, mudaliyārs*, this point cut both ways. In this period of weakened central rule, they now occupied a pivotal position: mass refusal to collaborate with the Portuguese colonial project would have brought it to a standstill, but many were quite ready to fight on behalf of the Portuguese captains.[151] On the other hand, many of the lascarin officers were decidedly not willing to collaborate in the destruction of Kandy. The Captain-General Jerónimo de Azevedo managed to assemble a huge force comprising 800 Portuguese and 12,000 lascarins for his invasion of Kandy in 1602–3, but once they had occupied Balana all but 1,000 of the lascarins deserted under Kāngara Āracci.[152] According to a Jesuit letter written some months afterwards it was no surprise: even before setting out the native lascarins had shown great reluctance to participate in a project that would leave the Portuguese 'absolute masters of the island'; hence many of them 'went with us against their will'.[153]

Forced to retreat to Colombo, Azevedo discovered the low country in turmoil too. After defecting to Kandy and taking on the title Vikramasiṃha, Kāngara Āracci had led his troops into Alutukuru Kōraḷē and inspired revolts in the Seven and Four Kōraḷēs. A few weeks later, another former lascarin leader (and former Christian), António Barreto, led an uprising in Kuruvita. The same letter tells us that 'the people were easily moved to rise in revolt with great joy and eagerness, for it seemed to them that they were rid of the yoke and subjection of the Portuguese,

147 See Queyroz: 561. It is tempting here to refer to the letter that Queyroz: 540, claims was sent by the people of the Seven and Four Kōraḷēs to Vimaladharmasūriya, which appealed to him as 'the universal King and Victorious Lord of this Lancab' in the name of 'the Nation of which you are the Restorer, Guardian, Relief and firm protector'. While the text does contain a few details that may relate to indigenous forms, Queirós' tendency to resort to fictional devices means that this must be considered unreliable evidence.

148 Furthermore, a prince of the Seven Kōraḷēs was called Vīdiyē Baṇḍāra. The names of legendary defiers of the Portuguese were thus popular in the 1590s, see Queyroz: 515–20, 537–8, 541, 549; Couto: 411, 416.

149 Queyroz: 557; Couto: 423–5.

150 On further, lesser defections, see Queyroz: 518–19, 549; Couto: 437. Abeyasinghe 1986: 21, says that when Sinhalese troops were deployed in Jaffna, by contrast, they did not defect.

151 See Abeyasinghe, 1966: 78–83, on the rise in power of these elites.

152 Queyroz: 566; Abeyasinghe 1966: 43. Flores 2001b: 28 has it that 20,000 lascarins deserted, while a royal letter of 1605 in Pato 1880–1935, I: 8, says 'all the black people' deserted. Of course, there were many reasons for lascarin defections beyond patriotic or cultural factors, including an opportunistic attempt to pre-judge success.

153 VP, II: 229.

which in truth is very great. . . .' To some contemporaries, and to later chroniclers, it seemed, once again, as if the 'whole island' had turned against them.[154] Churches were targeted, native Christians killed. As for the 1630 defection, that takes us beyond the scope of this book and into the period when Rājasiṃha II (1635–87) began to make his presence felt, but it is worth noting that here too a captain-general was forced to retreat to Colombo after his lascarins had deserted *en masse* in the highlands. Moreover, this was part of a conspiracy in which a group of Christian nobles in Colombo planned to mount a simultaneous coup there. They had marked out their allegiance to the ringleader through apostasy.[155]

The 1616–19 rebellions illustrate particularly neatly all our chief points.[156] When in December 1616 a man of Kōṭṭe assuming the name of Nikapiṭiye Baṇḍāra led a revolt against the Portuguese in the Seven Kōraḷēs, upcountry militiamen were quickly pushed into action under two former rebel leaders, Kāngara Āracci and Kuruvita Rāla (António Barreto, who was by this time Prince of Ūva). Nikapiṭiye found military success and drew many to his cause, but his ambition soon reached such a pitch that he deprecated Senarat by demanding a princess of Kandy as a wife.[157] Senarat felt so threatened by this over-mighty behaviour that he strove to make peace with the Portuguese, which was eventually concluded in 1617.[158] But the truce, which lasted less than three years, cost him dear: Kuruvita Rāla now rebelled against him because of it.[159] There was, thus, a brief mutual concern between Kandy and the Portuguese to undermine this disturbing upstart, which was strongly articulated in the poem *Kustantīnu Haṭana*.

This is the clearest example we have then of the way in which the interests of Kandy and lowlanders could diverge. For Senarat, the power of the Kandyan throne was the first priority; for lowlanders such as Nikapiṭiye and Kuruvita, expulsion of the Portuguese was the aim. Anti-Portuguese politics were independent from loyalty to the Kandyan monarchy or to any one political centre. Yet, if the argument for some sort of unified 'nationalist' sentiment is thereby compromised, the argument for indigenism is only strengthened. These revolts drew to them 'many principal men of Candia' according to a contemporary, and many lascarins were moved to defect – in other words to abandon their ties to both the Portuguese and the Kandyan monarchs – to the extent that, once again, it seemed as if 'practically the whole island was in revolt'.[160]

Whatever the specific infidelities, the generic ideal of monarchy remained of vital importance. Even the Portuguese policy of removing Sinhalese heirs could not staunch the appetite for royal blood: Kuruvita Rāla felt obliged to conspire

[154] VP, II: 229, 235–6; Queyroz: 580, 591.

[155] Queyroz: 753–5. These were all high-placed Christians by birth, and the ringleader had pretended to be a grandson of Rājasiṃha. C. R. de Silva 1972: 107, suggests as many as half may have stayed loyal. Quéré 1995, 45–6; Wickremesekera 2004: 134.

[156] For a detailed account of these rebellions see C. R. de Silva 1972.

[157] VP, II: 418. [158] Biker, I: 203–17.

[159] Trindade, III: 78; Queyroz: 710. On Kuruvita Rāla/Barreto's iconoclasm in Kandy, see Biker, I: 224.

[160] VP, II: 415–17.

with a scion of the Sītāvakan line residing in India, another Māyādunnē, bringing him over to act as a royal figurehead with which to challenge Senarat; Nikapiṭiye Baṇḍāra concocted an identity as Rājasiṃha's grandson of that name, whom we saw fleeing the island in 1594 and who had actually died in Coimbra in 1608. Drawing on persisting memories of heroic Sītāvakan opposition to the Portuguese in this way, he proclaimed himself king in Daṁbadeniya, and then emperor in Nakalagama.

These were desperate measures, and it is striking how effective they were given that they had to paper over deeply unimpressive realities. Kuruvita Rāla had been born into the Karāva caste, without a trace of noble blood, while Nikapiṭiye Baṇḍāra had begun life in the family of a minor village headman and passed into the service of Franciscan friars and the court of the Portuguese generals.[161] This emphasizes that we are dealing with anti-Portuguese rebels *per se*, rather than simply a continuation of traditional fissiparous politics on the part of royal successors and the higher nobility, or a continuation of the opportunistic ambitions of military leaders exploiting their new pivotal status since the 1590s. Whatever the personal motivations or loyalties of these men, they were taking advantage of a demand for leadership from below. If such leadership could not be found in the existing royal family, well, then royalty would have to be fabricated to that end.[162] And the details of that fabrication, in Nikapiṭiye Baṇḍāra's case, are exceptionally intriguing. He chose to defect from the Portuguese during an expedition to Jaffna. He made his way to Anurādhapura, and there grew his hair long and wore animal skins in the manner of a yogi [*jogue*], and announced himself to be Rājasiṃha's grandson returned from Portugal.[163]

This was conspicuous indigenization on a grand scale. The choice of Anurādhapura, far from the current centres of political activity, reveals how the long history of the Sinhalese kings as told in the Pāli and Sinhala chronicle traditions was still alive in popular consciousness of the landscape.[164] Such an extravagant gesture would have to have been widely understood: 'Nikapiṭiye Baṇḍāra' was announcing his ancestry atop the touchstone of Sinhalese royal tradition – with an all-island relevance, one might add, rather than for any one dynastic centre. Indeed, such reservoirs of symbolic power would become a concern of colonial policy. Queirós advised that a new *disāva* should be erected in the region, partly in order to 'prevent the pilgrimages to Anu-Raja-Pure [Anurādhapura], whither Pagans and Christians resort on the pretence of visiting those antiquities, and under such a plea a Rebellion was plotted there'.[165] Heritage tourism in the seventeenth century . . . But note, too, that the rebel arrived as a 'yogi'. While this reference

161 Bocarro, *Decada*: 497. *Kustantīnu Haṭana*: Nevill: Or. 6606(156).

162 VP, II: 412: 'For some time now a revolution was feared in the island, as the Chingalas were becoming restless; but for want of a leader, it did not take place till now.'

163 Bocarro, *Decada*: 497.

164 The Portuguese first reported on the ruins of Anurādhapura a decade or so after this rebellion, see Bocarro: 15, where feats of ancient kings were still remembered; Miranda: 55, 171. Anurādhapura appears as a as major centre of cult in Knox: 30. For the eighteenth and nineteenth centuries, see Sivasundaram 2007.

165 Queyroz: 1155.

may derive from a Portuguese misperception of an ascetic *bhikkhu*, it can serve here as a reminder not to assume that heritage as purely or simply Buddhist.[166]

This complex intertwining of traditions – so often blandly deposited under the rubric of tolerance – did not hinder the passions of religious antagonism. Consider what happened in the Christian centre of Mātiyagama in the first months of the rebellion of 1616. A group of lascarins sent by Kuruvita Rāla arrived there, apparently ignoring many other towns of greater strategic importance, and focused their fury on desecrating and destroying churches and killing its two Jesuits. It was reported that

> they killed the Fathers in revenge for the death of three Buddhist priests, executed by the Portuguese in the previous month. These *changatares* of Candia came to Alicur Corla and the adjoining villages, exciting the people against the fathers, deploring the numerous conversions to Christianity, and calling upon the people to return to the worship of the idols and give them alms for the decoration of the shrine of Candia. The poor and uncultured people were so moved by their clamours, that they truly gave up what they had: the farmer gave his scythe . . . When the general Nuno Alvarez Pereira was informed of this and of the tumult secretly caused by the priests . . . [he imprisoned them, one was thrown to the alligators, the other two were subjected to religious instruction]. In the opinion of many, this attempt to convert their priests gave great offence to the people and made them conceive great hostility to the Fathers and gave occasion to this murder.[167]

Here we see in action the Buddhist *saṃgha* only recently revivified under Vimaladharmasūriya, an institution that yet had an ancient sense of guardianship over the whole of the island and the Sinhalese people. We catch a glimpse of how it might work as a force for the cultural and emotional unification of low country and upcountry, of literate and illiterate, rich and poor.

It is not surprising then that the Sinhalese should have developed the reputation of being the most 'false and deceitful that there are in the whole of India', as Agostinho de Azevedo claimed in the 1580s.[168] The defection of 1630 set the seal on this reputation, and as the wars with Kandy claimed the lives of two Portuguese captain-generals in short succession (1630 and 1638), the inveterate treachery of the Sinhalese formed a major theme of a rush of treatises expounding and explaining the problem of Ceylon.[169] One aspect of this was personal: many

166 Perhaps then the ancestral Buddhist-Hindu religious practices, in all their multi-stranded glory, were being evoked here. But Portuguese sources sometimes fail and sometimes succeed in distinguishing between yogis and monks.

167 VP, II: 434. Care is required here, because the rhetorical burden of this letter is clearly to prove that the Jesuits had died a martyr's death at the hands of men killing them for their religion. Indeed this bias of perspective fed into the chronicle sources' accounts of religious violence: see Queyroz: 609 on his source Negrão. Yet, the simple facts of iconoclastic violence are persuasive. Mātiyagama may have been targeted because it was a great Christian centre developed by that double traitor, Simão Correa. See these details confirmed in VP, II: 408, 419–20, 425, 428, 473.

168 Azevedo: 238, repeated by Couto: 66; Queyroz: 185, 291, 321, 590, 603, 623, 706, 766, 826.

169 The post-1630 treatises include Bocarro: 17; Miranda: 52–4, 164; The *Expedition to Uva*, in Perera 1930: 31, 45; Saa y Menezes 1681, which was probably written before 1640; the comments of some lascarins themselves in 1636, in Queyroz: 1012. See also Cruz and Flores 2007, for further texts and an illuminating discussion of their context.

of the defectors were men whom Constantino de Sá de Noronha (Captain-General of Ceylon 1616–20, 1623–30) had drawn close to him as favourites.[170] Indeed, we need to be a little careful not to allow the weight of post-1630 evidence to dominate our view of the whole epoch.[171]

Given the events relayed above, it can hardly be doubted that the image of the rebellious Sinhalese owes more to the Sinhalese themselves than to European fantasies and preconceptions, but the latter undoubtedly helped fashion the emergent stereotype. The sources on Sri Lanka suggest that by the seventeenth century there was a common apprehension among Portuguese that, according to one writer, 'the desire for a native king and a government of their own people [*nação*] is a natural inclination among all those [peoples] of this world.'[172] In particular, it is likely that some Portuguese read on to Sinhalese behaviour their own sensibilities chafing under the Castilian Crown. Ribeiro, for example, listed the reasons why no quarter could be expected from Kandy – 'we are Christians, The King [Rājasiṃha II] and his people are Gentiles; we are white, they are black; we, are Portuguese, they Chingalas' – and then reminded his readers of how much they had hated the Castilians during the Union of the Crowns when 'we longed to drink the blood of everyone who belonged to that nation' – even though the Castilians were white and Christian![173]

From this passage nascent European ideas of race also emerge. We have not concentrated on those here, because while one may detect signs of racial pride and prejudice, there is very little racial theory evident in the earlier Portuguese sources directly relating to Sri Lanka. Ines Županov has recently elucidated the way in which the humoral principles of the prevalent Hippocratic-Galenic medical theory were already facilitating conceptual connections between the climate of India and the nature of mankind under such exaggerated conditions.[174] In the excessive decay and fertility of the tropics, the mind itself might become unstable, blooming and corrupting in quick succession.[175] Extrapolating from Županov's work, perhaps tendrils of this proto-climatic perspective reached our seventeenth-century writers and tightened their preoccupation with the changeability of the Lankan personality? Perhaps.[176] But in general the dominant geographical trope for Sri Lanka was its

[170] The *Jornada* of 1633, cited in Cruz and Flores 2007.

[171] These sweeping analyses had a strong influence on the perspectives of Queirós and Ribeiro, who were particularly informed by the feeling that not even Colombo Christian Sinhalese could be relied on. But the reputation had older roots. Bocarro's view is as much a product of the 1616–17 rebellions, which he analysed in detail in his Thirteenth Decade, and the views of his subject, Jerónimo de Azevedo, who in 1614 used a similar phraseology to describe the wavering Sinhalese: Abeyasinghe 1974: 43.

[172] In 1635, Bocarro, 1992: 220 (*O Livro das Plantas* . . . , translation different to Bocarro: 17). Winius' suggestion (1971: 29), that the Portuguese could not understand the 'anticolonial feeling of nationalism' that would explain Sinhala rebellions is therefore misleading.

[173] Ribeiro: 264, echoed by his contemporary, Queyroz: 577, 620, 1064–5.

[174] Županov 2005: 8–10.

[175] This was particularly useful for explaining the decadence of Portuguese society in India, and its renegades and apostates.

[176] This requires further investigation.

salubriousness, its image as an earthly paradise for all men.[177] In more general terms, there may be some profit in locating the theme of treachery within a Saidian account of the Occidental view of the Oriental as fickle and unmanly.[178] Certainly the familiarity of the 'natives are treacherous and they all hate us' trope suggests that it issues from a general psychology of colonialism. It also allowed moralizing Portuguese chroniclers to appeal to the loss of local support as a consequence of what they considered wrong or un-Christian about the imperial project.

But we must move beyond mere representational logics in order to properly understand the Sinhalese reputation for infidelity among later Portuguese observers. It must also reflect the disjuncture between European and Sinhalese ways of conceiving certain political and religious relationships. For the Sinhalese, the geographic boundaries of political authority were always more mutable, and the liege–vassal relationship always more contingent, as royal centres rose and fell by competing for manpower. The Portuguese were disturbed by the tumultuousness of these 'galactic polities', whose succession disputes and insubordinations made even European dynastic affairs seem sedate, and which meant that the Sinhalese could not even be trusted to hold to their own kings. According to Bocarro in 1635, their fickleness was such that they would kill their own fathers if they would profit by it: the 1521 assassination of Vijayabāhu VI and the rumoured parricide of Māyādunnē were still present in the memory.[179] The Portuguese had first been drawn into the island by the ceaseless fratricidal campaigns of Māyādunnē, who must have appeared to them a treasonous blackguard of the highest order. When Dharmapāla was finally raised to the throne as a malleable figurehead, his own father, Vīdiyē Baṇḍāra, shockingly, turned against the throne.

One problem, then, with isolating dynastic loyalty as the one force capable of organizing Sinhalese political sentiments in the pre-modern era, is that to many Europeans it was the *limits* to such loyalties that they found remarkable: that kingship should be so reified and yet so contingent, which we discussed in Chapter Eight. We may be able to see the logic behind the paradox: that highly developed rhetoric of sacred and hereditary exclusivity was precisely an attempt to contend with a political system which continually threatened to subvert the distinctiveness of sovereignty. It is also clear that the shift to direct dominion by the Portuguese from the mid-1590s only enhanced the need for fabricated leadership. But the ability of rebel leaders or regional chiefs to suddenly assume royal credentials was a source of frustration and wonder to the Portuguese.

We are reminded again that 'defection' and 'rebellion' were constants of Sinhalese history, rather than novel responses to the novelty of Portuguese rule. The political garden of Sri Lanka was inherently fecund: within minutes of the lawn being mown clear by a centralizing power, new weed-heads of political opposition

[177] VP: 334, 338. For Queyroz: 19, 21, the wonderful climate of Lanka explains the laziness of its inhabitants – but it is also conducive to the health of Portuguese (79, 1144).

[178] Queyroz: 284, considered their infidelity as a product of their gentleness, but without appealing to any explicit theoretical constructs.

[179] Bocarro: 16; Linschoten, I: 78. See also Pyrard de Laval, in Laval 1887–8, II, part one: 147.

would rear up in diverse regions. But there can be little doubt that the legitimacy of the centre was weakened in new ways by Portuguese direct rule: the effect was akin to pouring fertilizer on the ground so that new opponents sprang up with bewildering ease, until from a position of apparent mastery, suddenly the whole landscape could be choked up with threatening political overgrowth. Indeed, the scale of these movements – often appearing all but unanimous to the Portuguese – was indeed new. And they were magnetized in a subtly new way. After referring to the ease with which the Sinhalese vassals 'cross from us to the enemy, and return from the enemy to us', Bocarro goes on to say,

> But with [a] big difference, because when on our side they never refrain from being ready for any treachery against us, however obligated they may be [to us] for benefits received from the Portuguese. And also, so strong and firm are they in their hatred of us and [their] subjection, that even those who have showed themselves always faithful and have proved it with their own lives [in our service], confess that even unto the grave, they will not be able to give up that hatred . . .[180]

Moreover, whereas the Portuguese may be able to draw on the services of significant units of lascarins, 'during the rebellions everyone takes arms and fights against us.'[181] We can concur with Bocarro that behind this generic predisposition for 'infidelity' one can often discern a more selective one: a flickering antipathy to foreign dominion. Incidentally, to find a rebellion of comparable scope previous to the Portuguese period, one must go back to the *Siṃhalasaṃge* (Sinhala war) that broke out with the seizure of power by Bhuvanekabāhu VI (1469–77).[182] This was the key moment for the break-up of de facto Kōṭṭe overlordship and therefore the creation of the political scene in which our sixteenth-century actors played out their lives: Kandy and Jaffna won some sort of independence during his reign and much of the lowland territory revolted. It is plausible, if hardly certain, that here too the rebels had sought to gain support by appealing to indigenist sympathies.[183]

The stereotype of the 'unfaithful' Sinhalese also derived from bewilderment in the face of the different approach to religious identity among Sinhalese Buddhists. In the monotheistic worldview, to switch religious labels is to move between well-defined communities. It is also to break off or initiate a relationship with a human-like supernatural agent, analogous to a political 'lord', who demands obedience. Converting back and forth, which is what many Sinhalese did, was therefore seen as a form of repeated treachery. Whereas, for the Sinhalese, the

[180] Bocarro 1992: 219 (translation different to Bocarro: 16). This finds more than an echo in Queyroz: 23: 'in obeying their native Kings they have always been various and inconstant, but most stubborn in not admitting foreign domination, and . . . they did not hesitate to submit to any bold rebel, in order to recover their liberty.'

[181] Bocarro: 17.

[182] Dädigama inscription. See *EZ*, III: 280; IV: 8–9, 263. The *Alakeśvarayuddhaya*: 24/*Rājāvaliya*: 66, refers to the *Siṃhalaperaḷi* (Sinhala insurrection).

[183] Against a prince who was associated with foreign elites, notwithstanding the arguments of Gunawardana 1990: 67, and Somaratna 1975: 139–42, as I suggest in Strathern (forthcoming a).

practice of religious rites was not necessarily associated with one's soteriological status, and need not (although it might) denote any fundamental transition from one community to another.[184]

The Portuguese apprehension of Sinhalese religious behaviour reveals an intriguingly similar logic to their apprehension of Sinhalese political behaviour.[185] Here again both a generic infidelity and a specific bias to that infidelity were suspected. Where the former prevailed, it was claimed that the Sinhalese would easily become Christians and just as easily apostatize. This could generate optimism, as in the Bishop of Cochin's remark in 1598 that the whole island would soon become Christian, 'since the idea among them is that every man can reach salvation in his religion'.[186] But increasingly, this infidelity was identified as a force that was specifically harmful to the prospects of Christianity. The most painful examples, of course, were the various princes who had apparently received baptism only to reveal how meaningless they considered that rite to be. But this was routinely observed of the common people too, and it was borne out not just by their approach to Christianity but in the way they juggled Buddhism and Hinduism, which Queirós attributed to a deep-seated uncertainty and the idea that one can 'go to Heaven by many ways', an idea that was ultimately anti-Christian.[187] They were up against a form of religious identity that often seemed insubstantial and yielding, melting away like snow in the tropics, the waters of Buddhist, Hindu and Christian traditions running into each other. Yet in other conditions it seemed to be made of immovable ice: 'true' (exclusivist) conversions seemed so difficult to obtain, that of princes usually impossible, their pride in their traditions rarely humbled.

Such behaviour presented a serious psychological and spiritual threat. By this time, the Inquisition was firmly established in Goa and urgently applying itself to the unmasking of those who practised their ancestral Islamic or Jewish faith under the cover of Christianity.[188] Moreover, the cultural politics of apostasy – by which those who were most Lusitanized were those who most had to prove their indigenist loyalties – were particularly abhorrent to the Portuguese, who saw, time and again, those raised in the bosom of Colombo Catholic society suddenly transformed into exaggerated heathens. The rebel Nikapiṭiye Baṇḍāra, for example, had been honoured with a succession of highly intimate duties of service to the Portuguese, including palanquin-bearer to the Portuguese Captain-General.[189] It is understandable (if distasteful) that they thereby came to suspect the power of culture itself, seeing its work shockingly undone by loyalties and instincts that

[184] See above, pp. 135–6. [185] This is explicitly expressed in a letter from 1611: VP, II: 325.
[186] VP, II: 163. [187] Queyroz: 699–700; Ribeiro: 52.
[188] Bocarro was one such 'New Christian' who had secretly returned to Judaism before again becoming Christian and receiving absolution from the Inquisition in 1624 – which casts his comments on the religious fickleness of the Sinhalese in a different light . . . See C. R. de Silva 1996: xiv.
[189] Bocarro, *Decada*: 497. Such duties, however high-status, may have emphasized the general subservience of the Sinhalese. We can glimpse this through the event which triggered his revolt: punishment at the hands of friars for marital sins and, as Bocarro revealingly puts it, 'for being an impudent black'.

seemed bred in the bone. Of the defection of 1630, Ribeiro says that 'they had been brought up among us, yet they conspired with the King of Candia in such a manner that they were the cause of our total ruin, as we shall see, for in the end the blacks are all our enemies.'[190] The irony is that Christianization had often been urged as a policy of pacification, to form a natural bond between the rulers and ruled; but it also served to cleave them in two.[191]

[190] Ribeiro: 90. [191] See *APO*: 819.

CONCLUSION: SOME FINAL THOUGHTS ON INDIGENISM, IDENTITY AND KINGSHIP IN THE SIXTEENTH AND SEVENTEENTH CENTURIES

The traditionalist understandings of these issues have, in various forms, been part of Sri Lankan historiography throughout the twentieth century. One could say that they have formed part of the set of comfortably worn mental furniture upon which narratives of the 'Portuguese era' have tended to recline. It is important to recognize how much of this furniture has been inherited from the Portuguese sources themselves rather than the preoccupations of Victorian and Edwardian Orientalists of British education, or from the twentieth-century politics of Sinhalese nationalism.[1] By the time Queirós was writing, it was commonly implicit or explicit in Portuguese commentaries that there were bonds between low-country and upcountry Sinhalese rooted variously in blood, manners, religion and political aspiration, and that there were popular sentiments militating against the acceptance of foreign rule or religion. Although it would be peculiar to overlook the contemporary resonances with British rule in P. E. Pieris' writings, it does feel sometimes as if all he has done is to translate Queirós' interpretations into the language of his day: terms and phrases such as 'nation', 'intense pride of race', 'the ancient religion of his fathers', which inevitably imbued his account with subtly different meanings.[2] Abeyasinghe's work of the 1960s–1980s is more critical and careful, but assumes that a certain Sinhalese solidarity played its part.[3] Since then, C. R. de Silva has unobtrusively referred to the way in which that solidarity may have been enhanced by interaction with the Portuguese.[4]

[1] Not that the unwieldy genre of the Portuguese chronicle lent itself to the tight promulgation of consistent agendas; not even each text speaks with a single voice. Queirós acknowledges a range of motivations for lascarin defection, for example, including maltreatment by the Portuguese, blatant greed and individual ambition, a desire on the part of professional soldiers to stimulate demand for their services, see Queyroz: 579.

[2] Pieris 1983–92 I: 272, 277, 281, 315, 378.

[3] Abeyasinghe 1966: 47–51, and more strongly towards the end of his life in Abeyasinghe 1995: 150. Jorge Manuel Flores, in Flores 2001b: 27, arrives at a similar analysis of the lascarin defections, referring to the 'very strong linguistic, cultural, religious connections' between lowcountry and upcountry. Winius 1971: 29 is blunt. An exception is Biedermann 2005a, which shows how one can read sixteenth-century history without invoking religious, cultural or patriotic antipathies.

[4] This 'helped to sharpen indigenous self-perception and boundary consciousness' among the Sinhalese, see C. R. de Silva 2000: 280; 1983: 16; 1984: 4. One could say then that to previous historians, the weight of Portuguese evidence on such matters has been simply too great to ignore or to attribute entirely to the burden of Eurocentric precognitions.

However, it has only been in the last twenty years that the exciting and challenging theoretical work on identity has arisen. And this has focused on other eras and often issued from other disciplines altogether. This book has tried to train the spotlight of this new 'historicist' perspective onto the mental furniture of Portuguese-era historiography, which now ought to feel newly conspicuous and uncomfortable. It has found that much of this furniture remains, in a certain sense, indispensable, but in need of rearrangement and upholstering; it is present to us now in altered guises, some of them uncertain. The principal issue here concerns the nature and limits of the 'indigenism' that we saw beginning to make an impact in our period. How can we give this force its due without slipping into over-coherent readings of identity?

Ethnicity

This was an indigenism that was probably based upon a sense of Sinhalaness, but could also have derived from a more general sense of Lankanness.

To proceed from the political logic of the conflict with the Portuguese: *a priori* one can see how this might enhance the salience of Lankanness, emphasizing the legitimacy of all the communities who had traditionally resided on the island and been assimilated into its polities, or equally how it might enhance the salience of Sinhalaness as contrasted with all 'foreigners', thereby reinvoking sentiments previously generated by conflicts with South Indian forces. Perhaps sensations of community shifted fluidly between these two states, in an analogous manner to the way that feelings of Englishness and Britishness slosh incoherently but powerfully around the United Kingdom to this day.

The nature of pre-modern Sinhalese ethnicity remains a matter of great debate, which cannot be resolved here. It could, however, be advanced by greater attention to what the Portuguese sources have to contribute. In the Introduction we defended broad conceptions of ethnicity. One such is 'a group of people whose members share a common name and elements of culture, possess a myth of common origin and common historical memory, who associate themselves with a particular territory and possess a feeling of solidarity'.[5] It should not need spelling out that the sixteenth-century Sinhalese possessed many of these features, and the Portuguese picked up on them too. For example, the striking 'common historical memory' of the Sinhalese as embodied in textual traditions was a cause of concern for soldiers such as Sá de Miranda and chroniclers such as Queirós, who saw it as one reason why the spirit of rebellion never seemed to die out. Commenting on the sacking of Sītāvaka, Queirós wrote that this gave 'ample material for the writings which the Chingalaz preserved, reading them to their children to bring them up in hatred of the Portuguese'.[6]

[5] Barnard and Spencer 1996: 192. This is very similar to the list in A. D. Smith 1991: 21, 36, which also emphasizes the role of myths of ethnic election.

[6] Queyroz: 304, and see also 117, on verse composition.

That sentence evokes too the 'common name' of the ethnic group: 'chingalas' (spelt variously) is there in the correspondence from 1545 onwards.[7] Bhuvanekabāhu's ambassador and Brahman *purōhita* used the term in 1551, and he was the chief pivot on which intercultural communication turned, a go-between capable of both shaping Portuguese understandings of local conditions and introducing Portuguese concepts into the Kōṭṭe court.[8] The earliest Portuguese ethnological tract on Sri Lanka, in Barros' third Decade written in the 1550s, clearly established 'Chingálla' as a language and a people.[9]

Portuguese imperialism did not, as the British would do, seek to establish racial categories as the basis for governmental systems. From 1582 to 1619, the Jaffna region came under the purview of officials in Mannar, while the rest of the island was under the jurisdiction of Colombo. Contrary to some Sinhala visions (both early modern and – in a different form – modern) views of the natural coherence of the island, the Portuguese in this sense treated the far north as part of a different world. In the first instance, this probably reflected perceived strategic and commercial factors more than cultural distinctions *per se*, but the latter were clearly recognized, and the descriptive surveys and administrative reports by Portuguese officials and churchmen are careful to distinguish between Sinhalese and Tamils – sometimes with heavy emphasis.[10] In the seventeenth century, Dutchmen such as Spilbergen and Englishmen such as Knox used the term 'chingala' in the same way as the Portuguese, that is to refer to both the Sinhala language and the speakers of it. This is a term that encompasses both low-country and upcountry peoples but not the unintegrated immigrant groups nor the Tamils of Jaffna.[11] 'Chingala' was not defined by residency or political allegiance.[12] Classified in this quasi-racial manner, the Sinhalese were represented as having particular characteristics (proud, treacherous etc); a particular religious system, literary tradition, script, set of customs, and indeed ancestry. Queirós makes his rebel leaders inspire their men by holding before them their pride in the 'Chingala name and nation [*nação*, people]'.[13]

What do the Portuguese sources say on the question of ethnic origin myth? They are in fact horribly confused and confusing, often acknowledging bewilderment

[7] VP: 87, 290/SV: 581; VP, II: 43, 303, 341.

[8] As a Lisbon-returnee, he was able to compose this letter himself. VP: 277/SV: 564 ('chimguallas').

[9] Barros: 33.

[10] Miranda: 118–19, claimed the people of Jaffna were 'extremely weak/passive (*fraca)*', implicitly contrasting with the warlike Sinhalese, and 'neither in language nor religion are they similar to the Sinhalese'. This is the source for Queyroz: 50; also see 104, 110, 113, 152–3, 158, 184. See too Abeyasinghe 1986: 7, 17. See Flores 2001b: 36–49, for a discussion of 'ethnology' in the service of Portuguese government. On the British: Rogers 1995: 2004a.

[11] Knox: 187: 'but I am to speak only of the natural proper people of the island, which they call Chingulays', and which he distinguishes from the Malabars, who are assimilated into the state but are not the 'natural subjects' of the king.

[12] Spilbergen: 36: 'the *Candyan* Kingdom is very powerful and rich in inhabitants, mostly *Singales*'; further: 21, 42.

[13] Queyroz: 561, 763–4.

in the face of the diverse material to hand.[14] It is clear that certain caste groups had specific origin stories of their arrival to the island.[15] But the principal point to emerge is that the Vijaya myth, with its concatenation of various illustrious ancestors such as Mahāsammata, is presented as being an origin story for *both* Sinhalese royalty *and* the Sinhalese people. It was first redacted by Azevedo, who had heard the Kandyan prince Yamasiṃha chanting what appears to be a version of the *Rājāvaliya*. Vijaya is represented here and in subsequent texts as populating the island.[16] For Queirós, then, the obstreperous insistence on their rarefied and august lineage is a quality of the Sinhalese in general, as well as their kings.[17] This connection was reinforced by the awareness, first present in Sá de Miranda and Trindade (1630s), that the 'common name' for the people was derived from Vijaya's leonine parentage: Sinhala meaning 'blood of the lion'.[18] Interestingly, aspects of the Rāmāyana also found their way into the sources although they are somewhat ambiguous as to whether Rāvaṇa was a progenitor or not.[19]

The question remains, of course, to what extent the Portuguese were imposing their own conceptual grids on this dizzying surfeit of material: were they listening out for ethnic origins while their informants were relaying kingship ancestries and literary confections? Possibly, but we cannot dismiss out-of-hand the ethnological capabilities of our sources.[20] This debate must be put in perspective: the most analytically significant question is whether Sinhalaness (or perhaps indigenousness) existed as a mobilizing collective sentiment, a cultural template for organizing political action, not whether it conformed to definitions of ethnicity based on an assumption of common ancestry. Equally, however, concepts travelled both ways: what if local 'templates' and Portuguese 'grids' intermeshed? What if the 'Eurocentric' influenced the 'Sinhala-centric'?

Much scholarly energy has been expended on the epistemological ramifications of British imperialism in South Asia, but very little on the infiltration of Portuguese understandings. Yet we have seen that, particularly from the 1590s onwards, the greatest mobilizers of group sentiment against the Portuguese were those who had been most strongly exposed to Portuguese culture. Sometimes their origins lay so deep within Catholic Kōṭṭe that their transformation into rebel leaders must have involved almost an imitation of what they imagined might be traditional Sinhalese mores. Nikapiṭiye Baṇḍāra learnt how to simulate Sinhalese royalty

[14] For, e.g., the story of Chinese origins, apparently a product of mistranslation and etymological fancy, see Barros: 33; Couto: 66; Trindade, III: 5.

[15] Queyroz: 1018.

[16] Azevedo: 242; Couto: 101 (the latter comments: 'all their ancient events have been put into verse where they are chanted at their festivals'); Miranda: 162–3. See Queyroz: 6–7, contrasting with 48, on the later Indian origin of the Tamils of Jaffna.

[17] Queyroz: 6–7: these origin myths '. . . led both Kings and lieges to think they are the best blood of the East'.

[18] Trindade: 5–7; Miranda: 163; Queyroz: 7; compare with the *Mahāvaṃsa*: 531–3; *Rājāvaliya*: 14.

[19] Miranda: 162–3, Queyroz: 8. Indeed, to this day it is contested as to whether Rāvaṇa was a progenitor of the Sinhalese or merely of the non-human inhabitants whom Vijaya extirpated.

[20] Miranda: 104, for example, says that in writing his text he drew on his own experience as well as that of some persons who had become erudite in Sinhala letters while imprisoned in Kandy.

while attending a noblewoman at Malvāna.[21] Edirillē Rāla had been an interpreter to Dharmapāla, a post he had inherited from his father. Someone more versed in the conceptual subtleties of Portuguese political language and the ways these might map on to indigenous understandings one could not hope to find.[22] When Trindade, then, reports that Edirillē Rāla 'titled himself the liberator of the Chingala people' ('*se intitulou libertador da nação chingala*'), we cannot imagine any inherent dislocation between the author's language and that of his subject.[23]

In other words, it is plausible that Edirillē Rāla and certain other leaders considered the Sinhalese as a *nação* [people], in the same way that the Portuguese were a *nação*.[24] Equally, when our sources refer to the Sinhalese fighting for their 'liberty' they may have been reflecting a discourse of imperial dominion and resistance which Portuguese and Lusitanized Sinhalese shared.[25] In 1643, Prince Vijayapāla wrote to the viceroy: 'Though I am a Chingala by blood, I am a Portuguese in my ways and affections; it may well be that this is the chief reason for my losing my Kingdom. . . .'[26] Whether or not the concept of 'being Chingala by blood' had long been native, it was native now to such a prince who had been educated by the Franciscan Negrão. Vijayapāla's case reminds us that it was not only rebels who were Lusitanized, but also Kandyan royalty, from its re-founder, Vimaladharmasūriya, to his successors Senarat and Rājasiṃha II.[27]

We are presented here with an irony more than a paradox: transferences of political culture assisted the politicization of cultural difference. With the arrival of the *Sītāvaka Haṭana* (1585), and particularly the *haṭanas* of the mid seventeenth century, recently analysed by Michael Roberts, we are finally in a position to see how all this tallies with Sinhalese sources.[28] And it is striking how the flowering of this Sinhala genre in the 1630s coincides with the production of treatises on the 'Ceylon problem' by the Portuguese. The scorn and contempt that we find in the latter is redoubled in former. The coruscation of the Portuguese for their dietary habits is already present in the *Sītāvaka Haṭana*, and in the *Rājasiṃha Haṭana* (*c.* 1638) and the *Mahā Haṭana* (*c.* 1658), the politicization of cultural difference becomes unavoidable. The Portuguese are animals, demons, beef-eaters and alcohol-swiggers.[29] Bocarro narrates an episode during the 1616–17 rebellion, when a 'black' crept into the Portuguese camp and called out to the lascarins, asking them which side they were on, and

[21] Bocarro, *Decada*: 497. There are possible echoes of the Portuguese messianism surrounding King Sebastião in his 'return' to the island as Rājasiṃha's grandson.

[22] Queyroz: 474, 501.

[23] Trindade, III: 104, may have been drawing here on the lost chronicle/ethnology of Fr. Negrão, who was in the country from 1610 (VP, II: 290), and the tutor of Prince Vijayapāla.

[24] The term could take on a range of different connotations. Roberts 2004: 105–7, discusses different foreign and Sinhala terminology. He suggests that *jātiya* could have been used as a translation of *nação*.

[25] VP, II: 346 (from 1612); Bocarro, *Decada*: 497–8; Queyroz: 626.

[26] Pieris 2004: 31.

[27] On Rājasiṃha II, see Knox: 137. All spoke Portuguese.

[28] Roberts 2004.

[29] Young and Senanayaka 1998: 31–2 (and see 11–12), show how such dietary issues form a recurrent motif of Sinhalese objections to the disruptive influence of the Portuguese and Christianity in the sixteenth to eighteenth centuries.

called them vile names [*ruins nomes*], saying that while they might have no shame to go about with the Portuguese thieves, well, they should have, and that they should remember that they were Sinhalese [*chingallas*], and that only two leagues away was their king, their god, and Eye of the Sun, who had defeated the army of Manicavaré and that there were no Portuguese thieves on that island anymore, and that they should go to him [the king].[30]

We find ourselves here in the same world as that of the *haṭanas*, where we can look up those 'vile names' for collaborators, and find the same insistence on the illegitimacy of the Portuguese presence and the reverence accorded to the divine sun-like king.[31] The Sinhalese texts do not often explicitly champion the 'Sinhala' name. The term is certainly found, typically to refer to armies, but often it is the island of Lanka and the king's overlordship over it that is exalted.[32] Whether this is because it was taken for granted that the 'we' were Sinhalese, or because a propagandist emphasis on a broader king-centred indigenism was more useful, is difficult to ascertain. What does emerge, however, is that of a deep connection between the 'us' and the land of Lanka.

We find this reification of the soil echoed in a remark by a European visitor to the island in 1608 who reported that the islanders 'do not put the Portuguese [prisoners] to death, but merely cut off their noses and send them back; *for they say that they will not have their soil polluted with the bodies and blood of foreigners . . .*'[33] It is congruent too with the war poems' symbolic evocation of the Portuguese threat as biological and socio-cultural as well as political: they are not merely military enemies but pollutants and chaos-mongers. Those who fought for the Portuguese, consorted with them or were of mixed race were also reprehended. In the *Rājasiṃha Haṭana*, the battles with the Portuguese are compared with the ancient wars against Tamil (*demaḷa*) powers.[34]

Culture

This was an indigenism that co-existed with strong cosmopolitan tendencies. It was therefore associated with a xenophobia that was selective, inconsistent and spasmodic rather than generic.

Before we allow this evidence to colonize our understandings of centuries of cultural interaction, let us reiterate that the Sinhalese states, in common with many others in early modern Asia, were generally predisposed to both attract foreigners and find foreign fashions attractive.[35] The literati could be multi-literate, versed in Tamil and Pāli literature as well as Sinhala. In Chapter Four we outlined the local forces which sucked outsiders – particularly high-status groups with military

[30] Bocarro, *Decada*: 501.

[31] Compare too with the verse from the *Śrī Vikrama Ratnālankara* of 1614 on sun-like Senarat in Deraniyagala 1954: 171.

[32] See above, pp. 177–9, and *Rājāvaliya*: 92, 96–7; Roberts 2004: 105–7, 120–2.

[33] Laval 1887–8 II, part one: 147. This dates to the relatively un-aggressive rule of Senarat, but is reminiscent of Vimaladharmasūriya's nose amputations.

[34] Roberts 2004: 134.

[35] Remember that the *haṭanas* were court eulogies and military propaganda.

or commercial expertise – into the affairs of the Sinhalese states. In the earlier Kōṭṭe period this had led to a predominance at court of South Indian culture and personnel. There may then have been a certain disjuncture between a rather heavily Hinduized Kōṭṭe city and the hinterland. In the early modern state, it is not surprising to find court elites participating in a cosmopolitan culture, as conscious of their relations to corresponding elites in other regions as they are of their local standing. Indeed, such vagaries of fashion were not confined to Asians or elites: it is pleasing to find Queirós, for example, contrasting the stable integrity of dress among Eastern peoples with that of 'the Portuguese nation [*nação*] who, in spite of so great a conceit in themselves, adopt all foreign fashions'.[36] It is certainly not difficult to see how the personal habits and tastes of the rulers could tend further and further away from those of their subjects – as may have occurred with Rājasiṃha I. In Kōṭṭe, of course, the Portuguese replaced the South Indians as the most powerful of foreign military specialists, their missionaries an adornment of the court as Brahmans were.

Even when they began to arouse antipathy (a 'selective xenophobia'), this always remained one response among many. It is striking that Lusitanization was not simply a product of obvious power dynamics: it flowed outwards from Kōṭṭe to shape the court aesthetics of Kandy too. Elements of Portuguese culture retained their appeal even while Rājasiṃha II's courtiers were composing their propagandist assaults on Portuguese humanity. The politics of identity in this period were so complex, the play of signifiers so messy, as to confound interpretations driven by modern-day political impulses. Too prescriptive or dogmatic a vision of group identity, and we fail to understand a man such as Vimaladharmasūriya who dressed like a Christian and yet wanted to destroy the Christianity of his prisoners, who was a committed foe of the Portuguese yet wanted them in his service, who pursued a policy of partial conspicuous indigenization even though – or rather because – he was conspicuously Portugueseified.

Religion

This indigenism was associated with the reassertion of Buddhism, but may also at times have lent esteem to a vaguer notion of non-Christian Lankan practices.

In common with Christianity, the religions of Lanka had their origins in the transcendentalist revolutions of the Axial Age: they too asserted exportable religious truths that were rooted in written texts, promoted by ascetic-priestly literati, indissolubly associated with the moral order and subject to second-order reflection and debate. The set-piece disputations of 1543 would not have been possible otherwise. If intellectual conflict was therefore prefigured, it is rarely acknowledged in current discussions that so too had Sri Lanka witnessed periods when political conflict had acquired religious overtones. But the Indic institutionalizations

[36] Queyroz: 22. One theme of Leo Tolstoy's *War and Peace* is how Frenchified Russian high society had become during its wars with Napoleonic France.

of transcendentalism had led to different possibilities of identity: the boundaries around religious behaviour and belief were more permeable and not continuously re-etched into the fabric of everyday life by centralized bureaucracies such as the Church. Religious co-existence and intermingling were the norm.

The introduction of Christianity threatened this. Religious allegiance was emphasized and politicized in an altogether original manner – but this was the product of interplay between opportunistic locals and proselytizing Portuguese. From the late 1530s, locals dwelling close to the Portuguese and along the south-west coast converted in order to escape obligations to Sinhalese rulers, thereby altering their political identity through religious means. But it was with the arrival of the first mission in 1543 that the more radical implications were revealed as local kings sought to obtain Portuguese support through baptism. The Franciscan friars revealed a form of proselytization that was, again, quite unprecedented in its dynamism. Moreover, the missionaries were constantly pushing secular authorities to help further their spiritual ends. Christianity was swiftly associated with the penetration of Portuguese power.

This urgency, this martial vision of the advancing cross, owed something to the Catholic reform movements of late fifteenth- and early sixteenth-century Iberia. The same branch of friars who transformed the atmosphere of diplomacy in the 1540s and 1550s in Sri Lanka had taken the Word to Mexico, where they set about smashing 'idols' in great numbers, as offences in the eyes of God. This concept of abomination, also new to the island, only began to make an impact on Sri Lanka after the conversion of Dharmapāla in 1557, and the Counter-Reformation desire to Christianize Portuguese dominions took hold of ecclesiastical authorities in Lisbon and Goa.[37] We can, however, note that the Portuguese were not in a position to roll out such state policies across the land until the late 1590s: in previous decades temples were destroyed as part of military campaigns by Portuguese and Kōṭṭe men striking out from Colombo, when Christianity itself was under threat and a war of morale was under way. Nevertheless, we might be seeing faint echoes of the later sixteenth-century wars of religion in Europe reverberating in Sri Lanka. The island underwent its own version of 'confessionalism', that is the desire to make religious allegiance increasingly explicit and pervasive in all aspects of life and behaviour, and to make it a domain of political authority.

Sri Lankan history was certainly not, however, merely receiving the backwash of European tidal forces. The locals began playing their part very early: a fact that is sometimes obscured by modern-day readings. Within two years of the mission's arrival, Bhuvanekabāhu sought to protect his sovereignty by forbidding conversions and stripping convert properties, while Māyādunnē was reported to be impaling Christians.[38] Only a few years afterwards, in the campaigns of Vīdiyē Baṇḍāra, comes the first unequivocal evidence that political opposition to the Portuguese

[37] Elsewhere, however (Strathern unpublished), I show how such policies were formulated before the Counter-Reformation *per se*.

[38] VP: 122, see above, p. 108.

was being expressed through religious violence. This was before Dharmapāla's official conversion or the institutionalization of Christianity, but it did follow on from the first major act of religious violence by the Portuguese, the sacking of the Temple of the Tooth in 1551. Vīdiyē Baṇḍāra's campaigns lasted only a few years, but a Portuguese pictorial representation of the island from that time shows how they were seen as engulfing the lowlands.[39] And they seared themselves onto the memories of both Portuguese and Sinhalese for generations to come to judge by the great quantity of material about them preserved in both the *Conquista* and the later Sītāvakan sources such as the *Alakesvarayuddhaya* and *Sītāvaka Haṭana*.[40] Such was his impact on the politics of identity. Indeed his iconoclasm set the tone for future rebellions in the 1590s. It is unlikely to be a coincidence, however, that Vīdiyē Baṇḍāra had briefly been a Christian. His campaigns, like those of future rebels and Vimaladharmasūriya, seem to reveal the importation of Catholic concepts of religious identity.

Boundaries had hardened then on all sides. But around what precisely? Our question here mirrors that which we put to the problem of ethnicity. Did the Christian threat arouse feelings of loyalty merely to that which was non-Christian or did it harden pre-existing sensations of Buddhistness? Did it revivify or trounce previous religious antagonisms? De Silva has suggested that Buddhism *per se* received greater definition, with Saivite Hinduism more liable to be seen with suspicion.[41] This is plausible if we recall that even in the fifteenth century there had been *bhikkhus* ridiculing Saivism as grotesque and ill-founded. More work needs to be done to establish whether the Christian presence had begun to reconfigure intra-Indic religious relationships. There is the odd scrap of evidence to suggest that if the rebels were fighting for liberty, it was the liberty to practice the whole range of non-Christian religious practices that had been established on the island.[42] Nonetheless, it is reasonable to refer to the Sinhalese anti-Christian campaigns as implicitly defending Buddhism, if we understand by that the myriad and shifting forms of religious practice that were subsumed to a greater or lesser extent within a Theravādin soteriological framework. Whatever the religious tastes at court, the *saṃgha* clearly remained the hegemonic religious institution for all levels of Sinhalese society across the island. If the missionaries sought to drag political power into their concerns, there is some evidence that the *saṃgha* did likewise, helping to instigate the riots in Kōṭṭe of 1557, and the rebellions from the 1590s. The writers of the *Sītāvaka Haṭana* and the *Rājāvaliya* saw the *sāsana* (the institution of Buddhism) as betrayed by those who succumbed to the Portuguese mission.

39 See the map of Ceylon (1558–64) showing the 'Desbarado RibuliPamdar' (the defeat of Vīdiyē Baṇḍāra), and his capital at Pälaňda in Abreu 1992.

40 *Alakeśvarayuddhaya*: 35–40; *Rājāvaliya*: 76–82; *SH*, verses *c.* 580–830; Queyroz, 220–3, 254–5, 262–9, 288–94, 299–326.

41 C. R. de Silva 2000: 288–9, and see 1998.

42 VP: 346, 342; Bocarro, *Decada*: 497. In the 1630s Botelho saw Muslims and Buddhists as bound together in an anti-Catholic league: Cruz and Flores 2007.

If we were to plumb the depths of the power struggles in 1580s Kandy we would probably find the traditional wrangling of noble factions rolling around at the bottom. But what means of legitimizing their claims would each faction have employed? The evidence suggests that religion had been invoked, and that the claims of Buddhism ultimately proved more compelling.[43] This was a lasting victory, and from that time on it is likely that Buddhism was identified by both sides as the counterpart to Christianity. Certainly Filipe Botelho in 1633 saw Catholicism as locked in a desperate wrestling match with the 'sects that exist under the false Laws of Buddu'.[44]

But set this alongside the comments of the Franciscan chronicler Paulo da Trindade, also writing towards the end of Senarat's reign (1604–35). The Buddhist monks, 'though they are pagan, they are friendly towards our religious, since they consider them as men of the same profession, especially since, also like us, they go out each day and in great silence beg for alms from door to door.'[45] In this way a common language of transcendentalist asceticism could be found, and the long-standing equanimity towards other visions maintained. The transition from Vimaladharmasūriya to Senarat's more welcoming approach to Christianity suggests that European-style confessionalism had not been enduringly incorporated into the non-converted indigenous consciousness. If the irony is not too neat, it may be no coincidence that the more traditionally tolerant Senarat was an ex-*bhikkhu* and the more vehemently antagonistic Vimaladharmasūriya, an ex-Catholic.[46] Nor was such antagonism a major element of Rājasiṃha II's propaganda. It is perceptible in the *Rājasiṃha Haṭana*'s reference to the destruction of the Temple of the Tooth, but it was not the principal banner under which the poem exhorted the troops to march.[47] Instead a more secular aristocratic warrior ethos dominates the poem, just as it did the literary productions of Rājasiṃha II's Sītāvakan namesake.[48] Our fragmentary sources preserve shifts of consciousness between generations and divisions within them. But ultimately the long-term structure of religious intermingling remained predominant.

State

This was an indigenism that did not necessarily require reflection in a unitary state. The loyalties of this era were not only stimulated by particular royal families but by a generic reverence for indigenous high-status titles.

43 Re-founded Kandy may have drawn on anti-Saivite as well as anti-Christian sentiment.

44 Cruz and Flores 2007.

45 Trindade, III: 33 (an interpolation in his rendition of Gonzaga's account – compare VP: 46).

46 Although this may have been one reason why some rebels in the low country, where Christianization was in full swing, spurned his authority.

47 C. R. de Silva 2000: 187; Roberts 2004: 124. Beyond Rājasiṃha II's personal lack of interest in religious affairs, this may reflect the fact that the imposition of direct Portuguese rule over the lowlands had rendered political and religions boundaries more stable and consistent with each other: missionaries were no real threat in Kandy, while there were Christians in Kōṭṭe whom one might want to win over.

48 The religious dimension to conflict probably mattered less to the two Sītāvakan kings than it did to the Kōṭṭe rebels. Once again, notice that neither king had been Christian.

Dynastic sentiment is not incompatible with other solidarities. On the contrary, kings symbolize great populations in their person; ideally, they must defend and embody the collective vision that society has of itself. The ideal of Lanka unified under the canopy of one king remained of great importance throughout our period. It had been and may have again become an ingredient in the formation of a sense of Sinhalese identity and hegemony; it certainly drove the kings of Kōṭṭe to consort with the Portuguese in order to effect its realization, and the kings of Sītāvaka and seventeenth-century Kandy to repudiate the Portuguese with the same end in view. As Dharmapāla bequeathed his *cakravarti* title to Portugal, this merging of Kōṭṭe and Iberian imperial traditions thereby sought to render the independent centres of Sītāvaka and Kandy illegitimate upstarts.

But the mundane realities of political life then were often quite other. In the sixteenth century, the Sinhalese lived and died in various warring polities rather than any lasting unitary state. Any patriotic or indigenist sentiments such as there were, were not dependent on a desire for a single polity incorporating all Sinhalese (plus other minorities) in a manner equivalent to modern-day nationalism. Nor was there an absolute insistence on *sui generis* sovereignty: the Kōṭṭe kings routinely acknowledged the higher sovereignty of many external powers, whether Chinese or South Indian, in return for military and commercial advantages. The kings of Kōṭṭe, 'emperors of Sri Lanka', were official vassals of the Portuguese king from Vijayabāhu VI onwards, routinely articulating their subordination to Lisbon even if they conceived vassalage in subtly different ways.

While this final section has swung the spotlight onto indigenist sentiments, it was not so as to obscure the fact that the primary motors of political activity remained the conflicts between and within Sinhala states. Gunawardana's influential historicization of Sri Lankan identity politics has tended to present dynastic loyalty as the fundamental allegiance at work in the pre-modern era. This has significant analytical advantages: the loyalty of a section of the Kōṭṭe elite to Dharmapāla and the critical defections to his throne in the mid-1590s remain as illustrations of how dynastic authority could predominate over other group sentiments.[49] Perhaps the most significant loyalties of the sixteenth century remained personal ones – to their superiors in the status hierarchy, to their military leaders, to their kings and queens.

We have seen that much of the *Sītāvaka Haṭana* was devoted to emphasizing the illegitimacy of a Sinhalese rival to the Sītāvakan kings, Vīdiyē Baṇḍāra, even though he was the most forthright opponent of Christianity and the Portuguese of his day. Therein lay the potency of his threat, for Sītāvaka became intent on capturing that project for itself.[50] But the reality, which the poem obscures, was that Māyādunnē became an ally and vassal of the Portuguese in order to crush this rebel. The traditional rivalry of Lankan political centres continued throughout the sixteenth century, and all of them, without exception, proved willing to consort with the Portuguese to advance their own interests.

[49] Although realpolitik and self-interest can hardly be discounted here.

[50] Hence the poem has to present him as overmastered by the Buddhist vice of greed. See above, p. 182.

However, what do we understand by the 'dynasty'? Do we mean that the strongest claim on an individual's loyalties is made by his particular king? But in the polities of the sixteenth century it is the comparative contingency of such loyalties that stands out. What remained firm was a generic reverence for 'Sinhalese' royalty. The conditionality of vassalage is manifest in the great swings of support from Kōṭṭe to Sītāvaka in the 1540s and 1550s, and it is clearer still in the collapse of Sītāvaka in the mid-1590s. In the continual conflict of this brief period, it was often warlords such as Jayavīra Baṇḍāra who had the most immediate command of manpower. Some of these were themselves loyal only to their ambitions, but all sought to claim royal recognition or hankered after the status titles that only royalty could confer. The very fact that Sinhalese kingship became more readily fabricated in the seventeenth century, as rebels with modest backgrounds claimed royal origins, only serves to highlight its generic appeal. A Portuguese advisory document on Ceylon from 1611 actually suggests that rigorously policing the customary use of such titles – permitting 'only those that had the right' – would help prevent any old rebel gathering a following.[51] The increasing artificiality of kingship indicates more than the dwindling of royal stock. With the imposition of Portuguese direct rule, the conditions had changed. The rebellions were not called into being by dynastic glamour; dynastic glamour was called into being by the rebellions. This is one reason why we can refer to their leaders as 'rebels' rather than as the traditional pretenders of galactic politics or as fortune-seeking warmongers.

'Dynastic allegiance' thus also extended to the royal family tree that had branched out into the various competing seats of Kōṭṭe, Sītāvaka and Kandy as well as the odd lesser centre such as the Four Kōraḷēs. One discerns then here the shadow of unity, a pan-Sinhalese political 'system' of sorts, which lent a certain semantic frame to the jostlings within.[52] By the end of the century, Kandy was left as the sole indigenous claimant to the *cakravarti* title, and could attempt once more to lend patriotic sentiment a single political focus – with some success, as one observes a certain flickering loyalty to Kandy among the Sinhalese of the low country. This is best expressed by the fact that, while many low-country men were willing to fight for the Portuguese, they were typically unwilling to participate in the destruction of Kandy.[53] On the other hand, it was because all the rebels *were not* always acting out of devotion to the Kandyan dynasty that the theme of 'liberating the Sinhala nation' seemed most compelling to Portuguese observers. If they were not acting in the name of the king of Kandy, in whose name was it?[54]

[51] Pato 1880–1935, II: 84.

[52] To extend the analogy with the ancient Greeks (see above, p. 8, n. 26), each city-state might have its own origin myths, but these founders could nonetheless be tied into a broad family tree, which distinguished the Greeks from the really foreign such as the Persians.

[53] This is given fictional expression in Queyroz: 766.

[54] Hence we shall have to disagree with Hocart 1933: 272 that in Oriental wars 'Patriotism is not the incentive: the people fight merely to support the god who brings welfare. . . . Persian, Indian, Sinhalese armies, dispersed as soon as their leader was killed . . .' For patriotism can exist even where it can only be expressed through kingship, and can create leaders to serve its ends.

What we do not see in the sixteenth century is an importation of European visions of statehood into indigenous polities. The Portuguese sought to enhance their power through existing structures and they did this through a system of vassalage which had important features in common with the indigenous variety: the Portuguese model of overseas expansion was generally not to conquer and administrate substantial defined territories, but rather to exert influence over the elites of key political and economic centres.[55] All this changed, partly as a result of Castilian influence after the Union of the Crowns, in the mid-1590s.[56] The fissiparous nature of the Lankan state had facilitated Portuguese power, as each political centre could always be broken down into factions ready to overthrow the status quo and league with the newcomer. But now that same structure also served to obstruct the imposition of direct rule. Moreover, continual warfare enhanced the ability of military leaders of diverse origin to pursue their own ambitions while commanding strong loyalties among their men.

The origin of kings

This was an indigenism that abhorred intrusive foreign dominion but not the selective importation of foreign royal blood.

The Portuguese conquest propelled these centrifugal energies still further in so far as it weakened the legitimacy of the centre. There was an attempt to offset this by playing on the Kōṭṭe inheritance and preserving some semblance of continuity. This is most evident in Azevedo's court at Malvāna in which the captain-general was displayed in the manner of a local king. Senarat sometimes referred to him as 'King of Malvāna' or 'King of the Lowlands', indicating that the Portuguese presence had been conceptually incorporated, in a certain sense, within the frame of Lankan kingship.[57] The *Kustantīnu Haṭana's* eulogy (1619–20) to Constantino de Sá de Noronha shows that Portuguese captains could be assimilated to the indigenous heroic warrior ethos and lionized with the language of the *cakravarti*-esque.[58] The story of the Sinhalese Catholic community of Colombo is rarely told today, but by the seventeenth century it was just as much a part of Lanka as any other. They apparently felt comfortable with confessing loyalty to Christ and to their temporal lord Philip IV, the Spanish Habsburg king who had inherited the estates of the Portuguese king, and thus of the kings of Kōṭṭe, who had been latterly established in Colombo![59]

Most remarkable is a petition of 1636 made by 'the lascarins of the Island of Ceylon'. Faithful soldiers of the Portuguese, they still saw themselves as the heirs

55 For most of the sixteenth century, the Portuguese imperial model remained significantly different to Castilian conquistadorism, as Biedermann 2005a shows.

56 See Biedermann 2005a.

57 In the peace treaty of 1617: Biker, I: 213–14; compare with Roberts 2004: 78, 92, on how the Dutch were seen as vassals.

58 Deraniyagala 1954: 318.

59 See Cruz and Flores 2007, on Filipe Botelho, who argued, in traditional Lankan fashion, that the King of Kandy's claims were therefore illegitimate, but that he could nonetheless be kept *in situ*.

to a grand tradition 'wherewith our Kings fostered and preserved us, governing us for the space of 2,200 years and more, so long as the empire of the Island was in the hands of the Native Princes from Vijia Bau, the first King thereof, to the last Emperor of Cota, the aforesaid D. João of happy memory'. Furthermore, 'We beg to have in the arrayal a standard of banner of the arms of the ancient Kings of Cota . . . so as not to forget the memory of such great Lords.'[60] Of course, history had moved on by this time: these lascarins were Christians, the products of a conversion drive by which the Portuguese had set about rewriting the rules of political legitimacy for many thousands of lowland subjects. Their understanding of such matters differed from those of other contemporaries (Kandyans, rebels, the unconverted) as also from their counterparts of the 1590s, whose mentality in turn was different to those of the 1540s.

But more importantly, for many Sinhalese across the generations, there were fundamental limits to the Portuguese ability to slip into position as the inheritors of Lankan kingship. It hardly needs underlining that neither the Portuguese captain-general, nor the figure of the king in Madrid he ultimately represented, could claim the requisite ancestry or marriage ties, the traditional regalia or sacred imagery. Occasionally, the remnants of native dynasty could be wheeled in to fight fire with fire, as occurred at a critical point in the 1616–17 rebellions when a Lusitanized nobleman (Constantino) managed to halt some of the lascarin defections by claiming to be of royal blood, saying that 'if they were looking for their native king then they could find it here in him.'[61] Far more often, of course, it was Kandy that benefited from this esteem for native royalty. In 1625, an alarmed Portuguese commentator wrote about Senarat's three sons who had descended into the lowlands where the 'people [*gentes*] are more for them than for us . . . and as they consider them their native kings, they enter with fame and the name of liberators of the people [*povo*] and of the kingdom, saying that they want to liberate them from the many tyrannies and captivity of the Portuguese.'[62]

But what, precisely was understood by 'native' here? Whether or not the origins of both royalty and the people could be tied together in the Vijaya myth, a salient discourse of ancestry in our period served to separate the two by insisting on the uniquely exalted lineage and caste status of kings. 'Native' clearly did not then mean of pure indigenous blood, for kings routinely married brides – or were occasionally themselves imported – from abroad. The same could be said for much of early modern Europe, even for those kingdoms evolving into nascent nation-states: it is a routine feature of the dynastic state. But we cannot equate this with a generic indifference to the origins and cultural status of rulers. First, while the emphasis on *kṣatriya* status pertained to the royalties of certain peoples within the broader Indic ecumene, it excluded all those others who were unwilling and

[60] Queyroz: 1010, 1019–20. They support their claim by referring to 'the ancient books concerning the affairs of this island and of the Kings thereof, which are extant even today'. See also Ribeiro: 24–5.

[61] Bocarro, *Decada*: 498–9.

[62] Flores 2001b: 26. What does the distinction between 'people' and 'kingdom' imply here?

unable claim such a lineage. We can perhaps imagine different qualities of dynastic loyalty: shifting one's allegiance from one member of the Sinhalese royal family to another (Kōṭṭe to Sītāvaka) was not only conceivable but occurred en masse; shifting between two more heavily defined regions and loosely related families (Kōṭṭe to Kandy) perhaps more disruptive; shifting to a *kṣatriya* monarchy related by marriage but based outside the island would carry a different set of connotations; and of another order altogether would be obeisance to an entirely non-*kṣatriya*, non-Indic elite.

Second, in dynastic states some sort of symbolic indigenization is generally required of sovereigns or consorts. In Sri Lanka, one way this was expressed was through the transformative ritual of the consecration ceremony in which the Buddhist commitments of kingship were lent heavy emphasis. Third, rule is 'alien' when it refuses to accede to the traditional forms and customs of indigenous society, and when it is seen to work in the interests of a foreign conquest elite or metropole rather than the local people. The Sinhalese aristocracy expected their privileges and offices to be maintained, the castes their particular rights. The royal burden of responsibility for the welfare of society had anciently been emphasized, but it may have received particularly strong emphasis in the Kandyan rites of consecration in order to contrast with the 'unethical' rulership of the Portuguese. Turn once more to the lascarin petition of 1636 and we find that while it manifests the ghost of Kōṭṭe in the Portuguese imperial machine, it also reveals how insubstantial and ill-at-ease that presence was. The Portuguese had not, in fact, preserved the fabric of custom and law that the 'native princes' of old had protected; they had allowed opportunistic locals to set aside all precedent for the business of exploitation. Thus even these Catholic lascarins, loyal and true to their Iberian masters, held to their own variant of indigenism. Queirós lamented that in times of peace the Portuguese had treated the natives as common enemies, and in times of war all as rebels: in this way, he saw their Sinhalese opponents as the means by which their own sins were visited upon them.[63]

We are now arriving at a rather obvious distinction between invitation and conquest. To use an analogy from English history, if contemporaries considered it natural for Elizabeth I to look abroad for a husband in 1570s, it did not mean that they would consider with equanimity the prospect of the Spanish armada in the following decade. In Sri Lanka, the transition from invitation to conquest was long and ambiguous. It was only with hindsight that it seemed obvious and obviously located in the reign of Bhuvanekabāhu VII.[64] There is a sense, however, in which the identification of the 1540s as the pivotal decade embodies a historical insight. For it is in these years that the traditional practice of welcoming foreign groups into royal service began to segue into letting foreigners overwhelm the Sinhalese state. This is when the Portuguese – primarily as individual adventurers and entrepreneurs rather than officers of the *Estado* – revealed themselves to be

[63] See the coruscating critique of Portuguese imperialism in Queyroz: 1105.
[64] That is to the authors of the *Sītāvaka Haṭana* (1585), and the *Rājāvaliya*.

not just specialist servants or distant hegemons but an acid eating into indigenous sovereignty. It is not that Bhuvanekabāhu invited in foreigners which stimulates the scorn of the *Rājāvaliya*, but that he failed to harness them to his authority.[65]

Exactly the same logic organized relations in the spiritual realm too: from abiding by the practices of multi-religious patronage in the 1520s and 1530s, the sudden appearance of genuinely proselytizing Christianity in the shape of the 1543 mission immediately advertised a shift from assimilation to domination. It was only in these conditions, when the Portuguese seemed increasingly unwilling to play by the rules that had previously sustained cosmopolitan sensibilities, that indigenism came to acquire some relevance.[66] As early as the 1580s, the author of the *Sītāvaka Haṭana* could occlude the Portuguese quasi-accommodation to indigenous authority, representing them as the alien agents of political, religious and social destruction.[67]

Sacred kingship

This was an indigenism that assumed a link between the religious status of the people and that of their kings, without binding either to exclusivist understandings of religious practice and identity.

What most marked out the Portuguese as an alien force in the eyes of many of the unconverted was their abjuration of the religious aspects of kingship tradition. This was the primary means by which rulers of foreign origin were domesticated and accepted, but the Portuguese not only refused to acquiesce themselves but set about trying to wrest Buddhism from other rulers. We have given warning of the potential treachery of our Western sources on this point, whose analyses may have been shaped by the 'wars of religion' afflicting Europe.[68] It is striking – but may be mere coincidence – that these reached their height towards the end of the century, just as these issues become critical in Sri Lanka.[69] If European kings had been comparatively secure when set alongside their Lankan counterparts, what had suddenly rendered them vulnerable – to assassination, usurpation, war – was religious schism. Hence we find an explicit debate on the rights and wrongs of deposing rulers of heretical faith, on the relationship between one's duty as a subject of man and one's duty as a subject of God. In France, for example, Henri III was assassinated by a Dominican friar (1589) and Henri IV by a Huguenot

65 I owe this point to Biedermann 2005a: 105. See *Rājāvaliya*: 74: Bhuvanekabāhu 'had handed over the country to foreigners, having introduced unlawfulness to the people and shown contempt for the *Sāsana*'.

66 Queyroz: 579.

67 Taken up by the *Rājāvaliya*: 75–7, and compare with Young and Senanayaka 1998: 6–8, 13, 63, on Christianity as the product of Māra, the destroyer of Buddhist harmony. The dating of the *Rājāvaliya* interpolations is very problematic. They may belong to the final recension in Vimaladharmasūriya II's time, but there are reasons for thinking that they were first written under Senarat.

68 See above, pp. 164–5, on Queirós, who makes analogies with Europe during the Thirty Years War: Queyroz: 286, 483.

69 There is a slight suggestion that such European visions had penetrated local understandings of such matters: see above, p. 174, on Afonso Rasquinho.

(1610). As for England, Pope Pius V had excommunicated Elizabeth I in 1570 and encouraged the faithful to depose her, while the Catholic gunpowder plot (5 November 1605) had attempted to wipe out James I and the entire ruling elite.

It was against this broad ideological backdrop that the issue was highlighted in Queirós' treatment of his material; he pursued it in a manner that was sometimes anachronistic, dogmatic and fictitious. Yet we do not need to see him as a mere Don Quixote of Sri Lankan history, his precepts as impervious to percepts as a deluded itinerant who sees romances in dust clouds. For this book has concluded that a structure of the Lankan long term can be seen at work here – pulled about and tested to the limit by the upheavals of the sixteenth century, obscured by the apparent reduction of politics to the muddy business of the battlefield, all but invisible between 1585 and 1595 – but persisting still to shape the fortunes of kings. Queirós's text is not simply the residue of European fantasies but the offspring of an entanglement with a stubborn indigenous reality, and one which shaped rulers' responses to the mission from the very first encounters. The comparative religious tolerance of Lankan kings, their willingness to perform to the sacral expectations of many moral communities, can be dazzling to modern eyes. But it ought not to blind us to the presence of quite other boundaries, often irrelevant or submerged, but summoned to the surface when the relationship between kingship, *saṃgha* and people was placed in jeopardy. Sri Lankan Buddhism was, in this very specific sense, genuinely analogous to Christianity: ultimately both owed such intransigence to their origins in the conceptual revolutions of the Axial Age.[70]

It is fitting that the keenest contemporary insight into the relationship between political and religious authority – and the comparability of Buddhist and Christian traditions in this respect – can be found in the writings of a local Sinhalese Christian, Filipe Botelho, whose heritage looked both ways. He identified the role of Buddhism in thwarting Kōṭṭe–Portuguese power, and yet saw clearly that Constantino de Sá de Noronha's attacks on the sacred edifices of Kandy would rouse terrible opposition, 'disinterring a sleeping heresy' that would seep down the hillsides and into the lowlands, destroying churches, rebuilding temples, and tying together the kings and the monks in rejuvenated alliance.[71]

[70] It should be clear by now that this comparison works on an unusually abstract level only. The main historical contingencies to which such intransigence is subject are are outlined in Strathern (2007*b*).

[71] Cruz and Flores 2007.

Appendix
Regnal Dates of Rulers in Sri Lanka

The dates follow those in K. M. de Silva 1995.

Kings of Kōṭṭe

Parākramabāhu VI	1411–67
Jayavīra Parākramabāhu	1467–9
Bhuvanekabāhu VI	1469–77
Paṇḍita Parākramabāhu	1477
Vīra Parākramabāhu VIII	1477–89
Dharma Parākramabāhu IX	1489–1513
Vijayabāhu VI	1513–21
Bhuvanekabāhu VII	1521–51
Dharmapāla	1551–97

Kings of Sītāvaka

Māyādunnē	1521–81
Rājasiṃha I	1581–93
Rajasūriya	1593–4

Kings of Kandy

Senāsammata Vikramabāhu	1469–1511
Jayavīra	1511–52
Karaliyaddē	1552–82
Vimaladharmasūriya	1591–1604
Senarat	1604–35
Rājasiṃha II	1635–87
Vimaladharmasūriya II	1687–1707

Kings of Jaffna

(The regnal dates of previous rulers are unclear)

Caṇkili	1519–61
Puvirāja Paṇḍāram	1561–5, 1582–91
Periyapillai	1565–82
Ethirimanna ciṇkam	1591–1616
Caṇkili II	1616–20

BIBLIOGRAPHY

Manuscript sources

Archivo General de Simancas, Secretarías Provinciales, Portugal (AGS-SP): Códice 1551.

Arquivo Histórico Ultramarino, Lisbon (AHU): Códice 281.

Biblioteca da Ajuda, Lisbon (BA): 47-VIII-5; 51-II-20; 51-II-33; 51-VII-27 (no. 27: *Descripção Historica, geographica, e topographica da Ilha de Ceilão*); 51-VIII-40 (*Historia de Ceylão*).

Instituto dos Arquivos Nacionais/Torre do Tombo, Lisbon (IAN/TT): *Chancelaria de D. João III*, livros 25, 31; *Cartas dos Vice-Reis da Índia*, number 100; *Manuscritos da Livraria*, number 1104, *Corpo Cronólogico*, maço 107, doc. 51,

British Library, London (BL): Add. MS 28,432 (Mathias de Albuquerque, *Lembrança dos Galeões . . .* fols. 124–31); Add. MS 20,861.

Primary sources

Abeyasinghe, T. B. H. (1974) *A Study of Portuguese Regimentos on Sri Lanka at the Goa Archives*. Colombo.

(1978–9) 'Some Portuguese documents on the last days of the Sītāvaka Kingdom, 1593–4', *Journal of the Sri Lanka Branch of the Royal Asiatic Society*, n.s. 24: 86–91.

(tr., ed.) (1996) 'António Bocarro's Ceylon', with intr. by C. R. De Silva, *Journal of the Royal Asiatic Society of Sri Lanka*, n.s. 39.

Abeyawardhana, H. A. P. (1999) *Boundary Divisions of Medieval Sri Lanka*. Colombo.

Abreu, Lisuarte (1992) *Livro de Lisuarte de Abreu*, intr. by Luís de Albuquerque. Lisbon.

Albuquerque, Luís de, and Costa, José Pereira da (1990) 'Cartas de Serviços da Índia (1500–1550)', *Mare Liberum* 1: 309–96.

Alguns Documentos do Archivo Nacional da Torre do Tombo Ácerca das Navegações e Conquistas Portuguezas (1892). Lisbon.

Andrada, Francisco de (1976) *Crónica de D. João III*, ed. M. L. de Almeida. Porto.

Aubin, Jean (ed.) (1974) 'Francisco de Albuquerque, un Juif Castilian au service de l'Inde portuguaise', *Arquivos do Centro Cultural Português* 7: 189–202. (Contains the *Referir de Francesco dal Bocchier* of 1518.)

[Azevedo, Agostinho de] (1960) 'Estado da India e aonde tem o seu principio', printed as anonymous document in *Documentação Ultramarina Portuguesa* 1: 197–263.

Baião, A. (ed.) (1925) *História Quinhentista (inédita) do Segundo Cêrco de Dio*. Coimbra: 296–334.

Baldaeus, Philip (1752) 'A True and Exact Description of the Most Celebrated East-Indian Coast of Malabar and Coromandel; as also of the Isle of Ceylon', in *A Collection of Voyages and Travels*, ed. Awnshawm Churchill, vol. III. London.

Barbosa, Duarte (1918–21) *The Book of Duarte Barbosa*, trans. M. L. Dames (2 vols). London.

Barros, João de (1988) *Ásia de João de Barros: Dos Feitos que os Portugueses fizeram no Descobrimentos e Conquistas dos Mares e Terras do Oriente* (3 vols.). Lisbon.

Bell, H. C. P. (1904) *Report on the Kegalla District of the Province of Sabaragamuwa*. Colombo.

Biker, J. F. Júdice (1881–7) *Collecção de Tratados e Concertos de Pazes que o Estado da Índia Portugueza Fez com os Reis e Senhores com Quem Teve Relações nas Partes da Ásia e África Oriental desde o Principio da Conquista até ao Fim do Século XVIII* (14 vols.). Lisbon.

Bocarro, António (1876) *Década 13 da História da India*, ed. Rodrigo José de Lima Felner, Lisbon.

(1992) *O Livro das Plantas de Todas as Fortalezas, Cidades e Povoações do Estado da Índia Oriental* (3 vols.), vol. II. Lisbon.

Bodin, Jean (1992) *On Sovereignty*. Cambridge.

Bouchon, Geneviève (ed.) (1971) 'A letter: Cristóvão Lourenço Caração to D. Manuel, Cochin, 13 Jan 1522', *Mare Luso Indicum* 1: 163–8.

Brásio, António (1960) 'Uma carta inédita de Valentim Fernandes', *Boletim da Biblioteca da Universidade de Coimbra* 24: 5–25.

Cervantes, Miguel de (2005) *Don Quixote*, trans. Edith Grossman. London.

Castanheda, Fernão Lopes de (1924–33) *História do Descobrimento e Conquista da Índia pelos Portugueses* (9 vols.). Coimbra.

Correia, Gaspar (1858–64) *Lendas da Índia*, ed. Rodrigo José de Lima Felner (4 vols.). Lisbon.

Couto, Diogo do (1936) *Década Quinta da 'Ásia'*. Coimbra.

Cunha-Rivara, J. H. da (ed.) (1857–77) *Archivo Portuguez-Oriental* (6 vols.). New Goa.

Da Silva Cosme, O. M. (ed.) (1986) *Sri Lanka and the Portuguese (1541–1557)*. Colombo.

De Silva, S. (ed.) (1930) *Rājaratnākaraya*. Colombo.

Deraniyagala, P. E. P. (ed.) (1954) *Sinhalese Verse (Kavi)* (3 vols). Colombo.

Documentos sobre os Portugueses em Moçambigue e na África Central, 1497–1840 (1962–) (9 vols.). Lisbon.

Du Jarric, Pierre (1917–19) 'Ceylon according to Du Jarric', trans. E. Gaspard, *Ceylon Antiquary and Literary Register* 3: 163–73; 4: 5–18, 49–57.

Earle, T. F., and Villiers, John (eds.) (1990) *Albuquerque, Caesar of the East: Selected Letters of Afonso de Albuquerque and his Son*. Warminster.

Epigraphia Zeylanica, Being Lithic and other Inscriptions of Ceylon (1904–43), Ceylon Archaeological Survey (4 vols), vols. I-III (ed. Don Martino de Zilva Wickremasinghe), vol. IV (ed. H. W. Codrington and S. Paranavitana). London.

Faria e Sousa, M. (1665–75) *Asia Portuguesa* (3 vols.). Lisbon.

Felner, Rodrigo José de Lima (ed.) (1868) 'O Tombo do Estado da Índia', *Subsídios para a História da Índia Portugueza*. Lisbon.

Ferguson, D. (ed. and trans.) (1928) 'The earliest Dutch visits to Ceylon', *Journal of the Royal Asiatic Society (Ceylon Branch)* 31: 102–79.

(ed. and trans.) (1935–6) 'The Portuguese in Ceylon in the first half of the sixteenth century. Gaspar Correa's Account', *Ceylon Literary Register* 4: 141–61, 189–211, 265–73, 320–6, 359–66.

(ed. and trans.) (1993) *The History of Ceylon from the Earliest Times to 1600 AD As Related by João de Barros and Diogo do Couto*. New Delhi.

Flores, Jorge Manuel (ed.) (2001a) *Os Olhos do Rei: Desenhos e Descrições Portuguesas da Ilha de Ceilão (1624, 1638)*. Lisbon.

Foster, W. (ed.) (1921) *Early Travels in India 1583–1619*. London.

Freyre, António (1630) *Primor e Honra da Vida Soldadesca do Estado da India*. Lisbon.

Gavetas (As) da Torre do Tombo (1963), vol. III. Lisbon.

Geiger, W. (ed. and trans.) (1953) *Cūḷavaṃsa, Being the More Recent Part of the Mahāvaṃsa*, trans. from the German into English by C. M. Rickmers, part II. Colombo.

(ed. and trans.) (1993) *The Mahāvaṃsa or the Great Chronicle of Ceylon*, trans. from the German into English by M. H. Bode. New Delhi.

Gonzaga, Francesco (1603) *De Origine Seraphicae Religionis Franciscanae eiusque Progressibus*. vol. II. Venice.

Hobbes, Thomas (1991) *Leviathan*, ed. Richard Tuck. Cambridge.

Knox, Robert (1989) *An Historical Relation of the Island of Ceylon*, ed. J. H. O. Paulusz, 2nd edn., including interleaved notes (2 vols.), vol. II. Dehiwala.

Lafitau, Joseph-François (1733) *Histoire des découvertes et conquestes des Portugais dans le Nouveau Monde*. Paris.

Laval, François Pyrard de (1887–8) *The Voyage of François Pyrard of Laval*, trans. A. Grey (2 vols.). London.

Lawrie, A. C. (1896–8) *A Gazetteer of the Central Provinces of Ceylon* (2 vols.). Colombo.

Linschoten, J. H. van (1885) *The Voyage of John Huyghen van Linschoten to the East Indies from the Old English Translation of 1598*, ed. A. C. Burnell and P. A. Thiele (2 vols). London.

Lisboa, Marcos de (2001) *Crónicas da Ordem dos Frades Menores* (3 vols.). Porto.

Lobo, A. Costa (ed.) (1887) *Memórias de um Soldado da Índia. Compliladas de um Manuscrito Português do Museu Britânico*. Lisbon. (This contains Francisco Rodrigues Silveira, 'Reformação da milicia e governo da India oriental'.)

Locke, John (1964) *Two Treatises of Government*, ed. Peter Laslett. Cambridge.

Lucena, J. de (1600) *História de vida do padre Francisco de Xavier*. Lisbon.

Luz, Francisco P. Mendes da (ed.) (1953) 'Livro das Cidades e Fortalezas da Índia', *Boletim da Biblioteca da Universidade de Coimbra* 21: 1–144.

Matos, Luís de (1985) *Imagens do Oriente no Século XVI: Reprodução do Códice Português da Biblioteca Casanatense*. Lisbon.

Monforte, Manuel de (1751) *Chronica da Provincia da Piedade*. Lisbon.

Müller, Edward (ed.) (1883) *Ancient Inscriptions in Ceylon*. London.

Nanavimala, K. (ed.) (1946) *Saparagamuvē Päraṇi Liyavili*. Colombo.

Paranavitana, R. (ed.) (1999) *Sītāvaka Haṭana*. Colombo.

Pato, R. A. De Bulhão (1880–1935), *Documentos Remettidos da Índia ou Livros das Monções* (5 vols.). Lisbon.

Perera, S. G. (ed.) (1930) *The Expedition to Uva made in 1630 by Constantino de Sá de Noronha*. Colombo.

Perniola, V. (ed.) (1989–91), *The Catholic Church in Sri Lanka, The Portuguese Period.* Vol. I, *1505–1565*, Vol. II, *1566–1619*, Vol. III, *1620–1658*. Dehiwala.

Pessoa, António (1960) 'Livro que trata das cousas da Índia e do Japão', *Boletim da Biblioteca da Universidade de Coimbra* 24: 1–38. (Contains the report of António Pessoa from 1548.)

Pieris, P. E. (2004) *The Prince Vijaya Pala of Ceylon 1614–54*. New Delhi.

Pieris, P. E., and Fitzler, M. A. H. (1927a) *Ceylon and Portugal, Part I: Kings and Christians, 1539–1552*. Leipzig.

Pimenta, Nicholas (2004) 'Jesuit letters on Pegu in the early seventeenth century', *SOAS Bulletin of Burma Research* 2: 184–6.

Pires, Tomé (1978) *A Suma Oriental de Tomé Pires e o Livro de Francisco Rodrigues*, ed. Armando Cortesão. Coimbra.

Polo, Marco (1986) *The Travels*, trans. R. Latham. London.

Queiroz, Fernão de (1916) *Conquista Temporal e Espiritual de Ceylão*, ed. P. E. Pieris. Colombo.

[Queyroz, Fernão de], (1992) *The Temporal and Spiritual Conquest of Ceylon*, trans., and with intr. by S. G. Perera (3 vols.). New Delhi.

Rego, A. da Silva (ed.) (1947–58) *Documentação para a História das Missões do Padroado Português do Oriente* (12 vols.). Lisbon.

Reynolds, C. H. B. (ed.) (1970) *An Anthology of Sinhalese Literature up to 1815*. London.

Ribeiro, João (1948) *The Historic Tragedy of the Island of Ceilão*, ed. and trans. P. E. Pieris. Colombo.

Saa y Menezes, Juan Rodrigues de (1681) *Rebelion de Ceylan, y los Progressos de su Conquista en el Gobierno de Constantino de Saa y Noroña*. Lisbon.

Schurhammer, Georg, and Voretzsch, E. A. (eds.) (1928) *Ceylon zur Zeit des Konigs Bhuvaneka Bahu und Franz Xavers, 1539–1552* (2 vols.). Leipzig.

Schurhammer, Georg, and Wicki, J. (eds.) (1944–5) *Epistolae S. Francisci Xaverii*. (2 vols.). Rome.

Somadasa, K. D. (1987–95) *Catalogue of the Hugh Nevill Collection of Sinhalese Manuscripts in the British Library* (7 vols.). London.

Spilbergen, Joris van (1997) *Journal of Spilbergen, the First Dutch Envoy to Ceylon, 1602*, ed. and trans. K. D. Paranavitana. Colombo.

Suraweera, A. [Suravira, A.] (ed.) (1965) *Alakēśvarayuddhaya*. Colombo. (trans.) (2000) *Rājāvaliya*. Ratmalana.

Trindade, Paulo da (1962–67) *Conquista Espiritual do Oriente*, ed. Fernando Félix Lopes (3 parts). Lisbon.

Upham, E. (ed. and trans.) (1833) *The Mahavánsi, the Rájá-ratnácari, and the Rájávali, Forming the Sacred and Historical Books of Ceylon* (3 vols.). London.

Varthema, Ludovico di (1997) *The Itinerary of Ludovico di Varthema of Bologna from 1502 to 1508*, ed. and trans. John Winter Jones. New Delhi.

Wicki, J. (ed.) (1948–88) *Documenta Indica* (18 vols.). Rome.

Young, R. F., and Senanayaka, G. S. B. (eds.) (1998) *The Carpenter-Heretic: A Collection of Buddhist Stories about Christianity from 18th-Century Sri Lanka*. Colombo.

Secondary sources

Abeyasinghe, T. (1964) 'The myth of the Malvāna Convention', *Ceylon Journal of Historical and Social Studies* 7: 67–72.

(1966) *Portuguese Rule in Ceylon, 1594–1612*. Colombo.

(1973) 'The politics of survival: aspects of Kandyan external relations in the mid-sixteenth century', *Journal of the Royal Asiatic Society of Sri Lanka* 17: 11–21.

(1980–1) 'History as polemics and propaganda: an examination of Fernão de Queirós' "History of Ceylon"', *Journal of the Royal Asiatic Society (Sri Lanka Branch)* 25: 28–68.

(1986) *Jaffna under the Portuguese*. Colombo.

(1995) 'Portuguese rule in Kōṭṭe, 1594–1638', and 'The Kingdom of Kandy: foundations and foreign relations to 1638', in K. M. de Silva 1995: 123–61.

Albuquerque, Luís de (ed.) (1989) *Portugal no Mundo* (6 vols.) Lisbon.

Almeida, Carlos (2004) 'A primeira missão da Companhia de Jesus no Reino do Congo (1548–55)', in Carneiro and Matos 2004: 865–88.

Amarasinghe, Risiman (1998) *Sitāvaka Rājadhāniyē Unnatiyēda Avanatiyēda Samahara Aṃśa Piḷibaňda Vimarśanayak*. Colombo.

Andaya, Barbara Watson, 'Statecraft in the reign of Lu Tai of Sukhodaya (ca. 1347–1374)', in B. L. Smith 1978b: 2–19.

Ariyapala, M. B. (1968) *Society in Medieval Ceylon*. Colombo.

Ariyasena, K. (1987) 'The concept of the state as reflected in the Pāli canon', in *Buddhist Philosophy and Culture: Essays in Honour of M.A. Jayawickrema*, ed. David J. Kalupahana and W. G. Weeraratne. Colombo: 100–11.

Arnold, Thomas, F. (2000) 'Diverging military cultures of east and west. The very long sixteenth century', *Mare Liberum* 20: 57–70.

Atran, Scott (2002) *In Gods we Trust: The Evolutionary Landscape of Religion*. Oxford.

Barnard, Alan, and Spencer, Jonathan (eds.) (1996) *Encyclopedia of Social and Cultural Anthropology*. London.

Bayly, Susan (1989) *Saints, Goddesses and Kings: Muslims and Christians in South Indian Society 1700–1900*. Cambridge.

(1993) *Caste, Society and Politics in India from the Eighteenth Century to the Modern Age. The New Cambridge History of India*, Vol. IV. Cambridge.

Beozzo, J. Oscar (1993) 'O diálogo da conversão do gentio, a evangelização entre a persuasão e a força', in *Missionação Portuguesa* 1993, II: 551–87.

Bethencourt, Francisco and Chaudhuri, Kirti (eds.) (1998) *História da Expansão Portuguesa*, Vol. I. Navarre.

Biedermann, Zoltán, ''Do regressso do quarto império: a China de João de Barros e o imaginário imperial joanino', in Carneiro and Matos 2004: 103–20.

(2005*a*) 'A aprendizagem de Ceilão. A presença Portuguesa em Sri Lanka entre estratégia talassocrática e planos de conquista territorial (1506–1598)'. Ph.D. diss. Universidade Nova, Lisbon, and École Pratique des Hautes Études, Paris.

(2005*b*) 'Tribute, vassalage and warfare in early Luso-Lankan relations (1506–1545)', in *Indo-Portuguese History: Global Trends. Proceedings of the XIth International Seminar of Indo-Portuguese History*, ed. Fátima Gracias and Charles Borges. Goa: 185–206.

Blackburn, Anne M. (2001) *Buddhist Learning and Textual Practice in Eighteenth-Century Lankan Monastic Culture*. Princeton.

Bouchon, Geneviève (1971) 'Les Rois de Kōṭṭe au début du XVIe siècle', *Mare Luso-Indicum* 1: 65–96.

(1987) 'Sixteenth-century Malabar and the Indian Ocean', in Das Gupta and Pearson 1987: 162–84.

(1988) *'Regent of the Sea': Cannanore's Response to Portuguese Expansion, 1507–1528*. Delhi.

(1999) 'Calicut at the turn of the sixteenth century', in Bouchon, *Inde découverte, Inde retrouvée, 1498–1630*. Paris: 227–36.

Bourdon, Léon (1936) *Les Débuts de l'évangélisation de Ceylan vers le milieu du XVIe siècle*. Lisbon.

Boxer, C. R. (1960–1) 'A note on Portuguese missionary methods in the east', *Ceylon Historical Journal* 10: 77–90.

(1969) *The Portuguese Seaborne Empire 1415–1825*. London.

(1978) *The Church Militant and Iberian Expansion*. London.

Brading, D. A. (1991) *The First America: The Spanish Monarchy, Creole Patriots and the Liberal State 1492–1867*. Cambridge.

Carneiro, R. and Matos, A. Teodoro de (eds.) (2004). *D. João III e o Império: Actas*. Lisbon.

Carrithers, Michael (1987) 'Buddhists without history', *Contributions to Indian Sociology* 21: 165–68.

(2000) 'On polytropy: or the natural condition of spiritual cosmopolitanism in India: the Digambar Jain case', *Modern Asian Studies* 34: 831–61.

Clendinnen, Inga (1982) 'Disciplining the Indians: Franciscan ideology and missionary violence in sixteenth-century Yucatan', *Past and Present* 94: 27–48.

(1987) 'Franciscan missionaries in sixteenth-century Mexico', in *Disciplines of Faith: Studies in Religion, Politics and Patriarchy*, ed. Jim Obelkevich et al. London: 229–45.

Codrington, H. W. (1959) 'The decline of the medieval Sinhalese kingdom', *Journal of the Ceylon Branch of the Royal Asiatic Society* 7: 93–103.

Collins, Steven (1998) *Nirvana and other Buddhist Felicities: Utopias of the Pāli Imaginaire*. Cambridge.

Couto, Dejanirah Silva (2000) 'Some observations on Portuguese renegades in Asia in the sixteenth century', in Disney and Booth: 178–201.

Correia-Afonso, John (1969) *Jesuit Letters and Indian History 1542–1773*. Bombay.

(1989) 'As missões Católicas no oriente (1500–1650) em particular na Índia', in Albuquerque 1989, IV: 223–36.

Correia, J. M. (1998) *Os Portugueses no Malabar (1498–1580)*. Lisbon.

Coutinho, B. Xavier (1972) 'Portugal na arte e história de Ceilão', *Studia* 34–5: 1–99.

Cruz, M. Augusta Lima and Flores, Jorge (2007) 'A "tale of two cities", a "veteran Soldier" and the last years of Portuguese rule in Sri Lanka: the two *Jornadas de Huva* (1633, 1635) revisited', in Flores 2007: 95–124

Das Gupta, Ashin, and Pearson, M. N. (eds.) (1987) *India and the Indian Ocean, 1500–1800*. Calcutta.

Da Silva Cosme, O. M. (1990) *Fidalgos in the Kingdom of Kōṭṭe*. Colombo.

de Silva, C. R. (1971) 'Lançarote de Seixas and Mādampe: a Portuguese *casado* in a Sinhalese village', *Modern Ceylon Studies* 2: 18–34.

(1972) *The Portuguese in Ceylon, 1617–38*. Colombo.

(1975) 'The first Portuguese revenue register of the Kingdom of Kōṭṭe, 1599', *Ceylon Journal of Historical and Social Studies* 5: 71–153.

(1983) 'The historiography of the Portuguese in Sri Lanka: a survey of the Sinhala writings', *Samskrti* 17: 13–22.

(1984) 'Ethnicity, prejudice and the writing of history', G. C. Mendis Memorial lecture in *G. C. Mendis Memorial Edition*. Colombo.

(1990) 'Peddling trade, elephants and gems: some aspects of Sri Lanka's trading connections in the Indian Ocean in the sixteenth and early seventeenth Centuries', in *Asian Panorama: Essays in Asian History, Past and Present*, ed. K. M. de Silva, S. Kiribamune, and C. R de Silva. New Delhi: 287–302.

(1991a) 'Political and diplomatic relations of the Portuguese with the Kingdom of Kōṭṭe during the first half of the sixteenth century', *Revista da Cultura* 13/14: 220–32.

(1991b) 'Colonialism and trade: the cinnamon contract of 1533 between Bhuvanekabāhu, King of Kōṭṭe and António Pereira, Portuguese factor in Sri Lanka', *University of Colombo Review* 10: 27–34.

(1994) 'Beyond the Cape: the Portuguese encounter with the peoples of South Asia', in S. Schwarz 1994: 295–322.

(1995) 'Sri Lanka in the early sixteenth century: political conditions'; 'Sri Lanka in the early sixteenth century: economic and social conditions'; 'The rise and fall of the Kingdom of Sitawaka', in *University of Peradeniya History of Sri Lanka,* vol. II, *From c. 1500 to c. 1800*, ed. K. M. De Silva. Peradeniya: 11–104.

(1996) 'Historical introduction' to António Bocarro's description of Ceylon, trans. Tikiri Abeyasinghe, *Journal of the Royal Asiatic Society of Sri Lanka* n.s. 39 (1995, published 1996): pp. xii–xxvi.

(1998) 'Algumas reflexões sobre o impacto Português na religião entre os Singaleses durante os séculos XVI e XVII', *Oceanos* 34: 104–16.

(2000) 'Islands and beaches: indigenous interactions with the Portuguese in Sri Lanka after Vasco da Gama', in Disney and Booth 2000: 280–94.

(2001–2) 'Portuguese interactions with Sri Lanka and the Maldives in the sixteenth century: some parallels and divergences', *Sri Lanka Journal of the Humanities* 27–8: 1–23.

de Silva, C. R., and Bartholomeusz, Tessa J. (1998) 'Buddhist fundamentalism and identity in Sri Lanka', in *Buddhist Fundamentalism and Minority Identities in Sri Lanka*, ed. Bartholomeusz and De Silva. New York: 1–35.

De Silva, D. G. B. (1996) 'New light on vanniyas and their chieftancies based on folk historical tradition as found in palm-leaf MSS in the Hugh Nevill collection', *Journal of the Royal Asiatic Society of Sri Lanka* 41: 153–204.

De Silva, K. M. (ed.) (1995) *University of Peradeniya History of Sri Lanka,* vol. II, *From c. 1500 to c. 1800*. Peradeniya.

De Silva, K. M., Kiribamune, S., and de Silva, C. R. (eds.) (1990) *Asian Panorama: Essays in Asian History, Past and Present*. New Delhi.

De Silva, M. U. (1994) 'Land tenure, the caste system and *rājakāriya* under foreign rule: a review of change in Sri Lanka under Western powers', *Journal of the Royal Asiatic Society of Sri Lanka* 37: 1–38.

De Silva, P. H. D. H. (1975) *A Catalogue of Antiquities and Other Cultural Objects from Sri Lanka (Ceylon) Abroad.* Colombo.

Dewaraja, L. S. (1988) *The Kandyan Kingdom of Sri Lanka, 1707–1782*. Colombo.

(1995) 'Religion and the state in the Kandyan Kingdom: the 17th and 18th centuries', in K. M. De Silva 1995: 453–69.

Dharmadasa, K. N. O. (1992) *Language, Religion and Ethnic Awareness: The Growth of Sinhalese Nationalism in Sri Lanka*. Michigan.

(1995) 'Literature in Sri Lanka: the 16th, 17th and 18th centuries', in K. M. De Silva 1995: 471–90.

Dirks, Nicholas B. (2001) *Castes of Mind: Colonialism and the Making of Modern India*. Princeton.

Disney, Anthony (2001) 'What was the *Estado da Índia*? four contrasting images', *Indica* 38: 161–8.

Disney, Anthony, and Booth, Emily (eds.) (2000), *Vasco da Gama and the Linking of Europe and Asia*. New Delhi.

Don Peter, W. L. A. (1978) *Education in Sri Lanka under the Portuguese*. Colombo.

(1989) 'Portuguese influence on a Sinhalese poet', *Aquinas Journal* 6: 9–26.

Doyle, Michael W. (1986) *Empires*. Cornell.

Duncan, James. S. (1990) *The City as Text: The Politics of Landscape Interpretation in the Kandyan Kingdom*. Cambridge.

Eaton, Richard M. (1997) *The Rise of Islam and the Bengal Frontier, 1204–1760*. New Delhi.

Earle, T. F. (1990), 'Introduction: history, rhetoric and intertextuality', in and Earle and Villiers 1990: 2–49 (see Primary Sources).

Eisenstadt, Shmuel N. (ed.), (1986), *The Origins and Diversity of Axial Age Civilisations*. Albany.

Eisenstadt, Shmuel N., and Schluchter, Wolfgang (1998) 'Introduction: paths to early modernities – a comparative view', *Daedalus* 127: 1–18.

Eisenstadt, Shmuel N., Kahane, Reuven and Shulman, David. (eds.) (1984) *Orthodoxy, Heterodoxy and Dissent in India*. Berlin.

Flores, Jorge Manuel (1993) '"Um homem que tem muito crédito naquelas partes": Miguel Ferreira, 'os alevantados' do Coromandel e o Estado da Índia', *Mare Liberum* 5: 21–37.

(1994) 'Portuguese entrepreneurs in the Sea of Ceylon (mid-sixteenth century)', in *Maritime Asia. Profit Maximisation, Ethics and Trade Structure c. 1300–1800*, ed. Karl Anton Sprengard and Roderich Ptak. Wiesbaden: 125–50.

(1995) 'The straits of Ceylon, 1524–1539: the Portuguese–Mappilla struggle over a strategic area', *Santa Barbara Portuguese Studies* 2: 57–74.

(1998) *Os Portugueses e o Mar de Ceilão: Trato, Diplomacia e Guerra (1498–1543)*. Lisbon.

(2001b), 'Introduction', in Flores 2001a: 6–57 (see Primary Sources).

(2001c), *"Hum Curto Historia do Ceylan"; Five Hundred Years of Relations between Portugal and Sri Lanka*. Lisbon.

(ed.) (2007) *Re-exploring the Links: History and Constructed Histories between Portugal and Sri Lanka*. Wiesbaden.

Frazer, J. G. (1922) *The Golden Bough*. London.

Geertz, Clifford (1980) *Negara*. Princeton.

Geiger, Wilhelm (1960) *The Culture of Ceylon in Medieval Times*, ed. H. Bechert. Wiesbaden.

Godakumbura, C. E. (1955) *Sinhalese Literature*. Colombo.

(1966) 'Relations between Burma and Ceylon', *Journal of the Burma Research Society* 49: 145–62.

Goertz, R. O. W. (1986) 'The Portuguese in Cochin in the mid-sixteenth century', *Indica* 23: 63–78.

(1989) 'The Portuguese in Cochin in the mid-sixteenth century', *Studia* 49: 5–38.

Gombrich, Richard (1988) *Theravāda Buddhism: A Social History from Ancient Benares to Modern Colombo*. London.

Goonewardena, K. W. (1977) 'Kingship in seventeenth-century Sri Lanka', *Sri Lanka Journal of the Humanities* 3: 1–32.
Gschwend, Annemarie Jordan (1996) 'The marvels of the east: Renaissance curiosity collections in Portugal', in *The Heritage of Rauluchantim: Jewellery and Precious Objects from India to Portugal (XVI–XVIII Centuries)*, ed. Nuno Vassalo e Silva et al. Lisbon: 81–127.
Guedes, Maria Ana Marques (1994) *Interferência e Integração dos Portugueses na Birmânia, ca. 1580–1630*. Lisbon.
Gunasekera, Alex (1978) '*Rājākariya* or the duty to the king in the Kandyan Kingdom of Sri Lanka', in *The Concept of Duty in South Asia*, ed. Wendy Doniger O'Flaherty and J. Duncan M. Derret. New Delhi: 119–43.
Gunawardana, R. A. L. H. (1978) 'The kinsmen of the Buddha: myth as political charter in the ancient and early medieval kingdoms of Sri Lanka', in Smith 1978a: 96–106.
(1979) *Robe and Plough: Monasticism and Economic Interest in Early Medieval Sri Lanka*. Tucson.
(1990) 'The people of the lion: the Sinhala identity and ideology in history and historiography', in Spencer 1990: 45–86.
(1994) 'Colonialism, ethnicity and the construction of the past: the changing "ethnic identity" of the last four kings of the Kandyan kingdom', in *Pivot Politics: Changing Cultural Identities in Early State Formation Processes*, ed. Martin van Bakel, Renée Hagesteijn and Pieter van de Velde. Amsterdam: 197–221.
(1995) *Historiography in a Time of Ethnic Conflict: Construction of the Past in Contemporary Sri Lanka*. Colombo.
Hallisey, Charles (1988) 'Devotion in the Buddhist Literature of Medieval Sri Lanka', Ph.D. thesis, University of Chicago.
(1995) 'Roads taken and not taken in the study of Theravāda Buddhism', in *Curators of the Buddha: The Story of Buddhism Under Colonialism*, ed. Donald S. Lopez. Chicago: 31–61.
(2003) 'Works and persons in Sinhala literary culture', in *Literary Cultures in History: Reconstructions from South Asia*, ed. Sheldon Pollock. California: 689–745.
Hefner, Robert W. (ed.) (1993) *Conversion to Christianity: Historical and Anthropological Perspectives on a Great Transformation*. Berkeley.
Herath, D. (1994) *The Tooth Relic and The Crown*. Colombo.
Heusch, Luc de (2005) 'Forms of sacralized power in Africa', in Quigley 2005a: 25–37.
Hocart, A. M. (1927) *Kingship*. Oxford.
(1933) *The Progress of Man*. London.
Holt, John Clifford (1991) *Buddha in the Crown: Avalokiteśvara in the Buddhist Tradition of Sri Lanka*. Oxford.
(1996) *The Religious World of Kīrti Śrī: Buddhism, Art and Politics in Late Medieval Sri Lanka*. Oxford.
(2004) *The Buddhist Visnu: Religious Transformation, Politics and Culture*. New York.
(2007) 'Buddhist rebuttals: the changing of the gods and royal (re)legitimization in sixteenth and seventeenth century Sri Lanka', in Flores 2007: 145–69.
Holt, John Clifford, Kinnard, Jacob N., and Walters, Jonathan S. (eds.) (2003) *Constituting Communities: Theravāda Buddhism and the Religious Cultures of South and Southeast Asia*. New York.
Hsia, R. Po-chia (1998) *The World of Catholic Renewal, 1540–1770*. Cambridge.

Ilangasinha, H. B. M. (1992) *Buddhism in Medieval Sri Lanka*. Delhi.

Inden, Ronald, Walters, Jonathan, and Ali, Daud (eds.) (2000) *Querying the Medieval: Texts and the History of Practices in South Asia*. New York.

Jaffer, Amin (2004) 'Asia in Europe: furniture for the West', in *Encounters: The Meeting of Asia and Europe, 1500–1800*, ed. Anna Jackson and Amin Jaffer. London: 250–61.

Jaffer, Amin and Schwabe, Melanie Anne (1999) 'A group of sixteenth-century ivory caskets from Ceylon', *Apollo* 445: 3–14.

Jeganathan, Pradeep, and Ismail, Qadri (eds.) (1995) *Unmaking the Nation: The Politics of Identity and History in Modern Sri Lanka*. Colombo.

Kannangara, A. P. (1993) 'The rhetoric of caste status in modern Sri Lanka', in *Society and Ideology: Essays in South Asian History Presented to Professor K. A. Ballhatchet*, ed. Peter Robb. Delhi: 110–41.

Kantorowicz, E. H. (1957) *The King's Two Bodies: A Study in Medieval Political Theology*. Princeton.

Kapferer, B. (1988) *Legends of People, Myths of State*. Washington.

Keyes, Charles F. (1987) 'Theravāda Buddhism and its worldly transformations in Thailand: reflections on the work of S. J. Tambiah', *Contributions to Indian Sociology* 21: 123–45.

Kiribamune, Sirima (1978) 'Buddhism and royal prerogative in medieval Sri Lanka', in Smith 1978a: 107–11.

(1987) 'Trade patterns in the Indian Ocean and their impact on the politics of medieval Sri Lanka', *Modern Sri Lanka Studies* 2: 67–78.

Kriegel, Maurice, and Subrahmanyam, Sanjay (2000) 'The unity of opposites: Abraham Zacut, Vasco da Gama and the chronicler Gaspar Correia', in Disney and Booth: 48–71.

Kulasuriya, Ananda S. (1976) 'Regional independence and elite change in the politics of fourteenth-century Sri Lanka', *Journal of the Royal Asiatic Society of Great Britain and Ireland* 2: 136–55.

Levack, Brian P. (1995) *The Witch-Hunt in Early Modern Europe*. New York.

Lieberman, Victor (2003) *Strange Parallels: Southeast Asia in Global Context, c. 800–1830*. New York.

Liyanagamage, Amaradasa (1968) *The Decline of Polonnaruwa and the Rise of Dambadeniya, circa 1180–1270* AD Colombo.

Lockhart, James, (1994) 'Sightings: initial Nahua reactions to Spanish culture', in Schwarz 1994: 218–48.

Lopes, Fernando Félix (1949) *Fontes Narrativas e Textos Legais para a História da Ordem Franciscana em Portugal*. Lisbon.

(1962) 'Os Franciscanos no oriente Português de 1584 a 1590', *Studia* 9: 29–142.

(1967) 'A evangelização de Ceilão desde 1552 a 1602', *Studia* 20–2: 7–73.

Loureiro, Rui Manuel (1998) *A Biblioteca de Diogo do Couto*. Macao.

(2006) 'The matter of Ceylon in Diogo do Couto's Décadas da Ásia', in the (2007) 'The matter of Ceylon in Diogo do Couto's Décadas da Ásia', in Flores 2007: 79–93.

MacCormack, Sabine (1985) '"The heart has its reasons": predicaments of missionary Christianity in early colonial Peru', *Hispanic American Historical Review* 65: 443–66.

Malalasekera, G. P. (1994) *The Pāli Literature of Ceylon*. Kandy.

Malalgoda, K. (1976) *Buddhism in Sinhalese Society 1750–1900*. Berkeley.

(1997) 'Concepts and confrontations: a case study of *agama*', in Roberts 1997: 55–77.

(1999), '*Mandārampura Puvata*, an apocryphal chronicle', a paper presented to the Seventh Sri Lanka Studies Conference, Canberra, December 1999.

Manickam, S. (1983) 'The politico-economic implications of the religious conversions of the paravas in the gulf of Mannar, AD 1532–1552', *Tamil Civilization* 1: 57–73.

Mathew, K. S. (1989) 'The Portuguese and Malabar society during the sixteenth century: a study of mutual interaction', *Studia* 49: 39–68.

and Ahmed, Afzal (1990) *Emergence of Cochin in the Pre-Industrial Era: A Study of Portuguese Cochin*. Pondicherry.

McBrien, Richard P. (1994) *Catholicism*. London.

McPherson, Kenneth (1998) 'Uma história de duas conversões: deus, a cobiça e o desenvolvimento de novas comunidades na região do Oceano Índico', *Oceanos* 34: 74–85.

Mirando, A. H. (1985) *Buddhism in Sri Lanka in the Eighteenth and Nineteenth Centuries*. Dehiwala.

Missionação Portuguesa e Encontro de Culturas, Actas do Congresso Internacional de História (1993) (4 vols.). Braga.

Mulakara, G. (1986) *History of the Diocese of Cochin,* vol. I, *European Missionaries in Cochin (1292–1558)*. Rome.

Muldoon, James (1979) *Popes, Lawyers and Infidels*. Liverpool.

Mundadan, A. Mathias (1984) *History of Christianity in India,* vol. I, *From the Beginning up to the Middle of the Sixteenth Century*. Bangalore.

Muttukumaru, Anton (1987) *The Military History of Ceylon: An Outline*. Colombo.

Neill, Stephen Charles (1984) *A History of Christianity in India*. Cambridge.

Nissan, Elizabeth and Stirrat, R. L. (1990) 'The generation of communal identities', in Spencer 1990: 19–44.

Obeyesekere, Gananath (1979) 'Religion and polity in Theravāda Buddhism: continuity and change in a great tradition', *Comparative Studies in Society and History* 21: 626–39.

(1984) *The Cult of the Goddess Pattini*. Chicago.

(1995*a*) 'Buddhism, nationhood and cultural identity: a question of fundamentals', in *Fundamentalisms Comprehended*, ed. Martin E. Marty and R. Scott Appleby. Chicago: 231–56.

(1995*b*) 'On Buddhist identity in Sri Lanka', in *Ethnic Identity: Creation, Conflict and Accommodation*, ed. Lola Romanucci-Rossi and George A. de Vos. London: 222–41.

Oliveira e Costa, João Paulo (1994) 'Os Portugueses e a cristandade Siro-Malabar (1498–1530)', *Studia* 52: 121–78.

Oliveira e Costa, João Paulo, and Rodrigues, Victor Luís Gaspar (1992) *Portugal y Oriente: El Proyecto Indiano del Rey Juan*. Madrid.

Pagden, Anthony (1986) *The Fall of Natural Man: The American Indian and the Origins of Comparative Ethnology*. Cambridge.

Panabokke, G. (1993) *History of the Buddhist Sangha in Indian and Sri Lanka*. Colombo.

Paranavitana, S. (1953) *The Shrine of Upulvan at Devundara, Memoirs of the Royal Asiatic Survey of Ceylon*, vol. VI. Colombo.

(ed.) (1959–60), *University of Ceylon History of Ceylon*, 2 vols. Colombo.

Pathmanathan, S. (1982) 'South India and Sri Lanka, AD 1450–1650: political, commercial and cultural relations', *Journal of Tamil Studies* 21: 36–57.

Pearson, M. N. (1976) *Merchants and Rulers in Gujarat: The Response to the Portuguese in the Sixteenth Century*. Berkeley.

(1992) 'The search for the similar: early contacts between Portuguese and Indians', in *Clashes of Cultures: Essays in Honour of Niels Steensgard*, ed. Jens Christian V. Johansen, Erling Ladewig Petersen and Henrik Sternsberg. Odense: 144–59.

Pelikan, Jaroslav (1984) *The Christian Tradition: A History of the Development of Doctrine*, vol. VI, *Reformation of Church and Dogma*. Chicago.

Perera, E. W. (1910) 'The age of Śrī Parākrama Bāhu VI, 1412–1467', *Journal of the Royal Asiatic Society Colombo Branch* 22: 6–45.

Perera, S. G. (1951) *A History of Ceylon for Schools,* vol. I, *The Portuguese and Dutch Periods 1505–1796*. 5th edn. Colombo.

Perera, J. A. Will (1956) 'His patriotism: an appreciation', *Sir Paul Pieris Felicitation Volume*. Colombo: 21–3.

Phelan, John Leddy (1970) *The Millennial Kingdom of the Franciscans in the New World*. Berkeley.

Pieris, P. E. (1910–12) 'The date of King Bhuvaneka Bāhu VII', *Journal of the Royal Asiatic Society, Ceylon Branch* 22: 267–302.

(1983–92), *Ceylon: The Portuguese Era* (2 vols.). 2nd edn. (1st edn. 1913–14). Colombo.

Pieris, P. E., and Fitzler, M. A. H. (1927b), 'Introduction' to 1927a (see Primary Sources).

Pillay, K. K. (1963) *South India and* Ceylon. Madras.

Pollock, Sheldon (1998) 'India in the vernacular millennium: literary culture and polity, 1000–1500', *Daedalus* 127: 41–74.

Price, Pamela G. (1996) *Kingship and Political Practice in Colonial India*. Cambridge.

Quéré, Martin (1984) 'Francis Xavier and Sri Lanka', *Aquinas Journal* 1: 164–76.

(1987) 'Christianity in Kandy in the Portuguese period', *Aquinas Journal* 4: 52–79.

(1988a) 'Beginnings of the Portuguese mission in the Kingdom of Kōṭṭe', *Aquinas Journal* 5: 71–99.

(1988b) 'Christianity in the Kingdom of Kōṭṭe in the first years of Dharmapāla's Reign (1551–1558)', *Aquinas Journal* 5: 155–77.

(1995) *Christianity in Ceylon under the Portuguese Padroado, 1597–1658*. Colombo.

Quigley, Declan (ed.) (2005a) *The Character of Kingship*. Oxford.

(2005b) 'Introduction: The Character of Kingship' in Quigley 2005*a*: 1–23.

Raghavan, M. D. (1961) *The Karāva of Ceylon: Society and Culture*. Colombo.

(1964) *India in Ceylonese History, Society and Culture*. Bombay.

Rambukwelle, P. B. (1996) *The Period of Eight Kings*. Colombo.

Ranasinghe, Douglas D. (1969) *Kōṭṭe That Was*. Rajagiriya.

Raymond, Catherine (1995) 'Étude des relations religieuses entre le Sri Lanka et l'Arakan du XIIe au XVIIIe siècle: documentation historique et évidences achéologiques', *Journal Asiatique* 282: 469–501.

Rego, A. da Silva (1949) *História das Missões do Padroado Português do Oriente,* vol. I, *1500–42*. Lisbon.

Reid, Anthony (1988–93) *Southeast Asia in the Age of Commerce, 1450–1680* (2 vols.). Yale.

Reynolds, Craig J. (1995) 'A new look at old Southeast Asia', *Journal of Asian Studies* 54: 419–46.

Reynolds, Frank E. (1987) 'Trajectories in Theravāda studies with special reference to the works of S. Tambiah', *Contributions to Indian Sociology* 21: 113–21.

Ricard, Robert (1966) *The Spiritual Conquest of Mexico*. Berkeley.

Roberts, Michael (1984) 'Caste feudalism in Sri Lanka? A critique through the Asōkan persona and European contrasts', *Contributions to Indian Sociology* 18: 189–217.
(1995) *Caste Conflict and Elite Formation: The Rise of a Karāva Elite in Sri* Lanka. New Delhi.
(ed.) (1997) *Sri Lanka: Collective Identities Revisted*. Colombo.
(2001) 'Ethnicity after Said: Post-Orientalist failures in comprehending the Kandyan period of Lankan history', *Ethnic Studies Report* 19: 69–98.
(2004) *Sinhala Consciousness in the Kandyan period, 1590s–1815*. Colombo.
Roberts, Michael, Raheem, I., and Colin-Thomé, P. (1989) *People in Between,* vol. I, *The Burghers and the Middle Class in Transformations within Sri Lanka, 1790s–1960s*. Ratmalana.
Rogers, John D. (1994) 'Post-Orientalism and the interpretation of pre-modern and modern political identities: the case of Sri Lanka', *The Journal of Asian Studies* 53: 10–23.
(1995) 'Racial identities and politics in early modern Sri Lanka', in *The Concept of Race in South Asia*, ed. Peter Robb. Delhi: 146–64.
(2004a) 'Early British rule and social classification in Lanka', *Modern Asian Studies* 38: 625–47.
(2004b). 'Caste as a social category and identity in Colonial Lanka', *The Indian Economic and Social History Review* 41: 51–77
Rohandeera, Mendis (1996) 'Dharma Parākramabāhu IX: the false King of Ceylon inflated by Portuguese historians – a historiographical perspective', *Vidyodaya Journal of Social Sciences* 7: 13–45.
Rubiés, Joan-Pau (2000) *Travel and Ethnology in the Renaissance: South India through European Eyes*. Cambridge.
(2003) 'The Spanish contribution to the ethnology of Asia in the sixteenth and seventeenth centuries', *Renaissance Studies* 17: 418–48.
(2005) 'Oriental despotism and European orientalism: Botero to Montesquieu', *Journal of Early Modern History* 9: 109–80.
Ryan, B. (1993) *Caste in Modern Ceylon*. New Delhi.
Ryan, J. D. (1997) 'Conversion or baptism? European missionaries in Asia in the thirteenth and fourteenth centuries', in *Varieties of Religious Conversion in the Middle* Ages, ed. James Muldoon. Florida: 146–67.
Sabaratnam, Lakshmanan (2001) *Ethnic Attachments in Sri Lanka: Social Change and Cultural Continuity*. New York.
Sahlins, Marshall (1985) *Islands of History*. Chicago.
(1995) *How 'Natives' Think: About Captain Cook, for Example*. Chicago.
(2006) 'Depending on the kingness of strangers; or, elementary forms of the political life', a paper presented at the conference on 'Stranger-Kings in Southeast Asia and Elsewhere', Jakarta, 5–7 June 2006.
Saldanha, António Vasconcelos de (1991) 'O problema jurídico-político da incorporação de Ceilão na coroa de Portugal: os donativos dos reinos de Kōṭṭe, Kandy e Jaffna (1580–1633)', *Revista de Cultura* 13–14: 233–57.
(1993) 'Sobre o *officium missionandi* e a fundamentação jurídica da expansão Portuguesa', in *Missionação Portuguesa* 1993, III: 553–561.
(1997) *Iustum Imperium: Dos Tratados como Fundamento do Império dos Portugueses no Oriente*. Lisbon.
Sankaranarayan, K. C. (1994) *The Keralites and the Sinhalese*. Madras.

Santos, Catarina Madeira (1999) *Goa é a Chave de Todo a Índia: Perfil Político da Capital do Estado da Índia (1505–1570)*. Lisbon.

Schnepel, Burkhard (1995) *Twinned Beings: Kings and Effigies in Southern Sudan, East India and Renaissance France*. Göteborg.

(2005) 'Kings and tribes in East India: the internal political dimension', in Quigley 2005: 187–207.

Schurhammer, Georg (1973–82) *Francis Xavier: his Life, his Times*, trans. M. J. Costelloe (4 vols.). Rome.

Schwabe, Melanie Anne (2000) 'Schatzkunst auf Ceylon', in *Exotica: Portugals Entdeckungen im Spiegel fürstlicher Kunst- und Wunderkammern der Renaissance*, ed. Wilfried Seipel. Vienna: 101–4.

Schwarz, Benjamin I. (1975) 'The age of transcendence', *Daedalus* 104: 1–7.

Schwarz, S. (ed.) (1994) *Implicit Understandings: Observing, Reporting and Reflecting on the Encounters between European and Other Peoples in the Early Modern Era*. Cambridge

Scott, David (1994) *Formations of Ritual: Colonial and Anthropological Discourses on the Sinhala Yaktovil*. Minneapolis.

Seneviratne, H. L. (1978), *Rituals of the Kandyan State*. Cambridge.

(1987) 'Kingship and polity in Buddhism and Hinduism', *Contributions to Indian Sociology* 21: 147–55.

(ed.) (1997) *Identity, Consciousness and the Past: Forging of Caste and Community in India and Sri Lanka*. New Delhi.

Seneviratne, J., (1913) 'Berendi Kovil', *Ceylon Notes and Queries, Royal Asiatic Society Ceylon Branch*, part ii.

Silber, Ivana (1995) *Virtuosity, Charisma and Social Order: A Comparative Sociological Study of Monasticism in Theravada Buddhism and Medieval Catholicism*. Cambridge.

Singhaputhra-Coalition for the Preservation of the Sinhala Nation for LankaWeb (2004), 'The Wickremasinghe Betrayal of the Sinhala Nation' <http://www.lankaweb.com/news/items03/040103-2.html>, accessed 20 March 2004.

Siriweera, W. I. (1971) 'The theory of the king's ownership of land in ancient Ceylon: an essay in historical revision', *Ceylon Journal of Historical and Social Studies* 1: 48–61.

(1972) 'Land tenure and revenue in medieval Ceylon (AD 1000–1500), *Ceylon Journal of Historical and Social Studies* 2: 1–49.

(1993/5) 'The city of Jayawardena Kōṭṭe: history, form and functions', *Sri Lanka Journal of the Humanities* 19: 1–22.

(2002) *History of Sri Lanka*. Colombo.

Sivasundaram, Sujit (2007) 'Buddhist kingship, British archaeology and historicism in Sri Lanka, *c*. 1750–1850', *Past and Present* 197.

Smith, A.D. (1991) *National Identity*. London.

Smith, Bardwell L. (ed.) (1978a), *Religion and the Legitimation of Power in Sri Lanka*. Chambersburg.

(ed.) (1978b) *Religion and Legitimation of Power in Thailand, Laos and Burma*. Chambersburg.

(1978c) 'The ideal social order as portrayed in the chronicles of Ceylon', in Smith 1978a: 48–72.

(1978d) 'Kingship, the Sangha and the process of legitimation in Anurādhapura period Ceylon: an interpretative essay', in Smith 1978a: 73–95.

(1987) 'Varieties of religious assimilation in early medieval Sri Lanka', in *Buddhist Philosophy and Culture: Essays in Honour of N. A. Jayawickrema*, ed. David J. Kalupahana and W. G. Weeraratne. Colombo: 257–78.

Somaratna [or Somoratna], G. P. V. (1975) *Political History of the Kingdom of Kōṭṭe, 1400–1521*. Colombo.

(1991) 'Rules of succession to the throne of Kōṭṭe', *Aquinas Journal* 8:17–32.

Spencer, Jonathan (ed.) (1990) *Sri Lanka: History and the Roots of Conflict*. London.

(1995) 'The past in the present in Sri Lanka: a review article', *Comparative Studies in Society and History* 37: 358–67.

Stewart, Charles (1999) 'Syncretism and its synonyms: reflections on cultural mixture', *Diacritics* 19: 40–62.

Strathern, Alan (1998) 'Representing eastern religion: Queirós and Gonzaga on the first Christian–Buddhist debate in Sri Lanka, 1543', *Journal of the Royal Asiatic Society of Sri Lanka* 43: 39–70.

(2000) 'Re-reading Queirós: some neglected aspects of the *Conquista*', *Sri Lanka Journal of the Humanities* 26: 1–28.

(2002) 'Bhuvanekabāhu VII and the Portuguese: Temporal and Spiritual Encounters in Sri Lanka, 1521–1551', D.Phil. thesis, University of Oxford.

(2004a) 'Theoretical approaches to Sri Lankan history and the early Portuguese period', *Modern Asian Studies* 38: 189–226.

(2004b) '*Os Piedosos* and the mission in India and Sri Lanka in the 1540s', in Carneiro and Matos: 855–64.

(2005) 'Fernão de Queirós: history and theology', in *Anais de História de Além-mar* 6: 47–88.

(2006a), 'Towards the source-criticism of Sitavakan heroic literature, part one. *The Alakesvara Yuddhaya*: notes on a floating text', *Sri Lanka Journal of the Humanities* 32: 23–39.

(2006b), *The Royal 'We': Sinhala Identity in the Dynastic State*, a review of 'Sinhala Consciousness in the Kandyan Period 1590s to 1815' by Michael Roberts, reprinted from *Modern Asian Studies* 39 (2005): 1013–26, as a pamphlet for the Social Scientists' Association, Colombo.

(2007a) 'The conversion of rulers in Portuguese-era Sri Lanka', in Flores 2007: 127–43.

(2007b) 'Transcendentalist intransigence: why rulers rejected monotheism in early modern Southeast Asia and beyond', *Comparative Studies in Society and History* 49, 358–83.

(forthcoming a) 'A note on the role of Sinhala group identity in the "Sinhala rebellion", against Bhuvanekabāhu VI (1469–77)', in *Ethnic Studies Report*.

(forthcoming b) 'Towards the source-criticism of Sītāvakan heroic literature, part two. The *Sītāvaka Haṭana*: notes on a grounded text', in *Sri Lanka Journal of the Humanities*.

(forthcoming c) 'Sri Lanka in the long early modern period: its place in a comparative theory of second millennium Eurasian history', in *Modern Asian Studies*.

(unpublished) 'Sri Lanka in the Missionary Conjuncture of the 1540s'.

Sturm, Fred Gillette (1985) '"Estes têm alma como nós?"' Manuel de Nóbrega's view of the Brazilian Indians', in *Empire in Transition: The Portuguese World in the Time of Camões*, ed. Alfred Hower and Richard A. Preto-Rodas. Gainesville: 72–82.

Subrahmanyam, Sanjay (1987) 'Cochin in decline 1600–1650: myth and manipulation in the *Estado da Índia*', in *Portuguese Asia: Aspects in History and Economic History (Sixteenth and Seventeenth Centuries)*, ed. Roderich Ptak. Stuttgart: 59–85

(1990) 'The tail wags the dog: sub-imperialism and the *Estado da Índia*, 1570–1600', in *Improvising Empire: Portuguese Trade and Settlement in the Bay of Bengal, 1500–1700*, ed. Sanjay Subrahmanyam. Delhi: 137–60.

(1993) *The Portuguese Empire in Asia 1500–700: A Political and Economic History*. London.

(1997) 'Connected histories: notes towards a reconfiguration of Early Modern Eurasia', *Modern Asian Studies* 31: 735–62.

(2005a) *Explorations in Connected History: From the Tagus to the Ganges*. Oxford.

(2005b) *Explorations in Connected History: Mughals and Franks*. Oxford.

Tambiah, S. J. (1976) *World Conqueror and World Renouncer: A Study of Buddhism and Polity in Thailand against a Historical Background*. Cambridge.

(1985) *Culture, Thought and Social Action*. Harvard.

(1987) 'At the confluence of anthropology, history and indology', *Contributions to Indian Sociology* 21: 187–216.

(1992) *Buddhism Betrayed? Religion, Politics and Violence in Sri Lanka*. Chicago.

Tavim, José Alberto Rodrigues da Silva (1995) 'From Setúbal to the Sublime Porte: the wanderings of Jácome de Olivares, New Christian and merchant of Cochin (1540–1571)', *Santa Barbara Portuguese Studies* 2: 94–134.

(1997) *O Rei que foi em Peregrinação a Varanasi*. Lisbon.

Thomaz, Luís Filipe F. R. (1985) 'Estrutura política e administrativa do Estado da Índia no século XVI', in *II Seminário Internacional de História Indo-Portuguesa*, ed. Luís de Albuquerque and Inácio Guerreiro. Lisbon: 511–540.

(1993) 'Descobrimentos e evangelização: da cruzada à missão pacífica', in *Missionação Portuguesa* 1993, I: 81–129.

(1998) *A Questão da Pimenta em Meados do Século XVI: Um Debate Político do Governo de D. João de Castro*. Lisbon.

Thornton, J. (1984) 'The development of an African Catholic Church in the Kingdom of Kongo, 1491–1750', *Journal of African History* 25: 147–67.

Tolstoy, Leo (1997) *War and Peace*. London (Penguin Classics).

Vassallo e Silva, Nuno (2007) 'An art for export: Sinhalese ivory and crystal in the 16th and 17th centuries', in Flores 2007: 279–95.

Viterbo, Sousa (1904) *O Thesouro do Rei de Ceylão*. Lisbon.

Walters, Jonathan S. (1991–2) 'Vibhīṣaṇa and Vijayanagar: an essay on religion and geopolitics in medieval Sri Lanka', *Sri Lanka Journal of the Humanities* 12/13: 129–42.

(1995) 'Multireligion on the bus: beyond "influence" and "syncretism" in the study of religious meetings', in Jeganathan and Ismail: 24–54.

(1996) *The History of Kelaniya*. Colombo.

(2000) 'Buddhist history: the Sri Lankan Pāli vamsas and their community', in Inden, Walters and Ali: 99–164.

Weerasooria, N. E. (1970) *Ceylon and her People*, vol. I. Colombo.

Werake, K. M. M. (1987) 'A Re-examination of Chinese relations with Sri Lanka during the fifteenth century AD', *Modern Sri Lanka Studies* 2: 89–102.

Wickremesekera, Channa (2004) *Kandy at War: Indigenous Military Resistance to European Expansion in Sri Lanka, 1594–1818*. New Delhi.

Willis, John E. Jr. (2000) 'Was there a Vasco da Gama epoch? Recent historiography', in Disney and Booth: 350–60.

Winius, George D. (1971)*The Fatal History of Portuguese Ceylon*. Cambridge, Mass.

(1985) *The Black Legend of Portuguese India*. New Delhi.

(2000) 'Few thanks to the king: the building of Portuguese India', in Disney and Booth: 484–95.

and Diffie, Bailey (1977) *Foundations of the Portuguese Empire 1415–1580*. Minneapolis.

Xavier, Angela Barreto (2003) 'A Invenção de Goa – Poder Imperial e Converções Culturais nos Séculos XVI e XVII', Ph.D. diss., European University Institute, Florence.

(2004), '"Aparejo y dispoción para se reformar y criar otro nuevo mundo". A evangelização dos indianos e a política imperial joanina', in Carneiro and Matos: 783–805.

(unpublished) 'Uneasiness in the village: alliances, conflicts and conformity between Jesuits and local populations (Goa, 16th Century)'.

Yalman, Nur (1997) 'On royalty, caste and temples in Sri Lanka and South India', in *Identity, Consciousness and the Past: Forging of Caste and Community in India and Sri Lanka*, ed. H. L. Seneviratne. New Delhi: 136–46.

Young, R. F. (1989) 'Francis Xavier in the perspective of the Saivite Brahmins of Tiruchendur Temple', in *Hindu-Christian Dialogue: Perspectives and Encounters*, ed. Harold G. Coward. New York: 64–79.

and Somaratna, G. P. V. (1996) *Vain Debates: The Buddhist–Christian controversies of Nineteenth Century Ceylon*. Vienna.

Županov, Ines G. (2005) *Missionary Tropics. The Catholic Frontier in India (16th–17th centuries*. Ann Arbor.

INDEX

Arakan (Mrauk-U) 216
Asgiriye Talpatha 18, 192
Aśōka 146, 150
Axial Age 8–9, 12, 86, 125, 146, 149, 241, 251
Ayora, Francisco de 43, 108
Azevedo, Agostino de 15, 153, 186, 229, 238
Azevedo, Gaspar de 54, 66
Azevedo, Jerónimo de 197, 210–11, 224, 226, 230, 247

Bärändi Kōvil 184
Barbosa, Duarte 30, 32
Barbudo, Duarte 42, 100, 102, 103, 106, 108–9, 162
Barreto, António, see Kuruvita Rāla
Barreto, António Moniz 46, 80, 175
 expedition to Kandy 73, 156, 158, 160, 211
Barreto, M. Nunes, Rector of the Jesuit College of Cochin 88, 90, 95
Barros, João de 15, 103, 149, 237
Batticaloa 26, 96, 156, 158
 Prince or Chief of 24, 145, 156, 157
Bayinnaug, King of Burma 212
Bayly, Susan 93, 96
Bermúdez, Diego 110, 116, 168
bhikkhus 10, 86–7, 129–30, 131–2, 162, 164, 188–9, 190, 192, 216, 229, 244
Bhuvanekabāhu VI 127, 130, 232
Bhuvanekabāhu VII *passim*, and 2–3, 144, 212
 and acceptance of vassalage 24, 72
 age 24
 attitude towards conversion 85, 107, 119, 153, 161–3, 166
 character of 2–3, 63, 111, 166
  as sodomite 3, 122
  as tyrant 3, 63, 122–3
 coming to the throne 23–4, 26–7
 complaints against Portuguese 54, 56–7, 60
  in memorial of 1541 55–6, 62, 80, 99–100
 criticisms of, by locals 154–5, 249
 death 75, 80, 154, 167–8, 185
 mediation of letters 54, 128–9, 163
 patronage of and interest in Christianity 87, 109, 161
 patronage of Buddhism 130
 popularity and legitimacy amongst subjects 75–80, 99–105
 Portuguese representation of 34, 61
 personal religious beliefs 162, 166, 185
 religious policy 72, 99–112, 173, 187, 242
 sannas 17, 25, 31
 self-representation of his authority 61–4
 symbiotic relationship with Portuguese 49–51, 71, 72
 understanding of vassalage to Portuguese 63–4, 99
Biedermann, Zoltán 7, 16
Bintänna 30, 156, 160, 182, 216
Bocarro, António 230, 231, 232, 233, 239–40
bodhisattva 126, 133, 146, 150, 152, 216
Botelho, Filipe 243, 244, 247, 251
Botelho, Simão 37, 50, 216
Bragança, Constantino de 175
Brahmans 92, 93, 128, 144, 185, 191, 217, 237, 241
Brahmanization 96, 97, 99, 127–8, 135, 146, 155, 165
Brazil 115, 118, 120, 206
Buddha 152, 153, 165–6, 198, 225
 presence in Sri Lanka 5, 12, 154, 155, 183, 195
Buddhism 5, 10, 12–13, 98, 125, 158, 165–6, 170, 175, 184, 198, 202, 218, 229
 overview of soteriology 125–6
 and conversion, heresy 134–7, 146–8, 185, 188–9, 198, 219–21, 232–3, 243–4

Cabral, Jorge 50
Cabral, Pedro Álvares 22
cakravarti-ship, origins and nature of concept 25–6, 33, 146, 150, 179
Calicut 24, 37, 55, 71, 94
 Samorin of 21, 22–3, 32

Camões 199
Caṇkili, King of Jaffna 72, 95, 104–5, 107, 116, 156, 167–93
Cannanore 22, 34, 94
  Mamale of 22, 23
  Kōḷaṭhiri of Eli, a.k.a. King of Cannanore 22–3, 55, 90
Caração, Cristovão Lourenço 22, 30, 51, 100, 123
Carrithers, Michael 133
Carvalho, Miguel de 42
Casados and *moradores* 30
  acceptance of local norms 199
  commercial misdemeanours 55–6
  complaints about Bhuvanekabāhu 50, 63, 64, 108, 109–10
  imperial role 43–4
  oral traditions and mentality in later 16th century 170, 186, 190, 194–8, 218, 224
  trading opportunities in Colombo 55
Casal, António do 87, 110
caskets, Sri Lankan ivory 17, 27, 66, 73–5, 79, 136, 152, 162, 185, 215
casta 91, 98, 153
Castanheda, Fernão Lopes de 15, 32
caste, in India, and its consequences for conversion 91–4
caste, in Sri Lanka 7, 178–9, 207, 238, 248–9
  and conversion of rulers 152–3, 182
  overview 96–7
Castilians 167, 214, 230–1, 247
Castro, João de 42–3, 48, 55, 72, 73–5, 102, 108–9, 119, 144
Castro, Jorge de 50, 59–60, 75, 87, 211–12
Catarina, Princess of Kandy, a.k.a Kusumāsanadēvi 166, 214–15, 218
Catarina, Queen of Portugal 39
Cervantes 1
Chaliyam 22–3
changatar (saṃghatthēras) 128, 131, 132, 187, 229
Chaul 85
Chilaw 24, 56, 220
  Prince of 63, 78
China 65, 245
Cinnamon 21, 31, 33, 37, 43, 47, 48, 50, 56, 70, 176
  captain of cinnamon ship 43, 56, 63, 73
  contract of 1533 50, 70
  liberalization of trade 56
civility 45, 120–4
Cochin 10, 22, 33, 36, 37–40, 44, 54, 55, 61–2, 88–9, 90–1, 92, 94, 100, 161
  Raja of 22, 23, 34, 37–40, 44, 54, 55, 62, 66, 70, 71, 80–1, 88–9, 94, 100, 103, 111–12, 143, 161, 163, 183
  See Rāma Varma
Coimbra, Simão de 108, 109, 113, 117–18, 144, 145, 153, 156, 157, 211
Colombo 21, 80, 167–8, 215, 222, 223, 227, 237
  besieged 22, 176, 188, 190
  as a Catholic city 194–206, 223, 247
  depopulation 56, 57
  fort built, dismantled and rebuilt 23, 42, 47–8, 49, 70, 168
  location 31
  trade 40, 55
Comparison
  of Amerindian and Sinhalese society 120, 124
  of Ancient Greek and Lankan identity 8, 246
  of Britishness and Lankanness 236
  of Buddhist and Hindu sacred kingship 145–56
  of Koṭṭe and great territorial powers of India 24, 31
  of Malabar coastal kingdoms and Sri Lanka: *passim*, see Malabar, Cochin
  of monotheistic and Indic forms of transcendentalism 125, 126, 130, 251
  of *piedosos* and *bhikkhus* 86–7
  of Polynesia and Sri Lanka 14, 149
  of Portuguese and Sinhalese 10, 29, 39
    kingship and vassalage 51, 124, 141, 150, 231
    practices of overlordship, imperialism 64–5
    systems of land, property and inheritance 102–3, 123–4
  of Portuguese and British empires 46, 237, 238
  of Rājasiṃha and Alexander the Great 191
  of sacred kingship systems 8–10, 11–14, 174
  of sixteenth-century England and Sri Lanka 107, 249
  of Theravāda and Catholic monasticism 126, 129–30
    notion of identity 134–7, 232–3, 242
    religiosity 132–7, 164
Conde, João de Vila do 63, 72, 102, 106, 108, 110, 117, 119–20, 161
confessionalism 242, 244
Congo, King of 113, 122
contractualism
  political 29, 141–2, 146
  religious 142, 148, 149, 150, 151, 153, 250–1
conversion, *passim*
  academic definition 6–7
  and becoming Portuguese 90, 100, 104, 108, 120–4
  and exclusivist identity 9, 87, 136, 157, 158, 189, 233
  'forced' 113, 114, 118, 119, 218–21
Lankan conception of conversion 134–7, 188–9, 198, 199–205, 219–21, 224, 225, 232–3, 243–4

and marginality
to Christianity 157–8
cultural-religious 96, 97–8, 158–9
monarchical 159
political 160–1, 208–9, 213
social 95–6 (and see caste)
motivations for 88, 90, 95–6, 113–20, 143–5, 156–61, 196–210, 212, 213
organic conversion 86
and ostracization 91, 92, 153
and peoples of the sea 94–6, 97–8, 104–5, 158–9
Portuguese concept of 106, 111, 113–17, 120, 121, 172, 242
rate and extent of in Koṭṭe 86, 97–8, 112, 171, 196–7
and social separation 88–9, 121–2
and sequestration of property 91, 94, 100–4, 110, 112, 123–4, 242
conversion of rulers 8, 132, 156–61, 208–9, 212–14, 233
and the consequences for legitimacy 8, 14, 142, 145, 146–8, 153, 154–5, 161, 162, 164–75, 183–93, 213–14, 250–1
in return for Portuguese support 59, 85, 105, 107, 157–8, 160, 208–9, 212, 213
and popular displeasure in Malabar and Sri Lanka 143–5
converts, legal and political status of 88–91, 99–104, 105, 107, 242
elite of Koṭṭe 98–9, 182–3
persecution of 108, 109–11, *see* conversion and sequestration
Correa, Simão 223, 224–5, 229
Correia, Gaspar 15, 57, 78, 79
Counter-Reformation 85, 118, 197–8, 242
Coutinho, Gonçalo Vaz 50
Coutinho, Manuel Rodrigues 42, 50, 52
Coutinho, Manuel de Sousa 213
Couto, Diogo do 15, 16, 33, 164, 169, 170, 185, 186–7, 190–2, 195, 197, 220
Cranganore 22, 94
Cūḷavaṃsa 5, 147, 185, 188

Dantūrē, Battle of 215, 221, 223
dasarājadhamma 146, 155, 159
De Nobili, Roberto 92, 122, 205
De Silva, C. R. 6, 58, 171, 235, 243
Devinuvara 17, 110–11, 162, 187–8, 197
dhammadīpa 5, 183
Dharmapāla 3, 4, 52, 61, 66, 80, 104, 107, 176, 198–9, 207, 224, 231, 239, 248
Bequest of his imperial title to Portugal 27, 174, 198, 206, 210–11, 245
conversion and its consequences 131, 136, 144–5, 152, 153, 154–5, 168–9, 171–5, 184, 189, 194, 213, 242
Death 221
Defections to from Sītāvaka 189, 194, 206, 207, 208, 209, 210, 245
Marriage 160
Succession contested 79, 105–6
Vision of co-rule with Portuguese 210
diabolism 195, 218
Dias, António 57, 98, 131
Dias, Manuel 220
Dirks, Nicholas 92
disputation of 1543 120, 123, 162, 164, 166, 241
Diu, siege of 21, 42, 46, 73
Dominicans 116
Duarte, King of Portugal 120
Du Jarric, Pierre 15
Duncan, James S. 150
Dutch 16, 199, 216, 217, 219, 221–2, 237, 246–7
Duṭugämunu 13, 155
dynastic loyalty 14, 182, 211, 231, 244, 247

ear-piercing 218, 220–1, 223, 224
Edirillē Rāla
Edirimansūriya 154
Elizabeth I of England 249, 251
Estado da Índia (Portuguese 'empire' in Asia) 11, 56, 58, 60, 63, 75, 104, 111, 114, 116, 197, 206
corruption 41–2, 44–6
economic policy 46–8
as 'empire' 35
extent 35, 41
governor/viceroy, office of 41–2
heterogeneity of Portuguese expansion 46, 51
'imperial' vs. 'liberal' factions 47
numbers of Portuguese in East 35
policy towards Sri Lanka 47–8, 50, 56, 58, 197, 206, 212
problems of communication and governance 41–6, 64, 72
responding *ad hoc* to individuals 58–60
Estremadura, Province of San Gabriel de 86, 117
Ethnicity, ethnic identity/consciousness 75, 177, 179, 208, 211, 215, 221–2, 230–1, 235–40
defined 7–8, 236
Eutico, Padre 198
extra-territoriality and judicial boundaries 40–1, 55, 89, 99–100, 107, 111

factor (*feitor*) of Colombo 42, 43, 44, 49, 50, 52, 53–4, 56, 63, 64, 66, 72
Faria e Sousa, Manuel de 15
Federici, Cesare 176
Ferreira, António 57, 64
Ferreira, Miguel 3, 51, 53, 58
Filipe, Prince of Kandy, *see* Yamasiṃha
Filipe, Prince of Sītāvaka, *see* Nikapiṭiye Baṇḍāra
Flores, Jorge Manuel 6, 10, 42, 47, 58

Four Kōraḷēs 182, 225, 226, 246
Franciscans 15, 119–20, 143, 171, 195, 205, 210, 211, 214, 218–20, 223, 227–8, 242
attitude to conversion 114–15, 116–17, 220
requested by Bhuvanekabāhu 88
shaping Colombo mentality 195
See piedosos
Francisco mudali 189, 212
Frazer, James 11, 13

Gajabāhu II 147
galactic polity 27–31, 71, 78, 142, 146, 159, 222, 231
Galle 30, 59
Gama, Estevão da 39, 62
Gama, Vasco da 47
Garcês, João 47–8, 183
Geertz, Clifford 27
Goa
First Ecclesiastical Council of 114, 116, 197
Inquisition 224, 233
as manifestation of spiritual power 161, 171, 213
Sinhalese/refugees informants in 186, 190, 209, 212–13
Tightening of mission 168
Gonçalves, Diogo de 91
Gonzaga, Francesco 15, 98, 100, 101–2, 103, 106, 123, 131, 162, 166
Greeks, ancient and identity 8, 246
Guadalupe, Juan de 117, 130
Gunawardana, R. A. L. H. 221, 245

Hallisey, Charles 134
Hanvälla, battle of 208, 209
Hāpiṭigam Kōraḷē, rebellion in 78
Haṭanas 17, 176, 239, 240
heroic politics and ethos 7, 14
Hinduization 127, 151, 152, 158–9, 179, 183–93, 241
resisted, attacked 127, 134, 153, 155, 165, 189
historicism 5, 25–6, 91, 98, 126, 129, 133, 142, 148, 221–2, 224, 236, 245
Hobbes, Thomas 146
Hocart, A. M. 11
Holt, John Clifford 126, 132, 134, 187, 192

Ilangasinha, H. B. M. 97–8, 127, 131, 188
Indian immigration into Sri Lanka 32–3, 95, 127–8, 160, 176, 185, 215, 217, 241
Indic traditions 9, 12, 96, 133, 145–6, 149, 165, 166, 192
indigenism 8, 80, 167, 177, 196, 206, 207–8, 214, 215, 220, 227, 232, 233, 235–40, 241
conspicuous indigenization 220, 228, 241
defined 7
Indra 149, 152
Irava 92, 94, 96

Jaffer, Amin and Melanie Schwabe 73, 198
Jaffna 1, 26, 27, 63, 79, 80, 89, 104, 107, 108, 116, 127, 158, 167, 175, 177, 192, 226, 228, 232, 237
James, St 167, 195
Janavaṃsa 98
jāti(ya) 97, 178–9, 239
Jayavīra a.k.a. Vikramabāhu, King of Kandy 17, 29–31, 109, 143, 145, 155, 156, 157–8, 159, 160, 211–12
Jayavīra Baṇḍāra, *see* Manamperuma Mohottāla
Jesuits 15, 57, 85, 105–6, 112, 115, 118, 122, 128, 129, 131–2, 168, 196, 197, 205, 213, 219, 220, 226, 229
João, Prince of Koṭṭe 107, 108, 213
João, Prince, son of Yamasiṃha 186, 214
João, son of Bhuvanekabahu VII 144, 213
João III of Portugal 29, 37, 47, 62, 66, 70, 73, 94, 107, 108, 114, 120, 121
decrees of 1543 for Sri Lanka 56–7, 61, 62, 63, 99–100, 112
Jugo, Prince of Koṭṭe 29, 66, 105, 107, 116
Juzarte, Martim Afonso de Melo 33

kaḍaim pot 26
Kälaṇiya 75, 130, 167, 172, 182, 197
Kaňdurē Baṇḍāra 30, 78, 128, 160
Kaňdurē Baṇḍāravaliya 29, 32, 128, 160
Kandy 26, 27, 42, 72–3, 97, 99, 105, 110, 127, 141, 152, 155, 159–60, 166, 175, 192–3, 197, 208, 211–21, 232, 244, 245, 248
annexed by Sitavaka 1582 176, 186, 188, 189, 212
Christian experiment in 1589–90 193, 194, 211–15, 219
desertions/defections to 215, 221, 224, 226–7, 234, 246
hostility to Rājasiṃha 186, 189, 190
invaded by Koṭṭe/Portuguese 208
King of 17, 45, 46, 51, 65, 75, 78, 166, 192
flirts with conversion 59, 85, 106, 107, 109, 110, 116, 117, 119, 143–4, 145, 153, 155, 156–8, 162, 212
as overlord 27, 29, 156, 159, 160
patronage of Buddhism 159
requests vassalage 24
See Jayavīra, Vikramabāhu , Karaliyaddē, Vimaladharmasūriya etc
rebellion against Rājasiṃha 206, 212–14
relations with Arakan 216
relationship with anti-Portuguese rebellion 221–2, 225–8, 229, 230, 246

Kāngara Āracci 226, 227
Kapferer, Bruce 10, 12–13
Karaliyaddē Baṇḍāra 109, 118, 153, 212, 213, 214
as a Christian 157, 211–12, 217
Karāva 32, 52, 94–5, 97–8, 99, 127, 128, 159
mass conversion 1556–7 95–6, 98, 171
Karayār 95, 104; *see* Mannar
Kataragama 151, 177, 180–1
Kings, Kingship, Lankan
dynastic ancestry, solar lineage of 10, 11, 12, 142, 147, 152–3, 159, 162, 167, 182, 198, 207, 210, 215, 227–9, 238, 247
anthropology of 11–14
and persisting authority of royal family post-1590 225, 227–9, 246
and the control of manpower 141–2, 168, 169, 173, 189, 222, 231, 246, 249
fabrication of royalty 227–9, 231, 246
as fissiparous 30, 222, 228
and importance of queens 10, 207
and the 'king's two bodies' 14
and order 11–14, 146, 149, 154, 181
outside/within society 11–12, 141
and parricide 11, 231
and the problem of succession 10, 11, 30, 71, 78, 142, 161, 187, 206, 231
and the redistribution of wealth 10, 173, 181, 207, 208
rite of consecration, acclamation 141, 159, 210, 215, 249
sliding scale of rulership 142, 159, 224
symbolism of king-creation 11, 12
see legitimacy of rulers
Kingship, Portuguese 29, 51
Kingship, sacred imagery and discourses of 142, 145–56, 183–93, 196, 216, 250–1
and communal soteriology 155, 189
and cosmopolitan patronage 148–9, 184–5, 188, 218
as divine beings 149–50, 151, 191–2, 211
and the injunction to be Buddhist 146–8, 155, 174–5, 249
mystical connection to welfare of land 149, 154
tripartite typology of sacred kingship 149–50
Knox, Robert 97, 99, 124, 237
Kollam 22, 33, 40, 65, 70, 71, 89, 100
Konappu Baṇḍāra, *see* Vimaladharmasūriya
Kōṭṭe, *passim*
city of
abandoned 1565 152, 172, 194
archaeology and physical structures of 16, 129, 150–2
as Catholic city 194–206
revolt of 1557 172
strategic position 31
kingdom of
administrative system 51–3, 100–2, 141
chamberlain of, *see* Tammiṭa Sembaha Perumāl
Christian elite 98–9, 182–3, 196, 198–9, 206, 209, 223, 224–5, 227, 228, 233, 238, 247
'division' of 27
geographical extent of authority 26
military capability 32–3
nature of authority 25
purōhita of, see Śrī Rāmarakṣa Paṇḍita
resources and economic, commercial aspects 31–2
royal audience 53
royal guard of 52–3, 54, 63, 66, 71, 72, 128
kings of, chronology of reigns 23
princes of 24, 59, 72, 75, 85, 98, 105, 107–8, 161, 213
See also Jugo, Luís, etc.
kṣatriya 10, 149, 153, 159, 215, 248–9
kula, kulavadda 97, 135, 169
Kuruvita Rāla a.k.a António Barreto 226, 227–8, 229
Kustantinu Haṭana 227, 247

Lacerda, Afonso Pereira de 170
Lafitau, Joseph-François 15
land tenure 10–11, 56, 100–4, 123–4, 141
system of in Kōṭṭe 100–2
lascarins 97, 187, 213, 215, 229, 247–8, 249
defections 215, 221, 223, 226–7, 232, 234, 235, 246
Las Casas, Bartolomé de 114, 116
Laukika 125, 191, 218
legitimacy of rulers, principles of 10, 180–1, 189, 211, 215
notion of 'legitimization' 142–3
legitimacy of Portuguese rule 210–11, 214–15, 221–3, 232, 247
Lemos, Fernão Gomes de 49
Lieberman, Victor 206
Linschoten, J. H. van 16, 186, 189
Lisboa, Gaspar de 15
Lisbon 33, 38, 56, 61, 72, 86, 162, 173, 206, 218
Embassy to 1541–3 27, 39, 43, 52, 65–6, 73, 85, 88, 106, 111, 119, 128, 162–3
Locke, John 124
lōkōttara 125–6, 133, 218
Lomba, Afonso Dias de 218
Lucas, Fra. 219
Lucena, João de 15
Luís, Prince, of Portugal 39, 57, 62
Luís, Prince, of Koṭṭe 79, 107, 213
LTTE 4
Lusitanization 124, 136, 171, 217, 219, 223, 224, 233, 239, 241

Macedo, Duarte Teixeira de 43
Māgha 147, 188
Mahāsammata 146, 147, 152, 153–4, 198, 238
Mahasen Mahā Pāya 151
Mahāvaṃsa 5, 155, 183
Mahāyāna 133, 147
Magic, sorcery 190, 195
Malabar Coast 10–11, 21–4, 30, 31–2, 36–40, 55, 56, 104, 106, 123, 143–5, 146, 160, 161, 163, 176
 conversion movements in 96, 152
 supplying mercenaries 32–3
Malabar rites controversies 144, 220
Maldives 11, 116, 145
Malvāna 211, 239, 247
Manamperuma Mohottāla a.k.a. Ariṭṭa Kīvenḍu Perumāl a.k.a. Jayavīra Banḍāra 181, 185, 207–9, 210, 214–15, 246
 deserted by troops 207, 208
 xenophobic/religious reaction to 207–8
Mandārampura-Puvata 17, 188, 192
Māniyamgama temple in Avissāvēlla 18, 192
Mannar 196, 209, 212, 213, 214, 215, 237
 mass baptism 95, 104
 massacre 104–5, 116
 pearl fishery 32, 95
Manuel I, King of Portugal 11, 37, 38, 39, 47, 53, 119
Māppiḷas 21, 22, 26, 33–4, 39, 53, 90, 95, 151, 178
Marakkar, Pate 22, 24
martyrs 105, 170, 195, 196, 198, 218–19, 223, 229
Mātara 222–3
Mātiyagama 229
Māyādunnē, *passim*, and 3, 27, 30, 33–4, 41, 57, 72, 73, 129, 154, 168, 169–71, 177, 180–1, 211–12
 alliance with Bhuvanekabāhu 73, 80, 107–8
 alliance with Māppiḷas 24
 alliance with and vassalage to Portuguese 24, 73, 80, 171, 175, 245
 annexation of Rayigama 31
 character 3
 death 185, 187, 188, 192, 231
 defections to 79–80, 97, 168, 169, 172, 173, 184, 194, 246
 drawing on anti-Portuguese sentiment 79–80
 recruiting Portuguese 59–60
 religious policy and persecution of Christians 107–8, 110, 145, 163, 174–5, 184, 185, 242
Māyādunnē, chief of Denavaka 226
Māyādunnē, prince 228
Melo, Diogo de 172
mercenaries, Lankan use of 31, 32–3, 52–3, 65
messianism 198, 239
Mexico (New Spain) 86, 114, 115, 117, 119, 242
militarization 8, 33, 71, 176, 207, 216, 224, 228, 247
millenarianism 119–20
miracles 106, 195–6
mission, *passim*
 missionary criticisms of the Portuguese 48, 110, 111, 231, 249
 political and social impact 63, 87, 108–9, 110–11, 250
 understanding and reception of Christianity in Sri Lanka 132–7, 157–8, 199–205
modernization theory 8
Monforte, Manuel de 15
Monteprandone, Francisco de 117, 158
Morais, Manuel 57, 131–2
moral community 10, 149
Mukkara Haṭana 32
Mukkuvās 32, 92–3, 94–5, 96, 98, 104, 158, 178
Mullēriyāva, battle of 181
Munnēśvaram 197

Nandabayin, King of Pegu 191
nationalism 2, 7, 222, 227, 230–1, 245
 proto-nationalism 25
Nāyaks 90, 105, 176, 217
Negrão, Francisco 73, 218, 229, 239
Negombo 24
Nevill, Hugh 17, 188
New World 114, 121, 165, 206
Nikapiṭiye Banḍāra a.k.a Prince Filipe of Sītāvaka 186, 207, 209, 213
Nikapiṭiye Banḍāra, rebel 227–9, 233, 238
Nissan, Elizabeth and R. L Stirrat 27
Niśśanka Malla 147, 149
Nóbrega, Manuel de 115, 118, 120
Noronha, Afonso de 43–4, 46, 54, 60, 73, 110–11, 119, 144–5, 150, 168–9, 170, 171, 175, 182, 211
 involvement in Bhuvanekabāhu's death 75, 167–8
Noronha, Diogo de 59–60

Obeyesekere, Gananath 147
oriental despotism 103, 122, 123, 124, 186–7

Padmā, junior queen of Bhuvanekabāhu 66, 78, 79, 98
Padrão, António 59, 73, 87, 109, 117–18, 119, 144, 158, 211
Padroado, Portuguese 111
Palkuṁbura Sannas 17, 31, 129, 131, 188, 212
Panḍita, Śrī Rāmarakṣa 52, 73, 99, 110, 128, 171, 237
Parākramabāhu I 147
Parākramabāhu VI 25, 53, 127, 129, 135, 150–2, 153

Parākramabāhu IX, Dharma 23, 24, 30, 130
and first diplomacy with the Portuguese, 1506 36–7, 78
Parākramabāhu, Vīra VIII 23, 130, 159
Paravas 90, 94–5, 104, 113, 159, 171, 196
patriotism 182–3, 245, 246–7
defined 7
Perahära 148, 180
Pereira, Afonso 171
Pereira, António 50
Pereira, Nuno Álvares 58–9, 80, 85, 117, 118, 119, 153, 156, 157–8, 163
Pereira, Gaspar de Leão 197
Pereira, Pedro Homem 207
Perera, S. G. 3
Perniola, Vito 3, 14
'personality of law' 89, 124, 217
Perumāl, Tammiṭa Sembaha (chamberlain) 52, 62, 99, 171
Perumpadappanud 22
Pessoa, António 48, 49–50, 103, 168
Philip II 210–11
Philip IV 247
Philippines 206
Piedosos 15, 100, 110, 119–20, 130, 144
background of 85, 86, 116–17
compared and contrasted with *bhikkhus* 86–7
Pieris, P. E. 2–3, 36–7, 164, 235
Polo, Marco 32
Portuguese, *passim*
as bringers of chaos 4, 13, 154
conquest of lowlands 206–11, 221–4, 247
colonial injustices 222, 223, 231, 248
as destroyers of sacred buildings 3, 4, 169, 175, 187, 192, 197–8, 222, 242, 251
empire in Asia: see *Estado da Índia*
era, historiography of 3, 46, 113, 235–6
as inheritors of Kōṭṭe tradition 210–11, 247
military superiority of 21
naval power of 21, 41
treaties, imperial law 36–41 (*See* vassalage)
understanding of religious and political allegiance 164–7, 197, 242, 250–1
viewed by the Sinhalese 177–8
post-Orientalism. 4, 91
'primary group' theory 224
primordialism 5
prophecy 119, 167, 195, 198
providentialism 119–20, 163, 167, 183, 195, 196, 205
Pūjāvaliya 135, 147–8, 155

Queirós [Queyroz], Fernão de 2, 36, 47, 53, 60, 75, 79, 80, 91, 104, 105, 121, 124, 132, 133, 136, 169, 183, 186, 192, 194, 207, 223–4, 228, 230, 235, 236, 237–8, 241
criticism of the Portuguese 48, 166, 167, 249
'Hindustanic' perspective 97, 128
inventing sources 37, 226
perspective on religious and religio-political conflict 129, 132, 142, 158, 162, 164–7, 172, 174–5, 196, 213–14, 251
sources of his *Conquista* 15–16, 105, 185, 195, 196
spelling of name 2

Race 16, 235, 237
and climate 91, 230–1
mixed-race 178, 197, 240
See casta
rājakāriya 69, 101
Raja Mahāvihāraya 131
Rājaratnākaraya 17, 128, 130, 131, 155–6, 159
Rājasiṃha, Chief of Ūva 226
Rājasiṃha I 21, 73, 152, 154, 173, 176–7, 178, 183–93, 195, 209, 212, 214, 217, 218, 227, 228, 239, 241
alleged murder of Māyādunnē 185, 187, 188, 192, 231
attitude to Christianity 184, 220
death 190, 206, 207
divinization 191–2
loss of popularity and manpower 189–93
modern reputation 3
parentage 13, 186
patronage of Buddhism 184, 189
persecution of Buddhism 185, 187, 188–9, 191, 192
psychology 191
recruiting Portuguese 176
rise to power 180–2
saivism 13, 183–93
sieges of Colombo 176, 188, 190, 191
as tyrant 13, 124, 186–7, 190–1
Rājasiṃha II 17, 26, 52, 227, 230, 241, 244
Rājasiṃha, Kīrti Śrī 180, 193
Rājasūriya 207
Rājāvaliya 2, 5, 17, 34, 78, 99, 111, 131, 153, 155, 175, 186, 190, 208, 215, 225, 238, 243, 250
Rāma Varma 38, 39, 40, 61–2, 104
Rāmāyana 152, 179, 238
Ranasinghe, Douglas 151
Rasquinho, Afonso 60, 174, 250
Rāvaṇa 179–80
Rayigama 27, 31, 197
Rayigam Baṇḍāra 27, 30
rebel apostate, cultural logic of the 171, 219, 223–4, 233
rebellion 127, 189, 212–14, 231
against the Portuguese 167, 207, 210, 215, 221–34, 246
of 1616–19 227–9, 239, 248
of 1630 225, 227, 229–30, 234

rebellion (*cont.*)
cultural symbolism of 223, 224
geography of 222–3
political allegiances of rebels 224–8
and Portuguese stereotype of treacherousness 229–34
religious virtuosi 10, 126
renegades and rebels, Portuguese 45, 46, 60, 184, 217, 220, 230
Ribeiro, João 97, 230, 234
Roberts, Michael 8, 95, 180, 239–40
Rogers, John 221

Sá, Garcia de 48, 50, 103
Sá de Miranda, Constantino de 16, 97, 196, 236, 238, 247
Sá de Noronha, Constantino de 192, 199, 230, 251
Sabaragamuva 29, 223, 225
Sahlins, Marshall 11–12, 14
Said, Edward 231
saivism 13, 14, 127, 133, 134, 147, 153, 158, 183–93, 207, 208, 217, 243, 244
Sakalakalāvallaba 23, 159
Śakra 5, 149, 150, 152, 153–4, 177, 199
Saldanha, António Vasconcelos de 40
Saman 151, 184
Samarakōne, a.k.a. Fernando Mudaliyār 224
samaya 135
saṃgha. 9, 97, 146, 155, 184, 185, 187, 188–9, 191, 192, 209
described by Europeans 131–2
institutional vitality in 16th and early 17th century 126–32, 188, 216, 217, 229, 243, 244
standards of ordination 130–1
sāsana 126, 135, 146, 148, 154–5, 243, 250
Samudrādēvi 52, 79
Saparagamuvē Päraṇi Liyavili 175, 185, 188
Sapumal, Prince 127
Schipano, António 219
Sea of Ceylon 11, 24, 42, 58, 70, 90, 94
Sebastião, King of Portugal 198, 239
Senarat, King of Kandy 86, 188, 202, 216, 227, 239, 240, 244, 247, 248, 250
Seneviratmuḷa *mahāsāmi* 131
Seven Kōraḷēs 190, [206,209, rebels against Raj] 224
Prince of 24, 30, 154, 159, 170, 226
offers baptism 156, 209
see Sotupāla/Jotupāla Baṇḍāra
rebellion in 222, 225, 226, 227
Shunzhi, Emperor of China 165–7
Silva, Bento da 73, 195, 224
Silva, Francisco da 214
Silveira, Francisco Rodrigues 189
Siṃhalasaṃge 232
Sinhala/ Sinhalese, *passim*, and
'civility' of 121–4
historical memory of 4, 13, 14, 228–9, 236, 238, 247–8
identity, Sinhalaness 7, 75, 177–9, 215, 221–2, 235–40, 245
and ancestry, ethnic origin myth 237–8
as 'chingalas' in Portuguese sources 158, 167, 198, 207, 215, 220, 225, 228, 230, 236–7, 239, 240
as distinguished from Tamils 177, 237, 238
influenced by Portuguese notions 237, 238–50
sources in Sinhala 16–18
viewed and characterized by Portuguese 32–3, 102–3, 121–4, 131–2, 166, 167, 213–14, 229–34, 237
Silber, Ivana 129–30
Sītāvaka, *passim* and 17, 53, 108, 154, 176–83, 207–9, 245
and anti-Portuguese rebellion post-1590 223, 226, 228
creation of 27, 179–80
as 'early modern' state 176
resources 31
sackings of 162, 175, 185, 236
Sītāvaka Haṭana 13, 16–17, 25, 97, 99, 135, 152, 153, 154, 169–70, 176–83, 184, 188, 189, 191, 239, 243, 245, 250
Sitāvaka Rājasiṃha Rājja Kālaya 18, 192
Śiva 151, 184, 188, 189
see saivism
Skanda 151
slavery 55, 109, 115–16
Soares, Lopo 37
Sotupāla/Jotupāla Baṇḍāra 190, 209
Sousa, André de 58–9, 85, 105–6, 107, 108, 119, 161, 162
expedition to Kandy 72, 117, 119, 143, 145, 156, 211
Sousa, Martim Afonso de 50, 51, 58–9, 94, 100, 105, 107, 108, 161
Sousa, Pero Lopes de 214–15
Sousa, Thomé de 187
Spilbergen, Joris van 16, 186, 215, 216, 217–18, 219, 220, 237
Sri Lanka, *passim* and
as a Buddhist sacred space 154, 183
as a Christian sacred space 106, 107, 119, 161, 167, 183, 195, 196
Lankanness 236
political significance of island boundaries and ideal unity 5, 13, 25–6, 29, 46, 179, 181–2, 227, 228, 237, 240, 244–7
as a 'social frontier' 42, 58, 63
strategic role in Portuguese empire 31, 49
Śrī Rāhula of Toṭagamuva 127

state, Lankan
nature of boundaries 25–6, 27
and forces sucking in outsiders 71
and generation of conflict 7, 231
and noble factionalism 78–9, 222
segmentary 27
see contractualism, kingship, vassalage, etc
stranger-king myth 12, 180
Subrahmanyam, Sanjay 58
svarṇābhiṣēka 26

Tabarija, king of Maluku 85
Tambiah, S. J. 27, 146, 148
Tamil, as court language 128–9, 240
Taniyavallabāhu of Mādampe 30
Tanor, raja of 85, 143–4, 145, 157, 173
Taprobane 1
Teixeira, Duarte 41, 43, 49–50, 63, 72, 108
theological diplomacy 6, 113, 116, 119, 157–8, 209
Thomas, St 195, 196
Christians 89, 93
Thomaz, Luís Filipe F. R. 35, 47
Tiṁbiripola, a.k.a Palē Pandār 186
Tolstoy, Leo 14, 241
Tooth Relic 10, 150–1, 170, 172, 175, 184, 189, 212, 216
Temple of (Daḷadā Māligāva), in Kōṭṭe 150–1
sacked and made into Christian church 169, 172, 243
torture 195, 197, 218–19, 224, 240
traditionalism 5, 91, 142, 148, 164, 235
transcendentalism 8–10, 12, 14, 87, 125, 126, 130, 133, 135, 145–6, 157, 241, 244
non-transcendentalism 9, 12, 14, 149
transcendentalist intransigence 8, 10, 143, 145, 168
Travancore 90
Travassos, Pero Vaz 53–4
Trent, Council of 114, 115
Trincomalee 24, 26, 105, 156, 158–9, 160, 185, 197, 212
Chief of, offers baptism 156, 209
Prince Afonso of 213
Trindade, Paulo da 15, 16, 119, 170, 172, 195, 218, 223, 238, 239, 244
trīsiṃhalā/trīsiṃhalādhiśvara 25, 26, 29, 179
Turks 21, 107
tyranny 122–3, 124, 141, 186–7, 190–1

Union of Crowns 167, 230, 247
'unverified sources' 17, 18, 188, 192, 217
Upulvan 17, 111, 149, 162, 187–8, 197

väddās 26, 160, 178, 209
vadugai, a.k.a. badagas 34, 178, 185, 217
vasinava 127, 128, 133, 134, 153
Valencia, Martín de 86, 117, 120
Valignano, Alessandro 91, 93–4, 173, 196, 205
Valgampāya, Mahā Thēra of 17
vaṃsa texts, ideology 5, 10, 129, 142, 155, 216
see also *Mahāvaṃsa*, *Cūḷavaṃsa*
vanniyār chiefs 26, 29, 127, 149, 156, 158, 198–9
Varthema, Ludovico di 32
Vasconcelos, João Fernandes de 43
vassalage, Portuguese concept and practice of 23, 36–41, 111, 247
and *amizade* (friendship) 36, 37, 38, 56, 70, 71, 162
imperial and European versions 40
and responsibility for operation of succession 39, 61–2, 65–71
and tribute 36–8, 43, 47, 65, 70, 104
and vassal's right of protection 37–8, 70, 71, 73, 81, 104
vassalage, Sinhalese concept and practice of 13, 28–30, 64, 141–2, 231
external, to regional hegemons 65, 245
meaning of 1506 tribute 36, 65
and personalization of relationships 39
see under various kings.
Vaz, Miguel 89, 92, 94, 104
Vellassa 24, 26, 30, 156, 160, 182
Vēṇād, royal family of 22
Vibhīṣaṇa 158
Vīdāgama Maitreya 127, 153, 155, 165
Vīdiyē Baṇḍāra 34, 52, 73, 79, 105, 129, 154, 169–71, 175, 177, 180–2, 189, 192, 219, 231, 245
iconoclastic violence 4, 170–1, 197, 242–3
Vīdiyē Baṇḍāra, Prince of Seven Kōraḷēs 209, 226
Vijaya 11–13, 180, 238, 248
Vijayabāhu VI 13, 23, 24, 26, 30, 32, 33, 37, 51, 52, 70, 127, 130, 180, 183, 231, 245
acceptance of vassalage 23, 32, 36, 37, 38, 61–2
Vikramabāhu I 147
Vikramabāhu, Senāsammata, King of Kandy 17, 27–31, 131, 155, 159
Vikramasiṃha Mudali 184, 190
Vimaladharmasūriya I, a.k.a Konappu Baṇḍāra, a.k.a João D'Austria 1, 124, 192–3, 208, 209, 214–21, 241, 243
baptism 214
Buddhism restored 186, 194, 215, 229
attitude to Christianity 217–21, 224, 244
Lusitanization 217, 239
in Portuguese eyes 195–6
recruitment of foreigners, Portuguese 217
relationship with anti-Portuguese rebels 225–6
rise to power 215

Vijayanagar 24, 45, 65, 66, 90, 105, 127
Vijayapāla, Prince 239
Vīrasundara Baṇḍāra 189, 212, 217
Vīrasūriya 78
Virgin, Holy 195
Viṣnu 133–4, 149, 151, 187, 199
Vitoria, Francisco de 115, 141

Walters, Jonathan 158
Wars of Religion in Europe 164, 242, 250–1
Wickremasinghe, Ranil, Prime Minister 3

Xavier, Francis 15, 94, 95, 104, 105, 106–7, 161, 166, 195
Xenophobia 75, 176, 177–8, 217, 240, 241

Yala 26
Yamasiṃha, a.k.a. Prince Filipe 186, 190, 209, 211, 212–14, 238
Yogis ('jogues') 128, 172, 185, 228

Županov, Ines 230

University of Cambridge
Oriental Publications published for the
Faculty of Oriental Studies

1. *Averroes' commentary on Plato's Republic*, edited and translated by E. I. J. Rosenthal
2. *FitzGerald's 'Salaman and Absal'*, edited by A. J. Arberry
3. *Ihara Saikaku: the Japanese family storehouse*, translated and edited by G. W. Sargent
4. *The Avestan Hymn to Mithra*, edited and translated by Ilya Gershevitch
5. *The Fuṣūl al-Madanī of al-Fārābī*, edited by D. M. Dunlop (out of print)
6. *Dun Karn, poet of Malta*, texts chosen and translated by A. J, Arberry; introduction, notes and glossary by P. Grech
7. *The political writings of Ogyū Sorai*, by J. R. McEwan
8. *Financial administration under the T'ang dynasty*, by D. C. Twitchett
9. *Neolithic cattle-keepers of south India: a study of the Deccan Ashmounds, by F. R. Allchin*
10. *The Japanese enlightenment: a study of the writings of Fukuzawa Yukichi,* by Carmen Blacker
11. *Records of Han administration.* Vol. I, *Historical assessment*, by M. Loewe
12. *Records of Han administration.* Vol. II, *Documents*, by M. Loewe
13. *The language of Indrajit of Orchā: a study of early Braj Bhāṣā prose*, by R. S. McGregor
14. *Japan's first general election, 1890*, by R. H. P. Mason
15. *A collection of tales from Uji: a study and translation of 'Uji Shūi Monogatari'*, by D. E. Mills
16. *Studia semitica.* Vol. I, *Jewish themes*, by E. I. J. Rosenthal
17. *Studia semitica.* Vol. II, *Islamic themes*, by E. I. J. Rosenthal
18. *A Nestorian collection of Christological texts.* Vol. I, *Syraic text*, by Luise Abramowski and Alan E. Goodman
19. *A Nestorian collection of Christological texts.* Vol. II, *Introduction, translation, indexes*, by Luise Abramowski and Alan E. Goodman
20. *The Syraic version of the Pseudo-Nonnos mythological scholia*, by Sebastian Brock
21. *Water rights and irrigation practices in Lajih*, by A. M. A. Maktari
22. *The commentary of Rabbi David Kimhi on Psalms cxx-cl*, edited and translated by Joshua Baker and Ernest W. Nicholson
23. *Jalāl al-dīn al-Suyūtī.* Vol. I, *Biography and background*, by E. M. Sartain
24. *Jalāl al-dīn al-Suyūtī.* Vol. II, *Al-Tahadduth bini'mat allāh*, Arabic text, by E. M. Sartain
25. *Origen and the Jews: studies in Jewish–Christian relations in third-century Palestine*, by N. R. M. de Lange
26. *The Vīsaladevarāsa: a restoration of the text*, by John D. Smith
27. *Shabbethai Sofer and his prayer-book*, by Stefan C. Reif

28. *Mori Ōgai and the modernization of Japanese culture*, by Richard John Bowring
29. *The rebel lands: an investigation into the origins of early Mesopotamian mythology*. by J. V. Kinnier Wilson
30. *Saladin: the politics of the holy war*, by Malcolm C. Lyons and David Jackson
31. *Khotanese Buddhist texts* (revised edition), edited by H. W. Bailey
32. *Interpreting the Hebrew Bible: essays in honour of E. I. J. Rosenthal*, edited by J. A. Emerton and Stefan C. Reif
33. *The traditional interpretation of the Apocalypse of St John in the Ethiopian orthodox church*, by Roger W. Cowley
34. *South Asian archaeology 1981: proceedings of the Sixth International Conference of South Asian Archaeologists in Western Europe*, edited by Bridget Allchin (with assistance from Raymond Allchin and Miriam Sidell)
35. *God's conflict with the dragon and the sea. Echoes of a Canaanite myth in the Old Testament*, by John Day
36. *Land and sovereignty in India. Agrarian society and politics under the eighteenth-century Maratha Svarājya*, by André Wink
37. *God's caliph: religious authority in the first centuries of Islam*, by Patricia Crone and Martin Hinds
38. *Ethiopian Biblical interpretation: a study in exegetical tradition and hermeneutics*, by Roger W. Cowley
39. *Monk and mason on the Tigris frontier: the early history of Ṭur 'Abdin*, by Andrew Palmer
40. *Early Japanese books in Cambridge University library: a catalogue of the Aston, Satow and Von Siebold collections*, by Nozumu Hayashi and Peter Kornicki
41. *Molech: a god of human sacrifice in the Old Testament*, by John Day
42. *Arabian studies*, edited by R. B. Serjeant and R. L. Bidwewll
43. *Naukar, Rajput and Sepoy: the ethnohistory of the military labour market in Hindustan, 1450–1850*, by Dirk H. A. Kolff
44. *The epic of Pabūjī: a study, transcription and translation*, by John D. Smith
45. *Anti-Christian polemic in Early Islam: Abū 'Īsā al-Warrāq's 'Against the Trinity'*, by David Thomas
46. *Devotional literature in South Asia: current research, 1985–8. Papers of the Fourth Conference on Devotional Literature in New Indo-Aryan Languages*, ed.? etc.
47. *Genizah research after ninety years: the case of Judaeo-Arabic. Papers read at the Third Congress of the Society for Judaeo-Arabic Studies*, edited by Joshua Blau and Stefan C. Reif
48. *Divination, mythology and monarchy in Han China*, by Michael Loewe
49. *The Arabian epic: heroic and oral storytelling*. Vols. I–III, by M. C. Lyons
50. *Religion in Japan: arrows to heaven and earth*, edited by P. F. Kornicki and I. J. McMullen
51. *Kingship and political practice in colonial India*, by Pamela G. Price

52. *Hebrew manuscripts at Cambridge University Library: a description and introduction*, by Stefan C. Reif
53. *Selected letters of Rabindranath Tagore*, edited by Krishna Dutta and Andrew Robinson
54. *State and court ritual in China*, edited by Joseph P. McDermott
55. *Indian semantic analysis: the* nirvacana *tradition*, by Eivind Kahrs
56. *The Syraic version of the Old Testament: an introduction*, by M. P. Weitzman
57. *The cult of Asharah in ancient Israel and Judah: evidence for a Hebrew goddess*, by Judith M. Hadley
58. *The transformation of nomadic society in the Arab East*, edited by Martha Mundy and Basim Musallam
59. *Early Muslim polemic against Christianity: Abū 'Īsā al-Warrāq's 'Against the Incarnation'*, edited and translated by David Thomas
60. *Seeking Bāuls of Bengal*, by Jeanne Openshaw
61. *State and locality in Mughal lndia: Power relations in Western lndia. c. 1572–1730*, by Farhat Hasan
62. *Love in South Asia: a cultural history*, edited by Francesca Orsini
63. *Sorrow and joy among Muslim Women: the Pukhtuns of Northern Pakistan*, by Amineh Ahmed Hoti
64. *The God of Israel: studies of an inimitable deity*, by Robert P. Gordon
65. *Science and poetry in medieval Persia: the botany of Nizami's Khamsa*, by Christine van Ruymbeke
66. *Kingship and conversion in sixteenth-century Sri Lanka: Portuguese imperialism in a Buddhist land*, by Alan strathern